Derek Walcott

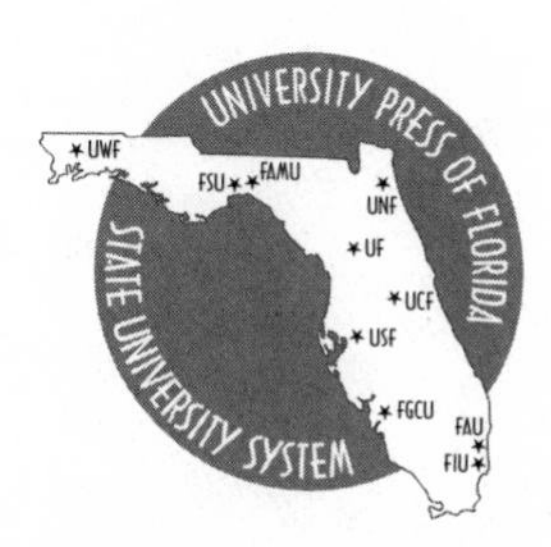

Florida A&M University, Tallahassee
Florida Atlantic University, Boca Raton
Florida Gulf Coast University, Ft. Myers
Florida International University, Miami
Florida State University, Tallahassee
University of Central Florida, Orlando
University of Florida, Gainesville
University of North Florida, Jacksonville
University of South Florida, Tampa
University of West Florida, Pensacola

Derek Walcott

Politics and Poetics

Paula Burnett

University Press of Florida
Gainesville · Tallahassee · Tampa · Boca Raton
Pensacola · Orlando · Miami · Jacksonville · Ft. Myers

05 04 03 02 01 00 6 5 4 3 2 1

Library of Congress Cataloging-in-Publication Data
Burnett, Paula, 1942–
Derek Walcott: politics and poetics / Paula Burnett.
p. cm.
Includes bibliographical references and index.
ISBN 0-8130-1882-X (cloth: alk. paper)
1. Walcott, Derek—Political and social views. 2. Politics and literature—Caribbean Area—History—20th century. 3. Caribbean Area—In literature. 4. West Indies—In literature. I. Title.
PR9272.9W3 Z55 2001
811'.54—dc21 00-064842

The University Press of Florida is the scholarly publishing agency for the State University System of Florida, comprising Florida A&M University, Florida Atlantic University, Florida Gulf Coast University, Florida International University, Florida State University, University of Central Florida, University of Florida, University of North Florida, University of South Florida, and University of West Florida.

University Press of Florida
15 Northwest 15th Street
Gainesville, FL 32611–2079
http://www.upf.com

For Louis
with gratitude and affection
and for Matthew, Joanna, and Daniel
with love and thanks

Contents

Preface

This study aims to do two things that I feel existing critiques miss: to read Walcott's work in the light of his own views and to map some of his aesthetic strategies. Clearly, neither of these can be exhaustive, but I hope that some fresh approaches will perhaps shed a clearer light on the world of Walcott's art.

The first part of the book examines Walcott's ideology, paying particular attention to his own exposition of his thinking, in his essays, public appearances, and interviews, and relating his discursive strategy to a range of the literature. It shows him as a mythopoeic writer, engaged both in the dialectics of counterdiscourse and in the initiation of new practices, marking Caribbean difference. The second part, with his craft as its theme, begins with a focus on his approach to language and then gives some more detailed readings of the crafting of particular works, some of them familiar, others less so. My overall intention is to grapple with some of the meanings of "epic" in relation to what is now an extensive and extraordinary oeuvre, produced over half a century of consistent and original literary production, profound, historically important, and continually of memorable beauty. Poems and plays are included on an equal basis, since it is central to my intention to consider the drama alongside the poetry. There is a tendency for these to be discussed as radically distinct areas of endeavor and to be evaluated according to different criteria, when in fact they have been synchronic, mutually involved, and reciprocally reinforcing throughout Walcott's career. In the first part, each chapter involves reference to all kinds of texts; in the second, critiques of individual works are organized into a poem group and a drama group, each at every stage illustrating the argument of the first half. The conclusion I hope reinforces the overall sense of a single oeuvre, variously explored.

This study is presented as a thematic survey, not a chronological one, partly because there are now some useful introductory works arranged on historical principles and because there is an unmet need for some kind of overview that responds to the work as a whole and to its abiding concerns. Given the length of his career and its productivity, Walcott's writing in fact displays a remarkable degree of interior consistency. Each work can be situated in the corpus and in the wider historical moment, but each also bears unmistakably the Walcott stamp. Conventional wisdom on Walcott is that he often contradicts himself, but this study grows from an increasing conviction, arising from long reflection on his works, that their inner diversity is not a mark of conflictedness but rather of plural approaches to a single philosophy—the multiple perspective providing in-depth focus. Everything he has written can be regarded as part of his ongoing epic project to name Caribbeanness to the world and, in so doing, to name the world. He offers not only a burial rite for empire (or perhaps a "putting it to bed," as publishers say) but a praise-song for Caribbean people's survival and for the freshness and richness of their culture—for their rootedness in the conviction that the solitary self finds meaning in its sharing with the other, which is the basis of community. The Rastafarian pronoun "I-an-I"—a coinage that refuses the distinction of singular and plural—provides masts for my ship. This study suggests that it symbolizes a radically different approach to identity from the modern orthodoxy and that it bears a profoundly optimistic message.

Shakespeare, who also combined the arts of poetry and drama, named *his* world at the beginning of the empire called English. I borrow his *Tempest,* which shows an uncanny awareness of the implications of the political world that was then just beginning, to rope the rigging of my argument. Its reef-knots tying the chapters lead also to the framing idea, set out in the introduction: the idea of the island as apple, as gift, as place of culture and of art. I hope it says something about love and about health, about giving and receiving, as well as about vision. For although punning is often scorned, Walcott knows that it is the soul of humor in a language and demonstrates its riches. His work, after all, is an act of homage to the English language—the great republic—in all its diversity, its odyssey still unfolding. Its bounty was his inheritance, and he has returned it enriched. The introduction sets up the whole book, situating my address to Walcott's work in a reading of *The Tempest.* The gap between the social map of Prospero's island and Gonzalo's dream commonwealth is seen as a mark of a potentiality that art, like idealism, can model. Drawing on a remark of Gonzalo's, the introduction establishes my focus on the Edenic fruit, the apple, as symbol of the health-giving gift (its meanings rooted in the island) that is Walcott's art.

The section on ideology charts Walcott's conceptualization of his aesthetic project. In chapter 1, this art is considered as modeling a different kind of subjectivity from that familiar to Western psychological theories. Using the Rastafarian grammatical subject-formation "I-an-I," it argues that Walcott rejects the tragic reading of human consciousness as irredeemably alienated from others, figuring instead a Caribbean subject for whom difference is integrated to community, and showing his commitment to a Caribbean aesthetic in which art demonstrates its ability to call "home" into being. The second chapter explores Walcott's mapping of a sense of place. It shows both how he centers his work on the trope of the island, celebrating the Caribbean's natural beauty and its people as a counter to metropolitan marginalization, and how from that center he also maps the wider world, interrogating the northern values in a dialectics of location. History is the focus of the third chapter, which examines Walcott's ambivalent address to it in various works and considers ways in which the apparently conflicting attitudes may be part of an overarching strategy to minimize its pain. The exploration of ideology reaches its destination in the fourth chapter, on myth. Walcott's view that, since myth's synchronic time offers liberation from the shackles of history, the imperative is therefore to create a mythopoeic art is contextualized in current theory and followed by illustrative examples of that method in action. His originality lies in both recording the world as mystery and demystifying it politically.

The fifth chapter introduces the second half of the book, on Walcott's craft, with a focus on his language practice. His approach to language is shown as essentially demotic and ludic, making symbolic play of the humble pun, for instance, and other forms of linguistic doubling, as part of his perception that the link between word and meaning is never closed. Since the remaining chapters focus on specific works, the discussion on poems and plays here separates, with chapters on selected plays after those on the poetry. Walcott's epic method in his long poems is analyzed in chapter 6 in terms of a metalanguage of imagery, a mythopoeic method. The poem "The Fortunate Traveller" and its companion piece "The Season of Phantasmal Peace" are the topic of the seventh chapter. This focuses on intertextuality as method and considers the aesthetic and polemical implications of such allusiveness.

Chapter 8 introduces the concluding section by discussing Walcott's ideas on theater and relating them to Brecht's epic theater. The four plays under discussion in the final chapters are not the best known but illustrate with particular clarity his lifelong project to create his own epic drama. The ninth chapter discusses the early pageant-play commissioned to commemorate the founding of the short-lived West Indies Federation, *Drums and Colours,* which makes particular use of carnival as indigenous theater. The subject of chapter 10 is another carnival-inflected drama addressing questions of empire, culture, and change, *The Last Carnival,* a play restlessly revised over several decades. The drama under discussion in the eleventh chapter, the unpublished *Ghost Dance,* shows Walcott engaging with a North American topic and exploring the use of myth to give epic expression to the tragic history of the Sioux nation. The final drama chosen, for chapter 12, is his adaptation of Homer's *Odyssey,* showing both the intertextual method and the ongoing commitment to poetry in the theater. Here the epic address to the whole Western tradition is felt in the makeover of the Homeric, with its parallel exposure of the African contribution to ancient Mediterranean culture and to the contemporary cultures of the Atlantic. It provides a fitting final instance of Walcott's craft in action and of his project to bring into play all of the cultures to which, as a Caribbean, he is heir, and I hope it demonstrates the distinctive way in which he makes them his own. A concluding chapter pulls together again what I hope has been a coherent if extensive study of an oeuvre that, if it is any one thing, is its author's praise-song for the Caribbean.

I thank Derek Walcott for the kindnesses that enabled me to feel less of an outsider and for the pleasure his work has given me, a steady delight over many years. I shall not forget my first night in Jamaica, reading *Ti-Jean and His Brothers* in the warm, musical darkness, while the children, then little, slept—moved and amazed and wondering why I had never heard of this writer. Now the whole literary world has heard of him. It has been a privilege to be alive, now, among the first readers of some of the great works in the English language, as they were being written, published, and performed, and to have had the opportunity to talk about them with their author.

I thank Joan Tucker for putting the *Dream on Monkey Mountain* volume in my hands that first day back in 1978 and all those who made us feel welcome in the Caribbean. In the two decades since, my biggest debt has been to my family. Without their good-humored patience and help of all kinds, this book would never have happened. I owe Joanna a special thank-you for her tireless practical assistance in the final stages, not to mention her unflagging moral support. Friends, too, have been important, and the work has made me many new ones. I have fond memories of Chris Conniff, who first suggested I could handle something this big, but it would never have happened if my early work on Caribbean literature had not received generously welcoming responses from many people, among them Kamau Brathwaite, Mervyn Morris, Edward Baugh, Louise Bennett, Evan Jones, James Berry, Lloyd Brown, Archie Markham, Abdul Malik, Linton Kwesi Johnson, Jean Binta Breeze, John Figueroa, Wilson Harris, Hena Maes-Jelinek, John Agard, Grace Nichols, Fred D'Aguiar, A. J. Seymour, and Ann Boys. In particular, the welcoming hospitality in St. Lucia of Robert Lee, Kendel Hippolyte, Jane King, the Charles family, and Mr.

Augustus Justin, who kindly allowed me to see the house where Walcott grew up, is warmly appreciated. I thank the many Walcott scholars before me whose work may not be directly acknowledged here (the secondary bibliography being confined, for reasons of space, to works cited) but whose various critiques have stimulated me over the years to formulate my own.

Where would I have been without John La Rose and Sarah White and their invaluable institution known as New Beacon Books? The staff of another invaluable London institution, the Commonwealth Institute's literature library, whom I also count as friends, have been major facilitators. My heartfelt thanks go particularly to Christiane Keane, Ronald Warwick, Paola Marchionni, and Marie Bastiampillai, as well as to Alastair Niven (then of the Arts Council, now of the British Council), who stepped in more than a decade ago with funding to save the library from imminent destruction resulting from government indifference and continues to support what used to be known as Commonwealth Literature. When I began this project, I did not expect that the planned new British Library at St. Pancras would be up and running before I finished. My thanks are due to the staff there and at the fondly remembered British Museum site, and at other libraries, particularly the Wimbledon public library and those of the Universities of London and Kent. I am grateful to the British Academy for its support in the early stages of this project and to the University of Kent at Canterbury for according me a humane tolerance in the best of university traditions.

I thank also my colleagues first at West London Institute and then Brunel University for their personal and professional encouragement, not least by giving me some time in which to take this forward. Many academics elsewhere have shared helpful information and ideas, but warm thanks are due particularly to David Dabydeen, Stewart Brown, Laurence Breiner, and Abdulrazak Gurnah for their perceptive and constructive comments on the manuscript, and to Robert Bensen, Duncan Smith, and Robin Hanford for kindly allowing me to quote them. Above all I remain indebted to Louis James, for sharing his expertise, for his many kindnesses, and for his gentle tenacity in coaxing me to see this through, despite what at times seemed long odds. We have gone rather gray in the process, and the children have all grown up, but for me it has been worth it.

The Apple of His Island: Introduction

> *Sebastian:* I think he will carry this island home in his pocket and give it his son for an apple.
>
> *Antonio:* And, sowing the kernels of it in the sea, bring forth more islands.
>
> *The Tempest,* II.i.95–98

The apple is the symbol of knowledge, of experience, the fruit of all fruits with a crucial but ambivalent place in the Western tradition's mythification of the human condition. After its consumption there is no innocence. Yet when Shakespeare's *Tempest* invites us to consider the island legacy as an apple to be given to the next generation, to the children, it remains a positive idea, for all its framing in the scornful irony of Sebastian, its speaker. The quality of the idea transcends its pejorative contextualization. This is the pattern for Gonzalo's role in the play: the ideas he speaks transcend the immediate context of their utterance. As Peter Hulme observes, "he is, as it were, both actor and critic, a combination which allows the play to discuss its own meaning in an almost Brechtian fashion."[1] The degenerate social map of Prospero's island is ultimately powerless to cancel the dream of a better one. Utopias such as Gonzalo's dream of the ideal society as "commonwealth" still haunt the imagination in our time, as the popularity of works such as John Lennon's song "Imagine" testifies. In relation to the specifically racialized Atlantic societies, the dream to which Martin Luther King gave voice will not be forgotten, nor will Nelson Mandela's faith in the idea of the "rainbow nation" of South Africa, however imperfect, as yet, their delivery.[2]

Nor is Prospero's abuse of magic as power able to destroy the "real" magic of the island, as trope of imaginative potentiality and natural beauty, capable of replicating itself elsewhere. As Antonio's sarcasm has it, one may by "sowing the kernels of it in the sea, bring forth more islands:" an absurd proposition, clearly, at the materialist level of the speaker's thought, but not to a creative thinker. Crucially, the exchange serves as a reminder that meaning cannot be controlled: the "intended" meaning of Sebastian and Antonio is not the only one and cannot prevent the hearer from investing their words with other meanings. Gonzalo's discourse is inserted into the play for a reason and, although mocked within the drama, remains open to being given different significance. At the core also of Walcott's aesthetic is an awareness that language is always radically unclosed and therefore an inherently revolutionary practice, endlessly open to the new.

The gift is given but the receiver can also give. The artist returns the gift of art with new art. Walcott's own cultural situation, the island—as social, spiritual, geographical, and historical space—is one of the gifts offered to the world through his art. *The Tempest* is also one of the givens, which can be handed on, invested with new meanings. Walcott has said of his own maturation as artist, "I needed to become omnivorous about the art and literature of Europe to understand my own world. I write 'my own world' because I had no doubt that it was mine, that it was given to me, by God, not by history, with my gift."[3]

In his writing, Walcott sometimes uses the figure of fruit to engage with the Caribbean experience, offering opposite the northern "ice-apple," imported to the Caribbean, indigenous fruit such as the star-apple, the "pomme cythère" (the apple of Venus's island, the pomegranate), and the "pomme arac" (the apple of the Aruacs, who were there first). As a poet of the New World he distinguishes the longing for innocence as the nostalgia of the Old World:

> The great poetry of the New World does not pretend to such innocence, its vision is not naïve. Rather, like its fruits, its savour is a mixture of the acid and the sweet, the apples of its second Eden have the tartness of experience. In such poetry there is a bitter memory and it is the bitterness that dries last on the tongue. It is the acidulous that supplies its energy. The golden apples of this sun are shot with acid. . . . For us in the archipelago the tribal memory is salted with the bitter memory of migration.[4]

The world itself is likened to a great fruit, history to its splitting and reassembling in the archipelago. Walcott ends his essay "The Muse of History" with a rite of homage to the twin ancestry, black and white, he shares with his people: "I give the strange and bitter and yet ennobling thanks for the monumental groaning and soldering of two great worlds, like the halves of a fruit seamed by its own bitter juice, that exiled from your own Edens you have placed me in the wonder of another, and that was my inheritance and your gift."[5]

There is cultural particularity hidden in the image. Writing of his first ten years in Trinidad, Walcott records the persistence in the Port of Spain townscape of "the same plump East Indian woman opposite the Queen's

Royal College tower slicing and salting oranges whose halves some Spanish poet has compared to a cathedral window. That acridness is the real tropical savour, hidden in sapodillas, plums, pommes cytheres and pommes aracs."[6] The same essay describes the homesickness for Trinidad induced in him as a young man in New York, by a screening of Satyajit Ray's film about rural India, *Pather Panchali,* which made Walcott aware of how much Trinidad, in all its cultural pluralism, had become a version of home:

> it confirmed my exile, and my adoption. I was adrift, I had my own loss, but this homesickness for Trinidad anchored me. And since then I have preserved a nostalgia for the loss of my own India, and I wish it will widen towards all who begin here, Portuguese, Jew, Chinese and Levantine. The fear of finding Trinidad so cosmopolitan that it seemed characterless had gone.[7]

The "fruit seamed by its own bitter juice" is a riposte to the bifurcating colonial discourse—the discourse of scorn for the Caribbean communities as inferior, and the romantic discourse that trades on the illusion of the region as a hedonist paradise of pleasure (part of what David Dabydeen calls "the pornography of empire").[8] Walcott's is an eloquent image of ambivalence, of the bittersweet simultaneous recognition of exile and home, of destruction and creation, of wrong and redemption—of experience. It is not self-deceiving but is about self-knowledge. The salted juice has its own new flavor, unlike anything else. For all its tartness, the gift of such a fruit remains, like Gonzalo's apple, a benign legacy, offering nourishment.

For Walcott, maturity is the "assimilation of the features of every ancestor,"[9] the artist self-empowering as assimilator not assimilated, not taken over by another's hegemonic project. The distinction is crucial. In the words of Wilson Harris, "We are the first potential parents who can contain the ancestral house."[10] Focused on language—the gift which is "irretrievably given"[11]—the desire to respond to the colonizing project produces certain options. Walcott rejects both the literature of recrimination (of the descendents of the slave) and the literature of remorse (of descendents of the colonizer) because they remain locked in a Manichean dialectics, reinscribing and perpetuating a negative pattern. His own position is a primary identification with the first group, the mixed-race self (his grandfathers were white and his grandmothers black) focused on the predominance of black people in its community. "Our symbol is not Ariel," argues Roberto Retamar, "but Caliban. This is something which we the 'mestizos,' who live in these islands where Caliban lived, perceive with particular clarity. . . . What is our history, what is our culture but the history, but the culture of Caliban?"[12] The Caribbean artist's sense that s/he serves the community is typically acute. When Derek Walcott received the Nobel Prize for literature, he named that self-identification with the people, although with an ironic sense of his difference: "This is the benediction that is celebrated, a fresh language and a fresh people, and this is the frightening duty owed," he said. "I stand here in their name, if not their image."[13]

But it is particularly, as Shakespearean commentators have observed, Caliban's language on which *The Tempest*'s meanings bear down. Learning to curse is the language lesson he voices to Prospero as the product of empire, but this version of his language practice takes no account of his poetry, as Walcott points out. It is only by stepping outside the blighted perspective of the power-abusers that a more convincing and complete map of Caliban's experience and practice can be perceived. As Sebastian comments when Gonzalo decodes his combative interruption within the compass of his own intended meaning, "You have taken it wiselier than I meant you should."[14] Walcott uses precisely this strategy—inviting us to "take it wiselier"—to demonstrate the uniquely redemptive power of language, relying on "the faith of using the old names anew."[15] Caliban enters the play cursing Prospero and proceeds to expound the monstrosity of his dispossession and abuse by him. Caribbean people, like Caliban, have good reason for wanting revenge on their exploiters, past and present. Walcott proposes instead the refusal of revenge and of its verbal mode, curse, but as a positive rather than a negative movement, a marker of a greater humanity. It enables Froude's infamous, late-nineteenth-century slur on the region—"There are no people there in the true sense of the word, with a character and purpose of their own"—to be finally cancelled.[16] Walcott models the archetypal Caribbean self who is not "nobody" but a "nation." V. S. Naipaul's equally infamous claim that "nothing was created in the West Indies" (an early remark which his own achievements belie) is revised as a triumphant something.[17] In 1966, the Barbadian novelist and political thinker George Lamming anatomized the cultural ambivalence—the split in the sense of self that Walcott and others have dubbed "schizophrenia"—caused by colonialism: "the West Indian sensibility shows the scars of this fracture, reveals the acuteness of this crisis to a degree that is, in my view, unique in the modern world. Hence the dramatic search for identity which, starting with an awareness of having *nothing,* encourages and promotes an appetite for comprehending *everything.* The West Indian artist with a fortunate range of gifts is a man who functions always in a spiritual state of extremism."[18] In language it is possible to transcend the competitive, reactionary stance: the Caribbean artist naming his people's experience is a Daedalus on an unconfined project. If his work soars above that of his exemplars, that is his gift to the world, the proffered apple.

Walcott distances himself from those Caribbean writers who "cannot separate the rage of Caliban from the beauty of his speech." To Walcott, the crux is that "the speeches of Caliban are equal in their elemental power to those of his tutor." When, in this way, the "language of the torturer [is] mastered by the victim," this should be seen not as "servitude" but as "victory."[19] This is the key to his art. The empowering stance is neither the refusal of language nor the use of it for revenge, but the use of it to transcend its deployment by the oppressor. Margaret Paul Joseph argues that Caliban "verbalizes the truth of actual experience, because doing so has therapeutic effect."[20] This is part of the truth, the part that relates to the mimetic project. But there is another side to it in Walcott's formulation: the aesthetics that equal in "elemental power" those of the oppressor.

Shakespeare's *Tempest* has acquired a special significance for the postcolonial world, as well as having long held a special place in the Shakespeare canon and in the Shakespeare myth. It was one of the earliest mythifications of European overseas empire. Although thought to be his last play, it was chosen by John Heming and Henry Condell to head the posthumous collected edition of the plays in 1623. Since 1905, it has also been placed first in the widely distributed Oxford edition of the complete works, with the Oxford University Press escutcheon on the title page showing an open book, with seven seals. Contemporary readers would have recognized it as the sacred book described in Revelation, the final section of the Bible. The opening of its first six seals produces the apocalypse of destruction, but the seventh initiates peace—for half an hour. The OUP emblem displays, as the text visible on the open book, the Latin Vulgate text, "DOMINUS ILLUMINATIO MEA" [Lord, my light].[21] Walcott ironizes its symbolism for the colonial, cherishing no illusions about the "civilizing" mission:

> The tongues above our prayers utter the pain of entire races to the darkness of a Manichean God: *Dominus illuminatio mea,* for what was brought to this New World under the guise of divine light, the

> light of the sword blade and the light of *dominus illuminatio mea,* was the same iridescent serpent brought by a contaminating Adam, the same tortured Christ exhibited with Christian exhaustion, but what was also brought in the seeded entrails of the slave was a new nothing, a darkness which intensified the old faith.[22]

The "darkness"[23]—Prospero's term—of Caliban (whose name is usually given an etymology from "Carib" although it also contains the older English term "ban," which meant both "summon to arms" and "curse") is here seen not as opposed to the vaunted "light" of the Christian mission but as its "intensifier." Walcott shows how the colonized of the Caribbean took over Christianity and made it their own. He deconstructs the imperial project, as did Shakespeare (who called his power-wielder Prospero, a name, unfamiliar as a personal name in English, that ironizes his role by sounding like a Latinate "I shall prosper"). In Walcott's work, both counterterms of "civilization" in colonial discourse, the binary opposites of its light and fullness, namely darkness and nothingness, are reinvested with positive meaning. Language, he perceives, is not locked to the past.

The Tempest is not only a principal text in the canonical hierarchy of English literature; it was given a lead role in the imperial project, as the place of revelation in the Shakespeare canon, as alpha and omega, printed first though written last. Its mythification of the colonial locus of European empire as a symbolic island experience has prompted all kinds of countercanonical engagements, the earliest being Ernest Renan's 1878 play, *Caliban: Suite de la Tempête,* which draws the figure of Caliban into a revolutionary foreground, but among the most conspicuous are those from Caribbean writers, who write with authority from their own island experience. George Lamming in 1960 theorized his extended creative engagement, as novelist, with Shakespeare's play in his collection of essays, *The Pleasures of Exile,* which both claims and renames the Calibanic experience. Like Walcott, he envisages the Caribbean Caliban's language as redemptive, using Prospero's "legacy of language—not to curse our meeting—but to push it further, reminding the descendants of both sides that what's done is done, and can only be seen as a soil from which other gifts, or the same gift endowed with different meanings, may grow towards a future which is colonised by our acts in this moment, but which must always remain open."[24]

In 1969, the Martinican poet and politician Aimé Césaire wrote his own intertextual drama, *Une Tempête,* "a critical reflection on the value system of Western humanism," which James Arnold sees as making "the valuable point that the white world needs to learn from the experience of the non-white world."[25] In the early 1990s, Kamau Brathwaite, in a lecture entitled "Caliban's Guarden" given in England at the University of Kent (the county known as the Garden of England), described Shakespeare's play as "written as if someone did internally understand the illogicalities of plantation and slavery," regarding the trope of the island as "guard eden" to which Europe brought its "alterRenaissance," the degenerate downside, for export, of its aesthetically and morally elevated project at home.[26]

Among the many critical works to focus on postcolonial revisions of Shakespeare's *Tempest,* Margaret Paul Joseph's *Caliban in Exile,* a study of Caribbean fiction, argues that Walcott, more than any other writer of his generation, "has the freedom within himself that Lamming mentions," being one who, in the quest to "find fertile soil for a fruitful future," is able to "respond positively to all that has gone before."[27] Postcolonial revisions of *The Tempest* have tended to focus on specific figures, particularly Caliban, Ariel, Miranda ("the innocent half of Caliban," to Lamming), and Sycorax.[28] Derek Walcott's work, however, is regarded here as an extended engagement with the totality of the play, as presided over not by Prospero but by Gonzalo, in which the heterogeneous island microcosm is brought under the lens of art, to examine not only the wider social organization of power but the great questions of the human condition.

"All my work has been about this island," said Walcott on his ceremonial return to St. Lucia after winning the Nobel Prize for literature.[29] In the second half of the twentieth century, he has inserted into the discourse of anglophone texts an extraordinary body of work, rooted firmly in the Caribbean, in the island, the "ocelle insularum," the "little eye" or "darling" of islands,[30] a phrase that unites the trope of the island as site of desire with the figure of the "apple of one's eye," and hence with Gonzalo. The corpus of poetry and plays, still unfolding, represents an epic project. From his youth, Walcott had a clear sense of his mission as an artist to give expression to his people's experience—in this sense, to produce "epic" (although Walcott uses the term also to denote a largeness of vision and is influenced by Brecht, who gave the word a special meaning). Writers of his generation born into colonial societies demanding independence saw themselves not just as articulators of the private and personal but as founders of a literature, conscious that the individual was inescapably generic, a social being, connected to the collective. Existing art, that of the colonial era, served only to displace the Caribbean person from self-knowledge, as in a distorting mirror. The new indigenous art was to provide different images, faithful to the inner reality of the Caribbean experience.

But it was to be a shaman's rite, rather than just a mirror. Louis James defines the Caribbean identity as "a catalytic genius, creating literatures defined not by form but by the ability to transform."[31] It needed to *celebrate* difference. "I'm glad to be peculiar," says David Dabydeen: "I'd prefer to be simply peculiar, and to get on with it, to live and write accordingly, but gladness is a forced response against the weight of insults, a throwing off of white man's burdens."[32] Part of the task is therefore dialectical, the establishment of a counterdiscourse, the task that Walter Rodney defined: "So long as there are people who deny our humanity as blacks then for so long must we proclaim and assert our humanity as blacks."[33] But Walcott's impetus has been to devise an inclusive solution. The strategies either of "redeeming the past" or of "anger" are, he has said recently (in Prospero's city, Milan), "dangerous or dishonest because they tend to exclude."[34] His own strategy has been to map a New World through art. It is part of the region's distinctive culture, which, in Antonio Benitez-Rojo's terms, "expresses the desire to sublimate social violence through referring itself to a space that can only be attained through the poetic."[35] Walcott envisions Caribbean art as a creative agent, a sacramental offering, a nourishing gift, an apple. And that apple of art, consecrated to the local community, is on offer to all who wish to share it.

Walcott writes first and unmistakably for Caribbeans, but he writes also to the wider community, a wise Gonzalo who, for all the sarcasm of Sebastian and Antonio, does indeed possess some special knowledge and gives the gift of his art for readers everywhere to pocket if they will and savor at their leisure. The island he pictures holds out the promise of different possibilities to set against some of the modern dystopias. In *The Tempest,* Gonzalo reports that the inhabitants of the island "are more gentle-kind than of / Our human generation you shall find / Many, nay, almost any."[36] The play constructs the island as place of alterity, where the norms of self-styled civilization can be interrogated and the possibility of founding human society on another basis explored. Gonzalo, the seer mocked and marginalized by his society, is kept in an ambivalent relation to the main action. His vision of the ideal society is simultaneously promoted and undercut by the way it is written into the play, yet it remains true that the dream of the ideal that it promulgates is strong enough to survive the ironization. The "commonwealth" Gonzalo envisages would have no "need of any empire," "riches, poverty, / And use of service, none," but "All things in common nature should produce," such as would "excel the golden age."[37] There will always be those who regard any kind of idealism as romantic and escapist. Walcott is no romantic, but he is an idealist, in the sense that he believes in the open-endedness of possibilities. He repudiates the tragic view of the human condition that sees it as unable to transcend the patterns evinced by the past, and he recognizes that the dream can lead the reality into amelioration. History as implementation tends to lag behind. For instance, he praises the commonwealth idea (not the social institution) as "one of the greatest achievements . . . of contemporary history."[38] His heritage as a Caribbean islander he identifies as the spur to optimism: the elation of the region's nature, the sense of being remote from geopolitical power, the knowledge that the people have survived a cruel history with their humanity intact, the ongoing genesis of cultural hybridity and innovation—these are the factors that give him the conviction that the Caribbean has something unique to offer.

This goes beyond narrow political objectives. Rather, it is the human condition that is addressed through the specifics of the Caribbean case—and this is where the dialectics come in. The Caribbean case is held up as exemplar in a counterdiscursive strategy. The hegemony of disastrous metropolitan-centered discourses that have facilitated such a trail of havoc through history is here challenged. Walcott's readers and audiences are invited to reflect that there may be other radically different possibilities secreted in the human personality, as demonstrated by the Caribbean case and that of other peoples of the South. In an inversion of the conventional metropolitan model, the Caribbean becomes a prism through which the fractured morality of the North can be re-envisioned. The goodness and strength of a culture that returns generosity for oppression, celebrating not only survival but solidarity, the faith that the value of the individual is the base for the value of society, is the "apple" that Walcott proffers to the world through his art. Crucially it is not utopian. Its positives have been tested in the crucible of a history tantamount to a worst-case scenario, and therefore the sheer fact of the community's faith in humane values has a moral authority at the opposite pole from romance. Walcott's art is first and foremost offered as a rite of homage to the people of the Caribbean. In parallel it is to the rest of the world, specifically the metropolitan North, which arrogates to itself the position of "center," that he extends his island-gift. There is a complex logic to this as well as a morality, and it is advisable that those occupying that "center" should not mistake its meaning. Lamming has set out his own version of it: "Caliban can contribute to widening that same horizon which belongs equally to him and his contemporary Prospero; for it is only when they work together in the context of that horizon that the psychological legacy of their original contract will have been annulled. Caliban's 'Yes' will then acquire its human validity of reason, and Prospero's 'No' will have achieved the genuine privilege of being free to offer an alternative. / That level of No and Yes is masterless and slaveless."[39] Walcott also speaks with the eloquence of the griot, the society's wordsmith, articulating the communal position to the stranger, and charged with a special responsibility as spokesman and translator. The wider listening world has the opportunity to open itself to the message. If that message is simply co-opted to preconceived models of hierarchized exchange, the world will be the loser. We do not read Derek Walcott aright if we see him as assimilated to a Western culture based on hegemony. His art is a different apple. Take it or leave it.

Part I

Ideology

1

"Becoming Home"

Modeling the Caribbean Subject

Gonzalo: In one voyage
Did Claribel her husband find at Tunis,
And Ferdinand, her brother, found a wife
Where he himself was lost; Prospero his dukedom
In a poor isle; and all of us ourselves,
When no man was his own.
The Tempest, V.ii.208–13

It is through Gonzalo that Shakespeare chooses to sum up *The Tempest* as a project of self-discovery, in terms that seem remarkably modern, anticipating twentieth-century ideas of psychological identity. At this authoritative point in the play, Gonzalo's wisdom is self-evident. Jacques Lacan has said with something like exasperation, "poets, as is well known, don't know what they're saying, yet they still manage to say things before anyone else."[1] An observation from Stephen Slemon elaborates some of the implications of this: "It has become commonplace in poststructuralist criticism to regard the critical text as essentially fictional, but the possibility that the fictional text might equally function as a work of literary criticism or as a genuinely theoretical document seems to be the occulted 'other' in the deconstruction of this particular binary."[2] To look to fiction for kinds of knowledge deemed nonfictional is unfamiliar, perhaps "unheimlich," the Freudian "uncanny" (literally "un-homely"), which disturbs as it disrupts a familiar order. To read off from fiction a psychological theory may seem perverse, yet the argument here is that Derek Walcott's work suggests nothing less than a different understanding of the human personality, and, by extension, of society—different, that is, from that currently prevalent in the Western establishment.

The work can be seen to encode profoundly innovative ideas, to be radically unorthodox, yet because the signs it uses encompass certain givens, such as those of the canon, it tends to be interpreted as evidence of assimilation to the Western bourgeois tradition. Just to draw on a tradition, however, is not necessarily to reinscribe its values. As Wilson Harris, the Guyanese novelist, poet, and philosopher, puts it, "Homer, Dante, Shakespeare, Goethe are as much the heritage of black men and women as of white men and women because the triggers of conflicting tradition . . . lie in . . . the cross-cultural psyche of humanity."[3] Writing such as that of Walcott and Harris may be the place to look for new models of possibility, for new understandings of our complex and hybrid individualities that are the building blocks of society. Lacan's arrogant presupposition that the wisdom of poets is not deployed consciously may be, rather, about defending the status of nonfictional inquiry. His acknowledgment of their lead (whether knowingly or not) is made in a context which historicizes Rimbaud's "*I* is an other" as precursor of Freudian psychology—an innovation which had "exactly the same implication of decentring as that brought about by the Copernican discovery."[4] It is used here to introduce an interpretation of Walcott because it obliquely confirms a rather unconventional approach. Julia Kristeva lists the three innovations in textual critique as the materiality of writing, its immersion in history, and its sexual overdetermination, which "orients it toward psychoanalysis, and through it toward the set of a corporeal, physical, and substantial 'order.'"[5] The topic of this chapter is the way Walcott's work can be read as proposing new insight into the psychological order—realizing Gonzalo's project of self-discovery—although it should be noted that he himself professes little interest in the "dead fish" of criticism.[6] He is convinced of *art*'s lead in identifying and developing the "cross-cultural psyche of humanity." It is a creole aesthetic.

"Home" is a term that is immediately problematized in relation to the postcolonial predicament. "Writing home," underneath its apparent symmetry with the idea of the empire writing back (to write home implying a subject position of not being at home, as the empire writing back implies a counterdiscursive position) raises a contrary notion. "Home," as well as being the indirect object of the participle "writing," is perhaps also its direct object—a matter not so much of address as of production. The ambiguity of the phrase "writing home" thus draws attention to the gap between the intentionality of writing as social practice and its product, the text, and raises the possibility of the text in some sense being able to make home happen, to call it into existence. Inevitably, it also raises the question of a dialectical relationship with the meaning of the phrase in colonial discourse. Under empire, "home" was constructed in relation to the imperial heartland (in the British case, the "home counties" remains a current usage), functioning as a centrist myth to alienate those who inhabit the colonial space from their own in-placeness. Counterdiscourses have identified the need to reclaim the notion of home, positing its pluralism, its openness to multiple determinations. These may involve differences of kind. Home may be a matter of psychology and of culture—to do with the construction of the subject—as much as a spatial concept. In essence, home may be the opposite of alienation.

Walcott "writes home" in a number of ways. Most obviously, he inscribes the particularity of his Caribbeanness into literary discourse to such a degree that his whole oeuvre can be read as an elaboration of the lines, "moi c'est gens Ste. Lucie. / C'est la moi sorti; / is there that I born,"[7] lines he chose to quote to the welcoming party on his first visit back home to St. Lucia after winning the 1992 Nobel Prize for literature.[8] As well as celebrating his own geographical in-placeness, however, he has eloquently addressed its antithesis, the migrant's displacement and hence ambivalence about place, shared with Caribbeans worldwide and with other emigrés. Unlike most writers of his generation, he refused for decades to seek his fortune in the North, making vigorous protestations of his commitment to the archipelago as home, in the sense of the location for utterance—"may I speak here"—but eventually in mid-life, he moved to America and to explorations of the condition of the "single, circling, homeless satellite," the emblem of mobile communication, remote, but articulating each to each.[9] It was, however, a migration driven more by personal crisis in the Caribbean than by desire for an elsewhere.

Concerns such as Revathi Krishnaswamy's, that the "metaphorization of postcolonial migrancy is becoming so overblown, overdetermined, and amorphous as to repudiate any meaningful specificity of historical location or interpretation,"[10] may be quietened by the interactive specificities of Walcott's epic poem *Omeros,* which brings these oppositional identities (of the in-place and the displaced subject) into relationship, reconciling them in a "homing" action on which the poem's intertextual relationship with Homer provides a kind of pun. The poem maps in-placeness as well as journeys, trauma as well as healing, and Seven Seas utters the wisdom that:

> there are two journeys
> in every odyssey, one on worried water,
>
> the other crouched and motionless, without noise.
> For both, the "I" is a mast; a desk is a raft
> for one, foaming with paper, and dipping the beak

of a pen in its foam, while an actual craft
carries the other to cities where people speak
a different language, or look at him differently.[11]

Seven Seas finally privileges stasis as "the right journey," because from travel "you have learnt no more than if you stood on that beach . . . except your skill with one oar." The text, stitching together the two shores of the Atlantic with its journey images, presents a double sign of the oar, with which Homer's Odysseus was to travel on until he reached a land where the people did not recognize it. It is a tragic cleaver in the African episode when it becomes a weapon wielded against the slavers, but it is transformed in the New World to the mast/pen emblem, repairing schism through the harmony of the text: not a utopian dream of oneness, but a seamed conjunction. The poem repeatedly models binary pairings between its personae, both within and across gender and racial groups, but these are never romantic. The toughness of the poem lies in its refusal of utopianism; its strength lies in its mapping of loving interpersonal relationships both despite and because of history. In this and other works, Walcott effectively remodels identity politics, placing alongside Western psychology's understanding of the individualist subject, constructed against alien others, a self that exhibits and seeks hybridity and pluralism as positive signs.

By implication, it thus calls into question the Freudian and post-Freudian interpretations of the psyche that have dominated twentieth-century thought, focusing on relations between the self and its others. Freud has enabled an exegesis of the modern condition as characterized by alienation, both individually and socially. In the phrase of Trinidadian poet Wayne Brown, it has been a "century of exile."[12] It would be an error, however, according to Fredric Jameson, to attribute "postmodern schizo-fragmentation," psychology's new "speculative mapping of fractured and multiple subject positions," to "some unimaginably complex new internal human nature rather than to the social templates that project them."[13] In the work of Julia Kristeva, a post-Freudian who studied with Lacan, the dynamic is inverted, with the difficulty of social relations derived from the difficulty of integrating the individual personality: "Living with the other, with the foreigner, confronts us with the possibility or not of *being an other.* It is not simply—humanistically—a matter of our being able to accept the other, but of *being in his place,* and this means to imagine and make oneself other for oneself. Rimbaud's 'Je est un autre' [I is an other] was not only the acknowledgement of the psychotic ghost that haunts poetry. The word foreshadowed the exile, the possibility or necessity to be foreign and to live in a foreign country. . . ."[14] The logic of Kristevan inquiry is to argue from recognition of the presence of the stranger within the self to acceptance of the stranger without: from the psychological to the social. For her, the route out of xenophobia (otherwise inescapable, omnipresent, even genetic) is acknowledgment of the alienation within the individual. This is close to a tragic philosophy, however, in which the individual consciousness collapses back on itself in despair of ever knowing itself or sharing with others. The best Kristeva can offer is the fatalism that "we are all 'others,' that hell is within us, that the foreigner is within us, that we must accept it," which is predicated on a xenophobic construction of the idea of the "étranger," translated here as "foreigner."[15] Perhaps at the point when the North's Freudianism has backed itself into a corner, the South, as Walcott presents it, can offer a way out, a fresh perspective on the problematic arising from the Freudian preoccupation with boundaries, principally with the delineation of the limit between selfhood and alterity—with difference.

Western thought traditionally proceeds by difference—it classifies by division, defining homogeneity by its antithetical relationships to otherness. Such systems of knowledge, however, tend to essentialize, suppressing difference within the groups being demarcated, in order to conceptualize the boundary with greater firmness and clarity. Scientific and social taxonomies appear to be conceptually accurate, recording real divisions between distinct classes, when in fact they often suppress other potential groupings and obliterate median positions. Notions of nation are conspicuously problematic in this way, as are those of race, the privileging of simplistic essentialisms functioning to obliterate, disparage, or suppress the hybrid and the plural. The conceptual basis of Western rationalism, now understood as a patriarchal hegemony, has real political consequences. Our understandings of the pernicious psychological effects of European imperialism, initiated by Frantz Fanon, Octave Mannoni, and Albert Memmi, are still developing. As Fanon anatomizes, it is at the most fundamental level that the colonial subject is traumatized. The imperial discourse (particularly in its racial dimension) prevented (prevents?) the healthily integrated construction of the ego, producing self-alienation: "It was no longer a question," he writes, "of being aware of my body in the third person but in a triple person. . . . I was not given one, but two, three places."[16] The colonial schizophrenia affects the colonized, the colonizer, and those in between. As Hawthorn puts it (discussing Jean Rhys's *Wide Sargasso Sea*), "in an exploitative society all involved are, in different ways, denied the possession of their full humanity."[17] It is this full humanity that Walcott aims to retrieve.

While the terminology of difference is the language through which we speak our perceptions of the world, we risk repeating the old myths. The dialectical embrace of the opposite pole to the dominant, while understandable, and perhaps a necessary phase, in the end is limited by its inscription within the old binary system, just as negritude is limited by its reciprocity: negritude "writes back" to hegemonic constructions of race as polarity by privileging the formerly negative pole, instead of rejecting polarization altogether. The need is rather to break out of the restrictive binaries. The particular usefulness of Walcott's aesthetic project is that it offers ways of reconceiving difference without either suppressing it in assimilationist taxonomies or allowing it to proliferate as absolutist fragmentation, the first tending conceptually toward fascism and the second toward balkanization.

To unite or to divide are not, after all, the only options; the continuum between them offers many median positions partaking in part of both one and the other. A region such as the Caribbean, fragmented as its communities are, geographically on small islands, historically by dislocation from ancestral communities, and culturally in terms of language, race, class, and background, nonetheless also exhibits shared sensibilities, its hugely various people having more in common than they have dividing them. It is therefore a case of both difference and sameness, simultaneously. It involves the recognition of otherness specifically as the point of sameness, of identification—of what I choose to call the sharedness of difference.[18] Walcott, I believe, reconstitutes the schizophrenic subject position as a plus—the West Indian position is one of "creative schizophrenia"—as the means to a richer selfhood than that postulated under the Western epistemology derived from Freudian and post-Freudian thought.[19] The Oedipus complex, as Gilles Deleuze and Felix Guattari point out, is not the only means of addressing the formation of the psychological subject.

They define the task of what they term "schizoanalysis" as both deconstruction—"tirelessly taking apart egos and their presuppositions" in order to liberate "the singularities they enclose and repress"—and construction—"assembling the desiring-machines that countersect everyone and group everyone with others."[20] Having exposed Oedipal psychology as a despotic monoculture internalized throughout society from microcosm to macrocosm, the argument of *Anti-Oedipus* revises the "breakdown" of the schizophrenic as a "breakthrough," an essentially creative and revolutionary process, a rejection of an intolerable order: "society is schizophrenizing at the level of its infrastructure, its mode of production, its most precise capitalist economic circuits."[21] The great artist is necessarily, in their view, of the schizophrenic party. Great writers, those "capable of performing a breakthrough in grammar and syntax, and of making all language a desire," speak "from the depths of psychosis" and demonstrate "for our benefit an eminently psychotic and revolutionary means of escape."[22] As opposed to the "oedipalization" of literature, which reduces it to "an object of consumption conforming to the established order, and incapable of causing anyone harm," the great author is the one who "cannot prevent himself from tracing flows . . . that necessarily nourish a revolutionary machine on the horizon. . . . For literature is like schizophrenia: a process and not a goal, a production and not an expression."[23] By privileging schizophrenia as revolutionary sign, Deleuze and Guattari postulate the disruption of the Western-defined "norm" in terms that resonate profoundly with the Caribbean experience, as expressed by artists such as Walcott.

Homi Bhabha applies the idea of the split to postcoloniality: "power must be thought in the hybridity of race and sexuality . . . nation must be reconceived liminally as the dynastic-in-the-democratic, race-difference doubling and splitting the teleology of class-consciousness."[24] Edward Said identifies the new ex-centric dynamic: "In a totally new way in Western culture, the interventions of non-European artists and scholars cannot be dismissed or silenced, and these interventions are not only an integral part of a political movement but, in many ways, the movement's *successfully* guiding imagination, intellectual and figurative energy reseeing and rethinking the terrain common to whites and non-whites."[25] Walcott, in inscribing his people's subject-position (writing home), addresses the world. His focal image is the tiny island of St. Lucia, from which he disrupts northern centrism with his etiolating discourse. Centrism attempts to preserve its dominance by privileging its own. Walcott challenges the constructions of race that serve that project. The one who is most on the margins of cultural constructions of identity, the person of mixed race, is psychologically most at risk, since, in Hawthorn's phrase, s/he "symbolizes the human internalization of external divisions in a racially divided society."[26] The imperialist construction of race exhibits the Manichean pattern very clearly: the privileged pole of so-called whiteness is defined by its antithesis, so-called blackness. The person of mixed race, like Walcott, therefore has a special authority to speak of race. Empire had a horror of the hybrid, because in the mixed-race person it recognized the destruction of its system of racial classification, the trampling of the boundaries, as its ever more hysterical devising of new terms of classification exhibits. As Robert Young notes, in the nineteenth century "racial difference became identified with other forms of sexual and social perversity as degeneracy, deformation or arrested embryological development. But none was so demonized as those of mixed race."[27] The theorization of the "between" as "unheimlich" (as noted, the Freudian term usually translated as "uncanny" but literally meaning "un-homely") is developed by Allon White in terms of Kristevan "abjection": "the abject feels split between a self and internalized otherness which s/he attempts to expel. This split or 'Ichspaltung' (Freud) destroys the fundamental subject-object boundary which both preserves subjective identity as such and keeps the world at bay. The abject is split between subject and object, neither fully an independent self nor completely determined by the objective realm, falling uncontrollably between both."[28] Such theorization, however, proceeds from a number of totalizing assumptions, such as the "fundamental" nature of the subject-object "boundary" and the presumed projection of hostility implicit in the need to "keep the world at bay." While these may be apt accounts of certain aspects of the construction of the psychological subject position, they are neither complete nor exclusive. The implicit politics of the denial of the validity or manageability of that which falls "between" is not addressed, yet it is acutely present and requires a response such as Walcott gives. Representations of both miscegenation and creolization (the bodily and linguistic hybridizations) are central to Walcott's creative project. The Caribbean personae he models are essentially plural and are shown engaging creatively with colonial trauma. The locus of "between" is, for him (in cultural just as in bodily terms), the site of fertility, product of interactive desire, where the generation of the new holds out the endless possibility of hope. Patriarchal Western preoccupations with origin, with retrospective lineage, are, in Walcott's aesthetic, countered with the privileging of originality, here and now. Dennis Plunkett in *Omeros* is engaged in the sterile search for an ancestor as putative son, but the poem ends with the image of the heterosexual couple and the implied promise of Helen's fetal child, whose lineage (the identity of its genetic father) is implicitly of relatively little significance compared with its future.

In suggesting that pluralism might be regarded as an empowering heritage, however, Walcott does not underplay the difficult reality, the product of socialized constructions of alterity as negative, and of the "between" as "abject." His Shabine persona in "The Schooner *Flight*," an implicit self-image, is a tragic figure of alienation, suffering a specifically mixed-race angst as his name suggests:

> After the white man, the niggers didn't want me
> when the power swing to their side.
> The first chain my hands and apologize, "History";
> the next said I wasn't black enough for their pride.[29]

Shabine is homeless, but a historically specific alienation, the legacy of a colonial displacement, informs his question:

> Where is my rest place, Jesus? Where is my harbour?
> Where is the pillow I will not have to pay for,
> and the window I can look from that frames my life?[30]

The colonial specificities simultaneously, however, open out to engage with the existential questions of our time. When Walcott names the origin as "that cry, / that terrible vowel, / that I!"[31] he addresses a crux of the human condition that goes beyond spatial and temporal categories and groupings of culture, race, or gender. Literacy, literature, culture, the poem indicates, are ultimately unimportant compared to the daring of the primal utterance of self-consciousness, an elemental "wild" voicing. The loneliness of that self-perception is real, but so also is the possibility of sharing, of the social: the poem's "I" migrates to "we" and from the oral to the scribal in the tracing of "our names." Walcott postulates that the continuum between individual and community requires *both* polarities to be given forceful representation, so that the multiplicity of intermediate possibilities can emerge.

The creole principle is evident not just in representations of the body (miscegenation) and in the language (creolization) but in Walcott's construction of the Caribbean subject position. His project of "writing home" is not like the empire writing back to the center but is an inscription of "home" in the sense of defining the in-placeness of the Caribbean person, the wholeness of the Caribbean subject in all her or his pluralism—after assimilating the features of each ancestor[32]—thus revisioning the centrist construction of Caribbeanness as alienation, locked in to trauma and tragedy. He does not deny the trauma—that would be romance—but reconceptualizes it in such a way that it opens out into both negative and positive, producing the balance of epic: at the end of *Omeros,* the sea is "still going on."

Clearly, the idea of alterity has been appropriated with enthusiasm by cultural producers of all kinds, in the project to counter totalizing discourses with inscriptions of heterogeneity, such that to give a skeptical critique of difference is to risk accusations of revisionist universalism. The task may be, however, to cherish heterogeneity while mapping congruence: the two are not necessarily incompatible. The binarism of self and other can be reconceived without implacable oppositionality. Walcott, as a twin, begins his approach to the world perhaps with a different relationship to alterity, and as a Caribbean person, inheriting both a hard history and a heartfelt humanity, he is able both to give expression to the loneliness of the "I" and to model the fundamental community I suggest is symbolized in "I-an-I," the Rastafarian pronoun that serves as both "I/me" and "we/us." This coinage offers an apt symbol of Walcott's practice, in its refusal to recognize a fixed boundary between self and other. It not only marks the dyad (and other multiples) without suppressing the individual, but it also preserves the subject position in all grammatical formations by its rejection of any differentiated object case. Historically, it was the repudiation of the commodification of the psychological subject implicit in the grammatical object case, understood as a semiotics of slavery, that led to the origination of the "I-an-I" formation in Rastafarian speech, which is a highly politicized discursive practice. Walcott (who has lived in Jamaica and took his degree at the Jamaican campus of the University of the West Indies) mines its significance in his Jamaican play *O Babylon!* He has Rude Bwoy explain that "in Rasta language / there is no accusative case. Dem feel not guilty," and ends with a final chorus that elaborates the dyad to a symbolically open-ended form of the first person plural, "I-and-I-and-I-and-I."[33]

Walcott thus sets alongside his explorations of the lonely individualist self a different concept of the subject, constructed by means of positive reciprocities in which the self-other formulation is less a problematic than an enrichment. Walcott's epic poems, as well as modeling images of community, make particular architectural use of emblematic dyads. In *Another Life,* the group of three is established by scenes in which the narrator makes "I-an-I" pairings both with Gregorias and with Anna; in *Omeros,* with its fishing-village community, Achille makes similar pairings with Hector, with Philoctete, and with Helen, while Helen is seen paired with Hector, with Achille, and with Dennis, who is himself paired with Maud. In addition, understood as the singular pronoun, "I-an-I" marks a complex sense of the plural individual which contests the Freudian notion of schizophrenia as pathology. For example, the narrator of *Another Life* and Achille, the protagonist of *Omeros,* are complex individuals whose creative response to the socially induced trauma of alienation enables them to outwit the conspiracy of history (like Anansi the spider-man trickster-hero of Caribbean folktale) to assert their full humanity, if anything enhanced by the depth of their suffering and the difficulty of working through the potentially crippling negatives. Healing is not easy, but it is possible, and in *Omeros* it is enacted, through the Philoctete story, in the faith that the language rite may have the "magic" power to deliver that which it narrates. The particular difficulty of constructing a masculine subject-position in colonial and neocolonial cultures is addressed in *Omeros,* culminating in the symbolic androgyny of Achille's and Philoctete's masquerade. Instead of being "unheimlich," the median of gender—the Tiresias figure, which is both genders rather than neither, a Jungian positive rather than a tragic negative—is modeled as heroic, the energy of the cross-gender creative act showing an alternative to the stark choice between either phallic violence or emasculation.

The revolutionary nature of this aesthetic can be seen not only against the discourse of Western psychology but against traditional constructions of Caribbeanness (although it is reflected in some of the most recent Caribbean thinking). The Caribbean experience has a particular place in postcolonial discourse, and Walcott's work has an interrogative place in both. Within the global postcolonial story, the region is often cast in a Cinderella role, foregrounding the painful dislocations and alienations suffered historically by the Caribbean people. Philip Sherlock, a Jamaican poet and intellectual who did so much to nurture the Caribbean cultural flowering of the second half of the twentieth century, put it forcefully: "Colonialism, however important, was an incident in the history of Nigeria and Ghana, Kenya or Uganda; but it is the whole history of the West Indies."[34] The authors of *The Empire Writes Back* use the region as negative pole in the scale of colonial experience: "The West Indian situation combines all the most violent and destructive effects of the colonizing process."[35] The extremity of the West Indian condition within the British empire extends in this formulation even to language: "English," say these Australians, "had a much more tainted historical role in the Caribbean."[36] That it should be the terminology of impurity, of "taint," which comes to mind to express the particularity of the West Indian language story is indicative of the tenacity of old ideologies, even among the most aware thinkers. For while the West Indians lived the extreme of language-as-power, they also generated the opposite pole of language-as-creative-survival, and of language-as-subversion (as the authors go on to acknowledge). It was in the fire of language in the West Indies that the creative response to tyranny was tempered, and that a uniquely hybrid culture was forged.

Walcott is not alone in placing a high value on that uniqueness. John Hearne, the late Jamaican novelist, made the large claim that the people of the Caribbean are "the last hope of a nearly beaten human race, because we, the hybrids, were beaten into the ground and have risen, furnished with an obstinate belief in the *person*—in the man, woman and child—that astonishes the institutionalised world."[37] Walcott shares with Hearne, a close friend, the conviction that to read Caribbeanness as locked into a psychology of alienation and an aesthetics of loss and suffering is not the only way to formulate its particularity in the global cultural story. As Walcott puts it in a miniature epic poem, "that was just Lamentations, / it was not History;".[38]

The boldness of claims such as Hearne's implicitly casts any artist who expresses that culture in a potentially overreaching role. Walcott, aware of the risks, has repeatedly stepped back from the "hubris" of his self-styled role as priestlike artist serving his community, for instance, by taking the figure of the "light of the world," sanctified in Christian discourse, and boldly undercutting it with irony. Used in *Another Life*, the phrase represents the near blasphemous daring and faith of the young artists' commitment as like a drunken passion, "lit" with alcohol. In his more recent "The Light of the World," when the poet-narrator shows himself as left behind in the dark by the transport (a minibus) that takes his fellow St. Lucians onward in a capsule of light and records his humble recognition that in the cultural economy of human exchange they lacked nothing he had to offer. His only gift, of doubtful advantage to them, is the global attention that art can evoke: "There was nothing they wanted, nothing I could give them / but this thing I have called 'The Light of the World.'" This expresses a genuinely revolutionary moment.[39] The supposed superiority of the poet—literate, educated, well traveled, revisiting a home projected by centrism as marginal—is deconstructed as relatively lacking—as locus of the desiring subject—while the ordinary citizens of the island, the objects of desire, are given superior status in both wisdom and spirituality. The poem's narrator, apparently Walcott himself, is both at home and away—a sharer but also different, othered by his intellectual role. The originality of his perception is the realization that to the extent that the individual shares, s/he does so as the gift of the group; it is not something s/he can claim. Only through the generosity of the group can the loneliness of the "I" be assuaged.

A poem that marked Walcott's move in the late 1970s into the alienation of exile, "The Schooner *Flight*," explores the pluralism within. It contains the twinned paradoxes, "I have Dutch, nigger, and English in me, / and either I'm nobody, or I'm a nation" and "I had no nation now but the imagination."[40] The idea of the miscegenated individual as "a nation," and its doubling with the idea of the life of the imagination as being in some sense a country or an identity, offers an important counter to reductive ideas both of the individual and of the social. As Walcott has said, "I'm constantly running into this idea . . . that I'm not sure which world I'm in, that I don't know who I am. I know very precisely. You can only dissect and understand the spiritual instability of the West Indian if your hands are calm. . . . But perhaps to an American living in such an atmosphere as black-is-black and white-is-white and never-the-twain-shall-meet, a mixed person like myself has to be seen as a mixed-up person."[41] He asserts it as a distinctive condition of Caribbean people, however humble—"Fisherman and peasant know who they are and what they are"—and calls himself "this neither proud nor ashamed bastard, this hybrid, this West Indian."[42]

The reading of the Caribbean experience as tragic, with schizoid distress the product of past exploitation, is thus revealed as conspiring with the neocolonial project, which it is the artist's and intellectual's task to counter. Fanon, also a Caribbean, argues that the "colonized man who writes for his people ought to use the past with the intention of opening the future, as an invitation to action and a basis for hope," in a revolutionary practice that "aims at a fundamentally different set of relations between men."[43] Walcott endorses Hearne's claim that the "fundamentally different" human relations are not just a matter of aspiration but of reality. Jamaican social theorist Rex Nettleford relates it to a global position: "The Caribbean . . . has no reason to indulge the now endemic doubts about its self-worth since it demonstrates its capacity for having all modes of artistic cultural expression, classical, popular and ancestral, which coexist in cyclical dynamic inter-relationship. This is a good enough basis for the region's call for a new international cultural order. . . ."[44] In his formulation, it is the writers, "literate, healthily schizophrenic, insightful," who have been "truly among the first to explain formally the Caribbean to itself,"[45] and he mentions Walcott as among those who have "something unique to say about the human condition, and where they come from and how they were socialized and bred just happens to give that something a special pitch and tone of importance and relevance to a North Atlantic world, itself in search of new patterns and new designs for its continuing existence."[46] Walcott writes for the Caribbean first, but he offers the good news of Caribbean "I-an-I" humanity to the wider world, inverting, with a fine irony, the old missionary project. This is not a Manichean counter-discourse but something of much more intricate pluralism, accepting and counterbalancing in one deft movement.

Bhabha, in an evaluation of Walcott's poem "Sainte Lucie," quotes Richard Rorty's phrase that "solidarity has to be constructed out of little pieces, rather than found already waiting" and concludes, "from the little pieces of the poem, its going and coming, there rises the great history of the languages and landscapes of migration and diaspora."[47] This recalls Walter Benjamin's figure for translation: "Fragments of a vessel which are to be glued together must match one another in the smallest details, although they need not be like one another. In the same way a translation, instead of resembling the meaning of the original, must lovingly and in detail incorporate the original's mode of signification, thus making both the original and the translation recognizable as fragments of a greater language, just as fragments are part of a vessel."[48] The image—of a whole composed of different but congruent parts—shadows Deleuze and Guattari. After defining the task of "schizoanalysis" as "assembling the desiring-machines that countersect everyone and group everyone with others," they go on: "For everyone is a little group ('un groupuscule') and must live as such—or rather, like the Zen tea box broken in a hundred places, whose every crack is repaired with cement made of gold."[49] Walcott uses a memorably developed variant of the metaphor in his Nobel speech, to explain the distinctively Caribbean cultural synthesis:

> Break a vase, and the love that reassembles the fragments is stronger than that love which took its symmetry for granted when it was whole. . . . It is such a love that reassembles our African and Asiatic fragments, the cracked heirlooms whose restoration shows its white scars. This gathering of broken pieces is the care and pain of the Antilles, and if the pieces are disparate, ill-fitting, they contain more pain than their original sculpture, those icons and sacred vessels taken for granted in their ancestral places. Antillean art is this restoration of our shattered histories, our shards of vocabulary, our archipelago becoming a synonym for pieces broken off from the original continent.[50]

The *Ramleela* drama, a folk ritual enacted in rural Trinidad, is such a fragment, used differently in a new time and place, as part of a different, plural culture. As he says, "Fragments survive. Most languages survive in fragments anyway, they don't survive entire, and so that access, that tonal access, makes the Caribbean, just because of history, logically a place that is going to create an immensely fertile, varied and different kind of literature."[51] The task of writing, the task of "creative schizophrenia," is "the god assembled cane by cane, reed by weaving reed, line by plaited line."[52] The artist is the community's shaman, its servant, not its master. S/he articulates the community to itself. The Caribbean artist articulates a plural identity, of fragments tightly knit into a new whole, each individual bearing the pluralism of the ancestral presences at the heart of her or his uniqueness and bringing the riches of that diverse self to share with the community. And the proffered wisdom is that this is not a condition unique to the Caribbean; that we are all plural in this way, bearing many selves within us, functioning within hybrid cultures, using languages that continually creolize.

As well as writing home in *Omeros* by articulating his vision of St. Lucianness as plural identity both to his own people and to the world, Walcott gives expression to his faith in the individual's power of creation, the power to defeat alienation by creating a symbolic "home," in whatever external conditions life may be lived. Instead of modeling Caribbeanness on nostalgia for a lost Africa, he shows the African ancestors, drawn by desire to see their descendents, crossing the Atlantic to watch as a silent, ghostly audience to their posterity. The whole poem may be seen as centered on a passage of metamorphic magic, creating home. It boldly disrupts the epic meter—the Dantean "terza rima" with its resonating hexameters—by shifting gear into the binary rhythms and insistent rhymes of the traditional English spell, an oral genre. It comes, significantly, at the heart of the poem, in the third section of Chapter 33, suggesting a numerological "magic" that Renaissance writers would have recognized, and is an incantation to turn a hostile house into a home. Walcott empowers the unhappy, alienated consciousness to transform its exile to in-placeness, teaching that it is available to each of us to use creativity to bring into being the world of aspiration.

The rite begins by naming the House of Horror, which we all recognize, the house of fear, memories, and broken relationships, a manmade environment that isolates the senses from the natural—the "Unlucky house that I uncurse / by rites of genuflecting verse." The relationship between place and consciousness is then inverted in a carnivalesque transformation: "I do not live in you, I bear / my house inside me, everywhere". In the concluding lines of the spell, which deliver the magic, there is a potent echo of George Herbert's dramatization of his faith in a hospitable God, rejoined in the ultimate homecoming:[53]

> House that lets in, at last, those fears
> that are its guests, to sit on chairs
>
> feasts on their human faces, and
> takes pity simply by the hand
>
> shows her her room, and feels the hum
> of wood and brick becoming home.[54]

The rite of transformation is enacted not as a "deus ex machina" with all its politics of hierarchy but as a popular appropriation, a magic that is demonstrated as available to anyone, specifically through the creative practice of language. The unhoused soul—always, in Walcott's metaphysics, in a kind of exile when embodied away from its creator in the world—can, by an act of mind, create its home. For the migrant, the moment of beginning to feel at home in a new location is symbolic. The spell at the heart of *Omeros* functions in the historical as well as the metaphysical plane, for as well as social application it has an etiolating mythic significance. Likewise the Jon Konnu dance for Christmas of Achille and Philoctete hangs like a Gemini constellation over the whole, figuring the "I-an-I" model of human consciousness.

Thus the insight as to psychological alienation, which Lacan traces back beyond Freud to Rimbaud's tragic insight, is balanced by Walcott with a parallel insight, comedic (to use his term). In the late twentieth century, he has shown how the burden of utterance, of naming the self, the "I," in all its loneliness and paranoia, is only one aspect of our psychological self-perception. Not only can the individual be creatively "schizophrenic," but variants of community, the sharedness of difference, are endless. To rephrase Kristeva: we all share each other, heaven is within us, we must celebrate it. As Rastafarian wisdom demonstrates, "I-an-I" is a speech practice of openly political symbolism, and the meaning of "dread" can be remade.

2

"Is There That I Born"

The Gift of Place

> *Gonzalo:* How lush and lusty the grass looks! how green!
>
> *Caliban:* I'll bring thee where crabs grow.
>
> *Caliban:* This island's mine.
> ***The Tempest,* II.i.55; II.ii.180; I.ii.331**

Gonzalo, the *arrivant,* is amazed by the beauty of the island, perceptible to him because he is open to the beautiful in ways that his companions are not, but Caliban loves and knows his island with a quite different joy, the joy of home. Its natural riches are his sustenance, bodily and spiritually, and the inspiration to his poetry. His deepest humanity is evident in his willingness to share them, not hoard them. Whether we interpret "crabs" as crustaceans or fruit (crab apples) will probably depend on our own cultural experience. For Caribbean people, naturally, the crustaceans will be signified, rather than the European fruit, for a particular geography, with all its flora, fauna, topography, and weather, confers a particularity of cultural identity, evident in the words for its cherished variety. All his work had been about the island, about "my love of it, my love of its people," said Derek Walcott to fellow St. Lucians, gathered to greet him on his first return to the island of his birth after winning the Nobel Prize for literature. As Stuart Hall puts it, "St. Lucia remains the source of his inspiration and his true home."[1] It is the place in which he spent the first eighteen years of his life, to which he has returned whenever he could, and in which he has, since the Nobel, built his own house. In Walcott's geography, the island space is first and foremost a privileged place of origin because of its natural beauty and the humanity of its people. It evokes elation, independently of any comparatives or any dialectics. As noted earlier, it is his "ocelle insularum," the apple of his eye, his "darling" ("dear-ling," the diminutive which marks affection).[2] To be in the islands is, for Walcott, to feel blessed. His work can indeed be regarded as an extended praise-song (a genre characteristic of Africa), a rite celebrating the gift of that particular heritage.

The islands' second property follows from this first one: their function as a therapeutic space. The archipelago can relieve the troubled soul, heal the wounded psyche. The paradox is that it is precisely in the site of a history of terror and humiliation that its cure is available. Walcott tries to show that the promise of healing is not romance. It does not depend on ignoring or playing down either suffering or poverty within the island community. On the contrary, the serious weight he gives the all-too-real negatives serves to make his assertions of positives the more authoritative. The third quality which Walcott attributes to the islands is a dialectical one, a multiple counter to a metropolitan-centered discourse that designates them as an inferior, marginal space. Walcott repudiates the centrist evaluation by reversing its relative terms. Inversion and ironization are therefore central to the rhetoric of "writing back."

Importantly, however, Walcott does not just "write back." His representation of the island space cannot be contained as a species of pastoral, in which a "locus amoenus" is held up in opposition to a metropolitan society as a means of interrogating the latter. Its primary motor is, rather, an assertion of its own particularity, for its own sake, and for its own community. But like the island of *The Tempest,* the island space that Walcott maps is a place of difference, of refuge even, from which the rest of the world can be seen anew. "There seems to be a quality in the island," writes Paul Brown of Caliban's dream, "beyond the requirements of the coloniser's powerful harmonics, a quality existing for itself, which the other may use to resist, if only in dream, the repressive reality which hails him as villain."[3] The repressive realities of the neocolonial world, which rouse Walcott's ire, pay testimony to the habitual abuse of power by those who have it, against others mythified as inferior. The small island, by definition devoid of geopolitical power, exemplifies other priorities, other nonhierarchical approaches to human interaction. As with Shakespeare's apple image, Walcott suggests that the islands' redemptive qualities are portable, showing how they can be translated to different places to work their special magic. As with *The Tempest*'s island, his portrayal of the Caribbean islands becomes itself a "place" in the world, an imaginative space, which can travel diachronically as well as spatially. It will survive the passing of the epoch and go beyond the boundaries of the society giving rise to it.

The Caribbean is unusual among the world's postcolonial regions in that as a result of the virtually total genocide of the indigenous inhabitants, its modern population is made up entirely of those whose forebears were *arrivants*. The knowledge of dislocation from an ancestral location is therefore common to all. As Walcott says, "we were all strangers here"; "The migratory West Indian feels rootless on his own earth, chafing at its beaches."[4] It has become axiomatic in postcolonial studies that place is of central importance. Bill Ashcroft, Gareth Griffiths, and Helen Tiffin suggest that the concern with place and displacement is a "major feature of post-colonial literatures": "epistemologies have developed which privilege space over time as the most important ordering concept of reality."[5] Edward Said, who has a particular preoccupation with privileging the condition of exile, importantly substitutes culture for location: "It is in culture that we can seek out the range of meanings and ideas conveyed by the phrases *belonging to* or *in a place,* being *at home in a place.*"[6] The naming of in-placeness in both senses (location or culture) is a primary task of any postcolonial writer, however, because the colonial experience inevitably involves displacement, culturally if not geographically. In the Caribbean islands, displacement has been both geographic and cultural. Walcott, however, counters the model of loss and fracture by drawing an umbilical link between the new location—the physical reality of the Caribbean region—and the emerging culture: "I think that this geography will continue to shape West Indian art more than anything else . . . the geography itself is an aesthetic."[7] Shifting the emphasis from ancestral displacement to the present location is a first step in challenging the discourse that reads the Caribbean as irremediably tragic because of its severed roots.

The region is also unusual because of the smallness of most of its political units, both geographically and socially, and because of the diversity of their landscape and culture. There is a fundamental paradox in the fact that some of the world's tiniest nations are also, within themselves, racially and culturally some of the most diverse. They exemplify the hyperbole of "multum in parvo," the microcosm that models the world. To map them in discourse is therefore no simple matter. Caribbean society has been modeled as dislocation compounded by fragmentation and marginalization under colonialism. Before the present century, and to a large extent still, the Caribbean islands, more perhaps than most other outreaches of empire, have been subjected to pejorative constructions from outside, which have simplified their intricate natural and social contours according to preconceived matrices of thought. The postcolonial project is to reverse that process. Instead of the blinkered and prejudiced gaze of the outsider, it is now the insider's gaze that is to survey the uncharted territory. Derek Walcott is an insider of a particular kind who is by virtue of his heritage and talents well placed to undertake the prodigious task of the mapmaker. He begins from the essentials: "the obvious thing is that this is an archipelago—the Caribbean is an archipelago—the whole presence of the sea, the variety of the islands, that any departure from an island means a return to it."[8] From these primal elements, which signify both topographically and socially, he constructs an epic art. Centering the idea of a balance between departure and return is another strategy to reconceive the otherwise tragic models of fracture and loss. It is his particular wisdom that in order best to map the microcosm, he should take on the mapping of the macrocosm too. The paradox is that the poles of scale are reversible. For the writer, Walcott says, "The more particular you get, the more universal you become."[9]

It is not his strategy naively to deny the tragic element of loss. On the contrary he gives it powerful expression, in *Omeros,* for example:

> Men take their colours
>
> as the trees do from the native soil of their birth,
> and once they are moved elsewhere, entire cultures
> lose the art of mimicry, and then, where the trees were,
>
> the fir, the palm, the olive, the cedar, a desert place
> widens in the heart. This is the first wisdom of Caesar,
> to change the ground under the bare soles of a race.[10]

The mirrored scenes of enforced mass migrations that *Omeros* so powerfully models give painful expression to the real tragedy of displacement. Epic, however, tends to valorize a community identity through a particular place of sacred belonging, often given the tragic tonality of exile. Homer's *Odyssey* is constructed on a powerful binarism, in which the desired locus—Ithaca, refuge of homeland and family—is positioned antithetically to the exilic voyage, as Walcott understands so well in adapting the poem to the stage. Likewise the topic of the *Iliad* involves Troy as home to Trojans but a place of exile to Greeks. Walcott has become a powerful poet of exile, particularly of the psychological exile in which faith in "harbours" has been lost, which strikes a chord in the modern consciousness:

> Slowly the sail will lose sight of islands;
> into a mist will go the belief in harbours
> of an entire race.
>
> The ten years war is finished.
> Helen's hair, a grey cloud.

Troy, a white ashpit
by the drizzling sea.[11]

Wayne Brown, the Trinidadian poet, has written of the present century as the "century of exile," generalizing from the specificities of a Caribbean identity to a global phenomenon, the modern ethos read as existential "angst."[12] He identifies a "fundamentally religious dissatisfaction with a world that is no longer clearly organized or with clear answers to offer," but, like Walcott, he turns to art as anchor: "the empires rise and fall . . . only the art stays." Walcott always resists nihilism and the aestheticizing of the tragic, insisting that it is a particular affliction of the Western scientific mind: "It is the vanity of metropolitan cultures to believe that they alone have the right to pessimism, just as they alone once held the rights to their opposites: elation, delight, conviction and faith. . . . The argument is: give a backward or provincial joy enough time and it will catch up with metropolitan tragedy."[13] Myths of exile remain manifestly powerful, however, as socially cohesive forces. A myth of exile has sustained the Jewish people through a diaspora lasting millennia, in the same way that the mythologizing of a lost Africa has sustained African Americans. For Walcott, Africa is still "heart-shaped."[14] But just as Virgil's self-appointed task was to affirm the in-placeness of the Romans in Italy as a consequence of the migration resulting from the fall of Troy, so the task that Walcott as artist of the New World sets himself is likewise to assert the in-placeness of such mixed communities as those that migration has brought together in the Caribbean. It is not enough just to claim the islands as home: he is acutely aware that a *myth* of the Caribbean home has to be created, of equal appeal to the myth of exile.

A Caribbean articulation of a sense of place is inevitably political, an act of resistance to the marginalization of colonial discourse. Frantz Fanon describes the displacement—from any right to identify with geographic place—that imperialism imposed: "The negro possesses a native land, has a place in a Union or a Commonwealth. Every account has to locate itself on the map of the phenomenon, but it is right there, once again, that we are relegated to remote perspectives."[15] The postcolonial era of independence and democracy may have made Fanon's dispossessed legally full citizens, but culturally they tend to be still displaced from the dominant discourse, a discourse disseminated not only in the West's centers of power but also in the geographic "margins." The literary mapping of place is a case in point. As Walcott has said, "There was no articulation of that vegetation. It was not sanctified by literature . . . that's the penalty of colonialism."[16] At the peak of the British empire, the colonial text implied an external center, like a focal point fixed disturbingly outside the frame, articulated through the potent myth of the metropolitan "home." The rhetoric of "home" was obviously initiated by white, migrant colonists for whom "back home" had real meaning as a signifier of Europe as place of personal origin, but it became a widespread usage also among indigenous colonials of all races, so successfully was it disseminated. As a verbal code, the discourse of "home" as the imperial "motherland," the "mother country," implicitly relegates all things colonial, including the indigenous people, to a secondary status, always overshadowed by the privileged, European (or Europe-oriented) center.

One of the first tasks, therefore, of the postcolonial writer has been to resist the pull of this exterior focus and to place the former colonial, marginal locus at the center of the text. This has involved countering the stereotypes of exoticism, which were part and parcel of the old portrayal, labeling the colonial location with the insidious negatives of excess—of overblownness, of oversensuality, of climatic extremes, disease and decay. (In implicit contrast, the tamed landscapes and moderate climate of southern England, the "home counties"—not, significantly, of Britain's northern or western reaches—featured as object and image of desire.) The sense of place created in postcolonial writing therefore typically subverts the colonial negative valuation, asserting the value and specialness of place for its own sake, with the identity of its geographical and social landscape, its climate, flora, and fauna, being centered in the new texts on its own terms. This phenomenon can be observed in new literatures whether of settler or plantation societies, but the situation is complicated in regions such as the Caribbean by the need for those postindependence communities that inherit a past of slavery to assert not only a right to but also a sense of belonging to the land that was the destination of ancestral abduction and the field of past suffering and humiliation. Ongoing alienation can be a real problem.

One sign of this is that from early Caribbean culture onward, the imperialist rhetoric of "home" found its mirror image in an independent and equally powerful counterdiscourse among the African-Caribbean community in which "home" signified Africa, the place of origin, to which the soul would return at death. This has acquired an urgent political momentum in modern times through the Rastafarian movement and the dialectics of black power, with reggae music such as Peter Tosh's "African" exporting it to a worldwide audience.[17] The imaginative construction of the actual locus in the Caribbean, the place of birth, paradoxically, as a place of exile—Babylon to Rastafarians—is therefore common to both standpoints. Walcott resists both self-marginalizations, although he records honestly the power of their appeal. "Where shall I turn, divided to the vein?" he asks in the poignantly titled "A Far Cry from Africa."[18] For him, it is no less damaging to a healthful sense of in-placeness to regard the birthplace as "exile" because Africa is "home" than because Europe is "home." In the Caribbean, the postcolonial writer has not only to give expression to the particularity of place as a means of canceling this privileged exterior reference to "home" but also to restore the sense of spiritual relationship with the country of birth—a relationship that is taken for granted in societies not distorted by colonialism or traumatized by slavery.

For Walcott, the task is to demonstrate the incorporation of multiple traditions in the Caribbean location, mythified as the site of hybridity. In the early years, this was posited against the dominant political discourse within the newly independent territories. In "What the Twilight Says," he repudiates "pastoralists of the African revival," asserting his own multiple heritage: "something prickles in me when I see the word 'Ashanti' as with the word 'Warwickshire,' both separately intimating my grandfathers' roots, both baptizing this neither proud nor ashamed bastard, this hybrid, this West Indian."[19] At this date, 1970, to insist on placing European roots alongside African ones was to display the moral courage of a heretic. African-Caribbean intellectuals who saw themselves as representative of the majority were vehemently orthodox in their exclusive emphasis on Africa, as exemplified, for instance, by Walter Rodney's influential polemic, *The Groundings with My Brothers,* and quick to marginalize those of other views, as Walcott dryly points out in *Another Life*—to "pronounce their measure / of toms, of traitors, of traditionals and Afro-Saxons."[20] "He is the true African," he has said, "who does not need to proclaim it."[21] Whatever view one takes of his politics (which in fact are more radical than they are often perceived to be), Walcott can be respected for his integrity in sticking to a sincere and defensible opinion and not capitulating to the pressure of the historical moment. Since an analogous refusal of fashionable views has marked his aesthetic choices, it is perhaps not surprising that he has often projected himself in his work as an isolated figure. He has felt the need to counter not only colonial discourse but the first phase of oppositional discourse, thus marginalizing himself for many years from both sectors of his community, those oriented to Europe and the West and those oriented to Africa. His position has not changed. He has argued throughout that both tendencies are nostalgic and de-centering, pathological even, when what is needed is an unequivocal celebration of the Caribbean as home.

In portraying the island "home" as "here," not "elsewhere," the postcolonial Caribbean text is not only asserting a geographical in-placeness, it is also expressing for the first time the sacredness that the Caribbean community can feel for the place in which it now finds itself. Speaking of his portrayal in *Omeros* of the Plunketts, postwar migrants to St. Lucia who make it their home and choose to remain there till death, Walcott has explained his view that a person not native to a place may become, through love of it, "spiritually native."[22] Even more significantly, in the same poem he makes Achille enact the ritual return to Africa (the rite Walcott had so long decried, in "What the Twilight Says," for instance). There is, however, no shift in attitude, as his purpose is to demystify the myth of a recoverable African identity. Achille through his dream-journey finds a tragic and mysterious Africa, which he recognizes as significant to him and where his ancestral father tells him his original name, but he is content to return to his New World identity, having laid his ghosts to rest. The important conclusion, for Walcott, is that Achille carries his Africa in him, through his genetic and cultural heritage; he does not have to incorporate its geographical reality into his life because it is naturalized into his Caribbeanness. Against the perception of tragic Caribbean loss, Walcott asserts the counterview, that the ancestral cultures are not lost but adapt and survive, learning to root themselves in a different soil, which then becomes as powerfully "native," and to name different trees. Walcott is telling fellow Caribbeans that they bear within them their ancestral culture, which derives from their ancestral location, as surely as the child carries the genes of its parents.

Alongside the assertion of the mobility and translatability of culture, the premise from which he starts is that personal identity derives from a particularity of place. It is as "gens Ste. Lucie"[23] that he collected the Nobel Prize.[24] The use of the island's French patois signals a cultural hybridity that reflects its social community. The poem articulates a powerfully felt identity with the island and with its culture. Not only is it the poet's place of origin, where he was born and grew up, but it is the originary model for his very identity as poet. His community's linguistic heritage gives him being as a writer, just as much as his genetic heritage from his parents, passed to him in this, their location, shapes him as a biological being. The sense of place is therefore central to his sense of identity—not, for Walcott, problematic, though complex. He wrote of his adolescent conflicts: "I was a knot of paradoxes: hating the Church and loving her rituals, learning to hate England as I worshipped her language, sanctifying A. the more I betrayed her, a Methodist-lecher, a near Catholic-ascetic, loving the island, and wishing [I] could get the hell out of it."[25] E. A. Markham has asserted, "Few West Indians are so self-contained as to regard the island/territory of birth as fulfilling the sum total of their aspirations," but Walcott's conflicted desires resolved themselves in choosing to stay in the region: "One worked to have the 'feel' of the island, bow, gunwales, and stern as jealously as the fisherman knew his boat, and, despite the intimacy of its size, to be as free as a canoe out on the ocean."[26] He was and is at ease with his clear knowledge of his Caribbeanness. In his Nobel speech, he spoke of the region through the prisms of both St. Lucia and Trinidad (publicity material about the Nobel Prize issued by the Swedish Academy in October 1992 in fact described him as Trinidadian, a part-truth that became disseminated around the world), and both islands inform his work.

Walcott is one for whom his native land is hallowed ground. He has spoken of "the intensity that I feel, just the sacredness to me of being in St. Lucia. It is a very holy thing for me simply because nature has made me feel that good, and you want to give something back to an experience that you've had, and to share—not even necessarily to share, just to give thanks to what you've been blessed with seeing or going through."[27] The reverence is thus deeply bound up with his creativity; the island seems to provide inexhaustible, fertile material for his work. In an early review of a Sam Selvon novel, he wrote, "The level of vision from which a writer records his observation of a society is fixed, sometimes permanently, in the environment of his youth."[28] For Walcott, his imagination was "fixed" as if in a photographer's bath (the image from the beginning of *Another Life*) by growing up on the island, until he left to study in Jamaica. That steady exposure to his own particular place was to condition his responses to the rest of the world, enriching them, but from a standpoint in which St. Lucia was unshakably "home." In Jamaica as a student and subsequently in Trinidad, he felt himself to be the kind of outsider dubbed locally a "small-islander," but after twelve years in Trinidad he could write that though he had chosen Port of Spain "as a fugitive collapses against a cul-de-sac, but preparing, though I did not see how, to abandon the islands," he had grown "naturalized": "The only defence of a small island identity is refusal to become a citizen, but the conversion is complete. I fake being an outsider, but both have made him Trinidadian."[29] From the beginning, Walcott affirmed his commitment to the Caribbean, resisting the siren call of metropolitan centers. As he put it firmly in an early poem, "may I speak here," and later with a poignant sense of the cost, "I stayed with my own."[30]

Not until he was nearing fifty did he leave the Caribbean region to reside (other than briefly as a student) in America, but once he had established an academic routine at Boston University, he made a point of spending a significant part of each year back in the Caribbean. The St. Lucia house has become very important to him. While there, he produces plays, writes, and paints, although when asked where he wrote *Omeros,* after mentioning Boston and the Caribbean he added that when he was actually in St. Lucia, because of its beauty and the strength of his feelings for it, it "seemed almost irreverent to try to write about it."[31] His work celebrates to an extraordinary degree this sacred sense of belonging. Not only does he write with a painter's eye for light, color, and contour, he responds to the natural beauty of the region at every level, giving far-ranging historical and mythical readings of place which are all the more potent for being precisely rooted in the immediate physical actuality. He traces his vocation as a dramatist to hearing as a child with his brother on a St. Lucian hillside the performed folktales of Sidone, which are "part of our memory as writers": "a memory that . . . generated in the theater particularly . . . the impulse to tell stories based on the folk imagination and the folk memory, and in a setting that was turbulently beautiful in terms of what the landscape looked like, particularly at night in the moonlight."[32] Crucially, the cultural experience is remembered as a part of the landscape.

But to site an epic art in a very small island immediately suggests hyperbole: the scale of the idea, or work, over the scale of the location, connotes excess. The banal expectation would be of failure, that it could work only in an ironic or ludic vein (mock-heroic like Pope's "Rape of the Lock"), never in a serious and "high" style. Yet such an expectation, which implies that the Homeric poems were some sort of freak occurrence, betrays itself as a blinkered centrist view. Walcott, like Homer, has demonstrated that to have an archipelago of small islands as subject is no bar to an epic art. His two great epics are rooted continuously in the island experience. The Polish writer Zbigniew Herbert (whom Walcott mentions in *Omeros*) has suggested in an essay on the proliferation of Dutch landscape painting in the seventeenth century (a phenomenon unparalleled in the contemporary art of other bigger countries) that there may be an axiomatic relationship between a shortage of geographical space and the urge to create artistic space: "painting in Holland was omnipresent. It seems that the artists tried to augment the visible world of their small country and to multiply reality by the thousands, tens of thousands of canvases on which they recorded seashores, floodwaters, dunes, canals, distant vast horizons, and the views of cities."[33] It may also be partly out of resistance to the wider world's presumption that a very small island is an improbable or impossible subject for epic that a writer such as Walcott insists. From a very young age, he knew that he must refuse the imposed and internalized limits of colonial ambition, and having refused them, there was nothing to stop him from sticking to the scale of his imagination.

In fact, far from acknowledging any disparity between the grandeur of his artistic project and the smallness of the island of his birth, Walcott paradoxically asserts topographic decorum on account of the epic scale of the omnipresent sea, against which the human figure is offset as heroic: "The Caribbean is really the sea. It's not the islands. . . . So you have the sense of immensity that is there, and all immensity creates awe."[34] This bears particularly on the consciousness of the artist. Asked about the disproportionate number of internationally known writers the Caribbean has produced, given the numerical smallness of the society, Walcott has said:

> islands perhaps may make that happen, because islands are kinds of concentric experiences, in which there's some kind of a pivot around which you look. I think the island experience of writers in some way contributes to a larger sense of space, and of time, and even of history in the Caribbean. No matter how minor the Caribbean poet, in a sense he is an epic poet simply because of the scale of what surrounds him. If you live on a rock in Barbuda you are really in an immense ocean—an immense sea, actually, the Caribbean—and in an immense sky, and that vertical figure of the individual person is within large elements of physical feeling.[35]

Walcott's epic presentation of the Caribbean as geographical place is rooted in two primary physical properties: the essential drama implied in "island," of the interface between land and sea, and the plurality implicit in "archipelago," in which separateness is consonant with commonality. The first is a binary concept, in which the two worlds of land and sea are rhetorically contrasted: the one firm, fixed, solid, delimitable, the other yielding, changing, formless, as if ubiquitous. The beach, their interface, is a place of endless drama—of friction, movement, and music, as each impacts on the other—and the thought-provoking scenario of many of Walcott's poems. And yet the nature of the island landscape is such that even this fundamental binarism is blurred, as the leaf-covered land is also wet, soft, and moving. Walcott's verse sometimes collapses the distinction between land and sea by metaphorically linking forest with ocean, as in the portrayal of Harry Simmons's house, built "within a sea of roaring leaves."[36] Both teem with life, are infinitely various, and, in storm, present similar images of chaos.

The other primal concept is that of the archipelago, in which the separate units are reconceived as part of a group—the apparently disjunct units linked by repetition and, by implication, physically joined below the water. Lloyd Brown identifies the "separate-but-communal implications of the archipelago archetype" as one of the themes of postwar West Indian poetry extended by Walcott, but he argues (in 1984) that in his poetry, "people *are* islands unto themselves."[37] Patrick Taylor is of the view that "much of Walcott's poetry remains tragic," but while it is obvious that Walcott gives vibrant expression to the experience of isolation and pain, the poetry as a whole cannot, in my view, sustain these readings.[38] The distinctive epic balance is achieved precisely through the counterbalancing of the isolation with the sense of connectedness, and although *Omeros* provides particularly memorable images of this, I do not think it is a case of reading the earlier work with hindsight to assert that a similar poise is evident there too. The archipelago allegory is at least as important as the island trope as vehicle for his modeling of subjectivity. It is the "I-an-I" archetype of simultaneous difference and similitude, for in particular it is through culture, through art, that the isolated consciousness is able to enter communion with others. For Walcott, the Antilles invite parallels with the Greek islands, with the corollary of comparable aesthetic flowering: it's a "marine culture, it's an island culture, in Greece, and it's the same thing in the Caribbean."[39] Walcott's friend Dunstan St. Omer, the painter, is portrayed repeatedly in *Another Life* as a black Greek, a New World artist as talented and original as the artists of the Old World's mythic Greek origins. Walcott resists any tendency to read Caribbean art as filial to the Aegean: "the shape, the geographic reality of the Caribbean, is the cultural reality of the Caribbean, and the cultural reality of Greece is the geographic reality of the Aegean, the archipelago . . . the Caribbean islands existed at the same time; they didn't decide to imitate the Aegean, they were there at the same time."[40] The isomorphism is aesthetic, not dynastic. Now Walcott, as Caribbean poet, speaks across the ocean in his own voice, not only to Homer but also to writers of modern Greek epic.

The ubiquity of the sea is important to Walcott. Instead of cutting off, the sea unites, the same water washing all the shores of the world. The concept of "isol-ation"—which constructs the sea as threat, a sundering stormy sea, "Whirring me from my friends," in Shakespeare's phrase,[41] and makes the island (*isola*) itself a locus of deprivation, apart from the "world," as "desert island"—is foreign to him. The Caribbean island resists the stereotypes of barrenness with its prolific fertility, turning every ascetic into a St. Francis. To him neither island nor ocean connotes loneliness. In a characteristically apt metaphor, Walcott's perception is that the world's oceans above all transmit rhythm from one continent to another, the rhythm of poetry as much as the wave-rhythm. Addressing the modern Greek poet George Seferis, in "From This Far" he progresses from the idea of the sea as divider to its role as communicator, as the grand narratives are washed up in new lands:

> ocean divides: a bronze door.
> In the wash the trunks of warriors
> roll and recede.
> Great lines, Seferis, have heaved them this far.[42]

The image is echoed in a poem in *Midsummer,* dedicated to Robert Fitzgerald, which engages with the act of translating the classics from old world to new:

> his pulse starts the gavel
> of hexametrical time, the V's of each lifted blade
> pull from Connecticut, like the hammers of a piano
> without the sound, as the wake, reaching gravel,
> recites in American: "Arma virumque cano."[43]

The waves on the beach are, first and last, a maritime people's first lesson in rhythm, in natural "meter," and that environment naturally generates other cultural givens, imprinted deeply on a people's psyche. "The rhythm of the *Odyssey,*" Walcott has said, "is the metre of the lift and dip of oars going into the water. . . . I came from a cultural context where rowing was a daily thing."[44]

Inland, the precipitous tree-hung heights of islands such as St. Lucia, rising sheer from the water, offer an image of magical apartness, of inaccessibility. It is a wild, uncultivated environment that appeals to Walcott most (the lowland plantation landscapes tend to be passed over as too burdened by a tragic history). The island contains places of an Edenic, untouched nature, "slopes where nobody has been," which are "absolutely virginal."[45] To give literary expression (language being the uniquely human gift) to places that are still as nature made them is to play Adam to the island's paradise: "Now if as a writer you look at that place and you just name that mountain, . . . you're not just naming the mountain, it's like it still remains unexplored and untouched—you know, Adam's task of giving things their names."[46] More than twenty-five years on from *Another Life,* where this phrasing of "Adam's task," quoted from fellow Caribbean writer Alejo Carpentier, was first given prominence, it still rings true to Walcott.[47] The different trees with their various leaves and separate music are often evoked (defined by the particular eloquence of their St. Lucian French names), the blue distances of tree-clad heights and ravines, and bluer distances of the sea, as well as the vividness of water at first hand, of waterfalls down rocks, of the sliding world of wave and wind. Sounds and smells as well as sights are used evocatively. In his loving portrait of the island, "Sainte Lucie," he writes, for instance, of "the wet leather reek / of the hill donkey" and of "the evening deep / as coffee / the morning powerful / important coffee."[48] All sorts of creatures—birds, lizards, monkeys, insects, crabs, fish—are woven into his poetic narratives and are even given parts in his plays. This is a kind of naturalism, as he has explained: "in *Ti-Jean* the chorus is an audible chorus of a frog, a cricket, and a bird. When I was doing this story, I thought: Okay, we need musicians so we'll have a frog doing the bass, a cricket playing the maracas, and a bird doing the flute. . . . Those songs are there in the Caribbean night. If you heard the orchestration of the Caribbean night, you'd be amazed how rich it is in terms of the sound that goes on."[49] In a symbolic assertion of the identity that comes from geographical, natural place—which is also social—Walcott narrates in his poetry a small drama in which an irascible teacher summons an account of the stars from his pupils, only to be told in precise, local terms that they look like "fireflies caught in molasses."[50] This line, which concludes the poem, exemplifies the rhetorical shift which the postcolonial project of mapping involves: the task is not only to name an immediate locale, but the universe in terms of that locale, and from the perspective of its subject's gaze. The moment is epic, though tiny. Through its cruel juxtaposition of the fragile, elusive beauty of fireflies with the sugar industry's smothering molasses, it becomes a powerful symbol, encapsulating the region's predatory colonial history. It marks the pathos of its losses but redeems its tragedy into comedy by voicing it through a child's innocence. In the freshness of his response to the particularity of place that is his birthright, the pain of the image dissolves like sugar on the tongue.

There is a sense in which Walcott's work is like a taxonomy. In his early work, in particular, he often explores the visual particularity and associative significance of certain creatures as if in a medieval bestiary (one of the sequences in *The Castaway* is titled "Tropical Bestiary"), achieving a heraldic clarity of image that lends itself, like other aspects of his mapping of the island space, to symbolism. Recently, for example, he has given the iguana, which gave St. Lucia its first name, Iouanalao, "the place where the iguana is found,"[51] a heraldic place in the rich symbolism of *Omeros,* its hunched back mirroring that of the island it represents. There too the bird known in English as the African swift and in French as a swallow, the "hirondelle des antilles," is a central mythic symbol. It doubles the Homeric transformations of Athena to a swallow by implying the bird is an avatar of a later divinity, Christ. The poem reveals it as a Christian sign. With its wings in the shape of a cross, it is an emblem of restoration, expressed through a metaphor of stitching: "Her wing-beat carries these islands to Africa, / she sewed the Atlantic rift with a needle's line, / the rift in the soul."[52] The pervasive trope of the wound which traverses the poem—and of which the volcano at the heart and height of the island is another (Dantesque) symbol—is here given one last metamorphosis to healing, on a global geographic scale. The divided macrocosm, the world as halved fruit, split by the horizon or by the meridian, has its wound sewn up, in parallel with the healing of the protagonists' chronic sores in the island microcosm. Within the island, the magic is delivered by a magic herb, its medicinal properties located by Ma Kilman, but on the global scale, a bird delivers the therapeutic restoration. In other works, other natural figures are used. In "The Star-Apple Kingdom,"[53] for instance, the fruit known in Jamaica as star-apple (though in most other territories as "caimite" or "caimito")[54] is evoked not only for its physical shape, like a grenade, but for its proverbial connotations: "two-faced like star-apple leaf" symbolizes the poem's address to double standards, as the grenade metaphor does to its engagement with the problem of political violence, both urgent contemporary questions for Michael Manley's Jamaica. In "The Saddhu of Couva," the white cattle-egret with its long, thin legs is evoked, similarly, for two reasons.[55] Not only do the bird's shape and color resemble the old, white-dhoti-clad East Indian men in central Trinidad, but the bird too is an immigrant, and a more recent one, as it is only since the middle of the twentieth century that the bird has colonized the southern Caribbean. It emerges as a beautiful image to reconcile the human figures to their background as natural and right. Like the ocean whose waters unite the world, birds have long been favorite symbols of Walcott's.[56] Not only have they been used traditionally as cultural ciphers of spirituality, but in nature their migrations, very evident in the islands, serve as a seasonal reminder that mobility need not be seen as loss. If migration is natural, and cyclic, repeatable, then much of the mythification of the Caribbean experience in terms of tragic displacement and loss loses its sting.

Yet this tragic history is mirrored too in the islands' natural phenomena. As well as the "sore" of the volcano (the name "Soufrière," common to several Caribbean volcanoes, suggesting "sufferer" as much as "sulphur place"), threatening cataclysm, there is the tropical violence of hurricane or of sun. Walcott has been a powerful evoker of the power of nature, which creates in people's minds the habit of humility and awe, the necessary precursors of spirituality.[57] The reality is remote from tourism's idyll. Of St. Lucia Walcott has said, "her natural history was tragic. I had seen enough in childhood to believe it: a landslide that swallowed a mountain village after heavy rains, the memory of Saint Pierre, and, the year after I left school, a fire that destroyed half the town."[58] The end of the century has brought Montserrat's turn at apocalyptic destruction. Antonio Benitez-Rojo relates the region's character to chaos theory. The archipelago is an "island bridge" between North and South America, a place of "unstable condensations, turbulences, whirlpools, clumps of bubbles, frayed seaweed, sunken galleons, crashing breakers, flying fish, seagull squawks, downpours, nighttime phosphorescences, eddies and pools, uncertain voyages of signification." In short, the Caribbean is "suspended in a soup of signs."[59] Its plenitude is a reminder to Walcott of awe rather than fear, natural violence teaching that change is always possible, and the vigor of natural growth—so "lush" and "lusty," to use Gonzalo's terms—teaching that creative fertility can heal the scars of the human psyche, as of the landscape. The "soup of signs," both natural and cultural to Walcott, who habitually reads landscape through metaphors of textuality, is the given cornucopia.

As another strategy to counter the emphasis on lost origins, Walcott at times projects a metaphor of the female body onto the island, recuperating the idea of dispossession from a remote ancestral motherland to a local, immediately available alter/native. The island's topography invites such a symbolism. The internationally recognized icon for St. Lucia is the twin volcanic cones of the Pitons, rising from the sea: "Under the Pitons, the green / bay, dark as oil. / Breasts of a woman, serenely rising."[60] The notion of "motherland" associated in colonial discourse with Europe, and in counterdiscourses such as negritude with Africa or Asia, is by metaphorization of this kind indelibly imprinted on the local environment. It is not only the island itself but surrounding nature that is projected as female; the sea, as "mer," Walcott reminds us in *Omeros,* means "both mother and sea in our Antillean patois."[61] It is particularly the "body" of the land, however—the delimited small island (knowable, perhaps, in a way that larger territories conveying a sense of national identity to the individual citizen are not)—that is symbolized as female. Both of Walcott's long poems and several of his shorter ones give abstract ideas of nation or community expression through female personae, and *vice versa*. Nurture as female principle is involved, for instance, again through the island figure, in Walcott's tribute in *Another Life* to his second wife, Margaret, in whom children "settle . . . simply, like rhymes" and in whose arms he is "bayed"—which draws meaning both from the noun "bay" and the verb "to bay": "bayed in whose arms I bring my stifled howl." The wolf-howl suggests hunger, yearning, and distress; the image is developed to man-as-beast seeking ambiguous comfort from his desired home in the island/wife/mother:

> in whose side, in the grim times
> when I cannot see light for the deep leaves,
> sharing her depth, the whole lee ocean grieves.[62]

Physical love is to come home to the body of the other as the mariner comes home to the island, and it may be that Walcott holds out the promise of "homing" particularly to masculine identities, more traumatized and alienated, perhaps, than those of women, as his use of the wound as trope in *Omeros* suggests.

Walcott has said of his response to Homer, "The parts of the *Odyssey* I like are the parts I felt so immediately in terms of the Caribbean—water, light, a man's struggle to get home round the islands."[63] Here "home" is a destination, a place or body sought for the completion it will confer, relieving the loneliness of the traveling consciousness. The island identity, according to Lloyd Brown, is "rooted in the paradox of a cherished separateness and a strong need to merge with the other."[64] He relates this to Walcott's deployment of the Odysseus archetype (although he was not to know how comprehensively it would be developed in *Omeros* and the *Odyssey*). The power of this double impetus, simultaneously toward divergence and convergence, is that it is a universal dimension of human experience, illuminated by Walcott's (and others') creative address to the Caribbean condition. Such themes therefore resonate widely in readers whose personal and cultural starting point may be remote from the region.

Feminist criticism, however, has repudiated masculine discourse's capture of the trope of the female body as territory symbolizing the nation.[65] Elaine Savory (Fido) has been critical of Walcott's representation of women. Her generalized criticism that Walcott's "portrait of the Black woman . . . bears no relation to the feisty, emotionally various, strong, vulnerable and generally complex picture emerging by Black women themselves" takes no account of such personas as Helen and Ma Kilman in *Omeros,* who display all the qualities listed.[66] Savory (Fido), however, elsewhere acknowledges, as does Freud, that the figuring of the maternal body as landscape is a universal symbolism (although in the context she relates it exclusively to the mother/daughter relationship): "Mother who is the first country, the first known territory which lies outside. Mother, from whom we leave and to whom we return, the one who is the starting point of all journeys and the point of reference for all destinations. . . . Mother belongs to a culture and a country, which becomes ours, and gives us our first social identity."[67] The tensioned paradox of desire for reintegration simultaneously with the desire for separation is clearly part of the birthing experience, which can be used aesthetically in relation to the mother*land.*

One of the primary ambivalences of the human condition is thus given particularly clear expression in Walcott's work. In antithesis to the "homing" movement is the impetus toward parting. Both are equally strong and necessary, and they express the profound paradox of human experience. The isomorphism between the needs of the individual and those of society is exact but conflicted: both are built on the tension between the will to individual identity/independence and the desire for love/community. Walcott uses this ambivalence (a rather different thing from the postcolonial ambivalence Homi Bhabha describes) to achieve his distinctive tone of epic balance. In a passage used first in "Tales of the Islands" and later incorporated into *Another Life,* for instance, he portrays his first departure from the island, a symbolic rite of passage, of leaving to study in Jamaica. As the plane gains height, the dwindling island is sharply portrayed, the pathos of the moment acute, as if at parturition: "each mile / tightening us and all fidelity strained / till space would snap it."[68] The mothering island is delivered of her son. It is a necessary rupture. Savory (Fido) explores the social and cultural implications of migration: "It is possible to live in a foreign country, as an exile, without ever breaking the tie to the birth country. But truly cross-cultural living requires a need to break out of the circle of childhood experience and accept what is foreign and strange as one's own."[69] By investing his moment of departure with a ritual symbolism, Walcott gives imaginative expression not only to a universal (maturation through leaving home) but to that displacement which is the common ancestral heritage of his community. Crucially, in portraying his own leaving in terms suggesting parturition, he counters both colonial and postcolonial discourses that mythify the history of migration as tragic loss, by replacing such myth with a trope of the most natural and positive of all processes, birth. The separation of parturition is not only natural but vital; it is a precondition to individual survival. By implication, this moment contains all of the ancestral and continuing migrations and remodels them as births to new, mature, independent life.

Just as Walcott is secure in his identity as a St. Lucian wherever he is, so, he implies, others need not fear a loss of identity simply because of a change of place. Equilibrium is implicit in either comings or goings: "any departure from an island means a return to it."[70] This positive representation is itself, however, balanced by a negative one. In Walcott's work the "fortunate traveller," who like Gonzalo can be imagined carrying his island in his pocket to give it to his children like an apple, is doubled and ironized by the figure of the aching loneliness of homelessness (the circling satellite), a voice of exile conceived as tragic. These are not mutually canceling. Both are equally present and "true," just as the pain of parturition is real, for child and mother. They enact the same isometric balance as in the motif of the mariner, who leaves harbor to return. The Walcott who articulates so powerfully his own displacement in "The Schooner *Flight*" is the same Walcott who celebrates his own intact sense of belonging. As well as "gens Ste. Lucie," he is the one who asks,

> Where is my rest place, Jesus? Where is my harbour?
> Where is the pillow I will not have to pay for,
> and the window I can look from that frames my life?[71]

This homelessness, however, is that of the castaway, who has a home but cannot be in it. The sense of the islands as an Edenic community from which he has become in a sense estranged can be acute. In "The Light of the World," for instance, the returning narrator is left desolate and overwhelmed by humility, from the knowledge of his own redundancy, as the symbolic transport gathers up the blessed and takes them on to the place of desire.[72]

In *Omeros,* Walcott moves on from this tragic perception of loss (which reflects a particular phase of his life, the late 1970s when failed relationships prompted him at last to leave the islands), to a different equanimity, centering, as noted above, the incantation that empowers the speaker to turn any house, anywhere, into a home. The deracination of the idea of home is the logical conclusion of his long-standing assertion that the individual embodies an ancestral history and consciousness, such that identity need not feel threatened by a mere change of place. In keeping with Walcott's overall aesthetic, the word "home" can be invested with the meanings we choose: it is not a given. As he says in one of the poems of *Midsummer,* "exiles must make their own maps," and in some ways the detached perspective can be an advantage.[73] As Said notes of Auerbach's *Mimesis,* such an overview of a whole cultural tradition would hardly have been possible except from exile; it is "built on a critically important alienation from it"—as with James Joyce writing about Dublin from Trieste.[74] As noted, Walcott acknowledges the scruples he has had in later life about writing of St. Lucia in St. Lucia. His personal identity is anchored in the island—the only place in the world where a stranger can say, "so you is Walcott? / you is Roddy brother? / Teacher Alix son?"—but that validation is like an identity card that also admits him to the world, secure in his inalienable filiation.[75] His images are of the biblical ark, in which the pattern of the world was preserved, and that other castaway icon, the ship in a bottle:

> if I must go,
> make of my heart an ark,
> let my ribs bear
> all, doubled by
> memory, down to the emerald fly
> marrying this hand, and be
> the image of a young man on a pier,
> his heart a ship within a
> ship within a ship, a bottle
> where this wharf, these
> rotting roofs, this sea,
> sail, sealed in glass.[76]

Like the emblematic snail, Walcott presents in his work an image of the complete personality as nomad, at home in itself and therefore at home anywhere. In his drama *The Odyssey,* the trope of the turtle, mobile in its shell, is deployed as a marine equivalent. Once again the world's seas serve as the field in which the naturalness of migration can be validated. Turtles, like whales, another figure of Walcott's, wander the global oceans, but turtles find their way back to the beach of their hatching to lay their eggs. Migration in nature is often a cyclic process, as it can be for the human animal. It is, therefore, not only as natural landscapes that Walcott represents the islands, but as symbolic landscapes, offering a reminder of the untouched, Edenic world, and through metaphors of the body extending the dialectics of home and identity.

In addition, he also evokes the Caribbean as social landscape, undermining the paradisal evocations: as he points out dryly in "Sainte Lucie," "the valley of Roseau is not the Garden of Eden, / and those who inhabit it are not in heaven," although he nonetheless maintains his assertion that it is blessed.[77] He captures the ambivalence of a society in which most are desperately poor and yet strikingly rich in their relish of life, "because the nature around it is so exultant, so resolutely ecstatic, like its music."[78] It is a pattern repeated throughout the region that is his province. (As a federalist, Walcott continues to regret the fragmentation of the islands into separate nations; from his earliest work, he speaks as a Caribbean writer, of that particular kind known as St. Lucian.) His poems and plays include portrayals of the major anglophone societies of the region—not only St. Lucia, but Trinidad, Guyana, and Jamaica (his reticence in relation to Barbados perhaps an act of deference to Kamau Brathwaite)—plus the wider Caribbean region, including the central American and Gulf coasts. He distinguishes the particular identities of the French and Spanish Caribbean, and the Americanness of the Virgin Islands. He was also one of the first to foreground the multicultural nature of Caribbean societies, particularly Trinidad, giving early poetic expression, for example, to Trinidad's cane fields as signifiers of Hinduism, with their prayer flags and Hindi films and thin old men in white, as in "The Saddhu of Couva," and he has been prominent in raising consciousness of the Native American presence in the region.[79] His two long epics are both strikingly rooted in the Caribbean landscape, *Another Life* in St. Lucia and in the later chapters in Trinidad (with the Sauteurs myth borrowed from Grenada, as discussed below), while the central narrative of *Omeros* gives multilayered expression to St. Lucia, as the "home" from which to engage with the world.

The volcanic island, though so small, is also very diverse, with its lee and its Atlantic shores, and its precipitous, virgin heights, as Walcott describes in the essay "Leaving School." He takes his reader on a journey on the one road across the island from Castries, and along the east coast to the American-built airport, the village names "plaiting into each other like straw."[80] The island's topography functions as a generic representative of the archipelago, but so also does its community, typified by the devout poor who are at the center of Walcott's frame:

Maria, Maria,
your bows nod benediction,
the broken pier kneels,
sanctus, sanctus,
from the tonsured mountains
the slow stink of incense

from Soufrière's chancre
the volcano's
sulphurous censer,

Sancta Lucia,
an island brittle
as a Lenten biscuit, . . .[81]

Where in *Another Life* a clear connection is drawn between the church (the Catholic church of St. Lucia) and the poor, in *Omeros* the church is more obliquely presented as a sustaining mystery, as part of the poem's mythic resonances. The vehement portrayal of the poverty of villages surviving on little but willpower in the earlier epic is encompassed in the repeated suggestion that life for many on the islands is hell:

Qui côté c'est l'enfer?
Why, Father, on this coast.
Father, hell is

two hundred shacks on wooden stilts,
one bushy path to the night-soil pits.

Hell is this hole where the devil shits, . . .[82]

Such images are less prominent in the later epic, where more grief is derived from the symbolic suffering of history—the great howl of Philoctete, for example—and the representation of modern hardship is secondary. Yet the disproportion between the nuanced richness of Maud's environment and the apparent destitution of Helen and Achille, with their poverty of goods but richness of spirit, is clearly set out. The essential wisdom of the poem seems to be that there can be liberation in the freedom from materialism—a philosophy encapsulated, for instance, in the sensual and spiritual cleansing that their handmade, open-air shower arrangements give Helen and Achille, providing a richer experience than any luxury bathroom. Walcott has defended himself against charges of romanticizing poverty,[83] and with justification, as he has been an angry denouncer of the global order which imprisons the Two-Thirds World in economic hardship, but it is also true that in his antimaterialism he sometimes overvalues the old-fashioned and makeshift. In his Nobel lecture, for instance, he asserts provocatively that "in the Antilles poverty is poetry with a V, *une vie,* a condition of life as well as of imagination."[84]

It is also true that there is nostalgia in his portrayal of the *mores* of the society of his youth, which he contrasts with a present (America-oriented) materialism and finds more heroic because of its self-sufficiency and its unclouded prioritizing of human relationships above commodities. It is evident in the tone of his Nobel lecture:

> To be still in the nineteenth century, like horses, as Brodsky has written, may not be such a bad deal, and much of our life in the Antilles still seems to be in the rhythm of the last century, like the West Indian novel. . . . Before it is all gone, before only a few valleys are left, pockets of an older life, before development turns every artist into an anthropologist or folklorist, there are still cherishable places, little valleys that do not echo with ideas, a simplicity of rebeginnings, not yet corrupted by the dangers of change.[85]

The landscape in which he sites himself as observing subject, particularly in the two major epics, is informed by the pre-technological, old-fashioned world of his childhood. The modern world, in the shape of technologies such as word processors and jet planes, is acknowledged in his work, but the changes that it implies he sees as double-edged, and it is kept at the margins of his work's central concerns.

Just as he seems to be setting up the green island in rhetorical opposition to the urban environment, in a variant of the pastoral model, the binarism of this is dismantled to reveal a new distinction within the urban. Out of tune with the modern "first world" city, hating its gigantism and its materialism, he contrasts it with the scale of the island capitals. He enters the dialectics of utopia by opposing the modern mythologizing of the technical city—the space-age dream—with his own countermyth. His own region, he says,

> can still be transformed in some kind of simplicity, and certainly by its own architecture and a sense of the scale of the Caribbean. I mean if you see two skyscrapers downtown in Port of Spain trying to look like the twin towers of New York City, there's something wrong with that. And it's true in many parts of the world that that sort of standardized block of living is turning people into "zombie." And you

> don't want zombies in the Caribbean; there's too much light and air for that. It seems to be the fate of cities to mechanize people into going into certain concrete blocks, coming out of them, and living by that rhythm. And if we start to do that in the Caribbean, then there's something radically wrong in terms of what the ordinary vision of the politician should be.[86]

In his Nobel lecture he puts forward Port of Spain, the Caribbean city where he has spent most of his adult life, as the model for the ideal civilized city, painting a lyrical portrait of its human and humanizing scale:

> Cities create a culture, and all we have are those magnified market towns, so what are the proportions of the ideal Caribbean city? A surrounding, accessible countryside with leafy suburbs, and if the city is lucky, behind it, spacious plains. Behind it, fine mountains; before it, an indigo sea. Spires would pin its centre and around them would be leafy, shadowy parks. Pigeons would cross its sky in alphabetic patterns, carrying with them memories of a belief in augury, and at the heart of the city there would be horses, yes, horses. . . . [I]t would be so racially various that the cultures of the world . . . would be represented in it. . . . Its citizens would intermarry as they chose, from instinct, not tradition, until their children find it increasingly futile to trace their genealogy. . . . This is Port of Spain to me, a city ideal in its commercial and human proportions, where a citizen is a walker and not a pedestrian, and this is how Athens may have been before it became a cultural echo.[87]

Walcott's faith in the multicultural cities of the Caribbean as closer to the ideal city than are the metropoles of the North is shared by the Cuban writer Antonio Benitez-Rojo: "Every Caribbean city," he says, "carries deep within it other cities, which live as fetal, minuscule modules of turbulence that proliferate—each different from the last—through marinas, plazas, and alleys." He defines the Caribbean "yard" as "a result of the plantation" but simultaneously "the anti-plantation." The heterogeneous people whose home it is are distinguished, he says, by "[t]heir refined individualism and their peculiar sense of freedom."[88] This urban landscape is clearly not utopian in all kinds of important real ways, yet it has a special humanity, which Walcott like Benitez-Rojo celebrates.

Walcott resists the patronizing gaze of outsiders such as Claude Lévi-Strauss, who read an "elegiac pathos" into the Caribbean landscape, which is "ultimately wrong," a "misunderstanding of the light and the people on whom the light falls." He goes on, "These writers describe the ambitions of our unfinished cities, their unrealized, homiletic conclusion, but the Caribbean city may conclude just at that point where it is satisfied with its own scale, just as Caribbean culture is not evolving but already shaped. Its proportions are not to be measured by the traveller or the exile, but by its own citizenry and architecture. To be told you are not yet a city or a culture requires this response. I am not your city or your culture."[89] As an American resident, Walcott now seeks out the islands as refuge from the depersonalizing scale and style of the modern city and as communities where people still have time for each other, but he conveys also a sense that this difference is doomed, as the islands insidiously get to look, and be, like everywhere else.[90] In *Omeros,* he has said, he wanted "to capture something about the way of life of ordinary people" such as fishermen, which was "going now."[91]

"Home" therefore, the sacred image of the Caribbean, becomes a concept under siege. Tourism is a "benign blight," which "can infect all of those island nations, not gradually, but with imperceptible speed, until each rock is whitened by the guano of white-winged hotels, the arc and descent of progress."[92] Islands surrounded by hotels, he has said, are like film sets, unreal.[93] In *Another Life,* he gives an ironic portrayal of the kind of landscape that tourism produces: "Hotel, hotel, hotel, hotel, hotel and a club: The Bitter End."[94] In defense of his ideal, Walcott has entered into the arena of political arguments over development of the island, campaigning against the proposed development of the Pitons area. Walcott's early patriotic engagement in the struggle for independence is paralleled by this struggle in his sixties against the despoiling of the region in the name of development. Both battles are waged primarily in the field of art, although he is willing to lend his name to direct campaigning. He has spoken out, for instance, against the tourist development of more than a hundred bungalows between the landmark Pitons of St. Lucia as "like building a McDonald's next to Stonehenge,"[95] or "writing 'Fuck you' on a wall in Mecca—that's the kind of arrogance I'm talking about."[96] Sensitive to criticism that such scruples are an outsider's luxury because tourism means much-needed jobs, he argues that "It's greed posing as necessity." In "Litany to the Pitons," Walcott puns, "Jalousie is one of the Seven Deadly Sins / Greed is another."[97] Profits will be secured by bankers overseas, while the local population will be maneuvered to remain indefinitely in poorly paid jobs serving the affluent tourists. But Walcott adds: "even if the greed were to the benefit of an entire community it would still be wrong. There are some things that you just don't sell."[98] Moves to have the

Pitons declared a World Heritage site failed to stop the development, which is now up and running.

The critique of tourism incorporated in *Omeros* is informed by this campaigning stance. When Helen quits her waitress job because of sexual harassment, Walcott is drawing attention to the particular self-debasement that the economically vulnerable islands enact when they effectively prostitute themselves to the rich North as sites for tourism fueled by erotic fantasy. Helen, who symbolizes the island, is heroic in her refusal of tourism's degradations, though at personal cost, as if Walcott wishes to suggest that a stand can be made. The paradisal imagery by which the islands are marketed in the North is a distinctly ambiguous lure:

> in our tourist brochures the Caribbean is a blue pool into which the republic dangles the extended foot of Florida as inflated rubber islands bob and drinks with umbrellas float towards her on a raft. This is how the islands from the shame of necessity sell themselves; this is the seasonal erosion of their identity; that high-pitched repetition of the same images of service that cannot distinguish one island from the other, with a future of polluted marinas, land deals negotiated by ministers, and all of this conducted to the music of Happy Hour and the rictus of a smile.[99]

The impact of the tourism industry on the cultural self-perception of Caribbean people is of particular concern because it reinscribes the colonial discourse of exoticism as part of its realpolitik of exploitation. It is neocolonialism in action. In a recent interview, Walcott underlines the politics of the visual enchantment: "The Tourist Board vision is not to be mocked. Every photograph you take in the Caribbean is beautiful, the light makes it so—you just gasp continually. And what's beautiful often turns out to be what's poor: the colours of galvanized shacks near the blue sea." But this is more than just "visual surprise."[100] He asserts the "spiritual beauty of the place: you have a sense of the celestial in that light, a radiance without edges." To him this makes the impact of tourism approach sacrilege, "the desecration of a spiritual, self-evidently sacred place. Anybody approaching the Pitons is overwhelmed by a sensation beyond themselves. You don't violate that unless you're a barbarian, because the place communicates its own votive aura." With casinos now the next threat, Walcott's line is intransigent: "If I can summon up all the forces I can, it'll be a real fight."[101] Yet while championing such causes not as "nostalgic sites but occluded sanctities," he is aware of the two-edged nature of his efforts, that he is jeopardizing them by attracting international attention even as he tries to preserve them: they are places "as threatened by this prose as a headland is by the bulldozer or a sea almond grove by the surveyor's string, or from blight, the mountain laurel."[102]

Where civilization is understood in terms of humanitarian values, a sense of the sacred, and an absence of materialist greed, then the old "civilization-savagery" continuum can be reversed. The process of identifying barbarism becomes a corollary to that of praising and defending what the home community holds precious. In constructing a sense of the Caribbean location, Walcott therefore sets up a dialectical opposition with the "elsewhere" of the North, countering old myths and constructing new ones. Overall, he remakes the old Manichean binarism, switching its topographical values, so that as the southern archipelago is revisioned as locus of desire—as, in a real sense, civilized—the urban, northern environment is stripped of its self-appointed status as site of civilization and reconceived as barbaric. For Walcott, it is primarily a matter of humanitarian values. He finds them more in evidence in the communities of the Caribbean than in the northern centers of power, and he deduces that the North's moral predicament is the consequence of its abuse of power, and perhaps of its cold climate. The islands' very lack of power therefore becomes a primary virtue; the powerless are brought to an understanding about the truth of moral values, he argues, in a way that the discourse of power typical of the North and its culture willfully obscures. By definition, the poor of the South have a worldview in which the power myths of the North arrive already demystified. To be trapped in poverty is to have no illusions about the supposed benevolence of the global political structures that promote our entrapment. Conversely poverty can remind us that we share a predicament with our neighbor, and it confirms the importance of compassion, mutual support, and solidarity.

It may be that such a gritty optimism as Walcott's, salvaged from the teeth of pessimism, is a phenomenon of a particular period of Caribbean history. He grew up under empire, argued for and saw the liberation to independence, but has also seen the effects of international capitalism since independence. The distinct culture of human values that he identifies in the islands is, as he recognizes, being eroded by those effects. In his "Project Helen" series of watercolors, he is involved, he says, in "preserving traditional island scenes for posterity," and this is one way of regarding his work in general, as a time capsule of a way of life that is fading.[103] To what extent the culture of satellite television now sweeping the Caribbean, for instance, will undermine the distinctness of the culture remains to be seen. Walcott, interviewed in a documentary film about the impact of

American television on St. Lucia (which it said had sixteen channels, with local program content of less than 5 percent), identified the "rapidity" of change as a problem: it was "leaving a lot of stuff behind." He reiterated, "I'm not against the idea of development. I'm against the idea of believing that my development has to do with my selling what is virtually my spirit." On a local phone-in program, he restated his opposition to the Pitons development: "Everybody knows there are other places where hotels can be built. Why there? . . . you don't put any obscenity in the Grand Canyon . . . because you'd be laughed at. . . . How can that happen here unless people have such contempt for you that they wanted to do it, or the government has such self-contempt that they can even think of doing it?"[104] The matter comes down to one of self-respect, with the younger generation becoming as culturally alienated as were their colonial grandparents, the contemporaries of Fanon, who wrote, "I cannot go to a film without seeing myself. I wait for me. . . . A Negro groom is going to appear. My heart makes my head swim."[105] In stances such as that over the Pitons, the committed radicalism of Walcott's cultural politics is unmistakable. He gives full weight to the negatives under which Caribbean society labors and acknowledges the pressures that sometimes result in despair and suicide (as in the real-life stories narrated in *Another Life*), but he frames such explorations within an overall assertion of the miracle that hope remains irrepressibly at large in a community that, logically, should have given up hope long ago. In this he is in tune with another famous radical—and martyr—Walter Rodney, who wrote, "we have gone through a historical experience through which by all accounts we should have been wiped out. . . . Now not only have we survived as a people but the Black Brothers in Kingston, Jamaica in particular . . . are every day performing a miracle . . . they have a vitality of mind, they have a tremendous sense of humour, they have depth. How do they do that in the midst of the existing conditions? And they create. . . . Black people who have suffered all these years create. That is amazing."[106]

Walcott's attitude retains in fact a number of points of contact with the radical politics particularly of the 1960s and 1970s. He constructs his own "Babylon." The corollary to his assertion of the sacredness of the islands, both naturally and in terms of the spirituality of their people, is his resistance to the privileging of rationalist or scientific thought that he associates with the North and its degenerate ways. At a conference on "The Legacy of Europe," he said he was "scared of being too linear and connecting, because that would make me too European."[107] Like Wilson Harris, he values imaginative and intuitive lateral thinking and devises a symbolist and mythopoeic aesthetic.[108] He engages urgently with the persuasive re-mythologizing of mythographers such as Lévi-Strauss, whose structuralist anthropology has had a huge influence on postwar Western thought. Two of his works in particular have prompted ripostes from Walcott: *Tristes Tropiques,* published in English under its French title, which captures the elegiac nostalgia better than "sad tropics"; and *The Raw and the Cooked,* which distinguishes Third World oral cultures, as "raw," from the cultures of literate societies, which are "cooked." Walcott rightly identifies the centrist gaze behind Lévi-Strauss's dissections of societies which are radically unlike his own, metropolitan France.[109] In *Another Life,* he both captures what is truly sad in the poverty forced on communities such as those of the Caribbean and undermines Lévi-Strauss's position, in his reiterative parody, "*tristes, tristes tropiques.*"[110] In "North and South," a few years later, he makes it very plain that the implicit pejorative evaluation in Lévi-Strauss's use of "raw" is centrist, and he opposes it with his own powerful championing of the thereby marginalized culture as preferable to the "cooked" preciosity and decadence of the Western tradition.[111] He is, in a sense, demystifying Lévi-Strauss by showing him to be the Rousseau of contemporary thought, who reinscribes in scientific codes the old, damaging binarism by which societies regarded as radically different are marginalized by being construed as primitive—however nostalgically or romantically so—in relation to the center's appropriation of the civilized.

As with negritude, the locus of the other is then claimed and revalued: it is placed at the center of a different interpretation of the world from the dominant. The gaze from this new center produces a radically new mapping of the world. In Walcott's case, not only are cultural silences voiced, and absences made present, but the myths by which dominance is perpetuated are exposed. The moral consciousness, in flight from the new monsters of the North, political hegemonies where "mastodons force their systems through the snow," seeks out the South for a society still wearing a human face.[112] The North is the place of power bases, expressed through architectural styles claiming the validation of antiquity. It is the place of the museum, of the cathedral, of the "classical" with its hierarchical steps and columns, of the public institutions which are alike in their dwarfing of the individual. The difference between time and place is collapsed in a single monadic system designed to express dominance. Walcott has said, "History to me means vanity; the belief that man has belief in his destiny and that *I*'m supposed to share, delivered from a central, focal, pivotal place. The best example is the cathedral; awe is contained in them. . . . I'm scared of the vanity of an architecture that's supposed to be in praise of God but could be about man praising God." The age of some of the European cities, their "sense of destiny," rouses "fury in me, against possession. To even phrase the legacy of Europe is to imply that Europe is going to bequeath in its patronage something which we all have to inherit, or should be proud to inherit."[113]

Exposure of the nexus between culture and power is a recurrent theme in his poetry, conspicuously in *Omeros,* where in a key exposition of the relationship between representation in the dominant culture and the powerlessness of the oppressed, he mocks Herman Melville's racial representation—"Lawd, Lawd, Massa Melville, what could a nigger do / but go down dem steps in de dusk you done describe?"—and brings the section to a close in the symbolic replacement of the hieratic by the demotic, as dusk brings the dominion of blackness: "Streetlights came on. The museum windows went out."[114] Europe, to Walcott as an adolescent at the end of the war, was a negative, a countervalue, a place of terror: "The idea of Europe was like a huge devastation, a hole." His outsider's gaze produced the conclusion, "These white people are mad but they know what they're doing."[115] Experience of New York led to different terrors, of violence on the streets, as described in "God Rest Ye Merry, Gentlemen," and the dread of the nuclear holocaust. In "North and South," Dante's concluding revelation of the white rose of paradise is echoed in an ironic and demoniac inversion in which "white" is given a new, sinister racial value, "as those in the North all wait for that white glare / of the white rose of inferno, all the world's capitals."[116] Once again, the Walcott aesthetic insists on the power to invest the signifier with new meaning—and on the moral imperative of subverting the racist codes of colonial discourse. In this way he joins the throng of black artists who have since the middle of the century been devising ways of countering the denigration (even!) of blackness that the privileging of whiteness constructs.

In Walcott's countermythologizing of geography, differences of climate are expanded to moral distinctions. In the darkness of a New York winter, in "North and South," Conrad's *Heart of Darkness* is invoked as expressive of the demoniac quality of life—producing a dread and isolation that causes depression and suicide; this is then contrasted with the southern islands, characterized by warmth—of feeling and climate: "And, in this heart of darkness, I cannot believe / they are now talking over palings by the doddering / banana fences, or that seas can be warm."[117] In "The Fortunate Traveller," the play on Conrad's title is taken further, as discussed below, as part of Walcott's core aesthetic that the meaning of language is not fixed, that art can invest the terminology of the Old World with fresh significance, empowered by the "faith of using the old names anew."[118] In a subtle variant of this resistance dialectic, the language of climate is made an expressionist semiology of feeling by being reconnected to an older myth. The northern climate with its season of cold is repeatedly associated with coldness in human relations and the failure of compassion, while the tropics are, as in "North and South," the refuge of emotional warmth. Walcott thus tackles a northern myth of the South that he describes in his Nobel lecture: the dominant view that people of the tropics "inhabit a geography whose rhythm, like their music, is limited to two stresses: hot and wet, sun and rain, light and shadow, day and night, the limitations of an incomplete metre, and are therefore a people incapable of the subtleties of contradiction, of imaginative complexity. So be it. We cannot change contempt."[119] He counters this with a different symbolism, related to the ancient myth of mutability—changeability as sign of the fallen state of the world. As the Eden story relates the introduction of the seasons to the postlapsarian world, so Walcott emphasizes that the tropical climate is blessed in its constancy: "We don't have seasons in the Caribbean, and I don't think we should think in terms of seasons."[120] When contrasted with the northern seasons, cursed in their mutability, this draws in a new way on the old reading of the New World as paradise regained; but instead of the traditional East-West binarism, Walcott remodels it on a North-South division, and in such a way that the North is projected as place of moral degeneracy and the fallen condition.

The American term for autumn of course lends itself to the analogy between seasons and moral state and readily extends to metaphors of falling in battle, overlaid on the fall of the leaf. In *Omeros,* for instance, the section set in the North relates the American War of Independence to the fall, as "battalions of leaves kept falling in their blood," and moves on to the sinister onset of winter, as symbol of the dominion of the "red" Native American being usurped by the white man: "Red god gone with autumn and white winter early."[121] Even the conventional benign mythology of the northern spring is reversed in Walcott's portrayal; in "North and South," he writes of "winter branches . . . mined with buds," and "fields of March," which will "detonate the crocus," in an extended metaphor of the seasonal cycle as war. Winter, he says, "adds depth and darkness to life as well as to literature." In particular, the blankness of snow, often mythified as the artist's blank page, becomes the field not only for his own hieroglyphs but for those of nature: in "Forest of Europe," for instance, the winter trees are "tortured icons."[122] Gordon Rohlehr has used a color semiology for the cover of his book on Brathwaite, *Pathfinder,* using white letters on a black ground, because the "language that has been imposed on you is white. You use that language but you are using it on a black ground, which is actually a total reversal of the European image of making black marks in the white snow," but Walcott is concerned to mythify the black inscription.[123] He sees himself as using his own language in his own way, involved in writing the story of his own black community whether on a snowfield or a tropical landscape.

This preoccupation with a Manichean symbolism of North and South is reflected in the organization of two of his poetry collections from the 1980s, where the poems are subdivided under section headings according to their setting. *The Fortunate Traveller* has three parts, "North," "South," and "North" again; *The Arkansas Testament* is divided between "Here" and "Elsewhere," where the first is the Caribbean, as "home" location which establishes the gaze. A similar structure is evident in *Omeros* (which followed), where the "excursion" to northern locations is inserted in an antithetical relationship to the poem's base in St. Lucia. The collection titled *Midsummer* may be seen to resonate in both time and place: what the North calls midsummer, when holidays are timetabled, is the all-year norm of tropical Trinidad where the poems, which arise from a summer vacation visit, are chiefly set; but it also suggests the midlife stage that the poet's life has reached (echoing Dante's opening) and ambiguously hints that the autumnal decline, which is the only future the northern approach to life can predict for him, may mask another possibility, of a lasting well-being to come. The ludic manipulation of the rhetoric is therefore clearly not frivolous or narrowly competitive. It is evident that Walcott turns round such myths in his use of language not just because they are inaccurate, misleading, or psychologically damaging, but because, in his scheme of things, they misrepresent the essentials of the human condition and, as such, are mortal error.

For these reasons, it seems, Walcott, as part of the project to map the microcosm of St. Lucia, takes on the remapping of the macrocosm. As he increasingly visits other locations than the Caribbean in his poetry, he seems able to generate striking representations of places new to him. But when he takes on a fresh geography, he does so unmistakably from the ground on which he stands as a Caribbean person. His gaze is not theirs, as he interprets the visible world in the light of his own experience and concerns, bringing his own Caribbean pluralism (the Caribbean persona as microcosm of the world) back into a reciprocal relationship with the plural world that created it. Ireland, for instance, in *Omeros* becomes the place of ancient sanctity, of anticolonial resistance, of a politicized literature, and of the ongoing "troubles"; Wales is the site of ancient imperial conquests and of song; London is the unfeeling metropolis still fantasizing its empire, where immigrants and vagrants are marginalized. Even in the extension of his own identity to a broader American belonging, and in his increasing incorporation of North American topics and locations in his work, he writes still as an outsider, as a Caribbean American, with fresh angles to reveal. The matching of the brilliantly evoked visual detail, which is recognized as having the instant authority of a known truth, to the particularity of interpretation, which is likely to be not "standard," draws the reader into new perceptions and challenges stereotypes, bringing to bear a new sensibility that uses the aesthetic to access the ethical.

Walcott has successfully resisted the marginalizing of his place in the world by centering it in his work and then centering his work in the world. From such strong imprinting of a local identity, it is natural for nationalism to grow, but the term itself requires some comment in this context. Nationalism has been a starting point of anticolonial resistance worldwide, especially for Walcott's generation, who grew up at the end of the World War II. Walcott embarked on his art out of a commitment to his own region's struggle for political and cultural independence, but terms such as patriotism and nationalism are tainted with the dramas and struggles of power, while, as he is always quick to point out, such small islands cannot pretend to power: "The Caribbean is powerless. It can't ever have important geopolitical power."[124] For him, power is always corrupting and tending toward fascism. His perception is that, economically and politically puny as they are, the Caribbean communities can, however, be potent in art—a thesis he himself has exemplified by establishing a worldwide readership for his poetry, and by winning formal accolades for his work. The coveted mark of international "arrival" in art, as writer—the Nobel Prize for literature—had meaning for him precisely in terms of his being "gens Ste. Lucie," an individual symbolizing the whole community, the "I-an-I" paradox: "Here, on the raft of this dais, there is the sound of the applauding surf: our landscape, our history recognized, 'at last.'"[125]

It is a potent illustration of the value of such postcolonial remapping of the world. Walcott's work demonstrates that it is not only fellow citizens of the Caribbean who benefit from such new angles of projection on the world we all share. When hitherto unrecorded places and societies are mapped from an insider's point of view, images replace the blank spaces in the story of the world, and some of the old maps based on superstition can be torn up and thrown away. But as one who is well aware of the power of myth, Walcott realizes that the most effective resistance to a memorable myth is a countermyth. He sites his portrayal of his own geographical and social landscape and his radical questioning of the *mores* of the North in the core of language, investing some of the terms of colonial discourse with different meanings. This is indeed to redraw the world. Yet Walcott is adamant that his optimism is not romance, as his political engagement demonstrates: "I am not re-creating Eden; I mean, by 'the Antilles,' the reality of light, of work, of survival. I mean a house on the side of a country road, I mean the Caribbean Sea, whose smell is the smell of refreshing possibility as well as survival."[126] It is that possibility which, according to Walcott, the Caribbean proposes as counter to the burden of the past. Ultimately he sees the writer's objective as to reach "the vision that sees all earth as sacred, including his birthplace, and old people as valuable. . . ."[127]

3

"Where Else to Row, but Backward?"

Dealing with History

Ariel: Full fathom five thy father lies. . . .
Those are pearls that were his eyes.

Gonzalo: This Tunis, sir, was Carthage.

Antonio: The latter end of his commonwealth forgets the begin ning.
***The Tempest,* I.ii.394–96; II.i.87, 164**

Griot Mamadou Kouyaté: We are vessels of speech . . . we are the memory of mankind.
Niane, ed., *Sundiata,* 1.

Ariel's song is echoed in Walcott's: "Where is your tribal memory?/ Sirs, / in that grey vault. The sea. The sea / has locked them up. The sea is History."[1] In the Caribbean, Walcott's historiography shows, the tragic ancestors are long gone yet survive transformed to something precious in the present: "Those are pearls." Yet his aesthetic project is also in tune with Gonzalo's addition of a historical perspective to present experience. Gonzalo's hearers mock him for a fool, convinced that Tunis is not Carthage. *The Tempest* does not settle the question and allows skepticism as to Gonzalo's wisdom to remain. Those possessed of historical knowledge, however, will know that Gonzalo is right: modern Tunis is indeed on the site of ancient Carthage. Gonzalo, it seems, is no fool after all. The moment is a crucial determinant of how reliable a witness he is perceived to be in general. It is part of that awareness of the subjective nature of discourse which the play promotes. As Peter Hulme points out, "right from the beginning Prospero's narrative is distinguished from the play's: we are made aware that Caliban has his own story and that it does not begin where Prospero's begins. A space is opened, as it were, behind Prospero's narrative, a gap that allows us to see that Prospero's narrative is not simply history, not simply the way things were, but a particular *version.*"[2]

Gonzalo's uncovering of a hidden past that alters the understanding of the present is the key to the future, because it opens the utopian dream he goes on to express, the dream of the "commonwealth," to possibility.[3] As figure of desire, his commonwealth is ridiculed as absurd by his companions, but the fact that he is right about Carthage causes us to wonder if he is right about the ideal society too. Antonio's sarcastic criticism that his commonwealth forgets its beginning may have a meaning which transcends that of its speaker: that for such a "brave new world" to be implemented, people would need a wholly transformed attitude to each other, that they would indeed have to forget the way of the world.

Gonzalo dreams of a future that might "excel the golden age."[4] To the Renaissance mind attuned to the classics, the golden age myth implied a degenerate present, an approach to chronicity in harmony with Christian myth, which posits an origin in Eden, followed by a postlapsarian, fallen world. To envisage a future golden age is thus a countermyth of history. Walcott too is engaged in producing a counterhistoriography, but as well as paralleling both Gonzalo's dream and his retrieval of a suppressed history, he contests also the more recent discourse of "progress." His rhetorical strategy is thus multiple, but its overarching purpose is to code "history" as a negative term. The epic task situates the poet as articulator of the collective narrative, which makes *story* of the past, rather than history, with the emphasis on the "present" of living memory. The griot charged with memorizing and communicating the epic story of his people, the story of the hero of Mali, Sundiata, identifies himself among those who are not only "vessels of speech" but "the memory of mankind." The epic poet, whether African griot, ancient Homer, or Caribbean epic poet of today (and there are a striking number of them), acknowledges a responsibility to the present and future of his community that contains a responsibility to the past without being dominated by it. The apparent conflict between these two positions, one claiming a need to forget the past, the other remembering it, is therefore not substantive. Walcott's figure of the rower, introduced as a key image in *Another Life,* which seems at first to suggest a compulsive revisiting of the past, on reflection implies a more complex meaning. "Where else to row, but backward?" is a tricky, ludic figure but one that is actually quite clear: the rower in fact proceeds backwards into an unknown *future,* taking his bearings by his past.

Walcott has long adopted a quizzical stance over the discourse of history, problematizing its function and usefulness. His views, although complex, have remained remarkably consistent over a long career. In "The Muse of History," written in the 1970s, he spells out its rejection: "The truly tough aesthetic of the New World neither explains nor forgives history. It refuses to recognize it as a creative or culpable force."[5] In his Nobel speech in the 1990s, he returns to a similar theme: "We make too much of that long groan which underlines the past."[6] However, the implicit acknowledgment in this phraseology of the pain of the past reveals that his attitude to history is not so different from that famously expressed by James Joyce in *Ulysses:* "History is a nightmare from which I am trying to awake."[7] If, for Walcott, his geographic heritage is a kind of blessing, his historical heritage is, on the contrary, a problem to be dealt with, but the tendency to regard it as a kind of curse is, to him, illogical, since it is directly because of that history that the gift—the apple—of the islands has been inherited. His rhetoric of a stubborn refusal to respond to history is thus a defiant resistance rather than any straightforward assertion of its unimportance, for, far from being marginal, the question of history is central to his work. To deal with it, he offers several oppositional strategies to try to strip it of its still hurtful power.

The emblematic rower is a Janus figure whose attention tends simultaneously both ways, to the future and the past. As Janus presides over the turn of the year, so art is at the hinge between past and future, expressing the significance of the transition. Walcott, self-allegorizing as Janus with his January birthday—"my sign was Janus, / I saw with twin heads, / and everything I say is contradicted."—is at the juncture of epochs, the artist who has experienced the end of empire and the beginning of independence.[8] He perceives himself distinctively as a historical being, with a particularity of historical experience from which to speak. Renu Juneja identifies a duality in his response to history: "the need to be free of its burden and the need to reclaim it."[9] But these are compatible aims when perceived as about discourses and about constructions of identity. Traditional historical discourse, spoken from the imperial center, narrates only the suffering and humiliation of the people of the Caribbean. That is the burden that demands a response, but, for Walcott, to respond only by reaction is a mistake because it leaves in place the authority of the original discourse. His provocative and profound perception is that "by openly fighting tradition we perpetuate it."[10] He chooses instead a double strategy, of narrating history with different priorities, not reactively but from a wholly different standpoint, which relegates its standard discourse to relative insignificance. The result is a different story, accorded a different value. It is therefore exactly parallel to the strategy in *The Tempest,* on the one hand to give the longer view (reveal Carthage before Tunis, Caliban's story independently of Prospero's version) and on the other to "forget" history altogether, to leave it behind in the move to a different future, one that cherishes the ancestral "pearls" (a destination to which this argument will return).

The epic poet in particular addresses the collective present as threshold between past and future. New narratives of the past are sought by Walcott as part of a positive strategy for the future to which they contribute. As Joseph Brodsky, a close friend of Walcott, reminded an American audience at his inauguration as Poet Laureate of the United States, "It's often been said . . . that those who don't learn history are bound to repeat its mistakes. Poetry doesn't make such claims. Still, it has some things in common with history: it employs memory and it is of use for the future, not to mention the present."[11] Epic is a genre whose social functionalism is clear. Typically, it commemorates the history of a specific group or community, and commonly involves "an ostensible glorification of the past," displayed as heroic in contrast with a present time of narration, though, as Peter Toohey proceeds to point out, such dynamics are artifice: "Such a contrast between 'then and now' is a sleight of hand and requires the collusion of the listener."[12] Two aspects are crucial: the time of articulation as a point on the continuum between a connected past and future, and the act of articulation as a mediation between the specific and the general, or the individual and the group.

Both tend to confirm the articulator in a shamanic role to the community s/he serves—a symbolically significant figure, or hero, in the quest for significant figures, heroes, but both essentially acquiring heroic status only through the meaning invested in them by the group. The poet becomes the fulcrum on which the extensive and multiple revelation balances and through whom the meaning of one part to another is mediated. The rower's purpose is to move forward, the craft he propels parting the future with the present of its prow, but it is part of the emblematic meaning of the figure that the future is invisible to the subject, the rower—a desired objective, an unknown, which has to be approached in faith, once bearings are taken and the course set by a gaze fixed accurately on the known. As epic poet, Walcott is concerned to revisit the past only if it can help to deliver his people a better future. For example, he narrates his personal past, telling of his own growth to artisthood in *Another Life,* as exemplar of his belief that the special strength of his community's future lies in art; and he tells the story of Achille and his community in *Omeros* (a narration mainly of events set in the recent past), partly to prompt an urgent questioning of the pace and direction of change in the Caribbean. Above all, his work as a whole has the epic purpose of securing self-respect to the Caribbean people of the future, both in their own eyes and in the eyes of the world.

How then does Walcott relate to the general postcolonial address to history, which has been claimed to be radically different from that of metropolitans as it confronts, in Linda Hutcheon's phrase, "the amnesia of colonialism through the memory of post-colonialism"?[13] Walcott's resistance to history has involved a specific call *for* amnesia, notably in *Another Life*. His attitude to history is clearly not simple, but neither is it contradictory. The different strands of his aesthetic strategy in relation to history can be seen to compose a coherent whole. Caribbean people's lived reality reminds them that historical discourses are sites for the inscription of power; they do not need Michel Foucault's prompt. The grand narratives of the past self-evidently belong to the centers of power, which have successfully appropriated them to their own purposes, as they have appropriated the world through empire—a process in which the role of texts is, of course, central. Despite its claims to objectivity and "truth," historical discourse exhibits to an extreme degree the slipperiness of textuality and is endlessly self-referential, because the facticity to which it orients itself is, in all its complexity and mystery, terminated and inaccessible.

The glorification of the past embodied in the canonical texts that have been used to prop up power is problematic for postcolonial societies. People read classical epic, according to Toohey, because "[t]hese epics helped shape Greece and Rome (the Greeks thought that they learned from Homer) and they helped shape the European mind. Reading epic, therefore, allows one entry into the 'mind' of great ages."[14] The idea of the narratives of the past as offering access to a past greatness is not so appealing to those who have suffered under the achievements of the "European mind." Postcolonial writers, Walcott prominent among them, challenge the grand narratives' annexation of the right to define the past. Their primary task is to take control of the discourse to express a different community's subjectivity. Recognition of the partiality of historical discourses allows their substitution with a different selective version. In the shift from hegemonic, totalizing "history" with its large, ill-founded claims, to "her story" and its scale of memory,[15] the poet does not jettison "fact" for fiction but discloses the inadequacy of the written record and accounts based on it, in order to redress the balance toward a more complete picture, pieced out with the imagination.

Like other Caribbean artists and thinkers, Walcott is understandably skeptical of Western theorizations, which often read as neocolonial appropriations. Jamaican sociologist Rex Nettleford prefers to pinpoint the two-way stretch of history, noting that Caribbean writers are of interest to the world because they have "something unique to say," and that the region's colonial phase of psychological alienation, of displacement, is now being superseded, as the Caribbean is "challenged to fall back on the inner reserves of its own historical experience and cultural dynamic in order to exist on its own terms, which is partly what cultural identity is about."[16] Foucault does have certain useful insights to offer, however, as when he identifies in historiography "that theme of the origin, that promise of the return, by which we avoid the difference of our present." In foregrounding history as illusory continuity, Foucault's thought is in tune with that of Walcott. Foucault goes on to characterize his own discourse as "trying to operate a decentring that leaves no privilege to any centre" and argues: "The role of such a discourse is not to dissipate oblivion, to rediscover, in the depths of things said, at the very place in which they are silent, the moment of their birth . . . it does not set out to be a recollection of the original nor a memory of the truth. On the contrary, its task is to *make* differences . . . it is continually making *differentiations,* it is a diagnosis."[17] Walcott's address to history could be described in similar terms: he is interested in "diagnosis," in knowledge across difference, in mobile, portable knowledge, Gonzalo's apple. His aesthetic revisits the infinitely diverse field of the past not to discover origins but to contest the idea of a unified and inevitable continuity of the same, by uncovering and celebrating difference, then and now.

In that the recorded history of the Caribbean region presents one of the grimmest accounts of European imperialism, it confronts the writer with particular difficulties. In parallel with his rejection of history, Walcott acknowledges its power in calling it "that Medusa of the New World," and he asks, "who in the New World does not have a horror of the past, whether his ancestor was torturer or victim?"[18] His writing contains a range of strategies calculated to heal the trauma, which in the event involve not so much a rejection of history as a reconceiving of it in order to bring it under psychological control, to resist the hypnosis. In order to quell the Medusa's fatal stare, the postcolonial writer must appropriate the gaze. But this reconceiving starts from a firm rejection of the standard approach to history in terms of determinism and progress. For Walcott, "an obsession with progress is not within the psyche of the recently enslaved. . . . The vision of progress is the rational madness of history seen as sequential time, of a dominated future."[19] In a region where history has, as its headlines, the rapid genocide of the Native Americans, the centuries-long enslavement of Africans, and the near slavery perpetuated in the indenture system under which laborers from Asia were introduced, all against a background of intra-European warfare in the constant competition for control of the archipelago's political units, determinism, in which the future is seen as determined inexorably by the past, can imply only tragedy. As Walcott points out, "There were those who did not survive, not by weakness but by a process of imperialistic defoliation which blasted defiance; and this process, genocide, is what destroyed the original, destroyed the Aztec, and American Indian, and the Caribbean Indian."[20] For these peoples' history there is only the silence of the unknowable, the unrecoverable: one aspect of the region's past is lost forever, because when a race is exterminated its collective memory dies with it. Only fragments of words and artifacts are left. In *Omeros,* the unearthing of an Amerindian petroglyph is made a symbolic drama, articulating like a revenant both the buried suffering and the creative expression of the lost people who made it. Through the poem, their cry is heard once again. The articulation of the original genocide is, for Walcott, a synecdoche for the later genocide of slavery, for which the islands' present population has a much more direct grief.

Walcott also uses the longer historical view to deliver a seemingly more conventional sense of a cyclic history, tragically repeating itself, but the focus is on migration, the sine qua non of Caribbean pluralism, rather than on the cruelties and humiliations involved and can therefore be incorporated in the grand narrative of Caribbean odysseys and arrivals. In *Omeros,* the tragedy of forced migration is deepened in a series of related images, long-shots of anonymous linked figures, already a kind of heroic "I-an-I-an-I" community, in antithesis with the repeated solitary, grief-stricken "I" of the abandoned child. The two icons create a dynamic in which to remain is constructed as more tragic than to move (which is at least a shared, a communal experience). In "The Schooner *Flight,*" the genocide of the Caribbean's indigenous people is mirrored in the genocide of the Africans, as Shabine reminds Vince, and both are mirrored in another genocide carried out by Europeans, that of the Jews. This latter parallelism is unconventional but distinctively Walcott's. Since his early work he has repeatedly made an imaginative link between the fate of Africans in the New World and the fate of the Jews under Nazism. His own adolescence was marked by World War II and by the news of the concentration camps, a reminder of the human capacity for inhumanity, which became to him a symbol of the local and ancestral horrors perpetrated in the islands. He has spoken of his sense that the Holocaust should have been the last atrocity and (in a counter-Adorno position) of the moral imperative on art:

> I think there should have been nothing after the holocaust; nothing should have happened after the holocaust that was bad. One can say, well, that's how nations behave. If there is nothing to have been learnt from it then it was OK. And although you can say that is a very naive view of human conduct, that is not any more naive than the Declaration of Independence or the Communist Manifesto. So either everybody's naive or everybody's lying. And I think that the power that a writer can summon should have that passion in it. We should never stop writing poems about the holocaust no matter how tired the theme may become.[21]

The imperative is an ethical one, of refusal to accept the negative or cynical view of the human condition, as irredeemable. He presents this refusal of tragic determinism as characterizing the Caribbean outlook, recording, for instance, the Trinidad Theatre Workshop's actors' resistance to tragic drama: "their minds refuse to be disfigured."[22] The narration of history is *one* of the tools for the political, humanist project to improve the world, but because linear thinking applied to a region with such a history can anticipate only a tragic future of endless cycles of loss, Walcott attempts to avoid or avert such thinking, at all costs, by putting forward a different approach to history.

His sense of the relativity of historical time as organizing concept relieves the traumatic pressure:

> the Caribbean experience is not limited strictly to three hundred years, or whatever, of slavery only. It's not simply a matter of being optimistic and looking towards the future, or skipping slavery and looking back to some glorious past, or whatever. I just think that it can be absorbed in the Caribbean experience. And it is not the beginning of the Caribbean experience and therefore it should be treated as a passage of the Caribbean experience and not the entire experience of the Caribbean. And for that reason I think when you get a lot of protest poetry, or poetry of longing, or poetry of defiance and so on, that's simply one aspect of Caribbean history.[23]

By insisting on an epic poetry, he is able to transcend the limited view. Chronicity implies not only recorded history but prehistory, geological time, the gradualism of the evolutionary timescale, while culture, particularly epic, mobilizes the synchronic dimension, collapsing time difference altogether in the achronicity of myth. When, therefore, Walcott addresses the trauma of slavery, he does so in contexts shaped by the longer perspective, which enables the pain to be managed. He neither denies it nor allows it to be overwhelming. He simply "absorbs" it as one constituent of the Caribbean experience, a painful actuality, but not the sole event, and not the only topic for epic narrative.

Patrick Taylor marks out Walcott and George Lamming as writers most successfully "exploring Caliban's history" in their contributions to "the formation of a West Indian national culture." In particular, Taylor brackets Walcott's work politically with that of the socialist, Lamming, in his perception that "[t]he challenge of liberating narrative is to transform the sociopolitical reality so that lived history becomes open possibility."[24] Like David Hoegburg,[25] Taylor recognizes the radicalism of Walcott's art, for although Walcott often attacks political activists, he is in fact deeply engaged, in the political sense. He steers clear of political factionalism and has no illusions about the power of art to effect substantial change (in tune with Auden's "In Memory of W. B. Yeats," that "poetry makes nothing happen"), but he has no doubts about the moral imperative of the attempt. The irony is that because of his belief that the "better" the art the greater its chance of efficacy, his stance tends to be read as informed by a reactionary, patrician aestheticism rather than a radical politics. To the left, his downplaying of history is particularly heretical, given its centrality to Marxist discourse. Instead of seeing history as the key to the future, he regards it merely as "a kind of literature without morality."[26] Yet his ethics are essentially socialist. The idea of empire is to him like the "hubris" of Faust—man "bent on a path of self-destruction"—and he identifies with the oppressed everywhere,[27] displaying the solidarity that Edward Said identifies: "Every subjugated community in Europe, Australia, Africa, Asia, and the Americas has played the sorely tried and oppressed Caliban to some outside master like Prospero. To become aware of oneself as belonging to a subject people is the founding insight of anti-imperialist nationalism. . . . It is best when Caliban sees his own history as an aspect of the history of *all* subjugated men and women, and comprehends the complex truth of his own social and historical situation."[28] Walcott's work provides ample illustration of this. For instance, the pathos of lines such as these from *Omeros* is unmoored from historical specificities in marking those

who set out to found no cities; they were the found,
who were bound for no victories; they were the bound,
who levelled nothing before them, they were the ground.[29]

Walcott has extended his sense of St. Lucian identity to a Caribbeanness, and on to a clear pan-American identity, which leads on to a global self-identification with the human race, particularly its sufferers, in Said's analysis. Solidarity is the means to thwart the apparent imperative of despair.

The American experience, in all its heterogeneity, has therefore been Walcott's abiding topic, the Caribbean seen always as bracketing the Americas, its story a microcosm of the extended continental story. North America has continued to feature in his work, both in poetry (as is evident particularly since *The Fortunate Traveller* of 1981, his first collection after moving to the United States) and in drama (as in plays such as *The Ghost Dance* and the 1998 musical written with Paul Simon, *The Capeman*). Themes from recent and more distant history recur, underwritten by the abiding concern to read the present American landscape as palimpsest of the past, as in the islands. The priestlike role of the poet is particularly that of giving voice to the dead. Walcott has taken it upon himself to speak for the silenced Native Americans, in a memorial rite for the collective memory lost in genocide. In *Omeros* and *The Ghost Dance,* he adds the tragic story of the tribes of the great northern plains to his earlier narratives of the Caribs and Aruacs. Collective suffering can be seen as collective heroism, remodeled as positive through art. In *Another Life,* the mass suicide of Caribs at Sauteurs—Grenadian history generalized as a Caribbean icon—undergoes symbolic metamorphosis to the life-giving pouring of water, itself a symbol of the imagination.[30] In *Omeros,* the recurring symbol of history is the wound, signifying sacrifice but also redemption; and in *The Capeman* the real-life story of a young Puerto Rican, who was the victim of his social circumstances in a racialized, criminalized America, and who was nearly executed in the 1950s for murder at the age of sixteen, is given aesthetic shape through his growth to self-knowledge and redemptive self-expression: "And when I wrote my story / The words flew from the page / And my soul in solitary / Escaped its iron cage. . . . The politics of prison are a mirror of the street. / The poor endure oppression / The police control the state. // Correctional facility / That's what they call this place / But look around and you will see / The politics of race."[31] Even when he is focusing on the Caribbean bourgeoisie, Walcott is deconstructing its relations to the working class, as in *The Last Carnival,* while a play such as *Pantomime* is a classic exposé of the neocolonial interaction of race and class. Although he may at times seem to lay hieratic claim to the special position of artist, that status is defined as valid only through the artist's role as shaman to the people, as their servant.

Lamming selects three events as the great turning points of Caribbean history: the arrival of Columbus, the emancipation of the African slaves, with its consequence in the arrival of what he calls the "East," and the writing of the first Caribbean fiction.[32] For the writer, the third is the key: without self-representation in their own discourse, people are not truly independent. Walcott offers a counterdiscourse to the hegemonic portrayal of such historical turning points. In "The Fortunate Traveller," for instance, he deconstructs the speciously pious iconography of the arrival of the conquistadors, so often depicted in and since the Renaissance as kneeling on the New World shore to pray—"such heresy as the world's becoming holy from Crusoe's footprint or the imprint of Columbus's knee"[33]—revising it to a symbolic act of murderous rape, as "Ponce's armoured knees crush Florida / to the funereal fragrance of white lilies."[34] Similarly, the centrist mythification of the British empire as the empire on which the sun never sets is subverted by weighty closure. Gonzalo's reference in *The Tempest* to Carthage would have resonated (for the educated among the play's first audiences) with Cato's saw, "Delenda est Carthago" [Carthage is to be destroyed], which Walcott quotes in "North and South."[35] In Western culture, it has become a symbolic reminder of mutability, of the transience of sociopolitical power. Walcott tends to incorporate references to ancient empires, now gone, in his work to draw attention to the parallel inevitability of the decline of the European global empires. Each of his major epics enacts at its core the end of empire, the last lowering of the flag, as it were. In *Another Life,* it is performed through the imagery of sunset, and the narration of the apocalyptic fire that in 1948 destroyed much of Castries, mythified as the end of an era, a violent severance, the "century breaking in half."[36] In *Omeros,* it is dramatized through the ending of the Plunketts' era, with Dennis's nostalgic tribute to Maud functioning like a march-past of the romance of empire at her death. By ritualizing such closures, the poems enable those readers whose minds are still full of imperialist fantasies to open themselves to the necessity of the transition to the next long-awaited phase of history, as the island community, predominantly black, assumes democratic responsibility for its future.

In fact, Walcott stages not only the local political history but the metahistory of cultures. In *Another Life,* he presents the young artist protagonist's upbringing in a visual culture that emphasizes the body of the white woman as symbol of beauty, but he narrates the historic transition to a new aesthetic, taught by the "master" Harry Simmons and pioneered in his own painting by Dunstan St. Omer. The poem is alive not only to the sexual politics of race but to the politics of representation, with its ironic, punning allusion to Harry's "brushing young things from the country" (which has sexual as well as painterly implications) and to the protagonist's knowledge that he "betrayed" Andreuille, his young love, by seeing her in terms of the iconography of whiteness.[37] The poem shows that while Caribbean culture remains centered on foreign imagery it sustains the historic trauma. Like Lamming, Walcott knows that the act of appropriation of one's own through art is the real determinant of emancipation: "At last, islands not written about but writing themselves!"[38] The young artists of that generation set themselves to Adam's task of naming the specificities of their own community, with its own history.

In his strategy to take the longer view, Walcott does not pass over or ignore the era of European empire but engages directly both with colonial discourse and the counterdiscourse devised to oppose it. For him, the narration of the black experience from the standpoint of the sufferer is as damaging, paradoxically, as the triumphalism of the centrist narration of empire, because it leads only to self-consuming bitterness. The narrator of *Another Life* is "Sick of black angst. / Too many penitential histories passing / for poems."[39] He refuses the single focus on victimhood, with its sacrificial heroes stirring the desire for revenge, preferring instead the heroism of ordinary people's survival and narrating a history of shared enterprise, to which all those whose lives were lived in the archipelago have contributed. In *Omeros,* the portrayal of Achille's ancestor building a fort for Admiral Rodney, for instance, is a counter both to the centrist version, that Rodney built the fort, and to the reinscription of slavery as humiliation, still traumatic today. Instead, it displays the dignity, skill, and strength of the real builder of the fort, the enslaved African, now revealed as a hero. To drive home the emblematic scene's meaning, Walcott brings Dennis Plunkett—ironized within the poem as historian, obsessed with the sterile project to uncover an ancestor who becomes like a dead "son" in contrast to Helen's future-oriented pregnancy—to a politically punning deconstruction of Rodney's name as "Admiral / Rob-me."[40]

As Salman Rushdie has said, "The empire writes back to the centre": "those of us who did not have our origins in the countries of the mighty West, or North, had something in common—not, certainly, anything as simplistic as a unified 'third world' outlook, but at least some knowledge of what weakness was like, some awareness of the view from underneath, and of how it felt to be there, on the bottom, looking up at the descending heel."[41] Walcott's aesthetic is always oriented toward the ordinary people. In *Omeros,* for instance, he ironizes the centrist view that "'[a] few make History. The rest are witnesses'" and symbolically remaps certain key imperial events.[42] As a reminder of the role of force in the imperial mission, not only is the building of a fort seen from the point of view of the slaves, but the Battle of the Saints, which determined the eighteenth-century power relations between England and France, the cultural pluralism of several Caribbean communities, and the subsequent political and cultural shape of the Western world, is viewed literally as well as socially from underneath—from the perspective of a humble midshipman below decks on an English man-of-war. Class in European societies is shown as providing the model for the racialized inequity of the colonies. Dennis Plunkett (of humble origins in Britain but privileged in St. Lucia) voices the process to which the poem contributes: "History will be revised. . . . And when it's over / we'll be the bastards."[43] By making Dennis voice this, Walcott cleverly helps his white readers toward a recognition of its truth.

The representation of the white side of the colonial story is a particular conundrum. Walcott refuses to allow race to be essentialized as good or bad: his white characters, like his black characters, have good and bad qualities. He does, however, anatomize the social construction of personality—the Plunketts, for instance, are inevitably shaped by European culture—but he is not a determinist, insisting instead that the individual can grow beyond the cultural givens, particularly when exposed to a new social milieu. The focus on the Plunketts is a vital dimension of the poem's mapping of the island society. Its majority story is black and poor, and the poem does not disguise the essentially neocolonial relationship between the two. Plunkett employs black, poorly paid workers in a modern equivalent of the Rodney/Afolabe material relations. The poem invites readers to collapse the time difference: as Maud reminds her husband in a politically symbolic moment, "'Dennis. The bill.' But the bill had never been paid."[44] Walcott's portrayal of the Plunketts, for all its generosity, is misread if it is taken apolitically. The Janus-work faces both ways: it is a rite of homage to Caribbean people first, but, aware that the majority of his readers will be non-Caribbeans, many of them members of a white elite with time and taste for poetry, Walcott uses the opportunity to educate the "fortunate travellers."

As part of the same project, he demythologizes the ancient empires of Greece and Rome, exposing the slavery on which they built their prosperity, a fact that the grand narratives of history do not publicize. For instance, the brilliant extended metaphor in *Omeros* of the food market as slave market not only deconstructs the "glory" of the classical world, it brings painfully to full consciousness the realities of Atlantic slavery, which was valorized both by the myth of that classical culture and by the racism it authorized: "The stalls of the market contained the Antilles' / history as well as Rome's, the fruit of an evil." Beyond that, it devastatingly deconstructs capitalism, disclosing the full implications of a system in which nothing and nobody is out of reach of commodification:

> Where did it start? The iron roar of the market,
> with its crescent moons of Mohammedan melons,
> with hands of bananas from a Pharaoh's casket,
>
> lemons gold as the balls of Etruscan lions,
> the dead moon of a glaring mackerel; it increases
> its pain down the stalls, the curled heads of cabbages
>
> crammed on a tray to please implacable Caesars,
> slaves head-down on a hook, the gutted carcasses
> of crucified rebels, . . .[45]

Antonio Benitez-Rojo situates the Caribbean experience in the history of capitalism:

> the Atlantic is today the Atlantic (the navel of capitalism) because Europe, in its mercantilist laboratory, conceived the project of inseminating the Caribbean womb with the blood of Africa . . . without deliveries from the Caribbean womb Western capital accumulation would not have been sufficient to effect a move, within a little more than two centuries, from the so-called Mercantilist Revolution to the Industrial Revolution. In fact, the history of the Caribbean is one of the main strands in the history of capitalism.[46]

For Walcott, the only "commodity" that can counterbalance such Faustian transactions is the gift of compassion, figured in the "iron tear" of the market scales' weight. The poem evokes pity not only retrospectively in relation to the suffering of the past, but actively, in response to the analogous suffering caused by the global market system of today. The epic image serves finally as a political conscience-raiser, all the more authoritative because of its aesthetic power, which "recalls the spirit to arms."[47]

As well as tackling the centrist assumptions of Western discourse on empire, Walcott negotiates, critically, the counterdiscourse of recent decades. Obviously the crux is the representation of slavery. His revisiting of this past leaves the great and terrible truths of Caribbean slavery assumed rather than explored. The ghostly slave ships of the Middle Passage, for instance, which Shabine encounters in "The Schooner *Flight*," are conjured up but as rapidly spirited away. The imperial warship is presented as a context Shabine can identify with, as crewmen like himself—"those Shabines"—are ordered about on deck, but, in contrast, there is a deliberate standing off to blankness and lack of self-identification in the portrayal of the encounter with the slave ships:

> Next we pass slave ships. Flags of all nations,
> our fathers below deck too deep, I suppose,
> to hear us shouting. So we stop shouting. Who knows
> who his grandfather is, much less his name?[48]

To dwell on the experience of that "grandfather" is, to Walcott, to subvert the project to heal history, by reopening old wounds. He knows, it seems, from his own pain and bitterness which such reflection causes, that some aspects of history are best not (to use the image from the poem) "dredged" up to the light of art.

At the end of "Laventille," the condition of collective trauma that slavery imposed is expressed with a rare and memorable openness: the closure of the hatch, seen from inside the hold, is powerfully, if again fleetingly, evoked:

> We left
> somewhere a life we never found,
>
> customs and gods that are not born again,
> some crib, some grille of light
> clanged shut on us in bondage, and withheld
>
> us from that world below us and beyond,
> and in its swaddling cerements we're still bound.[49]

The paradox of "swaddling cerements"—the wrappings of birth and death—provides an eloquent symbol of the mythic historical moment of both loss and gain. In addition, since this poem is dedicated to V. S. Naipaul, it therefore, while locating itself precisely in the black shantytown of Laventille, Port of Spain, reaches out to include in its narrative voice (the "we") the Trinidad East Indian community, who shared the "horrors" of the "hot, corrugated-iron sea." The African and Asian histories of Caribbeanness are different, but they share certain essentials: the "I-an-I" model of simultaneous difference and similitude is sought here as the basis of community. Walcott acknowledges the pain of ancestral dislocation more perhaps in his reticence than do those who dwell on it.

It is true, however, that in this he sets himself apart from many other Caribbean writers, for whom slavery has been an obsessive topic. He criticizes much of the contemporary fiction addressing Caribbean history, which he regards as perpetuating the tragic pattern of history by repeatedly rehearsing it in bitterness: "In the New World servitude to the muse of history has produced a literature of recrimination and despair, a literature of revenge written by the descendants of slaves or a literature of remorse written by the descendants of masters."[50] Some of his most vitriolic words have been reserved for what is caricatured as this regressive, divisive and masochistic narrative practice:

> Those who peel, from their own leprous flesh, their names,
> who chafe and nurture the scars of rusted chains,
> like primates favouring scabs, those who charge tickets
> for another free ride on the middle passage . . .
> whose god is history . . .
> These are the dividers,
> they encompass our history . . .[51]

The stridency of the rhetoric testifies to his passion. The ethical key is the effect this revisiting of the past has on the future. He vilifies these "dividers" because they only generate an excess of bile, which is essentially self-destructive and backward-looking, locking Caribbean diversity into a pattern of tragic social rifts. The rejection of hatred is central to Walcott's ethic. Seeing others prompted to desire for vengeance by the re/membering of slavery, he prefers to cauterize that particular race-memory, for "We know that we owe Europe either revenge or nothing, and it is better to have nothing than revenge."[52]

By focusing his own art less on the specific trauma of slavery than on the trauma of migration that subsumes it, Walcott addresses the history of all Caribbean people rather than that of a single group. Typically he uses the symbol as a means to generalize meaning. The cry of grief is repeatedly evoked, in "The Star-Apple Kingdom," for instance, or in such passages as this from a climactic moment of *Another Life,* in which he is again careful to acknowledge the pain of Asian displacement alongside that from Africa:

that child who puts the shell's howl to his ear,
hears nothing, hears everything
that the historians cannot hear, the howls
all the races that crossed the water,
the howls of grandfathers drowned
in that intricately swivelled Babel,
hears the fellaheen, the Madrasi, the Mandingo, the Ashanti,
yes, and hears also the echoing green fissures of Canton, . . .[53]

Knowledge of loss can lead to a collective nostalgia, but this is strenuously resisted by Walcott as pathological. He attacks "[p]astoralists of the African revival" who play on nostalgia for a lost, historic Africa, and he rails against those Caribbean writers whose malaise is "an oceanic nostalgia for the older culture and a melancholy at the new, and this can go as deep as a rejection of the untamed landscape, a yearning for ruins."[54] He sees the psychological danger in fetishizing the relics of a tragic past, prompting desire for compensatory fascistic power and for revenge, and creates a counterdiscourse of taboo by disclosing its decadence.

With his typical double strategy, however, at the same time as deconstructing an existing discourse, investing it with negative value, he creates a new positive alongside it. In *Omeros,* Walcott enters a particular discourse of the black diaspora, but in a dialectical spirit, fetishizing instead of the "back-to-Africa" journey the *arrivants'* heritage of the Caribbean location, and the present of the natural world in all its ravishing beauty. He understands his task as to make the rhetoric of affirmation—the praise-song—outdo in appeal the rhetoric of grief that leads to recrimination. It is a matter of aesthetics as well as of ethics; the two are inextricable, the second accessible through the first, because to be persuaded of an idea's imaginative truth is to be halfway to understanding and entering the moral position it inscribes.

The desire to seek antecedents of heroism in the past may be normal, but it is not straightforward. In "What the Twilight Says," Walcott writes of Christophe's Haitian citadel, the landmark of the first New World republic, as the Caribbean's only "noble ruin," "something we could look up to. It was all we had," but even that was an ambiguous symbol, a "monument to egomania . . . an effort to reach God's height." In his Nobel lecture Walcott says, "The sigh of History rises over ruins, not over landscapes, and in the Antilles there are few ruins to sigh over, apart from the ruins of sugar estates and abandoned forts."[55] The error of nostalgia for a lost Africa or Asia is that it repeats an Old World retrospection that has functioned to entrench a culture centered on death, loss, and sacrifice. The cultures of the Old World are preoccupied with ruins, monuments, statues—with "mausoleum museums"—but Walcott remains firmly opposed to the privileging of such relics. As he says in *Omeros*, "what I preferred / was not statues but the bird in the statue's hair."[56] To him, Europe's history is written in suffering, Joyce's "nightmare," symbolized by the Holocaust and by the death of his own people's hopes. *Omeros* shows the hero of the Haitian revolution, Toussaint L'Ouverture, in a French prison, where he was to die: "A snow-headed Negro froze in the Pyrenees / an ape behind bars, to Napoleon's orders."[57] It is an iconic scene of his community's history, one to which Walcott has also given powerful expression in paint. This is not nostalgia, but clear-eyed recognition of tragedy.

Nostalgia, to him, is a way of seeing. In colonial art, it is the inaccurate representations that "are saddening rather than the tropics themselves. These delicate engravings of sugar mills and harbours, of native women in costume, are seen as a part of History, that History which looked over the shoulder of the engraver and, later, the photographer. History can alter the eye and the moving hand to conform a view of itself: it can rename places for the nostalgia in an echo; . . ."[58] Here nostalgia is something to be resisted because it distorts the truth. Lévi-Strauss's title *Tristes Tropiques*, which Walcott repeatedly ironizes, sums up for him the melancholic and essentially disparaging view of the Caribbean.[59] This outsider's view can promote in the insider an enervating acceptance of Froude's negative, itself a compressed "history,"[60] prompting a defensive nostalgia for ancestral romance and remote achievement that is subtly disabling: "The West Indian mind historically hungover, exhausted, prefers to take its revenge in nostalgia, to narrow its eyelids in a schizophrenic daydream of an Eden that existed before its exile."[61] This nostalgia can be resisted by a different emphasis, on the simple fact of the survival of the collective memory ("Those are pearls which were his eyes"), which offers an alternative to historic determinism. The tyranny of linear time is overthrown in the continuous present of lived culture and the democratic dissemination of the folk or tribal memory—"all that archaeology of fragments . . . vibrating not under the earth but in our raucous, demotic streets."[62] The concept thus becomes central to the artistic project to name a different history: the folk tradition of the *Ramleela* in Trinidad and the masquerade of Achille and Philoctete in *Omeros* exemplify ways in which the fragments of collective memory can form the basis of a new art.

Walcott's strategy in relation to history is thus multiple. The lacunae in historical discourse can be foregrounded, but likewise the representation of past events can be manipulated by selective naming and silences, so that a different contour map of history is revealed, based on "the partial recall of the race," the collective memory, which is selective.[63] Walcott accepts the great tragic peaks as the given, known to his people in all their harshness, but by mapping a various and wider landscape he gives them a context that includes the benign. Principally, the great counterweight he sets against the tragic—"lived history" as "open possibility"—is the epic event of survival. This by its very nature as infinitely plural, diverse, and ongoing undermines linear conventional history's attempt to impose a grand narrative, a monad centered on power. Instead of determinism, "the mere repetition of human error which passes for history," he asserts an alternative philosophy, based on the faith that "societies can be renewed."[64] The conventional discourse of Caribbean history in terms of fracture and loss—modes of death—is thus radically replaced with an assertion of survival and benign potential—life.

He also outmaneuvers the tyrannical past by initiating a radically new rhetoric, of amnesia: "the amnesia of the slave is an obliteration of the old linear idea of progress."[65] It is not just a negative concept but as a radical subversion of history is a positive substitution for it: "In time the slave surrendered to amnesia. That amnesia is the true history of the New World. That is our inheritance. . . ."[66] Most importantly, through the idea of amnesia Walcott reconceives the loss of a past (the conventional view of Caribbean history) as not a negative but the start of other possibilities and priorities. As he defined it in 1973, when he had not long finished *Another Life,* in which he gives poetic expression to the concept, "the degradations have already been endured; they have been endured to the point of irrelevancy. In the Caribbean history is irrelevant, not because it is not being created, or because it was sordid; but because it has never mattered. What has mattered is the loss of history, the amnesia of the races, what has become necessary is imagination, imagination as necessity, as invention."[67] This theory of compulsion to invention derives from the notion of limits, of extremity: Caribbean history was so terrifyingly bad that some sort of limit was reached, from which further movement was possible only in the reverse direction: "The New World originated in hypocrisy and genocide, so it is not a question for us, of returning to an Eden or of creating Utopia; out of the sordid and degrading beginning of the West Indies, we could only go further in decency and regret."[68] What is posited in poetic form in *Another Life* is the possibility of existing in a present consciousness, as other creatures do in the natural world, with not only no knowledge of the past, but no need or desire for it. The need is to lose ourselves in "this augury of ibises / flying at evening from the melting trees," while the light brings "nothing, then nothing, . . . and then nothing."[69] It is, as Edward Baugh observes, "no primitivism," but the poet's vision of "the original fertile nothingness out of which he can build a new world."[70] The ransacking of history for origins and purity, which is typical of the northern mentality, can be replaced by the tabula rasa of contemplation: the poet has "nothing, which is, / the loud world in his mind."[71] This embodies the truly revolutionary concept that origins and purity are within, part of our individual heritage, and are of the present. We can "begin again, / from what we have always known, nothing."[72] The difference of time, of past, present, and future, is now collapsed in a creative, transcendental present.

This has affinities to the continuous present, which is the temporal dimension inhabited by art, and which enables it to provide an alternative discourse to history. Homi Bhabha usefully defines a concept of "performative" time, with which the linear constraints of historical narrative can be sidestepped and a fluid and multiple concept of the nation narrated, "the people constructed in the performance of narrative, its enunciatory 'present' marked in the repetition and pulsation of the national sign."[73] For example, Bhabha's idea of the performative illuminates Walcott's use of carnival (as Trinidadian art form) for its collapsing of temporal distinctions: "best of all, on one stage, at any moment, the simultaneity of historical legends, epochs, characters, without historical sequence or propriety is accepted as a concept."[74] By obliterating hierarchy, such an art form is radically democratic and shows how the philosophy of amnesia can read as distinctively American.

This privileging of amnesia and emphasis on the present has obvious implications for the function of memory, to which Walcott has allocated a central, generative role: "What the Greeks said is absolutely true, that memory is the mother of poetry."[75] The conflict is more apparent than real, however. Memory, it seems, is simply to be reconceived on the natural scale of the oral society, to include the lifespan of personal memory (constantly fading to amnesia) and the mythic register of collective memory (the Jungian concept, manifest in cultural practice). The historical rite is then necessarily an act of *imaginative* recovery, replacing Clio, the muse of history, with Mnemosyne, memory, the mother of the Muses, and reconceived as art. For the present citizens of the Caribbean, by definition survivors and the children of survivors, the collective memory *is* epic. Although much of it too involves a painful acknowledgment of loss, the pain is contained by the knowledge of survival: "For us in the archipelago the tribal memory is salted with the bitter memory of migration."[76] The tragic fact of the human condition derived from history—represented by Julius Nyerere at the end of the twentieth century as one in which "internationally there is no democracy. . . . The laws of the jungle operate. The rich developed countries continue to get richer and more developed while the poor stay poor. . . . That is the World Order which the planet Earth was, and is, suffering from"—such a reality can only be radically remodeled both in art and through art's agency.[77]

Walcott's positivism is not naive. It is validated by his acknowledgment of the negative. He rages at what is dubbed "progress." His standpoint is radically different: the "recently enslaved" have no illusions about progress, history's "dirty joke."[78] Also, as he sees it, much of what was valuable in former ways of life has been lost, and much of what has replaced it is morally and spiritually bankrupt. The old-fashioned lives of the fishermen in *Omeros* have a dignity and integrity eroded by "progress," personified in the waiter, mockingly dubbed Lawrence of St. Lucia, and Hector driving his doomed transport. The general drift of history on the public scale he sees as unrelievedly tragic, as human society has moved from one calamitous act to another.

His depression at the apparent lack of improvement produces keen and bitter satire, as in "The Spoiler's Return," where the (real) calypsonian's name, Spoiler, puns ironically with those glib articulators of "progress" who in fact despoil, or in the insistent warning of "The Fortunate Traveller," which comes as near as Walcott ever gets to an apocalyptic tone warning of divine vengeance. He is particularly vehement about the failures of local politicians, working under "the illusion that we really contribute to the destiny of mankind," aligning themselves "to this bloc or that, to that way of life or the other," when really they are afflicted by "this tiredness, which falls so quickly on the powerless."[79] They are "trapped in the concept of a world proposed by those who rule it, and these politicians see progress as inevitability. They have forgotten the desperate authority of the man who has nothing. . . . Such politicians insist on describing potential in the same terms as those whom they must serve; they talk to us in the bewildering code of world markets, and so forth. They use, in short, the calculus of contemporary history."[80] This acceptance of a code that defines the Two-Thirds World from a remote center is unnecessary, he argues. Those who have nothing can afford to insist on their own *mores:* "Large sections of the population of this earth have nothing to lose after their history of slavery, colonialism, famine, economic exploitation, patronage, contempt."[81] His elevation of art as the means to salvation is made in the light of and because of the failure of other discourses, such as politics and history.

The absence of romance is paradoxically conspicuous in his reference to utopian myths. For instance, whenever he draws an Edenic parallel with the Caribbean, or with America, he points out the difference from the originary myth: "The shipwrecks of Crusoe and of the crew in *The Tempest* are the end of an Old World . . . the old vision of Paradise wrecks here."[82] The New World's literature, like its fruit, is bittersweet: "the apples of its second Eden have the tartness of experience."[83] America has to accept that "we cannot return to what we have never been."[84] The New World is in this sense not young but, initiated in experience, "older" than the old with its myth of an origin in innocence. Already fallen at its genesis, the American world is cynically aware of its derivation from "the same iridescent serpent brought by a contaminating Adam."[85] But as the Old World's myth of innocence spawned its inverse, the Fall, Walcott seems to suggest conversely that the New World's origin in the fallen condition may perhaps generate a rebirth to, if not innocence, then at least some kind of ethical originality or improvement—"the re-creation of the entire order, from religion to the simplest domestic rituals." And he looks to the artists to deliver this, to those who "reject ethnic ancestry for faith in elemental man," whose democratic vision "is not metaphorical, it is a social necessity."[86] This idea of social necessity is a key to Walcott's position: to him it is the historical circumstance that dictates the revolutionary thinking, anything else being untenable. The dream of a better world is not an empty fantasy.

To cut loose from the past, to "reject ethnic ancestry," is a first step. Unlike culture, which requires that every ancestral tradition must be assimilated[87] ("ancestors," in Walcott's phrase, being an aggregate of every constituent group of the society), personal ancestry offers ambivalent choices between affiliation and rejection. Walcott associates the symbolic mother with the homeland as bestower of identity, but the symbolic father is a different matter. Walcott introduces a clear distinction between generations, between "father" and "grandfather/s," the latter standing generally for the broader term "ancestry." To look beyond those personally known and loved (including those live to the imagination, as Walcott's dead father was to him) is to find only distress and betrayal. His suicidal white grandfather was of the generation who spurned their mixed-race children, as so painfully related in "The Schooner *Flight*," and was not far removed from the complicity in slavery a little further back. Beyond the immediately known are many ghosts who, Walcott suggests, it may be painful to encounter. In "The Schooner *Flight*," the grandfather, a "parchment Creole, with warts," is presented as "History" itself: "I met History once, but he ain't recognize me."[88] As the poem unfolds, it becomes clear that "recognize" means "choose to acknowledge." If history means a preoccupation with origins and purity of line, Shabine, smarting from his rebuff, is not interested. Forgetting can offer a real cure. In fact, as the imagery of an earlier statement makes plain, Walcott's position can seem more despairing: "The children of slaves must sear their memory with a torch."[89] The anguished image, which takes the branding of slavery and makes it the cauterizing that staunches bleeding, in the self-inflicted violence of a desperate measure, makes plain the degree of sharp and persistent pain that inhibits him from dwelling on the ancestral trauma of slavery, just as pain prompts others to finger the wound.

Following Nicolás Guillén's famous "Ballad of the Two Grandfathers," Walcott allocates himself in his writing a symbolic grandfather (ancestor) of each race (although both his actual grandfathers were white).[90] At the conclusion to his argument in "The Muse of History," he presents a controversial challenge to the familiar (and apt) model of slavery—with black victim offset against white tyrant—by paralleling the European who bought with an African who sold. He acknowledges a heritage from both, but in a complex ambivalence of acceptance and rejection:

> I say to the ancestor who sold me, and to the ancestor who bought me, I have no father, I want no such father, although I can understand you, black ghost, white ghost, when you both whisper "history," for if I attempt to forgive you both I am falling into your idea of history which justifies and explains and expiates, and it is not mine to forgive, my memory cannot summon any filial love, since your features are anonymous and erased and I have no wish and no power to pardon.[91]

But having accepted them as "men acting as men, with the cruelty of men," he does, despite this, move on to acknowledge them as "inwardly forgiven grandfathers." He then introduces a third figure, a "father" (in contrast to grandfathers, who are more remote). This father is the victim "in the filth-ridden gut of the slave ship," with every reason to hate the two to whom he owes his wretchedness, yet Walcott shows even him accepting them as "men, acting as men," with the cruelty that traverses racial difference. The important perception that the fallen condition is common to all humanity and not the prerogative of one race alone is echoed in *Another Life,* where he draws attention to the cruelty of the pre-Columbian cultures of the Americas as well as to those of the invaders. Since all historical epochs have evinced a failure of compassion, Walcott looks to the future to enact the dream of improvement that his work inscribes. Finally he takes the sting out of the past by ingeniously reevaluating it as the enabler of the present. Improbably but impressively, he concludes by offering his two guilty grandfathers thanks: "the strange and bitter and yet ennobling thanks for the monumental groaning and soldering of two great worlds, like the halves of a fruit seamed by its own bitter juice, that exiled from your own Edens you have placed me in the wonder of another, and that was my inheritance and your gift."[92] The conventional model of Caribbean history in terms of destructive fracture is thus both rehearsed and revised: the fruit is both split and reunited by what was shed at its splitting, the monumental "groaning" and "soldering" suggesting also a painful sexual union, but one from which remarkable offspring would come. The ambiguous symbols of Eden are still central to a discourse that keeps harping on history, for all its rhetoric of amnesia. The insistent memory of the tragic collective experience also seeds celebration: "To such survivors, to all the decimated tribes of the New World who did not suffer extinction, their degraded arrival must be seen as the beginning, not the end of, our history."[93] By such conceptualization, Walcott is reversing the habitually negative reading of the great transformation, the moment of colonization itself. If it can be seen not as the tragic closure of a lost past but as an origin, it frees itself (in part, at least) from the trauma of history as loss.

By privileging the mythic pattern of the end seeding the beginning, Walcott's thought (like Foucault's in its preference for the proliferation of difference) implicitly challenges a philosophy of history embodied in a conspicuous text, both product and powerful agent of centrist determinism, Francis Fukuyama's controversial but influential interpretation of world history, *The End of History and the Last Man.* Fukuyama's thesis, that Western liberal democracy is the inevitable goal of all societies, privileges a social model, that of his own society, the United States, and orders the rest of the world in relation to it. His grand final metaphor, of history as that American myth, the wagon train, strung out along a long road but with each wagon arriving eventually in town, refuels old prejudices as to the linear progress from "primitivism" to "civilization," in which some societies are deemed further advanced than others, the offensive inference being that, given time, the stragglers will arrive at the inevitable destination. Fukuyama rests his argument on opinions presented eventually as truths. He speaks of the "fact" that "history is being driven in a coherent direction by rational desire and rational recognition" and the "fact" that "liberal democracy in reality constitutes the best possible solution to the human problem." Indeed, Fukuyama makes the very large claim that cultural relativism, or multiculturalism, may become nothing more than a historical curiosity in a monocultural world.[94] The implications of this are sinister in the extreme. His professedly utopian projection may seem from other perspectives to be conspicuously dystopian, repeating precisely the cognitive split, characteristic of empire, the myth of its benign face being progressively divorced from the reality as perceived from below.

In fact, Fukuyama's text inscribes and valorizes a new form of cultural imperialism. In his code of values, any difference from the model of Western liberal democracy (deemed superior) is a temporary and aberrant condition. To put it crudely, what it implies, for the purposes of the argument here, is that the people of the Caribbean will only have achieved their destiny when they are indistinguishable from Americans, both politically and culturally. Such attitudes summon up a fiercely resistant response, from both theoreticians and artists. Edward Said has taken issue with the helplessness implicit in the model's thesis of inevitability: "far from being at the end of history, we are in a position to do something about our own present and future history, whether we live inside or outside the metropolitan world."[95] One way of answering Fukuyama is to demystify the seductive claim of a "natural" law at work by exposing neocolonialism for the essentialist, self-interested manipulation it is, and by showing the continuity between past and present. As C. L. R. James, the Trinidadian philosopher and Marxist much admired by Walcott, put it in 1964, early in the independence of the former British West Indies: "This new system of independence is only the old colonial system writ large."[96]

Neocolonialism can be recognized for what it is only if the colonialism of the past is understood. Walcott tackles the new hegemony, in "A Colonial's-Eye View of the Empire," for instance, a 1986 address to an American audience:

> America contains in it a colony. It is an empire that contains a huge colony, and that colony, whether it is black, or Puerto Rican, or whatever it is . . . that colony obliquely, quietly, politely, gently, even

> encouragingly, is kept within its frontiers. That is a peculiar thing about this empire; and it *is* an empire. The point is also that this empire has a tremendous conscience as well about the rest of the world, but what we ourselves outside the boundaries of that empire cannot understand is the American conscience and passion for freedom which somehow is fine when it is exported—there is tremendous concern about the liberty of others—but there does not seem to me to be enough *care,* or enough imaginative concern, about the admission of the truth that this empire does contain and rule a colony within itself. And for me, as a colonial, it is very easy to see that.[97]

As he says, colonials are quick to notice such splits between rhetoric and practice: "one sees very simply from the experience of being a colonial what kind of situation exists politically around the world."[98] Despite his fierce criticism of some socialist regimes, made from a context of anti-totalitarianism whether of the left or the right, and his apparent disillusionment with the left at the point when he left the islands (indicated by thinly disguised personal statements such as Shabine's in "The Schooner *Flight,*" "I no longer believed in the revolution"), Walcott has been and remains more in tune with socialist philosophy than with right-wing thinking.[99] The reordering of time in cultural narrative is an act analogous to the social reordering; Walcott, in his writing, manipulates time to make it a revolutionary signifier. Terry Eagleton presents Walter Benjamin's reading of contemporary history in terms not just of a simple dislocation from the past, but of a transformation of it, so giving what he provocatively calls an "after-life" to history's "continuous tragedy": "we have a revolutionary chance to redeem the past by imbuing it through political action with retroactive meaning and value."[100] Walcott in effect translates this assertion of a chance to redeem the past, from the political sphere to that of art.

Fictional discourse, which can alter people's perception both of their historical predicament and of their potential futures, can therefore contribute to the realization of a different future, a better future that will redeem the tragic past. Both of Walcott's long poems illustrate this redemptive process. They question the pain of the Caribbean experience and show it in metamorphosis to the positive. In *Omeros,* he addresses the tragic core of that experience through the traversing trope of the wound—specifically through the great howl of Philoctete, like Lear's, which is the howl of all the enslaved, of a tragic history—but he moves this on, as a drama, to the enactment and celebration of healing. In *Another Life,* the simultaneity of metaphor provides the transformation. The tragic moment of history, of folk memory kept alive in the naming of place (Morne des Sauteurs means Mountain of the Leapers, denoting the collective suicide of forty Caribs at Sauteurs in flight from European imperialism), is given awesome representation, but the act of tragic ending (for the Caribs) is transformed to signify simultaneously and paradoxically faith in the future (for Caribbeans of the present), death becoming life.[101] In neither poem is the tragic ignored or suppressed. Rather, it is addressed and answered, enlisted to Eagleton's project to "redeem the past."

The weight of the tragic history is real and constant, but it is matched by an opposing and equal force, that of awe and delight, resulting in a kind of equilibrium—on balance, positive. As John Hearne put it, "History is the angel with whom all we Caribbean Jacobs have to wrestle, sooner or later, if we hope for a blessing."[102] By using this metaphor, Hearne shrewdly points to the gains to be had from the challenge: the struggle to come to terms with the past is an opportunity for moral and spiritual growth of a heroic order. Martin Carter's words seem apt: "Laocoon, for all the snakes, struggled well."[103] Ultimately, after all his subtle strategies to address, subvert, suppress, or reconceive history, the answer the Laocoon-Walcott gives to the "long groan which underlines the past" is the present reality that the "Caribbean sensibility is not marinated in the past."[104] He takes forward Joyce's concept of history as nightmare from which he is "trying to awake" to a calm assertion of having awoken: "For every poet it is always morning in the world. History a forgotten, insomniac night; History and elemental awe are always our early beginning, because the fate of poetry is to fall in love with the world, in spite of History."[105] But with his watchful eye on the dangerous seductions of romance, Walcott reinscribes the presence of history precisely in the place where amnesia is sought:

> It is not that History is obliterated by this sunrise. It is there in Antillean geography, in the vegetation itself. The sea sighs with the drowned from the Middle Passage, the butchery of its aborigines, Carib and Aruac and Taino, bleeds in the scarlet of the immortelle, and even the actions of surf on sand cannot erase the African memory, or the lances of cane as a green prison where indentured Asians, the ancestors of Felicity, are still serving time. . . . Decimation from the Aruac downwards is the blasted root of Antillean history. . . .[106]

Since the expressionist geography insists on a historical reading simultaneously with the elation it offers, there is relief from history only in the combined effects of geography and culture: "These two visions, the *Ramleela* and the arrowing flocks of scarlet ibises, blent into a single gasp of gratitude. Visual surprise is natural in the Caribbean; it comes with the landscape, and faced with its beauty, the sigh of History dissolves."[107] The place is called Felicity for good reason.

This is the secret of arrival, of hybridity, of creolization, of naturalization—of the future. As Robert Young sagely remarks, "History cannot be done away with any more than metaphysics: but its conditions of impossibility are also necessarily its conditions of possibility."[108] On the one hand there is the reordering of history to present alterity: different stories and other priorities than the hegemonic version provides, in the quest for what Chinweizu calls "a vitalizing perception of our history."[109] Walcott shifts the emphasis particularly from the lost to the found, to the vision of man as "a being inhabited by presences, not chained to his past."[110] On the other hand, there is the model of reordering it toward forgetting (in the name of the dream of the future)—the antihistory, which, like Gonzalo, Walcott presents so positively—which inserts a new rhetoric into historical discourse, as it celebrates "the possibility of the individual Caribbean man, African, European, or Asian in ancestry, the enormous, gently opening morning of his possibility . . . his memory, whether of grandeur or of pain, gradually erasing itself as recurrent drizzles cleanse the ancestral or tribal markings from the coral skull. . . ."[111]

4

"The Mind . . . Sees Its Mythopoeic Coast"

Manipulating Myth

Miranda: O brave new world,
That has such people in't!
The Tempest, V.i.183

Miranda's exclamation at her first sight of wider human society is often taken as an example of tragic irony, the individuals before her being, as the audience well knows, chiefly corrupt and base. Prospero's cynical rejoinder, "'Tis new to thee," is, however, only one possible response. The play's movement toward a redemptive closure is in part conditioned by the influence of her gaze, her innocent expectation of goodness (although she knows her own history), which, on the logic the play explores, may have the power to bring into being the world in which it has faith. This is not just fanciful. *The Tempest* investigates very seriously not only the subjectivity of perception but the transformative power of perception on lived reality. Its naming of the possibility of a brave new world, not just through Miranda but through Gonzalo and through the dreams of its various personae, constitutes its myth. Prospero's island is carefully made nonutopian, but the image of a better place presides over it imaginatively. "I cried to dream again," says Caliban.[1] Walcott's work is about his own nonutopian brave new world, modeled in the faith that the Caribbean community has special qualities, which a mythopoeic art can articulate, and which the world can share. The gist of the last two chapters culminates in this one: it is as myth that the specificity of place and culture is celebrated, and through myth that history can be reconceived: "In a big, powerful country with a 'history,' the ruins are more important than the people. We don't have that, because we weren't 'great' in that sense. And it's good: it annihilates the idea of history as progress, a march. Here there's only the primal, blessed experience of waking up to the reality of the earth."[2] That idea of the sacredness of one's world, as gift, to be celebrated in art, makes of the aesthetic a sacral rite, for Walcott. This chapter explores the meaning of myth to him, and his sense of language practice as rite, but it also examines his work in the light of a wider concept of myth, adopting Roland Barthes's concept of myth as metalanguage, a "second-order semiological system," that is, a cultural phenomenon, not necessarily related to belief in the transcendental, but "a pure ideographic system."[3] Individual texts as well as cultures can have their own metalanguage, and these can combine distinctively in the work of one artist, as they do in Walcott's oeuvre. When Walcott wrote in the early poem "Origins," epic in tone, "The mind, among sea-wrack, sees its mythopoeic coast, / Seeks, like the polyp, to take root in itself," he was identifying the originality and self-reliance that the artists of the Caribbean would need, to build a literature from scratch. But he knew from that early stage that such an art would use as building blocks the cultures of the world, which have hybridized and rooted to grow differently in their Caribbean location. The new world given to Caribbean poets to name is "brave" in both senses: it is resplendent in its geography and courageous in its human society. It is no paradise to its inhabitants, but it has special strengths that art can identify and hold up to the world as example. One of those is its faith in the good dream of human community, as opposed to Joyce's "nightmare" of history.

One of the tasks is to conceptualize community, not just through mimesis but to imagine it as possibility. Epic has traditionally been a conspicuous site for the narration of a belief system, just as for the narration of history, both having a complex confirmatory relationship with a community's identity. Myth's role in epic reflects both meanings: the stories (epics) a community tells itself to confirm its sense of identity and its will to embark on the future place a high value on the sacred narratives of the past, and themselves constitute a mythic discourse, in that they sign a symbolic meaning to the community (a second-order semiology). Epic both represents myth and generates myth: it is perpetually at the hinge between the cultural past and the cultural future. And it is myth that always signs plural meaning, Walcott's "crystal of ambiguities."[4] The meaning of myth is never fixed, as Robert Graves recognized, coining the term "iconotropy" for such change, "found in every body of sacred literature which sets the seal upon a radical reform of ancient beliefs."[5] Walcott has committed his mythopoeic, iconotropic art to his epic project with a singleness of purpose that has not wavered over fifty years.

Myth is a cultural given, but it is also a cultural tool. Existing myth can be harnessed to new purposes and new myth generated to address new social conditions or objectives. A mythopoeic art is related to symbolism but does not confine itself to fixed correspondences as symbolism tends to do. Rather, its characteristic mode is narratological; it unfolds and develops meanings in process, in an open-ended continuum. Franco Moretti relates it to what he calls "modern epic," the product of "the desire of contemporary societies for 'meaning,' imagination, *re-enchantment.*" His argument is that "rewriting an event in mythical form is tantamount to making it *meaningful:* freeing it from the profane world of causes and effects, and projecting into it the symbolic richness of the archetype."[6] Even Barthes, whose definition of myth in the 1957 essay "Myth Today" is principally hostile (he sees myth as retrogressive, bourgeois, and antipolitical), acknowledges a role for creativity, that "the best weapon against myth is perhaps to mythify it in its turn, and to produce an *artificial myth:* and this reconstituted myth will in fact be a mythology. . . . All that is needed is to use it as the departure point for a third semiological chain, to take its signification as the first term of a second myth."[7] Although this terminology has negative connotations ("artificial" and "reconstituted" give no inkling of the vigor of mythopoeia), the idea is useful.

Some of Walcott's most interesting and memorable strategies are those involving a third-order semiology, creating a language from existing myth to express new significance. It is a heterodox and essentially revolutionary practice, which gives rise to moments of startling beauty. Whether responses to their intense aesthetic effect involve the ethical or the transcendental will depend on individual habits of thought. Religious people will respond to Walcott's work differently from other readers, but no group need feel itself excluded. A mythopoeic art is essentially about culture—in Walcott's case, cultures. His work addresses faith as one of many factors in the human condition, analogous with love, or desire, or awe. He has his own beliefs, of course, but in a profound sense they become irrelevant to the work, which is itself. Although his texts constantly allude to ideas of the spiritual and of the divine, central as they are to culture (in the Caribbean particularly), it is as literature that they exist, and as literature that they participate (if at all) in the sacred. The obvious truth, so easily forgotten, is that the rite is the writing.

Walcott defines myth as "the alternative to history because it doesn't have linear time, chronological time—it's the opposite of reason, rational behavior, opposite to hierarchy," and he tends to situate it in the context of spirituality: "Myth is religion. The death of belief certainly annihilates myth."[8] This has implications for his own artistic use of religious myth. His reactions to the classical pantheon when working on his Homeric works were problematic: "The gods seemed totally contradictory. It all got very silly to me. They didn't seem to have any moral conduct I could follow, not a belief I could share in. There was the same difficulty with the African pantheon—because I'm a Caribbean person and don't share that."[9] He made a similar point about the writing of the *Odyssey:* "I had to be absolutely true to my own belief in the play. . . . I can't believe in the mythology and I cannot write if I don't believe in the mythology."[10] To Walcott, myths confer cultural identity: "You cannot create a mythology, and there's no culture that doesn't have a mythology."[11] Distinctively, he sees geography as the determinant: "Where have cultures originated? By the force of natural surroundings. You build according to the topography of where you live. . . . [Y]ou create what you need spiritually, a god for each need."[12] This essentially local idea of the spiritual is close to animism and in keeping with mythographies tracing the sense of the spiritual back to evolutionary nature.

He describes Caribbean culture as young compared to some cultures but unique, "a cultural goldmine":[13] "there has never been a place that has had such concentration in a tight space of all the cultures of the world," arising from "a race, in the Caribbean, made of all the various races." It represents in human terms a "multicultural possibility" of great creativity, for it is "multiplicity that . . . unifies the whole idea of the Caribbean."[14] This idea of Caribbeanness can be related to Benedict Anderson's definition of the nation as "an imagined political community"; "regardless of the actual inequality and exploitation that may prevail in each, the nation is always conceived as a deep horizontal comradeship."[15] Walcott's work can be regarded as an epic project to name the Caribbean nation to itself and to the world, his two great epic poems providing distinct variants on this. *Another Life* expresses the possibility of a society founded on the values of art, with the artist constructed as national archetype, through the twin protagonists, and *Omeros* models the self-sufficient, nondependent community of "deep horizontal comradeship" such as Anderson describes, without dynasties and, in the fishing community, without hierarchies (though with male rivalry over a woman). It is characterized instead by benign relations of mutual support and celebration, a nonviolent society again using paired friends as the overarching archetype, the "I-an-I" model, which is the building block of community.

Walcott has said of archetypes, however, "There are probably only four or five types, in terms of reality, or literature: somebody's in charge, somebody's a victim . . . that's only two."[16] Wole Soyinka sees both the politics and the metaphysics of this fundamental drama, the questioning of authority: it is within the "framework" of the gods that "traditional society poses its social questions or formulates its moralities." He describes the stage as "the ritual arena of confrontation," the "symbolic chthonic space," in which "the presence of the challenger" is "the earliest physical expression of man's fearful awareness of the cosmic content of his existence."[17] Walcott observes:

> there's always one figure in the folk imagination who is kind of a protestant figure, an elusive figure, who is not part of the cosmology and upsets the hierarchy somehow, either by defiance, or by wit, or by solving challenges. Like most of the West Indian jokes, which are based on African stories, [there is] somebody always challenging Tiger, always making an idiot out of Tiger . . . and in a sense the Tiger represents a kind of deity. And this person who is sceptical and smart and avoids the power of the Tiger is really a kind of protest against . . . or query or scepticism [of] . . . omniscience or power.[18]

His use of the term "protestant" here is interesting in that it connects with his own self-perception as a St. Lucian, a member of a nonconformist minority within his home community predominantly of Catholics, but the possessor of a difference that was essentially engaged, not just private. This helps to explain his own aesthetic practice as challenger of myths, of whichever side. He refuses blind acquiescence, sticking to his own perceptions however unpopular they may make him, on both sides of the political fence. His self-imposed imperative is one of great daring: as a mythopoeic artist he spins, Anansi-like, his own vision into a worldwide web.

Walcott famously wrote in *Another Life* of his epic project to "make of these foresters and fishermen / heraldic men!"[19] He has spoken more recently of his quest for (Jungian) archetypes as personae to represent his society: "One of the things we have to grit our teeth and endure is the arrogance of transforming your own people into emblems—that it is your business to make emblems, or archetypes, out of [them]."[20] Although the pronoun is plural or neutral, it is clear that he is speaking of his own aesthetic practice, for although such "emblematic temptations" bear the risk of arrogance, he sees the facts as "so strong," "so epically powerful" that they require recognition: "The West Indian people . . . are physical survivors of enormous punishment. That alone is heroic, because of the survival." He developed the point in terms of myth: "It is mythical that somebody should be in . . . the Middle Passage. The endurance *is* mythical, it *is* epical." He instanced "the galley slave who becomes Spartacus," distinguishing secular from sacred myth: this was "not myth in the interior sense of a presence." His own interest, he said, is "in the arrival at what becomes the archetype." This is an important exposition of Walcott's self-perception as a mythopoeic writer: that it is not that the art creates the archetype so much as that it uncovers it, allowing it to emerge, become perceptible aesthetically.

His acute self-awareness that this naming might be seen as arrogant is in fact the guarantee of its essential humility. The archetypes, to Walcott, are lived human realities, not fabrications, the role of the artist being to articulate them, to mediate them between the home community and the wider world. His plebeian heroes thus originate in mimesis. The environment in which he grew up (that shaped his identity) provided the images of what he described in his Nobel lecture as "the grace of effort":

> The hard mahogany of woodcutters' faces, resinous men, charcoal burners . . . a man with a cutlass cradled across his forearm, who stands on the verge with the usual anonymous khaki dog . . . the fishermen, the footmen on trucks, groaning up mornes, all fragments of Africa originally but shaped and hardened and rooted now in the island's life, illiterate in the way leaves are illiterate; they do not read, they are there to be read, and if they are properly read, they create their own literature.[21]

The gaze may be the poet's but it contains no hegemony, no capture: it begins from a knowledge of its secondariness to the heroic reality of such people's lives. The poet sees himself as simply the medium—in a quasi-spiritual sense—through which such lives can be honored and marked, in the wider global community. The poet is, by virtue of his role, set apart (most people are not poets), but the important fact is that he is given that role because he shares in that community: "your duty is supplied by life around you. One guy plants bananas; another plants cocoa; I'm a writer, I plant lines."[22] As he wrote in "Mass Man," "someone must write your poems."[23] The poet provides a service to his community, like the grower of food; his produce, poetry, can be seen as "the bread that lasts."[24] Real lives are ephemeral, but art endures. It is the old wisdom, "ars longa, vita brevis," but given new impetus in the poet's responsibility to "translate" a new, unrecorded society into art. "If I go down to Gros Islet," says Walcott, of the fishing village mirrored in *Omeros,* "each face has its own sculpture, but they become a something beyond their own natural flesh—iconic, emblematic. There's a sense of their faces being grooved by the daily life we all share."[25]

Text-derived archetypes, emblems of the Western tradition, such as Helen, Adam, Crusoe, and Ulysses, are enlisted to the portrayal of these iconic figures (the "heraldic men" of *Another Life*) because Western culture is naturalized to the Caribbean, but Walcott's strategy in deploying each is different. J. M. Coetzee, as a South African writer, has his own perspective on a society based on exploitative power: "The answer to a myth of force is not necessarily counterforce, for if the myth predicts the counterforce, counterforce reinforces the myth. The science of mythography teaches us that a subtler counter is to subvert and revise the myth."[26] Walcott's resistance is constantly to subvert and revise myths, as well as to create them, as his own counter to neocolonialism, his own writing back to empire.

Homi Bhabha reconnects Walcott's linguistic practice to a modified idea of history, seen through his own lens of ambivalence. (Bhabha's identification of ambivalence as marker of the postcolonial should, perhaps, be seen in the light of Soyinka's observation that "[a]mbiguity, levelled at the writer, is very often a cover for the critic's own social evasion.")[27] Walcott, he says, "leads us to that moment of undecidability or unconditionality that constitutes the ambivalence of modernity as it executes its critical judgements, or seeks justification for its social facts. . . . History's *intermediacy* poses the future, once again, as an open question. It provides an agency of initiation that enables one to possess again and anew—as in the movement of Walcott's poem ["Names"]—the signs of survival, the terrain of other histories, the hybridity of cultures." He describes Walcott as opening up his poem to the "historical 'present,'" Walter Benjamin's present, which is "not a transition, but in which time stands still and has come to a stop." It defines, says Bhabha, "the present in which history is being written."[28] This is subtly adrift, however, from Walcott's own exposition of his use of chronicity. His dialectics brings history into opposition with myth in order to subvert the former. The reluctance of left-wing critics to acknowledge the full import of Walcott's skepticism of history as useful discourse marks chiefly their orthodoxy. In fact, Soyinka's charge that Barthes's Marxism is undermined by his complicity in the bourgeois values he criticizes[29] is applicable to the academy at large (including Soyinka himself, as Chinweizu is quick to point out). Even Patrick Taylor, who is a perceptive critic of Walcott's work, in co-opting *Pantomime,* aptly, to his category of "liberating narrative," defines such narrative as antimyth—it "attacks mythical and ideological categories for sustaining oppressive situations"—without perceiving that it is possible to have work that is *both* politically liberating *and* profoundly mythic.[30]

As the preceding chapter argues, for Walcott, as for the Caribbean in general, history is a problem to which, he believes, myth can offer a resolution. He is not alone in this view. The great writers of the New World, he says, "reject the idea of history as time for its original concept as myth."[31] The desire for facticity typical of the discourses of history and linear time is collapsed as "[f]act evaporates into myth."[32] Story, the self-shaping form, predominates, based on "the partial recall of the race," selective collective memory: "History, taught as morality, is religion. History, taught as action, is art. . . . Because we have no choice but to view history as fiction or as religion, then our use of it will be idiosyncratic, personal, and therefore, creative."[33] Great as the project of history is, it is subsumed in the greater project of myth, for when history is narrated *as* myth, its tragic determinism can be subverted.

Myth to an age dominated by atheism tends to seem inescapably archaic, but on its own terms it is urgently of the present and about the future. The language of history becomes just one of the discourses through which it can sign that urgency. The focus on myth is thus a dialectical response to history in the sense that the tragic determinism of history can only be subverted in a different kind of discourse. Walcott ponders the "reality" of naming, of the utterance of faith to make real that which it names (related to the African concept of "nommo" [sacred naming] discussed below): "O Thou, my Zero, is an impossible prayer, / utter extinction is still a doubtful conceit. / Though we pray to nothing, nothing cannot be there."[34] He is not "modern" in this sense but is continuing an ancient mythic discourse that offers a redemptive alternative (in fact he ironizes himself as "medieval"),[35] the words of faith having the power to conjure that which they express. But the meaning of faith to the community at large is in part historically constituted. As Northrop Frye has put it, "The point is that when any group of people feels as strongly about anything as slaves feel about slavery, history as such is dust and ashes: only myth, with its suggestion of an action that can contain the destinies of those who are contemplating it, can provide any hope or support at all . . . myth *redeems* history: assigns it to its real place in the human panorama."[36] Walcott speaks of "[n]o history, but flux, and the only sustenance, myth."[37]

Chronicity is replaced in the mythopoeic by synchronicity, a zone of contemplation in which time difference is collapsed, allowing new meanings to emerge from collocations absent from history. Walcott's "The Muse of History" has clear echoes of T. S. Eliot's 1923 review of Joyce's *Ulysses,* as deploying a "mythical method" that draws "a continuous parallel between contemporaneity and antiquity."[38] Walcott aligns himself with those writers of the Americas who have gone beyond confronting the

Medusa of history.[39] The continent's patrician writers "whose veneration of the Old is read as the idolatry of the mestizo" are misapprehended, he says, for what is not understood is that they fundamentally reconceive time: "their sense of the past is of a timeless, yet habitable moment," a time that can be perpetually now. As with Eliot's view of *Ulysses,* they can conduct us "from the mythology of the past to the present without a tremor of adjustment."[40]

To Frantz Fanon, however, the operation of myth in a dominated community functions only to shore up the power of the dominators: colonials "no longer really need to fight against [the colonizers] since what counts is the frightening enemy created by myths. We perceive that all is settled by a permanent confrontation on the phantasmic plane." The first step to political action, for Fanon, is therefore to bring the colonized out of this plane to recognize his historical circumstances: "the native discovers reality."[41] To Barthes, too, myth is first the problem. He defines it as "depoliticized speech," with "the task of giving an historical intention a natural justification, and making contingency appear eternal"; it is "constituted by the loss of the historical quality of things." This to him is dangerous: "The function of myth is to empty reality: it is, literally, a ceaseless flowing out, a haemorrhage, or perhaps an evaporation, in short a perceptible absence."[42] This model of myth, however, is subverted by Walcott's radical vision: for him, the mythic method "is the revolutionary spirit at its deepest; it recalls the spirit to arms," with its deeply rooted "revolutionary or cyclic vision."[43] The characteristic pun is not just frivolous.

To Walcott, the writers of the Americas are the true revolutionaries, who unchain the present from the past by collapsing time as causal: "for what they repeat to the New World is its simultaneity with the Old."[44] The relationships of power are reversed: the past, instead of dominating the present, is made to serve it as inspiration. The tragic model is replaced with an optimistic one. Walcott sets out a specifically American aesthetic, which transforms history's negatives to the positives offered by myth. St.-John Perse and Aimé Césaire, for example, "perceive this New World through mystery. . . . [W]hat astonishes us in both poets is their elation, their staggering elation in possibility"—the "brave new world" envisioned not as cynicism but as potentiality.[45] The "Muse of History" essay thus contains a complex refutation of the easy dismissal of the patrician writer as archaic and establishment-oriented, by demonstrating him to be more revolutionary than the self-styled revolutionaries, a position that has, of course, implications for how Walcott himself is perceived. The qualities he praises in these other writers are manifest in his own writing, and he conceives of his artistic project, like theirs, within a wider American endeavor in which others have also chosen the mythic alternative to history, particularly those of the francophone and hispanophone worlds who have placed their fictions in a magic realist, future-oriented present. Franco Moretti's point about Gabriel García Márquez is that he uses magic as belonging "*to the future:* to the West, to the core of the world-system."[46] Antonio Benitez-Rojo observes that "the whole Caribbean was grounded in mythology."[47] Barthes does finally come round to a compatible view, that "mythology *harmonizes* with the world, not as it is, but as it wants to create itself."[48] Walcott (like Wilson Harris, a kind of magic realist) sees art as helping the world to imagine not only its heterogeneity but its *potential* difference.

Walcott's focus on myth, however, makes him all the more adamant in his opposition to false mythographies. The writings of Claude Lévi-Strauss are of more urgent concern to him than those of historians precisely because they are about myth. While purporting to be voiced from a position of empathy with the communities whose myths they subject to structuralist analysis, they are, as Walcott perceives, a neocolonial appropriation based on an essentially hierarchized and prejudiced way of seeing. Mythography's roots in anthropology undoubtedly require it to be historicized as a cornerstone of colonial discourse, to which the reclaiming of their own myths by writers such as Walcott and Melville is a necessary and important counterforce. The difference between myth lived as faith and myth studied as semiology is like that between the living body and that on the dissecting table: crucial dimensions are absent. Walcott marks the loss of myth-as-faith that Caribbean history entailed: what emerged was "an Africa that was no longer home, and the dark, oracular mountain dying into mythology" (ironizing the popular meaning, "untrue belief").[49]

Yet he allows a place for retrieval through art. In his Nobel lecture, he anatomizes the task of reconstruction, the building of a new house for ancient myths. His figure is a double one. On the one hand, "Memory that yearns to join the centre, a limb remembering the body from which it has been severed, like those bamboo thighs of the god. In other words, the way that the Caribbean is still looked at, illegitimate, rootless, mongrelized," with Lévi-Strauss's "pathos" or plain "contempt"; on the other, the "making of poetry, or what should be called not its 'making' but its remaking, the fragmented memory, the armature that frames the god, even the rite that surrenders it to a final pyre; the god assembled cane by cane, reed by weaving reed, line by plaited line, as the artisans of Felicity would erect his holy echo."[50] It is, of course, from the earliest sacred rites that both poetry and theater spring. Actors, Walcott says, must undertake "the journey back from man to ape. Every actor should make this journey to articulate his origins."[51] But the concept of "a god for each need" endorses a natural polytheism, foreign to most world religions—which poses another problem: "monotheistic myth is not exactly too exciting as fiction."[52]

Yet the autobiographical element in his work often refers to his Christian upbringing, which has clearly shaped his outlook. Speaking to a largely Catholic audience, he jested about a rather "papal" chair, saying, "I'm a Protestant. Or was."[53] But asked on another occasion whether he used the language of religion as a literary device or out of faith, he replied, "I have never doubted. But if you are asking whether I am a Christian, or whatever, that is another matter."[54] Like his beloved James Joyce, he is deeply anticlerical. It seems that he maintains the position reported by Selden Rodman in the early 1970s: "My faith in God has never wavered—which doesn't mean I have any use for the Mafialike churches! . . . I pray. I give thanks. I don't ask God for things—that's childish."[55] Raised to worship, he still constantly uses language as rite: for invocation, praise, awe, all kinds of prayer, including thanks—even incantation, with the "spell" to turn a house into a home. Although Walcott's family was Methodist, he was educated at a Catholic secondary school, staffed in part by priests; his beliefs are fundamentally unorthodox, but his sympathies are broadly Christian:

> The imitation of Christ, the mimicry of God as a man, . . . must be carried into human life and social exchange, we are responsible for our brother, we are not responsible to ourselves but to God, and while this is admirable and true, how true is it that the imitation of God leads to human perfectibility, how necessary is it for us to mimic the supreme good, the perfect annihilation of present, past, and future since God is without them, so that a man who has achieved that spiritual mimicry immediately annihilates all sense of time. "Take no thought of the morrow" is the same as "history is bunk"; the first is from Christ, the second from Henry Ford. But Ford is the divine example of American materialist man.[56]

Ultimately, he says, "the ideal man does not need literature, religion, art, or even another, for there is only ideally himself and God" (an essentially Protestant metaphysics), but the ideal is elusive, and in the sublunary world, spinning language as mythopoeic literature he sees as having a role.[57] The supreme task of art, as Walcott sees it, is to record the world as mystery, a task that is paradoxically perfectly compatible with that of demystifying it politically. Clear vision is vital in both sociopolitical and metaphysical dimensions, as he sees it, and the two are facets of one whole.

It may be that he will come to be recognized as a poet of spirituality. His eclectic use of cross-cultural religious myth makes no concessions to those who are convinced of a single "truth," but the growing momentum, in the fin de siècle academy, of postmodernism's flight from its aridities into the sweet water of the transcendental may prove a propitious coincidence. Philippa Berry and Andrew Wernick describe the emergence of "a darker, more obscure way of seeing and thinking" in opposition to the dominant oculocentrism of Western thought.[58] The paradox is that writers such as Walcott have been around a long time, but have been "obscure" to centrist thinkers because of an intricate screen of cultural blinkers. Walcott does not engage with spirituality as an alternative to oculocentrism; quite the reverse. He creates the illusion, as does Dante, of leading the reader to epiphany (aesthetic or spiritual, as preferred) with eyes wide open.

His mythopoeic project is double, facing two ways like Janus. He narrates his people's story to them as rite of thanks and to counter history's legacy of self-contempt, and he narrates his people's story to the world to redress its absence from Western discourse and to challenge rationalism's legacy of lack of faith. The first is primarily secular (his awareness that Caribbean people do not need lessons in the sacred from him is acute);[59] the impetus of the second is toward spirituality, though as a dialectical engagement with sociopolitical reality, it involves the secular. The peculiar irony is that in large measure his use of myth is functionally mimetic: in representing his people's story to the world, he centers belief and imitates the sacred in the first place because these are their priorities, as well as his own. Ultimately, Walcott sees the task of art as to make manifest the transcendent; in comparison with this, every other aspect of its function, as he sees it, fades into insignificance.

Myths, of course, have histories. In "Origins," as since, Walcott describes how his colonial education taught him about the ancient Greeks—"Of Hector, bridler of horses, / Achilles, Aeneas, Ulysses"—but for the story of the ancient people of his own locality, only "[b]lank pages turn in the wind."[60] Ironically, because of this cultural exposure, it was easier to relate to the mythology of ancient Greece than to that of lost Amerindians or of the obscured traditions of Africa. In "What the Twilight Says," he describes how difficult it was for his theater company to relate to the Yoruba divinities of Soyinka's plays: "Ogun was an exotic for us, not a force." The actors knew their difference as Caribbeans: "our frenzy goes by another name." They were "Afro-Christians" for whom "the naming of the god estranged him."[61] In "From This Far," he writes, "in the soil of our islands no gods are buried. / They were shipped to us, Seferis, / dead on arrival."[62] Yet the task of Antillean art was to be, as Walcott defines it, the assimilation of the features of *every* ancestor: pluralism was its imperative, with each of the region's various cultures represented. The claim to the new location must be "wholly made," "[b]y all the races as one race," with the freshness of new beginnings that "gave the old names life, that charged an old language, from the depth of suffering, with awe." But awe, the impetus that leads to religion, is sought by the poet in "the ritual of the word in print."[63] Art is conceived as a quasi religion, in which the most profound hopes of the community can be expressed. A mythopoeic art evokes that awe which recognizes the openness of possibilities.

It is not prescriptive and knows nothing of closure. The myth that all communities seem to share is that of "eternal return," to use Mircea Eliade's phrase, the dream, in all its cultural variants, of the defeat of death.[64] This is the religious dream. But there is another dream, the secular one of the ideal society. The distinctively dystopian past of the Caribbean community demands a powerful counterforce. Walcott seems to be saying that its people have been constrained to value relations based on gentleness and generosity precisely by and through the appalling reality of their history. The writer has to make "creative use of his schizophrenia, an electric fusion of the old and the new."[65] The utopian dimension to Caribbean art is therefore not naive. When Walcott's drama enacts such rites as a healing, a quasi resurrection, as in *Dream on Monkey Mountain,* a miracle performed by the least respected person of a hierarchical racialized community, it does so as part of its strategy to mark the social deprivation but spiritual strength of a real, historic group.[66] When his poetry centers a benign horizontal community within the wider society, as in *Omeros,* it does so around the central symbol of the wound, denoting historic and ongoing suffering, which the text brings to healing. There is a real conjunction of revolution and revelation but a stringent refusal of the rhetoric of revenge, as of the glorification of suffering. Instead, Walcott's art identifies the heroism of survival and suggests that suffering can be transformed or redeemed.

The assertion of the "felicity" of the islands through the miracle of *cultural* survival is about belief in the value of shared culture, of community rite: the Hindu epic *Ramleela,* for instance, performed as community rite in central Trinidad. It was not "theatre" but "faith," not elegiac but celebratory: "Why should India be 'lost' when none of these villagers ever really knew it, and why not 'continuing,' why not the perpetuation of joy in Felicity?"[67] This is a case of myth itself as survival, but Walcott deploys it also in a dialectics of lineage, as countermyth to the mystification of dynasty and purity, which riddles the dominant culture of the West. The communal rite is different from its origin, its predecessors: it is creolizing in the new location. Walcott, in naming Caribbeanness to the world in the Nobel lecture, creates new myth by demonstrating the harmony between the island as site of a revelationary nature and as site of vigorous, hybrid culture: he metaphorizes the red-costumed child archers of the Hindu epic through the flight of scarlet ibises (the national bird of Trinidad) and *vice versa*. Each becomes a symbol of the other; together they become a new myth of Trinidad, one demonstrating how Hindu tradition is naturalized to the Caribbean.

The argument of this chapter, then, is necessarily linked to that of the preceding chapters. The elemental geography of the archipelago—the islands, the sea, the vegetation, the waterfalls, the weather, the creatures—these all lend themselves, and have lent themselves throughout the human story in that location, to myth. The Amerindian word "hurricane," an internationally used signifier now, has lost its meaning as the name of a god to become simply a weather word. Using it as marker of the lost Amerindian presence, Walcott in his poem "Hurucan" performs an act of cultural retrieval. The myth persists, still associated with awe-inspiring storm, but its true spiritual meaning has been evacuated. By writing his poem, then, Walcott reminds the Anglophone world of the word's sacred power. Its authority is that it reconnects the ancient mythic power to the language, reinvesting it as myth. The anthropomorphized force is imaged like a Carib warrior: "running / with tendons feathered with lightning," he is "havoc, reminder, ancestor," and finally "god."[68] A modification of this process is Walcott's politicized variant of a song from the African-Caribbean oral tradition: "One, two, three, the white man have plenty, / When thunder roll is a nigger belly empty."[69]

A further kind of persisting myth is that which had a historical origin but has passed into folk legend, as with the collective Carib suicide memorialized in the place-name Sauteurs and then in *Another Life*. It parallels the use of metaphor from nature in poems such as "The Saddhu of Couva."[70] A similar effect is observable in Walcott's use of the conjunction of tragic Amerindian history and myth in the story of the Sioux Ghost Dance, incorporated into *Omeros* and his play *The Ghost Dance*. Walcott deconstructs the politics of the historical moment simultaneously with his reinscription of the sacredness of the rite of faith: the Ghost Dance did not save the Sioux (indeed, determinists might say it contributed to their demise), and the past cannot be undone, but because it can "call the spirit to arms," it may yet help to save the future. The redemptive promise remains real in art.

Walcott's deployment of myth as faith is distinctively cross-cultural. It is not difficult to trace, for instance, a chain of Christian iconography in his work, but it would be a mistake to ignore the often plural sign in which Christian myth is a participant but not the dominant element. In the climactic revelation of *Another Life,* for example, the Sauteurs/waterfall myth is developed by being matched with the biblical story of Moses striking the rock with his staff. The miraculous and life-giving water that gushed from the rock serves in the poem as a figure of the flow of creativity: the poet, like Moses, can lead his people to the promised land—again a figure calculated to reduce the pain of diaspora. But the downward movements of this are balanced by the ascending movement (an echo of the closure of "The Saddhu of Couva") of the Hindu funeral pyre, which releases the soul to another life—the final metamorphosis of the poem's exploration of its title's meanings, "another life" as "reincarnation." In both the water image (Sauteurs/waterfall) and the fire image (pyre/sun), a death trope is remade as figure of creativity. The narrator as poet declares "I shared, I shared, / I was struck like rock, and I opened / to His gift!" as well as "I sit in the roar of that sun / like a lotus yogi folded on his bed of coals," reciting "hare Krishna."[71] There is personal and collective history in this as well as myth, the history of the grandfather who committed suicide by fire, and the new-age culture of Western youth (*Another Life* was published in 1973), turning to the East for spiritual values lacking in their own world. From the Caribbean perspective, such values were to hand, an integral part of the "home" society already naturalized to the West. The Age of Aquarius, a countermyth of modernity that also informs the poem, reinvests the ancient idea of the zodiac with a different semiology, again associated with a personal history, since Walcott, whose birthday is in late January, comes under the star sign of Aquarius in popularized astrology, with its familiar icon of the water pourer, as in the poem. Janus, too, is named in the passage, presiding over its ambivalence. It is a very 1970s amalgam of mythic registers, which could easily have been bathetic, but the way the language of the final chapters captures and holds the passion that resolves the poem's long narration of what it meant to a particular generation to be West Indian and to have faith in art is still astonishing and beautiful.

Omeros also deploys a cross-cultural mythopoeia, structured on a doubling of the mythology of the ancient Greeks with that of Christianity: the oracular bird, African swift or Antillean swallow, is in the shape of a cross, but its role is to unite the guardian spirit of Athena in Homer with that of the dove of Christian revelation. The poem also includes other collocations. In "Hurucan," Walcott makes the Amerindian god refuse to respond to the name of the Yoruba storm god Shango—"you rage / till we get your name right"[72]—but in *Omeros* he assembles intercultural gods for a distinctively celebratory and terrifying party. The cross-cultural mythography is no academic exercise but spirited and witty. The hybridizing culture of the Caribbean is produced as an aesthetic space where West African and Caribbean divinities meet those of ancient Greece, dancing and drinking: "Ogun can fire one with his partner Zeus" ("fire one" punning not only on the deities' thunderbolts but also on the swallowing of a shot of alcoholic spirits). They are staged in a fête of storm that has Shango, Neptune, and the (now Caribbean) goddess of love Erzulie, partying "as their huge feet thudded on the ceiling."[73] There is also a complex inter-American engagement in the naming of the fisherman's canoe *In God We Troust.* "Leave it!" says Achille, "Is God' spelling and mine."[74] It is a plural signifier: of Caribbean difference within the Americas; of the power of American money ("In God We Trust" being inscribed on every U.S. dollar note); of challenged faith, with its resonance with "joust"; of the transcendence of faith over acquired skills such as literacy; and of the text's simultaneous humility and largeness of claim—the poem itself is a kind of alternative "gospel" or "god-spell," both using and making myth.

The persistence of Greek myths is, of course, a contingency of the Western cultural tradition. To Walcott they are "echoes that have been in my head,"[75] but he is careful to counter the tendency to read his art as neo-Greek mimicry. The myths of the Greeks are only one dimension of the Caribbean heritage. This cross-culturality reflects Walcott's personal beliefs: "Every aspect of culture contributes to another culture." The "African aspect" may be more important than "the machine," because "any spiritual contribution, to any civilization, is far more important than any technical contribution." Likewise the "contribution of the American Indian, which has never been absorbed by the American pioneer, to his cost—*to his cost*" is important to environmentalists because the "American Indian had these values," "the same sacramental idea . . . about not touching anything that doesn't belong to you—that is not yours. That belongs to God—that's not yours but of the gods."[76]

Walcott brings a revisionist historiography to bear on a particular crux of Caribbean selfhood, that Christianity came with empire. Instead of seeing Caribbean Christianity as the imposition of empire, with its double project of Bible and sword, he inverts the model, arguing unconventionally that no race is converted against its will and that it was less a matter of being given religion than of taking it over: "their own God was being taken away from merchant and missionary by a submerged force that rose at ritual gatherings, where the subconscious rhythm rose and took possession and where, in fact, the Hebraic-European God was changing colour, for the names of the sub-deities did not matter, Saint Ursula or Saint Urzulie; the Catholic pantheon adapted easily to African pantheism. Catholic mystery adapted easily to African magic."[77] This is syncretism in action, the creolization of faith. When, therefore, in *Another Life* he writes that in the St. Lucia of his childhood, "One step behind the church door stood the devil," it is the *closeness* of the two spiritual worlds he is emphasizing, despite the church's opposition and its demonizing terminology for beliefs it termed pagan.[78] As with carnival, the hegemony was being subverted, as "the tribe in bondage learned to fortify itself by cunning assimilation of the religion of the Old World. What seemed to be surrender was redemption. What seemed the loss of tradition was its renewal. What seemed the death of faith was its rebirth."[79] As with Walcott's dismantling of the hegemonic discourse of Caribbean history in terms of fracture and loss, he here subverts the accepted model of cultural assimilation: not to be assimilated, but to assimilate. He argues, crucially, that "no race is converted against its will"; on the contrary, "The slave converted himself, he changed weapons, spiritual weapons."[80] The slave, so glibly conceived from the metropolitan center as in both physical and mental bondage, is reconstrued as bound in body but free in mind. The slave as object is reestablished as subject (as in the Rastafarian "I" usage), reinvigorating what was declining in the hands of the Old World's "exhausted, hypocritical Christian."[81]

This appropriation is shown to be at the heart of New World spirituality. African Americans renewed Christianity, says Walcott, using the period after the American Civil War as example: "the blacks, instead of turning on their oppressors, magnanimously adopted the White Man's God, the God of their enemy and went far beyond the whites—who were then making a mockery of Christ's teachings by completing their butchery of the Indians—by going back in their spirituals to the core of Christianity."[82] Spirituality is the pervasive quality of Caribbean culture that Walcott celebrates and holds up as example: "We colonials can't exercise power, but we can exert spiritual strength through our culture and religion."

Like an animist or pantheist, Walcott prefers to suggest spirituality in the open air. Even when he evokes a scene of worship in a building, he tends to develop this with an exterior scene, for example in the section on the Roseau Valley altarpiece by his friend Dunstan St. Omer, in "Sainte Lucie," which contemplates the mural from within the body of the Jacmel church but as an etiolatory symbol, radiating out to the valley outside, or the portrayal of Ma Kilman in church in *Omeros* before she climbs the mountain in quest of the healing herb (the blurring of categories of interior and exterior is also, of course, mimetic of tropical life). The vigor of a syncretist faith is mythified as distinctively Caribbean, and by unmooring his representation from the architecture of religions he frees his work from competing orthodoxies. Of his decision to place the Circe episode in his play *The Odyssey* in a pantheistic New World society, he has said that for the audience and particularly for the actors, "if you provide the society that is pantheistic, then they can enter it and believe it, and then *you* believe it."[83] The two facets of Ma Kilman's religious belief are shown to be seamless: the ant-messenger signs to her actually inside the church, summoning her as she kneels in prayer to the world of nature outside, which is not passive or indifferent to the human predicament. Such belief is "an atavism stronger than their Mass, / stronger than chapel, whose / tubers gripped the rooted middle class, / beginning where Africa began: / in the body's memory."[84] To show the hybridity of religious beliefs and rituals is as important as to demonstrate the creative fusion in other spheres of cultural practice. This is mythopoeia as mimesis. The syncretism makes the art more rather than less mythic. In *Omeros,* for instance, the bush-bath that Ma Kilman gives Philoctete to heal him, and from which he emerges as if an innocent child again, is the more powerful for its doubling of a folk ritual with the idea of Christian baptism. But this too mimics personal experience, lived social practice, the memory, recalled in the early poem "Origins," of "my warm, malarial bush-bath, / The wet leaves leeched to my flesh." Ma Kilman seems reminiscent of the same passage's "sibyl," who "bears in her black hand a white frangipani, with berries of blood" and "gibbers with the cries / Of the Guinean odyssey."[85] Since she is dubbed "mother of memory," it may be a memory of Walcott's own early childhood—of a fever treated by a myal-woman with traditional herbal remedies—that has been expanded to the core epic drama of *Omeros,* the rite of healing, made to signify as myth, as the healing of a race, closing the wound of history. The local tradition's alternative medicine is the same thing as its alternative religion. Both are recognized as rites requiring faith but dealing with reality. Metropolitan culture has tried to drive a wedge between ideas of "truth" and of "magic," but Caribbean culture has never lost sight of their interconnectedness.

Clearly the myths of Christianity are deeply written into the collective Caribbean experience, but they are creolized, Walcott says, adapted to their new social and natural setting. Their social environment includes beliefs and practices of "a life older than geography" (that is, the life lived by the people before they encountered the Caribbean geography), the surviving culture of "Africa, heart-shaped."[86] This includes the lore of "tribal medicine" as well as communal rites such as the cross-dressed dance of Achille and Philoctete (a West African tradition naturalized to the Caribbean), but what survives most crucially is the centrality of the spiritual in perceptions of reality. Ben Okri says of West African belief that "there's really no division between the living and the dead. They're just, as it were, spheres of reality that you can travel between."[87] This African attitude to the human condition has survived to root itself in the Caribbean. Maryse Condé defines Caribbeanness as distinguished by simultaneous political solidarity and spirituality:

> a commitment to the world, the problems of the world, the difficulty of being alive, the oppression of our people, the dependency towards Europe and so on, and a commitment to the other world, the invisible world, meanings that will explain the world, not only in a sort of logical or rationalist sense but we understand that between the earth and the sky there are so many things that you cannot explain. If you want to render the complexity of life in a book you have to deal with all these elements, the rational ones, the irrational, and try to build a philosophy which includes all these possibilities.[88]

Such inclusive levels of reality and vision typify Walcott's work.

In the Caribbean, however, although the sensibility is still unquestionably mythic, the distinctive culture of pluralist faith is now under siege. Walcott admits that "[w]e're teaching in our schools the pursuit of material power, as everywhere else in the West. The same philosophy that is crippling the world."[89] This he sees as emblematic of a global pattern: though increasingly beleaguered by materialism, the spirituality of the South is the last bastion against the powerful North. Walcott dissects the modern metropolitan condition as "Voltaire confronting Nietzsche: 'It is necessary to invent God,' and 'God is dead.' Join both, and that is our twentieth-century credo. 'It is necessary to invent a God who is dead.'"[90] "Modern nonreligious man," says Eliade, "assumes a new existential situation; he regards himself solely as the subject and agent of history, and he refuses all appeals to transcendence." The new ideology is that "Man *makes himself,* and he only makes himself completely in proportion as he desacralizes himself and the world." The end position is that "[h]e will not be truly free until he has killed the last god." Eliade's observation is that "modern nonreligious man assumes a tragic existence."[91] This concept of the modern is inscribed in "The Fortunate Traveller" as the negative to which the opposite is the faith kept alive in the "dark" heart. Walcott takes it further, distinguishing cultural approaches to faith: "It's a difference in religion," he says, contrasting the American Indian who "celebrates" the world by "blending into the earth and air" with the settler saying "I own this earth": "the emphasis on the capital 'I' in Western religion has caused a lot of damage—though Christ didn't preach the aggression of an 'I.'"[92] In the "I-an-I" community, the figure adopted in this study, the emphasis is on the self as sharer. Walcott's writing is thus both mimetic of a culture of faith and a counterdiscourse to a generally growing lack of faith, fuelled by a materialist politics.

The rest of this chapter offers an indicative survey of a few of the mythic figures Walcott deploys in his writing, beginning with some derived from oral traditions. Guyanese novelist Roy Heath writes of the region's "persistence of a mythic preoccupation in storytelling, all but dead in Europe and amongst Americans of European extraction."[93] The oral culture, now fading, has its unique fund of stories, in which mythic figures proliferate. Walcott tells of the old women—today Sesenne, and long ago, Sidone—whom he and his brother would visit as children to hear her "strange croaking of Christian and African songs."[94] Her stories were "the libraries of the Caribbean," an oral resource that could be translated to the literature: "In the gully of her voice / shadows stood up and walked, her voice travels my shelves."[95] The "thrill" was for her to "scare you with stories about the African night that was there in the country in Saint Lucia, in the fireflies and the funny-looking banana trees and the superstitions, or what people call superstitions and which are myths."[96] The "true folk tale" had "a structure as universal as the skeleton": "It had sprung from hearthside or lamplit hut door in an age when the night outside was a force, inimical, infested with devils, wood demons, a country for the journey of the soul."[97] Ti-Jean (Little-John) was the hero of a group of these stories, told throughout the Francophone Antilles. Walcott relates how the particular Ti-Jean story he used as the basis for *Ti-Jean and His Brothers* was told to him as a schoolboy by a friend known as Mock, "short for Democracy, because he was an orator," "a very fast talker, very agitated." The story might have been one of Sidone's, "but this is one Mock knew," and he "would tell it beautifully," in French Creole. The story is "based on the exaggeration of a positive, comparative, superlative . . . three degrees in expression of anger"; "I built the play around this thing," says Walcott.[98]

But the story of the defeat of the devil by the youngest of three brothers is made not just a moral but a political fable by the parallelism that doubles the devil with the colonial plantation owner. Ti-Jean, with his song of "Bring down Goliath," is a classic trickster-hero, like the biblical David. He is a revolutionary who has no formal power but uses his wits to defeat the colonial system built with the white man's "bloody triumphs." His creed is solidarity, symbolized by the bundle of sticks, which together "are strong, / Apart, they are all rotten."[99] The defeat of power by the seemingly weak plebeian hero is a universal feature of folktales. *Ti-Jean* is perhaps as close as Walcott gets to endorsing vendetta, the racial politics of revenge. In the event he develops the anticipated ending—the triumph of the democratic hero—in unexpected and thought-provoking ways. First, the given of the story as told to Walcott is that Ti-Jean does not lose his temper: to become angry is to be defeated. This conforms to his view of racial rage: to give in to it, powerful and justifiable though the urge may be (and Gordon Rohlehr, for one, finds that a "countervailing energy of rage" gives strength to Walcott's *Castaway* poems), is in a profound sense to have been humiliated once again.[100] The empowering attitude is not fury at history and at on-going injustice but the calmness that takes control by ordering it as just a part of a larger, more important scheme. The historical and metaphysical registers of *Ti-Jean* symbolize this "translation"; the political fable is ultimately secondary to the spiritual one.

At one level, the play enacts the revolutionary overthrow of the plantocracy, but at others it is a morality play about the power of goodness and a psychological fable about the desire for life, even for a life of suffering. For this last, Walcott deploys a different folk myth of the French-Creole culture in the Caribbean, the bolom, a spirit figure of the aborted fetus that returns to haunt. Walcott explains, "The bolom is a figure—one of those words that you grow up saying but you don't know what they mean—only recently I realized that perhaps bolom is really 'beau-l'homme' [fine little man]."[101] In the play, the bolom begs for life, even though he is warned it will bring suffering and death. Even the devil, moved to unaccustomed tears by Ti-Jean's song, wonders whether this is what it means to be human:

> Tears! Tears! Then is this the
> Magnificence I have heard of, of

> Man, the chink in his armour, the destruction of the
> Self? Is this the strange, strange wonder that is
> Sorrow?[102]

The play closes with the twin revelations of the wisdom of the holy fool and the value of life, particularly for its godlike creativity.

The end of the play is echoed in the end of the poem "Adam's Song," where Walcott suggests that the human condition, given expression through art, can move even divinity to tears—a kind of heresy in that it suggests that the creator can learn from his creature. Adam sings "frightened / of the jealousy of God."[103] It is an old myth, the Orphic promise of the power of art to work magic. It positions the artist as a type of trickster-hero—an Anansi, the Caribbean spider-man derived from West African tradition. The postcolonial artist, in Walcott's scheme, enacts the trickster's triumph in two registers, the political and the metaphysical (this should not be confused with the colonial fantasy of the white man as god, which Caliban is made to endorse). George Lamming gives one version of the parallelism: "Caliban is Prospero's risk in the sense that Adam's awareness of a difference was a risk which God took with Man."[104] Walcott lives the double challenge: the politics of outwitting metropolitan centrism by going one better with his art, and the metaphysics of offering up his art as sacrament, as the greatest rite of celebration of which mankind is capable—and one that just might be superior to a monologic conception of divinity because of its heterogeneity, its eloquent combination of joy and sorrow. Walcott's view of the spirituality of the colonized is the opposite of Fanon's; instead of seeing it as disabling, he regards it as empowering. Faith opens a route to self-respect. It politicizes not in the name of reactive vendetta but in the name of the dream of a better world (like Gonzalo's or Miranda's), which can be built only by those who have "swallowed" their hates.[105] The awesome promise of art is that it can reach out to those without faith and thus contribute to this as a secular project. As Geoffrey Hartman points out in a largely faithless age, "If what remains of religion is its poetry, what remains of poetry is its heterodox theology, or mythmaking."[106]

The clear-eyed naming of the beloved island community combines realism and faith in the future, informed by the dream (in *Another Life*) of "a horned, sea-snoring island . . . without the shafts of palms stuck in her side."[107] Mythification of the island as figure of torture, borne like a saint, comes with history. In *Another Life,* Walcott reverses the designation of the island (traditionally assigned to Columbus) as "St. Lucia," the name of the blinded saint (commemorated on one of the darkest days of the northern year), by building his poem on an imagery of light and vision, and the visual arts, and in *Omeros,* he deploys the physicality of the island's volcano (Soufrière/"sufferer") as trope of the unhealed wound of history, which the poem closes. Dubbed the "Helen of the West Indies," the island was already mythified historically as "the cause of more blood-letting than was ever provoked by Helen of Troy."[108] Walcott says he was taught at school that it was the "Helen of the West," fought over and changing hands between the French and English thirteen times. It was a tragic story: "She had been regularly violated. . . . Her name was clouded with darkness and misfortune."[109] In the light of such cultural givens, and the daily reality of the "Plantation" (in Benitez-Rojo's sense), there was a real need for a countermyth of the island's identity. The Helen that Walcott creates in *Omeros* is a powerful positive to set against those negatives. The poem's female principle is in the form of a lunar triad, in ancient mythic tradition (including that of Africa), as analyzed by Robert Graves, with the triple aspects of the goddess figured as aged, mature, and immature woman.[110] Maud, the old moon, whose cycle (of white domination) is done, yields place to Helen, who is taking over, coming into her inheritance (hitherto denied her), like Cinderella, dangling, ironically, a clear plastic sandal, while the third figure, the nymph, is just coming into view as the girl, Christine, who arrives to help Ma Kilman, who unites all three, in the No Pain Café.[111] Ma Kilman takes on herself the suffering of the whole race in order to heal Philoctete. She is, it seems, the Christ figure in *Omeros,* a divinity of three-in-one and a figure of manifest sexuality and spiritual energy, in Walcott's radical remapping of moral and spiritual tradition. As Wilson Harris has said, "The woman priest is a very important ingredient in overturning the legacies of expectation."[112] Marian imagery is also recurrent in the work, particularly as a figure of the Catholic culture of St. Lucia, in works such as "Sainte Lucie" and *Another Life.* Not only is the island mythified through the female body to which the traumatized male can come home, but in *Omeros* the figuring of the island through the iguana as symbol reaches both for the pre-Columbian past, of Amerindian community, and for the innocent timelessness of nature, as well as for new art, new speech, as it emerges from the cannon's mouth as a benign "tongue." Walcott celebrates the heroic women of his community, seeing his task as to "give those feet a voice."[113]

His deployment of archetypes for his masculine personae will be the topic of the rest of this chapter. As noted above, it is important to read his use of figures such as Adam, Crusoe, or Ulysses (like Helen) as specifically

Caribbean, since they are naturalized to Caribbean culture, itself part of the Western tradition. The project to assimilate all ancestral traditions is, for Walcott, to uncover the archetypal heroes in ordinary Caribbean people, a democratizing aesthetic. When *Omeros* presents a St. Lucian fisherman named Achille, for instance, it is mimetic of Caribbean contemporary reality, not an applied classicism—although as the poem shows, there was a historical moment of "translation," when the name of the Greek hero was first allocated to an African-Caribbean as a mark of his heroism. Such names acquire local symbolism, "become real" for the community, "because they have the qualities of what's been ascribed to them, like an Achillean fisherman could look like Achilles who is a splendid figure."[114] This is confirmed by other art, such as Ian Macdonald's poem "Achilles," a portrait of a Caribbean teacher, yet "Achilles he was named at birth," and, in that he became a classics teacher, the poem seems to indicate that people can live up to their given names, becoming the heroes after whom they are named.[115]

The Adam persona is most conspicuous in Walcott's early work as a myth by which to explore the individuality of the Caribbean artist, but there is a double link with the Caribbean as geographical location, in that Adam, the first man, created in God's image, was placed in paradise (the islands often being mythified as Edenic), and through the discourse of American identity as Adamic. The mythification of the heritage of the American archipelago as, through history, the locus of loss—as not Africa, Asia, or Europe, the evacuation of meaningful location—is remodeled in Walcott's work as a divinely ordained "holy land" or "homeland," the site of plenty, of fullness of meaning. In the holy books of three great faiths—Judaism, Christianity, and Islam—paradise becomes the site of original sin and of expulsion, of forced migration. But Christian theology portrays the Genesis story, despite its tragic outcome of loss, as setting the whole narrative of Christian redemption in motion: Adam's sin loses him Eden but gains mankind redemption by Christ, thus being revisioned as the "felix culpa" [happy sin]. Original sin as concept derives from this biblical account of origin; the eating of the apple of knowledge results from a yielding, against divine law, to desire—a desire both for the sensuality implicit in the apple symbol and for the intellectual ambition, the "hubris," implicit in the idea of the tree of knowledge—Gonzalo's apple, perhaps.[116] In Dante and elsewhere, however, original sin is represented by the figure of the wound, prefiguring the wounds of Christ by which it will be redeemed.[117] The church's paradox of the "felix culpa" leads directly to the St. Lucian usage of "bless" to mean both "bless" and "consecrate by suffering," as in *Omeros*. It is not only the Adamic story. Defoe's Crusoe is a purgatorial figure, seeing himself as punished for his defiance of the law of the Father. The wounded Ulysses is part of an ancient and living tradition of seeing the evil of suffering as sacrificial, as a means of delivering good.

In Walcott's poetry of the 1960s and 1970s, Adam is used as figure of the poet, naming his world as Adam named paradise. *Another Life* mythifies this distinctively as not an Old World naming but a New World one, by borrowing fellow Caribbean writer Alejo Carpentier's phrase, "Adam's task of giving things their names."[118] This artistic naming, in Carpentier's text, is "the only task appropriate to the milieu that was slowly revealing to me its values," and the northern diaspora's artists find themselves unable to perform it on their return. The Adamic naming is thus translated into a crux of Central and South American culture: Walcott is mythifying the role of artists who chose to stay, through his narration of his own and Dunstan St. Omer's story, in an anti-diaspora politics. The figure of Adam, however, has long been naturalized to the Americas, especially in North American literary tradition, the paradisal perspective on the New World being central to colonial discourse. The "noble savage" ideology projected onto the indigenous people of the Americas as natural "Adams" was part of a classically derived dialectics of civilization and savagery that could lead only to Native Americans' marginalization, their "Adamic innocence" merely a referent serving the dominant discourse. It was not until American literature of the nineteenth century began to shape a national discourse that the "paradisal" landscape was equipped, in fiction, with a heroic Adam—crucially of European ancestry, not an indigene—at the center of texts in his own right. In 1955, R.W.B. Lewis's influential study interpreted early American literature in terms of the Adam figure.[119] When Walcott uses the Adam archetype, he does so very much as a post-Lewis writer of the Americas. Lewis argues that the myth of Adam has two parts, comic and tragic. Applied to America as "divinely granted second chance for the human race," the comic phase is embodied in a new hero, the "individual emancipated from history," who is "the poet par excellence."[120] Walcott now projects the *Caribbean* artist, liberated from history and origin into a creolized relationship with the new place, as hero.

The innocent Adam typified in Emerson's dictum, "Here's for the plain old Adam, the simple genuine self against the whole world," prompted, however, as Lewis describes, a resisting discourse: the Adam figure "was converted into the hero of a new kind of tragedy. . . . It was the tragedy inherent in his innocence and newness, and it established the pattern for

American fiction."[121] It is this fully mature awareness of the postlapsarian Adam that Walcott employs, the Edenic serpent portrayed as also an American *arrivant.* In *Omeros,* the sign of the serpent, s, is made a symbolic figure, linked with the U.S. dollar sign—although its shape also matches the poem's function as curative rite, in that the $ is the same as the caduceus, the healing rod of Hermes. Irony gives the edge to the Adam poems in the 1976 collection *Sea Grapes,* and his portrayal of the islands as Eden is always laced with a ruthless counterdiscourse that presents them as anti-paradisal myth—as hellish in their poverty and deprivation. Lewis's description of an "ironic temperament" typified by a "tragic optimism . . . [and] by an awareness of the heightened perception and humanity which suffering made possible" is also applicable to Walcott, who connects the strengths of the collective personality to its suffering.[122] Essentially American versions of the suffering hero, such as Melville's Billy Budd, can thus be seen as part of a pan-American tradition that Walcott is consciously extending. The concept of tragic optimism is particularly helpful; it gets a difficult balance right.

In Christian teaching, Christ, the supreme sufferer, is presented as the second Adam, the second incarnation, the two being closely connected by their antithetical roles. *Another Life* also plays with the idea of this second Adam, with its ironic references to the two young artists as "the light of the world,"[123] an image of the Christ-like, redemptive role of the artist, which Walcott revisits, again with a self-deprecating but high-claiming ambivalence, in *The Arkansas Testament.*[124] The artist as prophet is another figure that Walcott deploys, using the analogy with St. John the Divine in the early poem "As John to Patmos," where he sets out his commitment to awaiting the revelation of his art in the island of his birth, and in *Another Life* using the Moses myth in his assertion of the creative inspiration: "I was struck like rock, and I opened / to His gift!"[125] He does not identify the artist with the prophet here, however, but with the rock, the insentient part of nature, made to signify by divine intervention. In "The Arkansas Testament," he parallels his own epiphany as artist with that of the apostle Paul, the poem making creative use of the figure of Saul's revelation on the road to Damascus, matched to the poet's experience on U.S. Highway 71, as part of a profound meditation on the human condition (its "sure unshaven salvation"), alongside essentially political dilemmas, such as the mapping of a Caribbean within a U.S. identity.[126] Alongside the elevation of the artist to prophet is a critique of the society's attitude to its prophets. The suicide of Harry Simmons, for instance, in *Another Life,* is blamed on a philistine community that failed to recognize him as a "prophet," and the narrator's anger at the way fashionable cultural attitudes affect art and the populace gives a Juvenal-like acridness to Chapter 19.[127] In "The Schooner *Flight,*" the image is once again that of the hounded prophet, unrecognized in his own kingdom—a Ulyssean figure, as well as a Christian one.

In *Omeros,* the range of sufferers introduces a dialectical dimension to the symbolic: the reader is inevitably prompted to compare and consider. The extremity of Philoctete's suffering, so vividly expressed in his great howl in the Edenic yam garden, makes him seem a type of Adam, aware of the enormity of his loss. His is a postlapsarian cultivation of the yam, brought from Africa on the Middle Passage; he is the Adam forced to "delve," when before the Fall all he had to do was pluck the fruits of the garden. If Philoctete demonstrates the concept of Original Sin, then Ma Kilman represents its salvation, returning to the innocence of wild nature to pluck the wound's cure. Like the Christian second Adam, Christ, she too suffers: her howl on the mountain resonates with Gethsemane. It is only through her willingness to suffer that she is empowered to heal, the pattern of Christian redemption. The healing bath, an analogue of baptism, restores Philoctete to the innocence of childhood, specifically associated with sexual innocence through the image of the child's "shrimp-like prick," which enables a kind of Eden to be recovered in the restorative Christmas dance of Philoctete and Achille, paired in brotherly celebration.[128] Walcott is particularly drawn to Christianity's Christmas myth (here and in *Another Life*), which is in tune with his life-asserting spirituality. The cross-dressed dance of Achille and Philoctete, however, is drawn directly from African tradition. Just as the dream-book of *Omeros* shows Achille's visionary return to Africa, it shows, more importantly, the African ancestors making the reverse Atlantic crossing, their grass skirts rustling outside Philoctete's hut at night as he bathes his sore: "they gazed in / silence at the shadows of their lamplit children."[129] The symbolic swift crosses and recrosses the meridian.

The chain of mythic connectedness that unites both African and Caribbean practice and classical and Christian tradition extends in the modern era to literary myth. Walcott fastens particularly on the figure of Crusoe as a specifically Caribbean persona (Tobago being traditionally assumed to be "his" island) and deploys him as an Everyman on a symbolic odyssey to his God, but also, unusually, as emblem of the artist. His 1965 essay "The Figure of Crusoe" makes what he calls "a heretical reconciliation between the outer world, and the world of the hermit, between, if you wish, the poet and the objects surrounding him that are called society."[130] The

Crusoe archetype, to Walcott, is that of the hermit crouched over a bonfire, whether on a tropical beach, in the northern woods of "North and South," or as Omeros, but he is also a dialectical figure, an answer to the Froudian negative with his cry of "O happy desert!" and a counterimage to the searing of history—not to be burned, but to feed sticks to the fire, an active, controlling figure, not one of capture: "We contemplate our spirit by the detritus of the past."[131] To Walcott, Crusoe is the third Adam ("The second Adam since the fall"), the New World's third chance, after Adam the colonist who was given the American Eden by history, and Christ the redeemer whose teachings are ignored in the materialist scramble.[132] The Americas' third chance comes from the man of the islands, Crusoe the *arrivant,* who initiates the metaphysical difference, the heresy, of praying "[n]ot for God's love but human love instead." In these poems from the 1960s, Walcott uses Crusoe also dialectically, in a symbolic challenge to contemporary identifications with the Friday side of the story, which to him is governed by the humiliations of the colonial experience. To claim, instead, the central subjectivity of Crusoe is therefore the more subversive strategy. To some extent Crusoe represents a secularization of the mythic chain, as God's "protestant," a figure in the ultimate binary drama of the human challenge to the divine, but his chief symbolic importance to Walcott is as one who starts from scratch to build everything he needs, the archetypal solitary and contemplative person, the archetypal artist, whose isolation is his boon. Introducing his poem "The Castaway," Walcott said: "You can only create something you hope can be a work of art, alone, and in this case, it's set in the Caribbean, I imagine. But it's also the image of Crusoe as someone who has to begin again with whatever tools are around—and the tools may be a piece of paper or a pencil, or something, or canvas, or a brush—but I think that's what it's about, the isolation that is part of creativity."[133] As in his remark about cultures creating "a god for each need," the ideal of self-sufficiency is a dream of freedom; it defeats the tragic determinism of history, unlocking the vision of a fresh start. Great poets, in their elation, "reject ethnic ancestry for faith in elemental man." "The stripped and naked man," Walcott argues, "however abused, however disabused of old beliefs, instinctually, even desperately begins again as a craftsman." His art will have "real faith, mapless, History-less."[134] Crusoe is essentially a maker, a "poietes," used by Walcott to present art as a craft, an honorable toil, requiring patience and humility, and to initiate a Caribbean aesthetics in which remoteness from the metropolitan world can be reconceived not as marginalization but as blessing. In the poems, Crusoe has special significance as a Job-like overreacher brought to humility on the purgatory of his island, but he is given a different political resonance in *Pantomime* by Harry Trewe's pairing with Jackson Philip, and the inversions and ironizations which the play spins in its Anansi-like games, its carnivalesque testing of Defoe's (and Western culture's) assumptions. Its destination is the calypso wisdom "it go be man to man, and we go do it fine," which Bridget Jones describes as "a genuine shared humanity,"[135] or the "I-an-I" model threading through this study.

The Ulysses myth, in turn, is so powerful because it addresses head-on the fundamental narratives of human existence, of the tension between desire for home and for elsewhere, and of the desire for the erotic other. As Wilson Harris has said of it, "Ulysses is a spectral figure, like a star, the light-year that comes. We cannot seize the origination of that star."[136] Ulysses appealed to Walcott from his youth as a figure on which to project himself, recommending itself to him as the archetype of the seafarer whose home is an island. There is no "heraldic symbol" for Joyce's *Ulysses,* Leopold Bloom, he has said, but the "single stroke of a sail against a horizontal line" means Odysseus.[137] His own early self-dedication to remaining in the archipelago invited an easy self-identification with the Ithaca-seeker. The myth derives its power from an oppositional dynamic: it has "that simple rhythm," he has said, that "any departure from an island means a return to it."[138] As well as the Homeric *Odyssey,* it can be argued that the myth encodes an even more ancient story of a phallic hero, as I argue elsewhere.[139] His first long epic, *Another Life,* which matches Castries to Troy and alludes to Joyce's revisioning of the Ulysses myth, is less conspicuously Homeric than *Omeros,* but Lloyd Brown has made a persuasive case for a Ulyssean reading of the earlier poem as that in which (by 1978 at least) "the odyssey motif is most sustained, and most personal in its development": "The poet himself is such a 'lone Odysseus,' the one whose personality and individual development dominate and give shape to the work as a whole." In this he is symbolic of his community: "the poet's odyssey is a microcosm of the West Indian's quest for wholeness and creativity, and in turn, that quest represents what the New World experience can and should be."[140] The triumphant celebration of the young artists in *Another Life* reflects the concluding action of Homer's *Odyssey:* they are, in a powerful paradox, "firm / as conquerors who had discovered home."[141]

The defiantly solitary Ulysses figure of "The Schooner *Flight*" develops the double identification of the artist with the sea-wanderer, fleeing failed relationships. Moving down the islands, he becomes the Dantean figure of the mental voyager, free of all relationships except that with his God, and homeless, but for the prospect of his reunion with the divine in death. Like Dante's Ulysses, he anticipates his ultimate shipwreck. The sexual dilemma between loyalty and novelty is examined repeatedly in Walcott's work not just through the solitary Ulyssean persona, however, but through a diversity of gender relationships (of "I-an-I" pairings), in which women are often conspicuously dominant. In the play of the *Odyssey,* in particular, the Homeric givens are followed with a firm twist toward a feminist awareness. As Penelope emerges as a strong woman, so Ulysses shifts toward an Anansi-like resilient humanity, the solitary survivor who yearns for reintegration to his family. Overall, Walcott demonstrates both the durability and the flexibility of the myth, which addresses profound questions of masculine identity.

The paradox of the Homer is that the impulse "away," to seek out experience and the new self, is so finely balanced with the impulse "home," to eat bread with the wife, defining the self by old affective ties, that the journey, nominally of return home, in effect resists its own closure (all the more powerful emotionally when eventually accomplished). Writing after Dante and Tennyson, who develop a Ulysses like a transgressive Adam, a Crusoe defying the law of the father, Walcott builds *Omeros* on the twin perception that both the voyager and the one who stays at home are equally capable of creativity, open to epiphany, and susceptible to salvation. The inward journey of meditation is just as much of an odyssey as that of travel and bodily experience. Achille, who never leaves his island waters, is an epiphanic spiritual traveler, as is the ubiquitous Omeros, who is simultaneously the blind Seven Seas, stuck in the St. Lucian village. Plunkett's metaphysical journey is an allegorically Dantean drive to the volcanic core of the island, but, like an Icarus (symbol of intellectual daring), he has also tried flight and fallen (in his war experience, and by implication in the Nietzschean daring of the imperial project, which traumatizes the perpetrator as surely as it cripples its victims). After revisiting the Old World from the New, Plunkett returns sure of his place in the island which is now home, like Achille, who tries to find a new base for his life, by circling the island and in his dream-journey to Africa, but arrives only at his point of departure. The pattern encoded in the poem's narrative structures is set out toward the end in the words of Omeros/Seven Seas, telling of the fundamental paradox that there are "two journeys / in every odyssey, one on worried water, // the other crouched and motionless, without noise." The writer, ultimately, is a Ulyssean voyager required to find within himself the resources for survival and creation: "For both, the 'I' is a mast." The poem's epiphany is that

the right journey
is motionless; as the sea moves round an island

that appears to be moving, love moves round the heart—
with encircling salt, and the slowly travelling hand
knows it returns to the port from which it must start.[142]

The parallelism is eventually viewed as a difference, not only of kind but of moral value: the meditative, inner journey is, in the end, "right" and contains a profound acceptance of that return which is death.

The passage resonates back over Walcott's oeuvre, over his early Crusoe personae, and his later figure of the "fortunate traveller," of great philosophical significance, but also communicating a particularly Caribbean tension. It gives a limpid picture of the metaphysical importance to him of the island—not only "home" in the familiar domestic sense but a complex symbol of identity and the potentiality of community. As he says in the Nobel lecture, the "traveller cannot love, since love is stasis and travel is motion."[143] The devastating sense of the migrant's self-separation implicit in this is followed, however, by a corollary: "If he returns to what he loved in a landscape and stays there, he is no longer a traveller but in stasis and concentration, the lover of that particular part of earth, a native." The blessed persona of the in-place individual—whether nested in a geography, a relationship, or a faith—is never beyond reach. Walcott's comfort is his conviction that we are never beyond redemption. His mythopoeic engagement with the social animal, man, thus casts a fresh light on ancient ideas, as well as initiating new dreams. As the Husband says in his play *Malcochon, or The Six in the Rain,* "I am not God, Monsieur Chantal. And not a beast neither. . . . I am a fool with ordinary sins."[144] *Malcochon* was first performed by the St. Lucia Arts Guild, directed by Derek's twin brother, Roderick, in 1959 when they were twenty-nine. The brothers were already showing a precocious maturity, aware that their situation as St. Lucians was a rich endowment, placing them at the hub of the world's myths. The task of mythifying the Caribbean condition was therefore no parochial affair but a project with ripples spreading back across the world's oceans.

Even the one continent that might have seemed to have no part in the Caribbean story, Australia, has now been written into Derek Walcott's latest collection of poetry, *The Bounty,* which mythifies an obscured history of connections. First, the name "Australia" is a symbolic signifier of the South. Then, the idea of "bounty" is given many-layered significance, which includes Captain Bligh's ship, carrying breadfruit seedlings from the Pacific to feed the New World's slaves, as well as providing a St. Lucian joke, as Maya Jaggi observes, since Bounty is a local brand of rum.[145] Bountiful nature is once again celebrated, but the complex cultural consequence in the Caribbean, Walcott has said, is that the "truth of the reality of the noun 'breadfruit'" took a long time to be accepted without embarrassment.[146] His art is about recognizing the historical pain but also about salving it. The bounty is many things: the ship that was the scene of the necessary mutiny of Fletcher Christian, nature's provision of food, the "light's bounty on familiar things," the "glittering simplicities" of the blessed location in the islands to which the "blown tribes" have dispersed, and the bounty of love.[147] In a mind-expanding mapping, space and time are transformed into a wholly mythic register: "the soul's Australia is like the New Testament after the Old World, the code of an eye for an eye."[148] In *Malcochon,* the young poet gave voice to a somber philosophy:

> Like the staining of clear springs the mind of man,
> In blood he must end as in blood he began
> Like mist that rises from a muddy stream
> Between beasthood and Godhead groping in a dream.[149]

Now for Walcott at seventy, little has changed except emphasis. His perception is still that the human condition is somewhere between beasthood and godhead, and groping; what is perhaps different is his emphasis on the dream, the "willing of spiritual victory," his clear sense that holding fast to the idea of "bounty," as something both received and given, is the one thing that really matters—is the soul's Australia, its South, its brave new world.[150]

Part II

Craft

5

"The Smell of Our Own Speech"

The Tool of Language

Caliban: You taught me language; and my profit on't
Is, I know how to curse.

Caliban: 'Ban, 'Ban, Ca-Caliban,
Has a new master—Get a new man.
Freedom, high-day! high-day, freedom! freedom! high-day,
freedom!

***The Tempest,* I.ii.363–64; II.ii.197–200**

"Language is the perfect instrument of empire"—as a bishop said to the Queen of Spain in 1492 (so Peter Hulme reminds us).[1] While the bishop can hardly have dreamt quite how his claim would prove true, it follows that language is also the perfect instrument of anti-imperialism. As this study turns to a close focus on writing as craft, offering chapters devoted to specific works, a section on language is the inevitable starting point. But highlighting the poetics does not mean removing the spotlight from the politics. Walcott writes in *Omeros,* "this language carries its cure" as well as "its radiant affliction."[2] As Salman Rushdie has put it, "the empire writes back to the centre." The reflexiveness of this may be resented but may be inevitable. Toril Moi argues that "[w]e have to accept our position as already inserted into an order that precedes us and from which there is no escape. There is no other space from which we can speak: if we are able to speak at all, it will have to be within the framework of symbolic language."[3] Or, as in the epigraph Walcott used for his lecture "The Poet in the Theatre," quoting Sweeney, "I gotta use words when I talk to you."[4] But as he is at pains to point out, although language may be one of the givens of the world in which we inherit a place—a symbolic place in the symbolic order—we do not have a passive role in relation to that order. To return to Moi's phrase, there may be no escape from our starting position, but that does not mean that escape is not possible.

Walcott's revelation is that we can rewrite our position by altering the dynamic of the symbolic order; the past cannot be changed (although it can be revisioned), but from the present onwards we are able to speak our difference into the world of language. The separateness of the speaking "I" can, however, be encompassed in a joint project. Theater is one kind of collective utterance. Another is the praise-song, an African genre in which the poet as voice of the community expresses the collective praise. Much of Walcott's work can be seen as a Caribbean version of praise-song. In a memorable phrase, he speaks of "language's desire to enclose the loved world in its arms; . . ."[5] He takes very seriously his responsibility, as artist, to the community he serves, and while he is a skillful combatant in the carnivalesque "robber talk" mode of outperforming existing discourses, he is also a visionary poet, whose praise-song celebrates his people's special, spiritually oriented wisdom. His tendency to choose a metrical language for this task should not be co-opted to a notion of Eurocentrism, as his critics have sometimes argued. One of the reasons he has not written prose fiction, he says, is that the novel is "too much a single effort," whereas verse invites audience participation, in the African tradition naturalized to the Caribbean: it can "actually affect metre . . . in the storyteller, because at the end of every line there's an accommodating thing on the part of the audience listening, by making that sound. It can create metre."[6] Even for the solitary reader, the felt exchange is there, and Walcott's poetry often has the power to make us laugh out loud, as well as to weep with it, in its sense of the "lachrimae rerum."

Walcott's practice is heterodox: he engages with centrism, with the literary canon and with the symbols of hegemony, in order to subvert their dominance and inscribe his people's difference. He seeks, in a powerful Proustian sensory image,

> The smell of our own speech,
> the smell of baking bread,
> of drizzled asphalt, this
> odorous cedar.[7]

But since that difference also names likeness—different cultures share the smell of baking bread, for instance, and as *Another Life* puts it, "the taste of water is still shared everywhere"—a reciprocal movement is set up.[8]

Having appropriated the speaking position, the postcolonial writer names not only his own locus but the wider world, and not only his separateness within it but his sharing. He writes not for one side only of the Prospero/Caliban dynamic. George Lamming speaks of "the lie" of Prospero's self-presentation to Caliban, which tricked him into subjection. If there is to be a future, that has to be addressed: "If Prospero wants to demolish his own meaning, then he must find a new word, or alter his relation to the original lesson."[9] Walcott's (controversial) generosity is to offer Prospero strategies to locate that novelty and that alterity. At the same time, he is centrally and principally aware of the double relation of Caliban to language as Shakespeare presents it: "the great beautiful irony in *The Tempest* is that the best poetry in *The Tempest* is spoken by Caliban." For Walcott, the "peak of Caliban's speech goes beyond what he himself says" about learning to curse, which should be seen as ironizing a particular address: "'You taught me language and I know how to curse you.' And that's the limit of that particular experience. But he could just as easily have said, 'You taught me language and my profit on it is I know how to praise,' which would be just as natural, even more natural, than using his language to curse the person who taught him language." The idea of writing as rite is developed to a distinctive conclusion: "I think that since . . . the original idea of poetry was a votive idea of praise, a function to praise objects, to praise God, to praise whatever, that there's no distinction after a while between Prospero and Caliban."[10] This goes beyond Lamming's perception that Prospero "hates and fears and needs Caliban."[11] The perception that an oppositional relationship can be resolved in a common purpose is central to Walcott's philosophy.

Antonio Benitez-Rojo explores some related ideas in a discussion of Nicolás Guillén's work: Caliban and Prospero are "double signs that do not manage to exclude each other mutually, since each would secretly like to be in the other's place." Having posited this paradox, he argues that while it is "easy to establish binary oppositions between them," on the other hand "it's not hard to dismantle those oppositions in favor of a global ensemble of differences that might underwrite imperfect relations of coexistence in continuous transformation."[12] The "ensemble" of differences is perhaps another way of approaching the idea of sameness in difference and difference within the same, which informs the "I-an-I" figure used in this study. Caribbean language provides a striking example of heteroglossia, distinctively in process, unfinished, evolving. As V. S. Naipaul said (perhaps surprisingly), as long ago as 1965, "Culture is like language, ever developing. There is no right and wrong, no purity from which there is decline. Usage sanctions everything."[13] This is the essence of the Creole aesthetic. The resource of language for the Caribbean writer is a versatile tool. Calvin Bedient has said of Walcott's poetry that "heterogeneity is with him a grace, almost a way. . . . His powers long to travel and his sensibility enlarges everything to its widest limits. . . . At the level of style alone Walcott offers God's plenty."[14] He revels in his multiple language heritage but uses it to demonstrate potentiality. Above all he shows that meanings are constantly created and that there is no intrinsic link between signifier and signified. In unchaining the sign, he liberates language to difference, not with the arcane hermeticism of James Joyce's language in *Finnegans Wake* but with deceptively simple strategies of reinvesting words with meaning. In *The Fortunate Traveller*, for instance, he draws the mythified phrase "heart of darkness" through a sequence of changes or "translations." The parallel hope is that as the signifier relates to the signified in shifting, alterable ways, so the relationships between individuals and social contexts can also be remade.

Like Caliban, Walcott has a double project, to create a counterdiscourse and to initiate new expression—utterance, in Caliban's terms, polarized between curse and song, or between Caribbean "picong"[15] and praise-song—but both halves of this are themselves multiples. There is a need to answer the discourse of power, which was the tool of empire, but splitting off from this is the impulse to engage with his contemporaries' resistance. Walcott is generally not interested in using language to curse. His counterdiscourse opposing the power abuses and racism of colonial (and neocolonial) discourse is typically concerned to lead the wrong-headed to understanding and, hopefully, self-reform and is conducted in a spirit of protest that is anguished rather than angry. On the other hand, some of his most brilliantly vitriolic expression, his "picong," has been addressed to those on his own "side" whom he sees as traducing the project of reform. Factionalist in-fighting should not be regarded, however, as indicating any remoteness from the (linguistic) revolutionary cause. Rather the reverse. In the crucible of devising resistance, it is normal for the bitterest words to be reserved for colleagues. And as Walcott has pointed out, the Caribbean, like the Aegean, consists of intimate communities:

> Remember in the Caribbean, that basically, no matter how big they are, those towns and villages, you can walk up to someone and call him a damn fool. I mean really, personally, call him an idiot. It's very hard to do that in large cities, immense cities, where the power is remote. The possibility of change includes your ability to have a serious row with a minister over a drink or something. That is potential for change, and potential for making people realize that there is anger. I think that the immediacy of that kind of anger, which is almost pure vitriolic personal abuse, is much better than, say, that distance of remotely criticizing something through critical judgement or through sociological essays.

It is a playwright's wisdom applied to a profound morality: "The more constricted the passion within the arena that it's in, the more possibility there is."[16]

Walcott's difference from all but the most creative minds of the Caribbean, however, is in his perception that the most secure counter to the binary discourse of empire that deploys alterity to justify material exploitation is not a different binary discourse but one that transcends such classifications altogether. Shakespeare gives Caliban self-expression in English that goes way beyond imprecation. He is a poet, who makes song of his own desires, and celebrates his island and himself. Walcott refuses the hierarchy that Prospero's discourse parades, which postulates the inferiority of Caliban. To him, there is "no distinction"; both are men, imperfect, but most perfectible through their poetry. This is the ultimate gift of language, that as a field in which to articulate desire it enables us to approach our best selves and each other. As his friend Joseph Brodsky wrote admiringly of Walcott, "He acts out of the belief that language is greater than its master or its servants, that poetry, being its supreme version, is therefore an instrument of self-betterment for both; i.e., that it is a way to gain an identity superior to the confines of class, race, or ego. This is just plain common sense; this is also the most sound program of social change there is."[17] Walcott's metaphor is of the "tidal advance of the metropolitan language, of its empire. . . . It is the language which is the empire, and great poets are not its vassals but its princes."[18] To Seamus Heaney, Walcott has "imperious linguistic gifts": "There is a magnificence and pride about this art . . . that rebukes the old British notion of 'Commonwealth literature': Walcott possesses English more deeply and sonorously than most of the English themselves."[19] Although Heaney shows his sensitivity to the centrism concealed in the literary establishment's patronizing attitude to literatures not from Britain or America, Walcott's philosophy leads us to a realization that the term "commonwealth" can be used differently, as Gonzalo uses it, uncontaminated by hierarchy. The "Commonwealth idea," he has said, is "one of the greatest achievements . . . of conventional history":

> If one thinks of the Commonwealth as an extension of the empire then it's ridiculous; it's just a perpetuation of the idea of the empire. But if one thinks of it as a renewal of some kind of community of nations who are very diverse and are not linked simply by the idea of a Queen, but by the commonality of language, and by a commonality of experience that that language provides, it's a terrific thing, and it's a worthwhile thing.[20]

As Brodsky says, "language itself is an epic device"; everything Walcott touches "mushrooms with reverberations and perspectives, like magnetic waves whose acoustics are psychological, whose implications are echo-like."[21]

The accolades have been extraordinary from the beginning, and Walcott has always responded with great humility: "if I see my name, as I have seen recently, next to names that I revere, I really feel quite embarrassed. I feel I shouldn't be in that company."[22] When Robert Graves said in 1964 that Walcott handled English "with a closer understanding of its inner magic than most (if not any) of his English-born contemporaries,"[23] Walcott knew it was a "tremendous compliment": "I remember I came home from the beach and saw this letter from Jonathan Cape in which Graves had said that and I was astonished. What can you say, if someone the stature of Graves says that about you? You just swallow, and tears come to your eyes, and you say, My God, that's it!—you know, there's nothing more to say."[24] In 1986, Brodsky recognized in one memorable phrase both Walcott's stature and the difficulties he is up against, when he spoke of "the unwillingness of the critical profession to admit that the great poet of the English language is a black man."[25] In *Another Life,* Walcott ironizes his position as a "prodigy of the wrong age and colour."[26] The Nobel citation, made four hundred years after Columbus's first landfall in the Caribbean, referred to him as the "great poet" of Caribbean culture, with three abiding loyalties, to the Caribbean, to the English language, and to "his African origin"—a list in which the last seems subtly more a marker of the Swedish Academy's conditioning than of Walcott's priorities.

Heaney's choice of title for his essay on Walcott is a compact signifier. Where Brodsky had called his Walcott essay "The Sound of the Tide," Heaney ironizes it by choosing as his own title "The Murmur of Malvern," which is an intertextual signifier, foregrounding not Walcott's exoticism as seen from the white-dominated literary establishment but his in-placeness in the English literary tradition, since the Malvern allusion is to Langland's *Piers Plowman,* echoed in the opening of "The Schooner *Flight.*" Heaney sees Walcott as a sharer of the same tradition as himself, each with his own wry angle on the political meaning of Englishness, but each with a clear and incontrovertible knowledge that all that has been written in the language is his to enjoy and to use, from the beginning. As a young literature-lover Walcott was less interested in historicizing what he read than in the craft of how it was done: "The dust isn't on the language. The enjoyment is there, and I think the luck of that was knowing that poetry was its own element in terms of time, and was not manifested through epochs and schools and changes of style and so on. I think that has made me look stubborn or dated or whatever, but it doesn't bother me, you know."[27] The refusal is part of his revolutionary refusal to accept any externally imposed limits, whether social or aesthetic, a stance that has led directly to the epic sweep of an oeuvre that makes so much other writing look ephemeral or parochial. In *Another Life,* he accounts for the poem's ambitious tone by saying, "Provincialism loves the pseudo-epic," but the self-deprecation is unnecessary: his work is indeed epic.[28]

Since Joyce's *A Portrait of the Artist as a Young Man,* we have learned to see the languages of empire as contaminated with the discourse of power that they have contained: "My soul frets in the shadow of his language," says Stephen Dedalus.[29] The cultural politics poses real dilemmas: "The urge towards the metropolitan language," Walcott has said, "was the same as political deference to its centre."[30] Joyce's Stephen thinks of the Englishman he is speaking to, "How different are the words, *home, Christ, ale, master,* on his lips and on mine!" Walcott has said of Joyce that he "felt very close to the whole bitterness that is there," but at the same time that the "only god left to Joyce really is language—a sacral, self-surrendering, monastic idea." His achievement was to go beyond Shakespeare and Homer in undertaking "a history of language . . . a history of the origins of language."[31] Walcott describes Caribbean people as "ashamed of their speech"; like actors, they "awaited a language." They had, in fact, language aplenty, multiple registers of language, but the domestic language was felt to be unworthy, and the hierarchized metropolitan language was alien and reinscribed historic humiliations. What was needed was "the forging of a language that went beyond mimicry, a dialect which had the force of revelation as it invented names for things."[32] What was needed was a demonstration that the people already had a language that could express the fullness of their subjectivity—that the centrist scorn which induced them to feel ashamed of the Creole end of their language continuum was just racism and class prejudice, and that the metropolitan language, which was alien and pejorative, could be used differently and was open to metamorphosis, the stiff case of its historic meanings shed so that the rainbow imago of its diverse global communities could unfold new wings to the sun. In a climactic passage of *Another Life* echoing Joyce, Walcott names the history of language in his own community's new language:

O sun, on that morning,
did I not mutter towards your
holy, repetitive resurrection, "Hare,
hare Krishna," and then, politely,
"Thank you, life"? Not
to enter the knowledge of God
but to know that His name
had lain too familiar on my tongue,
as this one would say "bread,"
or "sun," or "wine," I staggered,
shaken at my remorse, as one
would say "bride," or "bread,"
or "sun," or "wine," to believe—[33]

Unlike the Joyce passage, the subject here is not alienation but over-familiarity reducing the sense of the sacred: the language is shown to be already fully possessed in his own culture. Walcott sees himself as like Aimé Césaire in reinvesting a metropolitan language with specifically Caribbean meaning: he translates, "Storm, I would say. River, I would command. Hurricane, I would say. I would utter 'leaf.' Tree. I would be drenched in all the rains, soaked in all the dews."[34] The sense of the naming as a sacred rite, as an analogue of creation, pervades the work of Caribbean poets and is, as Kamau Brathwaite has reminded us, an essentially African approach to the Word. Walcott writes, "this new Word / was here, attainable / to my own hand, / in the deep country it found the natural man, / generous, rooted."[35] The values enshrined in this language are essentially humanist.

As well as claiming his own language's difference, Joyce recognizes its derivation: "The language in which we are speaking is his before it is mine." The chronicity point orders sequence but not necessarily value. Only in a culture where origin is privileged through seniority does the remark invite a reading of Irish English as "lesser." The englishes (to borrow the Ashcroft, Griffiths, and Tiffin usage) now in use around the globe are not in a deferential relationship to British English.[36] As Walcott points out, what is needed is the "faith of using the old names anew," a process that is already under way: Caribbean people "gave the old names life" and "charged an old language, from the depth of suffering, with awe."[37] He sees his own work as part of a larger American project: "the inflexion of language is not English-accented but American-accented, and what we really are speaking, however defensively the English may feel about it, is we are all speaking American."[38] American English, he says, has the "vitality and vigour of dialect tone, of colloquial immediacy," which was found in Homeric language. With its "high colloquiality" and its "bad puns," Homer's Greek "is already energized by a kind of vulgarity, not by a kind of pomposity." Vulcan's task to "hammer at the shield / of language till the wound and the word fit" requires the finely controlled energy of the steelpan tuner. The world, which includes all texts and all art, is the oil drum, the raw material of the given, which can be made to give new music. The making of art is always a kind of translation, the American aesthetic distinctively peeling off the crustings of age and status to return something new-minted. The transatlantic translator of Virgil restarts time with the new language, as he "recites in American: '*Arma virumque cano . . .* '"[39] The phrase "high colloquiality" is useful as a term for Walcott's own linguistic practice, whether in verse or prose. It reconciles the twin dimensions of tone so often mythified in academic discourse as binary opposites.

Mikhail Bakhtin's distinction between the language of epic and of the novel, for instance, is based on such a false dichotomy. In Bakhtin's analysis, epic language provides a "monolithic and closed world," not the effect that Walcott seeks.[40] His language is an extreme polyglossia, combining disparate styles and registers. As Bakhtin notes, polyglossia, which for him is indicative of the novel, had "always existed (it is more ancient than pure, canonic monoglossia), but it had not been a factor in literary creation."[41] He goes on to pinpoint its effect: "The new cultural and creative consciousness lives in an entirely polyglot world. The world becomes polyglot, once and for all and irreversibly. The period of national languages, coexisting but closed and deaf to each other, comes to an end. Languages throw light on each other: one language can, after all, see itself only in the light of another language." It follows that those cultures and those individuals who inherit plural language traditions are in a better position to "throw light" than others. Bakhtin's perception that there is a kind of dialectical relationship between languages, as systems, illuminates Walcott's practice (which goes beyond Bakhtin's argument in demonstrating the use of polyglossia in epic, as discussed below). He ranges across all of the worlds available to him. John Figueroa identifies him as the first West Indian writer "willing to use all the resources of his culture."[42] Walcott demonstrates that standard modern aesthetic assumptions, such as that elevated language was possible in the Elizabethan and Jacobean eras but not now, or that colloquial language with an oral tone cannot signify a high seriousness or subtle thought, are meaningless.

The particular heritage of language comes down to very small identity groups. "What I hope I have never done is to go away from the sound of my own language," says Walcott.[43] Remaining faithful not just to his language but to the distinctiveness of its sound has been his lifelong project. He emphasizes the diversity of language practice in the Caribbean, defining himself as a Caribbean writer but within that group "specifically as a St. Lucian writer." Language is historically produced: "each Caribbean island has its own . . . history, and has a variety of linguistic experience," he says; "I don't think people are aware of the fact that within each island there is a whole insular experience of language and its own history, that can vary from island to island. The speech in Jamaica is different from that of Barbados and St. Lucia and Trinidad and so on."[44] This heteroglossia is a rich resource for the writer. Readers need an awareness that Caribbean language has many facets, as has every other dimension of the region. There is no place for a flattened concept of the Caribbean as some kind of monad. Walcott offers Trinidadian language as an extreme case:

> one look at the ideal in this multilinguistic situation would be Port of Spain, in which there are the Chinese, the Lebanese, Indian—Muslim and Hindu—and so on, so that even if they're all speaking in a Trinidad English dialect, it means that every race represented there has residues, or has an active language going on that may be spoken by grandparents or by people domestically. And that's what I find very exciting about Trinidad, that variety that is there.[45]

As Walcott said in his Nobel lecture, "I am only one-eighth the writer I might have been had I contained all the fragmented languages of Trinidad," in which Port of Spain is "a writer's heaven" with its "downtown babel of shop signs and streets, mongrelized, polyglot, a ferment without a history."[46] The characteristic canceling of history repeats a familiar prioritization and is not incompatible with the earlier historiography. Of course the linguistic present is the product of a particular past: the point is that that past pales into insignificance compared with the "ferment" of the now. A few lines earlier he recognized that "[d]eprived of their original language, the captured and indentured tribes create their own, accreting and secreting fragments of an old, an epic vocabulary, from Asia and from Africa, but to an ancestral, an ecstatic rhythm in the blood that cannot be subdued by slavery or indenture."[47] The point is that the language practices that have arisen from that history, in which the "original language dissolves from the exhaustion of distance like fog trying to cross an ocean," are vigorously creative: "The dialects of my archipelago seem as fresh to me as those raindrops," or, as he put it earlier in "What the Twilight Says," using a deliberately nonstandard idiom, "The power of the dew still shakes off of our dialects."[48] The image of the Caribbean as echo chamber needs to be transformed so that it evokes not diminishing resonance from a remote source but novel sound-encounters in a generation chamber, a new hybrid location inducing catalytic change. As with language, so with the metalanguage of intertextuality: the thought and art of the world are the artist's material as much as the natural or sociopolitical world of which s/he is a part. As Walcott has put it wryly, "Empires are smart enough to steal from the people they conquer. They steal the best things. And the people who have been conquered should have enough sense to steal back."[49] The signifying moment is always new and always symbolizes opportunity, whether couched in the oppositional language of Caliban or in his other language practice, of blessing by naming.

For Walcott as a St. Lucian, there is a heritage of two indigenous vernaculars, English and French Creole (or patois), as well as two standard European languages, in constant interplay with one another and not surprisingly producing new and unique meanings between them. The Caribbean language continuum for him thus has twin tracks in English and French, with complicated and interesting junctions. Conspicuously, his sense of the identity conferred by a particular geography is differentiated by language. He repeatedly recites the St. Lucian names for nature—trees, birds, and flowers—in patois, for instance, names that are "suppler, greener, more morning-stirred than English."[50] As he put it in *Another Life,* "certain roots refused English."[51] French Creole is central to his cultural identity. In "Sainte Lucie," it comes naturally: "moi c'est gens Ste. Lucie" is followed by a whole section presented as a patois folk song, which John Figueroa has claimed authoritatively is Walcott's composition.[52] As well as writing both St. Lucia and Trinidad into his Nobel lecture, he also offered a patois song to the international Stockholm audience as marker of his multiple linguistic heritage. St. Lucia, as he points out, is "closer to Martinique and Guadeloupe—linguistically, certainly—than it is, say, to Barbados."[53]

The French Creole experience, he says, "is something that's still not fully mined in Caribbean writing. . . . I don't just mean the dialect, I mean the whole feel of that experience. It's just beginning to be defined, I think."[54] It is evident that he has seriously considered writing more in patois: "I thought of this at one point of my life, that if I were writing in French there'd also be an audience for French, or for French Creole, so there's another whole unexplored area, I think, in me that could perhaps . . . I don't think it will ever develop, because I'm, perhaps, past that now, but certainly in terms of translating the plays that I have written in the English, French-accented dialect, that that could transfer quite easily to Martinique, to Guadeloupe and to Haiti, for instance."[55] But the idea of writing in French Creole has not gone away. In 1996 he said, "I would like at some time to write poems or songs in Creole. I did it once."[56] In a recent address, he has explained how central the French Creole is to *Ti-Jean and His Brothers.* The play is based on a verbal joke, as the story was narrated to him by a fellow schoolboy, which "doesn't work in an English translation."[57] His first conception of *Omeros,* in fact, was as a poem in French Creole: "I tried to do it in 'patois' . . . I ran out of vocabulary. That's ignorance of the language."[58] There is also the difficulty of class and race difference. The St. Lucian fishermen he was drawn to from his youth as his "material" were "blasphemous and bitter," a "sect which had evolved its own signs, a vocation which excluded the stranger."[59] There are problems in "putting it down on paper": "I don't want it to become a literary exercise." The task is to get the "melody"; the danger is "talking with an affected accent" or "pretending to be somebody else, including pretending to be somebody that sociologically I'm not—I am not a fisherman on a beach in Gros Ilet, that's not what I am. I am a professor of poetry at Boston University."[60]

The worry about appropriation and authenticity shows a commendable humility, but his evocation of a French Creole environment and his use of patois in *Omeros* and in other recent poems such as "The Light of the World" demonstrate complete assurance, producing extremely subtle poetic resonances. When at the start of *Omeros* Walcott glosses the exposition of Philoctete's wound, "*Moin blessé*" with "I am blest / wif this wound,"[61] acute observers may note that the English that reads as a translation appears to be more than that.[62] It seems to be an interpretation of the wound's spiritual meaning. What is less obvious is that the patois "blessé" has acquired a special meaning in St. Lucia from the influence of the similar-sounding English word "bless" and that the "translation" is just that: in St. Lucian patois, "moin blessé" can indeed mean "I am blest with this wound." Reading the patois from the metropolitan position of Standard French is to misconstrue. In fact, St. Lucian usage has returned both terms, in the English and French vernaculars, to their original sacred meaning: "bless" in English is cognate with the word "blood" and meant originally "to sacrifice, mark with blood," while the French "blessé" [wounded] has (in St. Lucia) drawn closer to the root idea of sanctifying. The mystery of the holiness of suffering is thus once again revealed in language, a syncretist re-creation, unique to St. Lucia, and the direct result of the tragic history and allegedly "nothing" culture of the islands. This is the "faith of using the old names anew." It is a collective act, not just that of the shaman-artist—and Caribbeans have a "total right of access to all the languages of the Caribbean," with no boundaries. The plenitude of language, in which each island has its own "tone," gives the poet access to a kind of "orchestration."[63]

Sometimes, however, oral difference can be obscured on the page, as with the word "conch," for example. It appears in Walcott's work as local object of natural beauty but also as symbol. It is a sacrificial emblem of life from death: like the paschal lamb it dies soundlessly but gives voice in death (like an Orphic head) from its "pink palate." Used in the shoreline cemeteries of St. Lucia to border graves, with its sculptural form like the female vulva, it becomes a fertility symbol representing the defeat of death. In recent Standard English, however, usage has changed. Most people now pronounce "conch" phonetically, although the *Shorter Oxford Dictionary,* published in 1933, records only the "conk" pronunciation as correct (the 1976 edition of the *Concise Oxford Dictionary* gives the "k" pronunciation as an alternative). Walcott follows Caribbean usage in pronouncing it "conk," which to a British ear returns its potential as symbol to the foreground, as it has a vernacular meaning in Britain as "nose," and increasingly, by extension and by contagion with expressions such as to "conk out" meaning "lose consciousness," "head."[64] It is yet another reminder both of the plurality of language influence in the Caribbean (the retention of the "k" ending in St. Lucia reflects the word's pronunciation in French, "conque," and in the romance languages generally, as in the Greek root) and of the way in which new meanings continually emerge. It matters because a line in a poem may have not only a different sound but a different rhythm. In one of the poems in *Midsummer,* for instance, the sentence (which probably begins with an editor's "amendment") "Conches move over the sea-floor" when read by Walcott begins with the monosyllabic "Conks," which weights the line with the molluscs' slowness.[65]

Walcott glosses some of the terms he knows will be unfamiliar. His awareness of the multiplicity of his readers' starting positions is acute, and he will frequently mediate the idiosyncrasies of usage by explanation or translation: "ciseau / the scissor-bird."[66] This is an essentially well-mannered practice, showing sensitivity to the pluralism of his readers' cultures (the implicit corollary of his assertion of the pluralism of his own aesthetic), as well as foregrounding for ideological reasons the formation and diverse practice of language itself. He *suggests* the vernacular rather than reproducing it exactly (which tends to make it impenetrable to outsiders): "One need not be faithful," he has said.[67] Sometimes, however, he seems to get caught out. The first question to Walcott from a member of the audience after a reading from *Omeros* at the National Theatre, London, was "What are 'coffles'?," one of the words in the passage read. After some difficulty in making out the question, Walcott looked surprised and said, "Feet-cuffs, chains for the feet."[68] It was a particularly poignant illustration of selective memory in language: in the seat of empire there was no memory of the tool of oppression, but it was well remembered in the former slave colony. Other terms have a precise period resonance in an international vernacular but will increasingly come to need footnotes. The procession of the language of empire that is used to mark Maud's death in *Omeros,* for instance, includes the phrase "tinkles in the jordan," for the sound of a china chamber pot in use, a familiar usage from the prewar period, which must have spread throughout the British empire.[69]

Whether he is working in a complex meter or free verse, Walcott regards his guiding principle as to be true to the tone of the language, which is oral: "There is no difference in the Caribbean between oral and written. No matter what the anthologists and the anthropologists may say, they are the same thing. Nor are there two languages; there's only one, one melody."[70] The "sound of the vernacular," he says, is "something which doesn't need the voice to go up on a platform."[71] It is therefore the natural vehicle for a democratic art. All great poetry, to Walcott, has an oral element—"You have to imagine . . . that somebody is capable of such speech"—but the vernacular carries "a true tone of the human voice in poetry."[72] Some of Walcott's influential first encounters with other Caribbean writing were oral, through Henry Swanzy's BBC World Service program, *Caribbean Voices,* and even some of the most hieratic of written literature was first heard rather than read: recordings of T. S. Eliot reading *The Four Quartets,* for instance.[73] Walcott was of that first generation for whom audio-technology was a norm, telescoping in some ways the distance from metropolitan centers of articulation and enabling the islands of the archipelago to speak to each other.

The notion of Standard English (or French) is, of course, a centrist construct, its normative influence tending away from the poetic, and from the creative use of language in general, and tending to down-value the local and regional. The vernacular polarity is characterized by Brathwaite as having a "person-centred, fluid/tidal rather than ideal/structured nature."[74] Although engaged in a rhetoric of promoting the oral tone as marker of Caribbean literature, Brathwaite is quite clear that the distinctive virtue of the region's creativity comes from drawing on all points of the continuum: "To confine our definitions of literature to written texts in a culture that remains ital in most of its people proceedings, is as limiting as its opposite: trying to define Caribbean literature as essentially orature—like eating avocado without its likkle salt."[75] Extraordinary linguistic innovation such as that of Rastafarian speech, which "flows directly from Rastafari philosophy and expresses a fundamental relationship of humans to nature and the universe," is the extreme version of a norm of creativity.[76] It performs both of the roles of Caliban's language, in opposing a damaging norm and inventing an alternative: it offers both "I-an-I" and "Babylon," which Gordon Rohlehr defines as "a portmanteau word which conveys the action of an unfair system of distribution; commercialism, and the subjection of human value to market value."[77] Walcott draws on Rastafarian language in *O Babylon!* and on a number of different local Caribbean vernaculars and class and group usages, particularly in his plays, yet a critical rhetoric has grown up that presents him as a writer predominantly uninterested in or hostile to the orality option. Concessions are made to his more recent experiments with it, but only as a refinement of the overall case of his fundamental antipathy. Rohlehr, for instance, argues that "Walcott instinctively resists the pressure of the oral tradition, making concessions to it only when it has through its own efforts gained in depth and dimension,"[78] while Chamberlin's assertion that "[t]he use of dialect did not come easily for Walcott" is seriously wide of the mark.[79]

From the very beginning of his career as a writer, Walcott in fact drew on the whole language continuum that he had inherited, just as much as did Brathwaite (who tends to be set up as the opposite to Walcott in this dialectic). The poetry of early plays such as *Ti-Jean and His Brothers* shows a remarkably inventive approach to St. Lucian vernacular speech, as vehicle for a literature already epic in intent and achievement. As a sustained deployment of the vernacular medium, *Ti-Jean* is actually more polarized on the Creole continuum than Brathwaite's *Arrivants* trilogy, which mixes Standard English with the vernacular. Walcott contests the language politics that sets up false choices between orality and the literary, split on class and race lines, and he ironizes his own position between them as "jumped on by both sides for pretentiousness or playing white." He is seen as "the mulatto of style. The traitor. The assimilator."[80] In recent years, the terms in which the metropolitan literary establishment has tended to couch its praise have exacerbated the problem at home: the more America and Europe have co-opted his work to an elitist model, the harder it has been for fellow Caribbeans to see it differently. The choice was false because both languages, that of the folk and that of Standard English, were given, were Caribbean, and were there to be used. The morality of his inclusiveness is spelled out: "If the language was contemptible, so was the people."[81]

The characteristically American refusal of monoglossia and of Europe's discourses of power brings the result that although the American epic may be on an ambitious scale, it tends to be saved from overreaching itself by internal diversity leading to irony. Bakhtin identifies the "multi-styled genre" as typically ironic and part of a process to "bring the world closer and familiarize it in order to investigate it fearlessly and freely."[82] Caribbean culture is distinctively self-ironizing. Benitez-Rojo defines the Caribbean novel and poem as "projects for ironizing a set of values taken as universal."[83] Its folk forms, such as calypso and carnivalesque "robber talk," make extravagant rhetorical play across the pleasure-ground of language. Walcott sees Caribbean rhetoric politically:

> It's historically inevitable that any suppressed utterance, as happened in slavery, when it does find release is going to find very voluble release. The hundreds of years of slavery in the Caribbean means that somebody was saying to the people "Don't talk," and when that ban, virtually—mental or otherwise—is released, there's going to be a lot of talk. Whatever's been repressed and prevented is going to suddenly explode.[84]

"Picong" [piquant, sharp, hot], as noted above, is the Trinidadian term for the language of abuse elevated to an art form, a specifically regional cultural marker that Walcott demonstrates in a number of his poems, such as "The Spoiler's Return."[85] His ability to catch a precise vernacular tone in a single ironic phrase is evidence of an acute ear. In *Omeros,* for instance, he deploys not just the vernacular of the Caribbean but the exactly caught language of upwardly mobile lower-middle-class England in the speech of Dennis Plunkett, and he mocks the racist portrayal of "black talk" in America in his satiric response to Melville's quoted *Moby Dick:*

> Heah's Cap'n Melville on de whiteness ob de whale—
> "*Having for the imperial colour the same imperial hue*
> *giving the white man ideal mastership over every dusky tribe.*"
> Lawd, Lawd, Massa Melville, what could a nigger do
> but go down dem steps in de dusk you done describe?[86]

In another compact and resonant juxtaposition in *Omeros,* he makes Odysseus's crew speak to him in the Caribbean vernacular, "This is we Calypso, / Captain, who treat we like swine," but he makes Odysseus reply in an archaic English, reminiscent of the now-forgotten, imperialist seafaring adventure fiction of authors such as Captain Marryat: "Cap'n, boy? Beg mercy / o' that breeze for a change."[87] As Bakhtin says, languages can only look at themselves in the light of another; that which is ironized can be evaluated. Even when his diction is apparently formal, however, Walcott's *tone* is nearly always oral, and paradoxically his adoption of the hexameter for *Omeros* enables him to work more rather than less easily with rhythms and structures typical of spoken language, as the above examples demonstrate. As a playwright he says he does not start with plot: his script "just comes out of somebody, a voice, and then another person answers, and something begins to grow around it."[88] Voice itself is an aesthetic.

The critical tendency to divide Walcott the poet from Walcott the dramatist leads to distortion of his work: the projects are twin, and he is as much a champion of poetry in the theater as he is a manipulator of the unfolding sequence of his poetry as drama, and an orality of tone permeates both. It is true that the bulk of his use of the vernacular has been in his drama, but this alone would be sufficient to warrant calling him a great Caribbean poet in the oral tradition if he had written nothing else. As it is, he has produced in addition an extraordinary corpus of poetry. A small but striking minority of his poems are voiced entirely in the vernacular, while a significant proportion of them draw on the orality end of the continuum within a Standard English framework. The early versions of the sonnet sequence "Tales of the Islands," for instance, show him experimenting with catching the intonations of speech in written language, which is essentially a dramatist's art. The 1962 collection *In a Green Night* contains other orally inflected poems, such as "Parang," which is entirely in a vernacular voice. Of his longer poems, two have also been voiced in a sustained vernacular, "The Schooner *Flight*" and "The Spoiler's Return," both remarkable proof of the oral language's capacity (if proof were needed), while others incorporate passages with an oral tone, or quasi-dramatic vernacular voices. Both of the long epics make striking use of the vernacular, particularly *Omeros,* which opens with it and, most memorably, has God speak to Achille in his own language. That this should have such a powerful effect is a salutory reminder of the remoteness of most religious discourse from ordinary speech, yet it is entirely logical that an individual's interior dialogue with his God would make use of his own language.

In the Nobel lecture, which sets out in effect a Caribbean aesthetic, Walcott gives thanks for "the benediction that is celebrated, a fresh language and a fresh people."[89] His is an inclusive language, which attempts to reflect Caribbean variety but in so doing reflects the world's variety, which it contains. The modernists were the first to assemble fragments of languages, quotations, snatches of quasi-dramatic speech and of popular song, and elements of different discourses; and to the extent that Eliot and Pound were its leaders, the modernist project was to a significant degree American. The "fragments" that, Eliot writes in *The Waste Land,* "I have shored against my ruins" are aesthetic parallels to the ancestrally secreted "fragments" that Walcott describes in his Nobel lecture.[90] His own use of this duality of cultural "quotation," a kind of "translation," can be illustrated from his references in *Another Life* to the operatic aria "O Paradiso."[91] At the surface level, the phrase is an invocation to paradise, in a language associated in anglophone culture with lyricism, that of an art-rich Italy, which as a young man he "flung round my shoulders like a robe."[92] In fact, the opera it comes from, Meyerbeer's *L'Africaine,* was written in French, so the form invoked is already a translation. It represents first an act of memory: in his childhood, Gigli's recording was popular with his elders who owned gramophones. But it records not only the personal nostalgia for lost childhood; it evokes a complex artistic moment, in which the art of the past, the art of a remote continent, the art of the historical oppressors, is co-opted to expressing a collective feeling of identification with the Caribbean location. It is evident from Walcott's introduction to his choice of the recording for BBC Radio's *Desert Island Discs* that his community related to it as an expression of delight in their own St. Lucian "paradise."[93] That Meyerbeer's opera displays an imprecise history and geography is no bar to that self-identification. The plot in fact tells of one of the first European explorers, Vasco da Gama, landing in an unspecified territory and of his romance with a local beauty. There are Asiatic overtones, but the opera is called *L'Africaine,* which would plausibly reflect the history of da Gama's landfalls in Mozambique and Malindi (now in Kenya) on the way to India in 1498. Historically Vasco da Gama did not undertake a voyage to the New World, and there is irony in Walcott's making Dunstan say in *Another Life,* "'Listen! Vasco da Gama kneels to the New World.'"[94] The "logic" of hegemony would identify this as "error," yet the elation of wonder at the new place and its inhabitants, which the music captures, is there for anyone, including St. Lucians.

The powerful dream of the locus of desire as attainable (which in the Old World tradition is locked to the concept of remoteness) becomes in the New World an image of the locus of desire attained, possessed. St. Lucians, who felt blessed by their location (particularly when, during Walcott's childhood, World War II seemed to engulf the rest of the world), wanted to celebrate their heritage of a particular geographical place in the world. Paradoxically, although the opera derives from imperialist discourse, the figure of the *arrivant* was one to which Caribbean people of all racial backgrounds could relate. The fact that the opera narrates as romance a fictionalized tragic history of imperialism, ending with the African beloved killing herself for love as da Gama sails away, becomes culturally irrelevant. In the age of mechanical reproduction, which Walter Benjamin was one of the first to address,[95] the opera loses its original significance and becomes open to new meanings through its new existence as a fragmented commodity. St. Lucians in general had no access to performances (or, probably, scores) of the opera as a whole, only the recording of the aria disseminated as a commodity and valorized by the star performer, Gigli. To inherit remoteness from a loosely defined cultural center (as Walcott says of his childhood, "Remember years must pass before he saw an orchestra, / a train, a theatre")[96] is not, he insists, to be disadvantaged. Imperial culture filtered through the Gigli record could be made to signify afresh, the act of interpretation investing the art with local meaning, the precise joy of natural blessing.

It is a very modern story, and one central to Walcott's perception of intercultural relations: the tragic reality of history can be transformed and redeemed through art. The community's appropriation of just the one fragment that could be co-opted to express a local joy reflects the obstinate creativity of optimism. The cultural event, the transformation, compressed in the phrase is extraordinary, given the relish of the imperial romance as tragedy, exhibited by the supremely romantic idiom of nineteenth-century opera, a distinctively European cultural product. Meyerbeer's opera invents the self-sacrifice of the African as closure, as a powerful valorizer of the myth of European patriarchal supremacy as destiny: the white man travels the world as figure of romantic desire, breaking hearts (and then lives) as he goes. Is it his fault if girls kill themselves, the opera seems to ask. But the potential meaning of the opera's closure as a kind of Brechtian symbol—historically the white man came and the indigenous people did indeed begin to die—is aborted by its ready meaning within a popular myth (of imperial patriarchy), which it then reinforces. The process of selection and reinvesting with meaning—of translation—

that the "O Paradiso" case illustrates can be seen as symbolizing a particularly American appropriation. In this example, the exploitative power relations immanent in the European art are discarded in the New World in favor of a cultural reading of it simply as praise-song. For the St. Lucian elders who played the record to the young Walcott, it was not distortion (they probably did not know the whole opera) or romance, but recognition: the aria captured an elation of place, which was theirs.

Cultural "quotation" is also naturalized by being locally re-voiced. In an epic poem largely about St. Lucia, it might be expected that to quote the capital's Latin motto, from Virgil, would lend a solemn and formal tone, but in *Another Life* Walcott rejuvenates the antique language by placing it in a dramatized schoolroom scene:

> "What is the motto of St. Lucia, boy?"
> "*Statio haud malefida carinis.*"
> "Sir!"
> "Sir!"
> "And what does that mean?"
> "Sir, a safe anchorage for sheeps!"[97]

The teacher's testing of the boy's knowledge enables Walcott (himself once a Latin teacher at his old school, overlooking the harbor) to teach his reader both the motto and its meaning, which the pupils already know, and to enhance awareness, through a significant example, of how a community can use archaic symbols, transmitted through education, to confirm (ambiguously) its sense of identity. The child's distinctive pronunciation of the word "ships" as "sheeps" is a subtly plural sign: a Brechtian ironization of colonial docility in the face of empire's appropriations (the island perceived from the center not as itself but as a tool of the controlling military machine, the fleet) and of the "herd" mentality that plays down the possibility of change; a reminder that English is not the first language to the majority of St. Lucians, so that boys in the Latin class are being taught a third, culturally valorized language, in contrast to their first language, banned from the classroom; a joke, using "incorrect" language (the plural of "sheep" is "sheep") to generate a surreal image (a fleet/flock of anchored sheep), a way of accessing the innocence and optimism of childhood; and a creation, that moment at which a distinctively local newness enters language practice. The lesson in translation is more than it appears to be. As so often in Walcott's work, an apparently simple moment, swiftly yielding a telling significance at first reading, repays reflective revisiting.

It can, however, be easy to mistake Walcott on first reading. When

Walcott ends an apparently gloomy portrayal of the island in the poem "Gros-Ilet" with the line "the language is that of slaves," the initial response, that a negative has been uttered, is inescapable. But in the pause that follows the poem, in the Brechtian moment of reflection, that assumption of a negative meaning is suddenly understood to be scandalous. The revelatory realization is carefully contrived by the poem, which states the island culture's difference from the Mediterranean "norm," leading the reader by negatives; it bids Elpenor (Odysseus's helmsman) to

> keep moving, there is nothing here for you.
> There are different candles and customs here, the dead
> are different. Different shells guard their graves.
> There are distinctions beyond the paradise
> of our horizon. This is not the grape-purple Aegean.
> There is no wine here, no cheese, the almonds are green,
> the sea grapes bitter, the language is that of slaves.[98]

Centrism's assumption of the right to label the different as inferior is addressed by the skillful strategy of manipulating the reader, by the powerful negative rhetoric, into an uncritical assent to the valuations, and having led her out into vulnerable exposure it spins her round to face the prejudice of her position: the still vilified language of the people is the context which has shaped the poet. It is not necessary to know that the etymology of "vernacular" is from the Latin "vernus" [slave]. Unlike Caliban, aware that the language given him by empire is a tool for cursing but unaware of his own poetry, this poet-Caliban is fully self-conscious of the qualities of his language. Echoing Caliban's "water with berries,"[99] already naturalized to the West Indies by Lamming's book of that name, the poem's speaker names his language:

> From this village, soaked like a grey rag in salt water,
> a language came, garnished with conch shells,
> with a suspicion of berries in its armpits
> and elbows like flexible oars.[100]

The language given by a tragic history begins as a conch-bordered grave but fruits in the unlikeliest places and becomes supple and mobile.

A similar technique, using irony as a key to new meaning, is seen in Walcott's address to the history of British racism and its present legacies. In *Omeros,* he shows a Britain "sharpening the grimaces of thin-lipped market towns, / whitewashing the walls of Brixton, darkening the grain / when coal-shadows cross it." The sense of a gloomy prognosis for a racially divided Britain is acute, confirmed, it seems, by the concluding phrase: "Dark future down darker street."[101] Only on reflection does this meaning split apart to reveal its inner opposite. Only if "dark" is a negative signifier does the future have to be seen as already tragically inscribed in the terms of the past. If "dark" is simply descriptive of a racially diversifying social landscape—if it can be reimagined without its racist connotations—then the future appears optimistic: "dark future down darker street" is transformed into a celebratory image of immigration and integration.

As Walcott makes Lestrade say in *Dream on Monkey Mountain,* "It is the crippled who believe in miracles. It's the slaves who believe in freedom."[102] The dialectics of hope and despair demands the reinvention of language: if "English is white" as Moustique suggests provocatively (as it would seem to a St. Lucian peasant like himself), it must be given a transfusion of "another life."[103] The discourse labeling the black man "Makak," "macaque," monkey, "as I so ugly," leaves him no choice but to name himself.[104] Walcott explains that he draws on personal experience:

> Makak in the play is based on a man I knew who terrified us when we were very young in Saint Lucia, a man called—and that's the tough thing about this—he was called Makak Roger. Roger was not his name. I think he may have worked for someone called Roger, so it really was this that people were calling him: "This is Roger's monkey," which is terrible. . . . I thought what a degrading thing for him to be called that. There was something in the man, however drunk and however degraded, that was extremely powerful.[105]

For the play's protagonist, then, to name himself "Felix," "happy," is to defeat the prejudice utterly and liberates him to name *himself* "monkey" if he pleases.[106] Since his mountain home is called *Morne Macaque,* his adoption of the name is thus freed to signify his in-placeness. It is this hero's freedom from racial and geographic alienation that the play celebrates finally: "He belong right here."[107] As Robert Fox comments, "The dream that transforms Makak is, in a very real sense, Walcott's own dream, his artist's vision which espies the potential for greatness in 'a degraded man' . . . Makak then becomes representative of the downtrodden and impoverished blacks who long to be redeemed."[108] It is, once again, at the heart of language itself that the process of redemption is initiated. "Makak" is stripped of its racist meaning and reinvested with a new positive significance; the sign is remade.

At every level, Walcott's approach to language is ludic: the play of the signifier across meanings and discourses is endlessly surprising and rich. In the first instance, he savors the quiddity of a word, its sound when voiced, and its pattern when written. His verse often incorporates concrete poetry. At the beginning of *Another Life,* for instance, he relishes the line "a moon ballooned up from the Wireless Station. O / mirror," in which the anticipatory "oo"s double the pleasure of the "moon-rise" at the end of the line (particularly satisfactory as the balloon with no strings attached, or "wireless").[109] In "To Return to the Trees," he makes concrete poetry of the printed "e," decoded as like a lidded eye: Seneca's heroes "see with the word / 'senex,' with its two eyes."[110] Again, in *Omeros,* he writes that "the 'I' is a mast," which, to the hull of the poem's line, it then becomes.[111] These games (and they proliferate in his work) explore the way texts exist in the world as visible and audible objects, for even more intriguing is the patterning of sound to evoke the visual. Like the French symbolists, Walcott is interested in the capacity of language to "translate" between the different senses: "the smell of our own speech." He uses an onomatopoeia that is not confined to sound. When, for instance, he writes "beer-bright Vermeer," the internal rhyme—"horizontal" syllables with the vertical "I" vowel between them—not only evokes the golden light in Vermeer's interiors but "paints" in words the amber of a glass of beer standing on a polished surface. The European tradition of still-life painting that the poem addresses, in which things "become / themselves," is summoned to the mind's eye by the four simple syllables. The still life genre may have symbolic meaning for a community establishing its in-placeness. As John Berger argues, "Still lifes tell about how certain things have come together and, despite their evident ephemerality, will stay together. They are images of residence, in every tense of the term."[112] Walcott is intrigued by the challenge of making language produce the illusionist effect of *trompe l'oeil* art. The technique is developed in relation to nature in the evocation of a St. Lucian waterfall: "we startle a place / where a waterfall crashes down rocks. Abounding grace!" The sound of the last phrase "enacts" the waterfall—the smooth leap of "abounding" finding its destination in the frothing pool. "I used the word 'lace' before," says Walcott, "so I just switched it, and I hope 'lace' is inside of 'grace' as well."[113] The related poem in *Midsummer* evokes the Spanish Caribbean:

> and down the Sunday promenade for miles
> the Civil Guard kept playing "La Paloma"
> and gulls, like doves, waltzed to the gusting lace
> and everyone wore white and there was grace.[114]

An extraordinary mental picture is created through the waltzing rhythm's effect on the pictorial images, ending in the swirling rhyme of "lace" with "grace." It is that painting with words in which Walcott is unparalleled. The interpenetration of art and the world is miraculously foregrounded: art both is and is not what it represents, and one of the pleasures it can give is in the exactness of that "translation." His acute self-awareness extends across an extensive oeuvre, a complex play of self-quotation and variation that is mythopoeic, as discussed below. One of his repeated tropes, both a concrete poem and a symbol that expresses a philosophy, is that of "reflection"—making a second line mirror a first, but with a wriggle of difference as if the upper one were reflected in the lower, as if in water. In *Another Life,* for instance, we read:

> I would wake every morning surprised
> by the framed yellow jungle of
> the groyned mangroves meeting
> the groyned mangroves repeating
> their unbroken water line.[115]

The way in which the visible world exhibits sameness in difference and difference in the same is part of the "I-an-I" paradox with its far-reaching implications. To Brodsky, "Water equals time and provides beauty with its double."[116] The ludic mystery of such a familiar phenomenon both gives delight and opens the mind to other mysteries.

It is particularly through its twinning potential that Walcott makes language express new similitude and new difference. Words are made to play different roles in the carnival of meaning according to those they stand beside. Doubling is an African linguistic practice, as an intensifier of meaning, that survives in Caribbean languages (for example, "sweet-sweet" means "very sweet"). Walcott is particularly interested in repetition that varies the first term slightly, creating the expectation of similitude but delivering difference as well, as when, for instance, he puts "Seashells" alongside "Seychelles" as a doublet, itself repeated, in *Omeros,* to give a special music ironizing the island idyll while reinforcing it: "One day the Mafia / will spin these islands round like roulette" is a real fear.[117] In *Ti-Jean and His Brothers,* he gives his chorus of animals, including the frog who starts it off, the refrain "Greek-croak,"[118] which modulates its own doubleness to embrace both the Grecian and the froglike (in homage to Aristophanes and his chorus of frogs), while simultaneously naming the Caribbean cultural tradition of storytelling, in which the teller calls "crick" to the audience's rapid "crack." The shape of the "crick crack" pair and its internal vowel modulation is echoed in "Greek-croak," which thus becomes a complex signifier of the doubleness of the Caribbean cultural heritage, both classical and folk. It is a "terrible, an embarrassing pun," says Walcott: "It's lousy but it's nice."[119] Relish of the comedy of language is a Walcott hallmark.

The practice of doubling is also applied to whole phrases, with a cliché new-minted by witty variation. Punch lines evoke a laugh or a wry smile: "Don't worry, kid, the wages of sin is birth," or "Youth is stronger than fiction."[120] The dynamic of the wit is in being simultaneously same and not-same; it lifts the newness of the phrases' meaning on an explosive charge. The givens of language are seen afresh, taken literally, subverted, and celebrated, as in the pair, "figment of the imagination, banana of the mind" in *Dream on Monkey Mountain,* which is both absurd and inspired and again naturalizes language to the Caribbean experience (which involves a lot of bananas but few figs).[121] That it should be Basil, the demonic figure in the play, who speaks the phrase, is appropriate: the anarchic power of wit is recognized in Caribbean folk culture—in carnival "robber talk," for example, and Anansi's running of verbal rings around Tiger, the authority figure. In Caribbean culture, to be voluble is to have a superior kind of power; real sociopolitical power may lie elsewhere, but the intellectual control that linguistic dexterity provides enables the downtrodden to turn the tables. There are "a lot of bad puns in Homer," Walcott notes. Like Ulysses, who adopts the name "Nobody" in order to outwit the tyrant Cyclops, the Caribbean writer takes his place in a tradition born of resistance: the slave who masters language ironizes his subjection and defeats it psychologically. Walcott sees it as a universal figure of the "folk imagination," the outsider who "upsets the hierarchy somehow, either by defiance, or by wit, or by solving challenges."[122] In that sense, he is himself a trickster-hero.

Walcott's aesthetic pairing of the same and not-same thus elevates to a high art the long-scorned pun. In a pun, ambiguity is sublimely ludic, in that two meanings coincide in the facticity of the sound only, not from any conceptual similarity, as in metaphor. Walcott is particularly interested in the puns that arise from the particularity of Caribbean linguistic pluralism. For instance, in *Omeros* he exploits the difference of meaning in two

Caribbean subcultures, that of Creole as against Standard English, to create dramatic irony. When Helen, the maid, answers Maud's question "So, how are you, Helen?" with "I dere," the sound of the phrase suggests two meanings: in the vernacular, Helen has answered straightforwardly, "I there" ("I am here, I am OK"), but Maud takes Helen's speech from the position of her own linguistic difference (a symbol of other differences) and interprets it from paranoia as meaning "I dare." Helen's simple statement of her presence is taken by Maud the imperial mistress as subversive: "At last. You dere. Of course you dare." But the meaning Maud gives acquires an independent life in the words, as potentially voiced by Helen: as if she said, "If you wish to read my presence as subversive, so be it, I have courage enough—I dare." The whole transaction of the end of empire—Maud's handing over to Helen—is symbolized in the simple pun. It enables the section to conclude in an assertion of Helen's survival, the heroic survival of the coal-carriers: "she'd last for ever, Helen."[123]

Sometimes the gap between two European language groups is mined. At the beginning of *Omeros,* Walcott plays on the French-English difference of pronunciation that crisscrosses between "canoe," "canot" [canoe, in French], and "cannot," in the marvelous line of Achille's prayer, "Tree! You can be a canoe! Or else you cannot!"[124] which when read to a fairly staid London audience brought a shout of laughter.[125] The beauty of it is that it appears to offer a choice of alternatives, but in the pun implicit in "cannot" (the French word for "canoe," "canot"), it tells the tree it is going to be a canoe in either case: a witty pun is in fact a profound statement about inevitability. Similarly in "North and South," a pun on "singe" and "singe," "monkey" in French, is used with deft grace in a moving exploration of white racism's effect and injustice:

> When
> I collect my change from a small-town pharmacy,
> the cashier's fingertips still wince from my hand
> as if it would singe hers—well, yes, *je suis un singe,*
> I am one of that tribe of frenetic or melancholy
> primates who made your music for many more moons
> than all the silver quarters in the till.[126]

The balancing of the ironic "black" imagery of the "singeing" and "monkey" ideas by the "white" imagery of moon and money, and the modulation of "singe" to the implicit "sing" that provides the link, parallels the first pun, "singe," with the second, "quarters," to present a sharply dialectical deconstruction of imperial power relations: black people give their art and are not paid but are made to suffer (singe) and howl; the white hand closes the till (withholds proper payment), as distant and unmoved as the moon. The final image is of the futility of the creature that bays at the moon (perhaps the futility of protesting in poetry or song)—and the sense of endlessness, such that the present (dis)order seems to have the immutability of a natural law. But in this deeply ironic closure, in the process of virtually canceling itself, the poem pulls off such a dazzling hat trick of ludic language that it asserts exuberantly that it is "not nothing," but a signifying "something." In the end, the virtuosity of the puns leads to the philosophical reflection that if language can bring two separate terms together creatively, then perhaps racially divided people can be brought together by art. Cultural constructions of ethnicity could be re-formed.

By extension, intertextuality is a kind of punning involving entire fictions, or parts of them. In "The Spoiler's Return," Walcott uses a method of ironized misquotation: the line, "Hell is a city much like Port of Spain," adapts Shelley's "Hell is a city much like London," changing it from tetrameter to pentameter such that it has, if anything, a more memorable rhythm, and placing Port of Spain and London in a mutually interrogatory relationship to the idea of the city and its potential for "civil-ization."[127] On the other hand, an example of the larger kind of intertextual pun is *Omeros,* which has an evident intertextuality with the Homeric texts and not just at the level of its title. The reader waits with pleasant anticipation, for example, for the poem to deliver the death of its character called Hector; but just as he is here the rival of Achilles in love, not war, so he dies in a road accident, not in battle. Once again, the intriguing coincidence of similitude with difference holds the attention and provokes pleasure.

Doubling is also involved in the sacred process of naming identity. The naming of the individual by the group is culturally of great significance in the Caribbean, a practice derived from Africa, the "*nommo* concept" from West Africa, of "belief in the mystical creative power of the word."[128] Names are allocated to young people in addition to the family name given at birth, in (usually ironic) acknowledgment of their particular qualities. Walcott's project of Adamic naming is therefore also a specifically Caribbean act. His opposition to the adoption of African names is based on his sense that they are not part of the living Caribbean linguistic experience but represent a nostalgia for a past that is lost just as surely as the European past is lost. He acknowledges the reality of the nostalgia in his response to proper names from both his ancestral cultures, "Ashanti" and "Warwickshire," but he resists its lure.[129] In *Another Life,* he gives at the climax a reprise of the exorcism scene from Chapter 4,[130] using a similar patois phrase, "Pour la dernière fois, nommez! Nommez!" to introduce a list of names—adopted African names followed by the European names they replace, as if the named were summoned to court:

> Abouberika Torre commonly called Joseph Samson.
> Hammadi Torrouke commonly called Louis Modeste.
> Mandingo servants offered Africa back,
> the boring process of repatriation.[131]

Implicitly, the presentation calls for the nostalgia for Africa to be exorcized, because it is as much a denial, as Walcott sees it, of a real Caribbean identity as any parallel aspiration to Europeanness might be. He prefers to use names that are already naturalized to the Caribbean—as he does in *Omeros* with "Achille," a classical hero's name that has, as he narrates, served to mark heroic qualities in Caribbean people for centuries. That is what he means by "the faith of using the old names anew."[132]

For these reasons, the indicative names allocated to the friend whose family name is Dunstan St. Omer are given prominence in *Another Life*. The poet, from his own appreciation of the Greek root of European culture, calls Dunstan the painter "Gregorias," a name that for him evokes a black Greek (and less a classical Greek than an Orthodox Christian name in its associations), with the reverence for art implicit in it, and also crucially, as the poem records, "because it echoes the blest thunders of the surf," and is therefore also local.[133] In the poem, he is routinely addressed as Gregorias, as Andreuille is Anna, but the poem closes in a dramatic cry of greeting, which puts alongside "Gregorias" not "Dunstan" but "Apilo!" which Edward Baugh identifies as "a nickname which St. Omer has had since schooldays and by which he is still popularly known in St. Lucia. He himself professes ignorance of its meaning."[134] St. Omer now acknowledges, Robin Hanford reports, that it means "pot-bellied" (it marked, presumably, a malnourished childhood), which seems wonderfully apt to the poem's parallelism between St. Omer and Harry Simmons—both artists, both closely related to the idea of suicide, above all both committed to the vision of an indigenous art and a Caribbean cultural renaissance.[135] Simmons is given a physical portrait twice, in the description opening the poem and repeated commemoratively at his death (another doubling), with the addition that he has "a dimpled pot for a belly from the red clay of Piaille."[136] In the beautiful passage that follows, the relationship of artist and intellectual to the community is expressed movingly as a mutual two-way exchange:

> People entered his understanding
> like a wayside country church,
> they had built him themselves.
> It was they who had smoothed the wall
> of his clay-coloured forehead,
> who made of his rotundity an earthy
> useful object
> holding the clear water of their simple troubles,
> he who returned their tribal names
> to the adze, mattock, midden, and cooking pot. . . .
> and he is a man no more
> but the fervour and intelligence
> of a whole country.[137]

The essential wisdom is that the community creates its artists to serve it, an idea that reflects exactly Walcott's lifelong perception of his own role in relation to that same St. Lucian community. In the final words of the poem, the twinned names by which St. Omer is greeted, "Gregorias, Apilo!" as well as each naming "a real and an ideal St. Omer" as Baugh notes, define his double role as an artist.[138] Through the poet's naming, he is linked with the European cultural tradition, on which he can draw with as much authority as any European, as it lives on, naturalized in St. Lucia; at the same time, through the group-given name he is linked with Simmons, as another pot-bellied clay vessel, which the community had "made . . . themselves," and who, like Simmons, would serve them by reflecting their folk culture in his art. The clay vessel theme is related in the next chapter to the poet himself, who is "a vase of water in its vase of clay"—part of the replication and extension of imagery that is Walcott's mythopoeic method.[139] The aesthetic informing the two names is not the doubleness of ambiguity but the twinning of joint presences. As Rohlehr has said of the following generation of Caribbean poets (it applies also to the visual arts),

> They have approached their heritage with a freedom rarely found in the pre-Independence era, seeking all available metaphors, sounds, rhythms and levels of sound and prosody. The Either/Or approach of the colonial era which had promoted English styled poetry and put down Caribbean orality was gradually replaced by the Both/And approach in which, as the situation demanded, writers varied freely along the continua between Folk and Modernist, Creole and Standard, Oral and Scribal.[140]

Walcott's intercultural juxtaposition—"Gregorias, Apilo!"—demonstrates him to be a leader in the process Rohlehr describes, rather than a reluctant yielder to it, as he claims. The inclusive culture of "Both/And," "I-an-I," is exactly Walcott's method.

Even such mythic names as "Homer" are opened up and looked at afresh by Walcott. We are made aware of the punning meaning of "Homer," "one who seeks home," which makes him an analogue (another kind of pun) of Odysseus. Alongside the familiar term "Homer" voiced in English, the poem places the newly rediscovered Greek vernacular form of the name "Omeros," which is broken down for us into a sequence of punning, symbolic syllables. The monadic myth of "Homer" is thus disrupted, split into binaries representing the "high" and "low" traditions—formal and informal, the standard and the vernacular, the canonical and the folk. This is an essentially dialectical process. Placing the vernacular term alongside the standard seems always to expose ideological functions of language that are normally hidden. In a memorable Freudian slip, C. L. R. James once, in a live broadcast discussion of Caribbean "dialect poets," began to talk of them as "dialectical poets."[141] Walcott is intrigued by spontaneous creativity, the aleatoric element in art's arrival at its form, such as in Auden's retention of a printer's error,[142] or in his own practice: "One can be astonished at what is being written because the process itself becomes astonished."[143] But as well as being open to chance and to the flow of unconscious creativity, he is very conscious of the labor, apprenticeship, skill, and will that poetry demands.

For Walcott, the "most exciting part of poetry" is its "craft."[144] It is a constant emphasis with him: "if you've made a good box it's like making a good poem. I mean, you really have to get the corners square if you're doing a quatrain."[145] Metaphors from carpentry, the craft of Christ, seem particularly to spring to his mind. Adapting the *Odyssey* to the stage was "a terrific technical challenge—to try to compress and stay with the Homer over the arc of the story as much as possible, so that it was like building a ship, that had to either sink or float."[146] In a different interview on the same day, he developed the trope in a fuller account of the dramatization as a poetic act:

> I made up my mind I was not going to have any long speeches. I was not going to do it in pentameter because that would have had Elizabethan echoes. I made up my mind I would do it in quatrains, for the discipline and containment of it, that I would do it in hexameters, and that what I was after was a huge poem. And I kept thinking of

> the shape, different images of lines, like lances laid down on racks, or perhaps a ship with its beams. . . . So you had to build. It was great fun to build a poem which had to be launched and performed, and whose—not direct model—but the echo of whose shape was from the original itself.[147]

The ancient meaning of "poet" as "maker" is refreshingly alive in this perception. It is what unites the poet with his people, not something that sets him apart: "The worst crime," Omeros tells us, "is to leave a man's hands empty. / Men are born makers."[148] The poet's material, language, is "both delicate and strong."[149] Walcott himself is a prolific worker. Greg Doran, who directed *The Odyssey* for the Royal Shakespeare Company, said that while the play was in rehearsal Walcott would respond by writing extensive new material, in the stichomythic quatrains that make the dialogue as quick as a game of squash.[150] He enjoys the process of collective shaping: "the evolution of the play is a great excitement for me, both when I'm directing it and when I'm watching it done."[151] The woodworking metaphor is a habitual trope, memorably incorporated into *Another Life:* "I watched the vowels curl from the tongue of the carpenter's plane, / resinous, fragrant / labials of our forests." The sanctity (filial, too, in that it evokes Christ in the workshop of his carpenter father) and the workmanlike ethos are distinctively of the Americas, informal and unpretentious, harking back to the puritan pioneers, but the figures of Pound and Hemingway in the passage connect American literature to the Old World of Paris in the 1920s, again with the timber imagery: the passage speaks of "the peeled ease of Hemingway's early prose."[152] The sound pattern has the plain rightness, the economy, of Hemingway at his best, a recurrent strength of this poem. Although he has been a scathing critic of "free-verse nightingales,"[153] he has himself used free verse to brilliant effect.

Walcott has drawn on many different meters but has felt free to vary or adapt traditional forms as he chose. For instance, the poems of *Midsummer* are informal sonnets, with the clarity and power of sonnets but without the regularities of length, meter, and rhyme. Orthodoxy for its own sake is never his choice. He is a powerful poet of pentameter, as some of his early work demonstrates, but he also recognizes that in pentameter it is difficult to avoid the "Shakespearean echo, and martial echoes."[154] Walcott has frequently been criticized for his adherence to formal meter. In accounts of Caribbean verse, Patricia Ismond's 1971 article has been influential in its polarization of Walcott against the supposedly more Caribbean rhythms of Brathwaite's verse. Rohlehr argues that Walcott "fails to recognize that a poetry based on the oral tradition would require, seek and create its own crafting," but, as Walcott points out, it comes down to the matter of how meter is used.[155] In "The Poet in the Theatre," he examines ways of capturing orality in formal meter, which he calls "liberating verse within the pentameter."[156] As he has asserted, "the lines I love have all their knots left in," which uses paradox, another ironic doubling, to make its point, since its praise of irregular rhythm is couched in a classically regular iambic pentameter.[157] A distinctive contribution of his own to English prosody is his importation of the Dantean "terza rima" in *Omeros,* a long-breathed line of great suppleness and variety in three-line rhymed stanzas, a meter that somehow is never long-winded. "It seems to me," he says, "that the flexibility of the hexameter gives you more of a prosaic speed than the trumpet and drum that comes with pentameter. Pentametrical translations of Homer don't seem to me to be right."[158] The hexameter has hitherto been rarely used in English, although it is established in other European languages. It is also the Homeric meter. Walcott perceives this radically differently from the aura of rather stuffy literariness it has acquired. He speculates that in the oral recitation of the epics in ancient Greece, the audience would voice a response—"that perhaps at the end of the hexameter there was approval."[159] His recent introduction of the twelve-syllabic hexameter is thus an act of active creolization, reinvigorating the language with a new/old orality. In this, and in so many other ways, English is enriched by his practice. He is a great original, refusing to follow received opinion or the convention of the day, refusing to limit his idea of the possible, in art as in life. He transports the idea of political independence into aesthetic practice. People who live in metropolitan centers, he says, are

> affected by fashion . . . by what's supposed to be "passé," what's supposed to be "avant-garde." Well, luckily I'm way beyond that, the reach of any of that. Take rhyme, for instance, or what people call "formal poetry"—as if there's any other thing but formal poetry—so that you don't feel bound or constricted by what's supposed to be the language of the epoch—twenty years ago it was T. S. Eliot, well this time it's somebody else, do you know . . . ? That sense of time simply because of distance, and also because of a rejection of the convention of historical judgement, I think, has made me feel that I can just write the way I want to write.[160]

The "marvellous thing about poetry," he says, "is its domination of time."[161] Empires are like grass, but poetry is "the bread that lasts when systems have decayed."[162] Poetry can create its own world, evoking by a quasi-magical rite the "thing itself." When, as noted above, he shifts gear in the middle of *Omeros* for the incantation to turn a house into a home, Walcott inserts into his poem in hexameter the strong, lyrical, binary stresses of the English spell, the folk poetry of the Middle Ages. It is both a rite of homage and an incantation: the faith in the power of rhythmic speech is real.

Crucially, Walcott refuses the idea of language being in any sense guilty. It is central to his refusal both of inferiority and superiority. Reflecting on the English pastoral of "those bastard grandsires," he says, "the worm that cores the rotting apple / of the world" in this Eden "cannot touch the words / of Shallow or Silence in their faded garden," because their "maker granted them a primal pardon."[163] The words are always already redeemed. His strategy is to accept the irreversibility of history through which the imperial language was "irretrievably given" but to refuse the model of that transaction as a one-way or passive process.[164] On the contrary, users of a language make it their own, mold it to their own experience. "English" is no simple but a plural, "Englishes," or "english," as suggested by Bill Ashcroft, Gareth Griffiths, and Helen Tiffin. On the one hand, "No language is neutral," but on the other, "the green oak of English is a murmurous cathedral / where some took umbrage, some peace, but every shade, all, / helped widen its shadow."[165] The wordplay within this (building on Joyce's idea of the negative shadow of the imperial language) is a powerful signifier of its thesis, the richness of the language's proliferating variety, the inclusiveness of its differences, whether Caliban's or Prospero's. In 1970, Walcott lamented his actors' hunger for what they thought of as "better speech" when their own had a "vigour that was going out of English."[166] In 1964, he had said, "The mnemonic use of words, of naming things and blessing them by naming, is something which has gone out of English, since it is possible that the more complicated in syntax a language becomes the more its original impulses, worship and communication weaken."[167] His own oeuvre since then has made good the deficiency in striking ways.

If the world is to go forward, the alterity which Prospero saw in Caliban and Caliban in Prospero needs to be differently envisioned, not to erase the guilt and suffering of the past, but to promote the twin projects, of demystifying surviving cultural myths which still promote abuse of power, and celebrating benign and mutually involved heterogeneity. It has to be both a No and a Yes, but the Yes must be bigger than the No. Where Joyce famously brings *Ulysses*—the "one book apart from the Bible or

Shakespeare" that Walcott chose to take with him to his "desert island" on radio's *Desert Island Discs*[168]—to a conclusion in Molly Bloom's Yes, Walcott's equivalent is not secular, but sacred. His admission of the other encompasses desire as eros with desire for faith. In the final poem of *Midsummer,* which is a meditation on death and exile, he uses the natural metamorphosis of the butterfly as a prompt to his doubting belief: "yellow butterflies rising on the road to Valencia / stuttering 'yes' to the resurrection; 'yes, yes is our answer.'"[169] It is in the shared address to the great questions that Prospero and Caliban or Crusoe and Friday, for all their historic and cherished differences, can devise a language of fellowship. As Seamus Heaney has said, "Walcott's poetry has passed the stage of self-questioning, self-exposure, self-healing, to become a common resource. What he would propagate is magnanimity and courage and I am sure that he would agree with Hopkins's affirmation that feeling, and in particular love, is the great power and spring of verse."[170] In the end, the poet loses any sense of the "I." Ultimately, the point is reached where, to turn Walcott's phrase on himself, "the genius of the poet has now entered the genius of the race."[171]

6

"A Crystal of Ambiguities"

The Craft of Mythopoeic Imagery

> *Ariel:* Him, that you term'd, sir, "The good old lord Gonzalo":
> His tears run down his beard, like winter's drops
> From eaves of reeds.
> ***The Tempest,*** V.i.15–17

To mark the tragic "way of the world," Shakespeare might have called his play not *The Tempest* but *The Grief of Gonzalo.* Such a title would, however, have altered it, radically and entirely, even if nothing else were changed. It would, for one thing, have brought the simile in this epigraph into an unmistakable prominence, whereas, as it is, its symbolism is easily passed over. In recording Gonzalo's grief through the image of winter rain dripping from thatch, Shakespeare is already qualifying and contextualizing it, translating it from a tragic resonance to a benign one. Rain is necessary to growth, and winter is the precursor of spring. In fact, the image serves as symbolic pointer to the drama's redemptive resolution, relegating the trials and tribulations of the "present" to necessary, purgatorial stages in the growth process, with a clear relevance to the drama's ethics. In other words, even as he portrays the grief of Gonzalo, the play's moral touchstone, Shakespeare is transforming or translating it, precisely through the chosen analogy, so *The Grief of Gonzalo* could never have stuck as its title. Walcott, like Shakespeare, understands well that metaphor and simile are essentially ludic practices, related to punning in drawing two or more terms into relationship but crucially able to transform the emotional or moral tone of the first term through the second. They are particularly apt to the Caribbean's "I-an-I" culture, in which the heterogeneous are brought into productive interplay. They are, it could be said, a linguistic equivalent of creolization. The ability to speak in metaphors is highly prized in the African rhetorical tradition: the wise man, the orator, perceives the similarities between different phenomena and derives new meaning, a third term, between the original ones brought together as a pair. It is an essentially oral practice, and it is perhaps this aspect of Caribbean culture to which Walcott refers when he says that for the New World poet, "metaphor was not a symbol but conversation."[1]

The practice is crucially different from the Miltonic epic simile, in which a hierarchical relationship is posited between a dominant term and its illustrative parallel. The practice of the metaphysical poets is closer to the African tradition and to Walcott's strategies, in that it is essentially generative not hierarchical, though within generally confined contexts. Walcott's work, however, demonstrates a play of similitude-in-difference spiraling on and outward, across an extensive epic oeuvre. Bruce King regards his use of "such commonplace images as sky, water, earth, south, and north" as "an elaborate system of private symbols," but perhaps "private" is the wrong word, in that it suggests hermeticism.[2] It is, rather, a "personal" system, but one that is accessible to readers, not requiring a private key.

His method is to construct a series of interrelated images, the meaning of which develops as the works develop. The design of individual works is unfailingly cohesive, though dynamic rather than static, and it is extended by the emerging design of the works as an oeuvre. Walcott, for all his phenomenal inventiveness, has been remarkably consistent over a long career. Some of Walcott's early metaphors showed already the instinct for the essence of relationships that has since characterized his work. After the fire that destroyed much of Castries, his hometown, when he was eighteen, for instance, he wrote, using an extraordinarily assured imagery, of turning from the ephemerality of the man-made to the enduring values of nature and spirituality: "In town, leaves were paper, but the hills were a flock of faiths."[3] Walcott's subsequent development of his metaphoric method has resulted in epic works of an extraordinary craftsmanlike cohesion. As he wrote in the now famous passage from *Another Life,*

> in every surface I sought
> the paradoxical flash of an instant
> in which every facet was caught
> in a crystal of ambiguities, . . .[4]

The context records his frustration at attempts to express himself through painting, which led to his concentration on poetry, the career he had envisaged for himself from his childhood. When Walcott was a twenty-year-old painter and poet sharing his first exhibition with Dunstan St. Omer, his mentor Harold Simmons, in a review of the show, had the perspicacity to say (with what was no doubt an influential pun), "Words and imagery are

Derek's forte; the brush with discipline will be Dunstan's citadel."[5] Walcott remains, however, distinctively a poet with a painter's eye. "Getting the light right," he says, "has been the hope of saints as well as of painters, of poets, from Augustine to Turner, to Wordsworth and Dante."[6] One of his great gifts is to unreel his story before the inner eye like a film, with an acute clarity of visual image: after a hurricane, for instance, the islanders emerge to find "big yellow tractors / tossed up the salad of trees."[7] "Every metaphor," he says, "can be drawn, graphically."[8] Ambiguity, therefore, should not be understood as uncertainty of meaning: it is not a case of "either/or" but of "both/and," and not even the conflicted meanings of ambivalence, but multiple meanings, clearly and simultaneously held in view. To return to the "I-an-I" model, the play of potential pairings is endless. There is delight in the paradox of the sharedness of difference, and what ultimately the creative use of correspondences can reveal is the inexhaustibility of mystery. Walcott goes on to develop his imagery to an entire metalanguage of symbolism—a mythopoeia—which enables his longest poems to soar in an arc of self-extending meanings. It is in this way that the word can become, in *The Tempest*'s phrase, "more than the miraculous harp."[9]

Epic is typically concerned with the collective. For Walcott the relation of the poet to his society is absolutely central, and what he describes is the shaman-like role associated with the epic poet: "the good poet is the proprietor of the experience of the race . . . he is and always has been the vessel, vates, rainmaker, the conscience of the king and the embodiment of society, even when society is unable to contain him."[10] His task is to give creative representation to the collective experience,[11] but its distinctive vehicle is to be metaphor: "In tribal, elemental poetry, the epic experience of the race is compressed in metaphor."[12] In *Omeros,* that task is worded as the paternal injunction "to give those feet a voice."[13] The coal-carrying women the father's ghost points to had had voices, indeed Walcott elsewhere describes their singing, but the key point is that *art,* the culture, had no representation of them, and therefore they were being forgotten. Crucially, Walcott saw himself, with his fellow artists, as not just writing poems or plays or painting but as founding an aesthetic for the region, writing the distinctive Caribbean experiences into the world of texts. One form of the "I-an-I" aesthetic is in the yoking of different tones, in an art that is not afraid to be both elevated and familiar simultaneously. Walcott's "high colloquiality," as noted above, enables him to sound multiple notes at once. *Omeros* is to a significant degree mock-Homeric rather than Homeric, for example, but it retains an epic ambition at the same time as ironizing the tradition, the irony it deploys being in part an insurance against pomposity, which paradoxically enhances rather than reduces the high seriousness. Interviewed by Luigi Sampietro, Walcott says about *Omeros,* "I did not want to write anything that was going to sort of *dignify* the Caribbean by ambition—by my own ambition."[14] The awareness of the risk of hubris does not, however, diminish the scale of the project. His concept of epic emerges from his comments on Whitman: "He's epic in the sense of width—and the subject. But he doesn't do what we know to be epic, in terms of a narrator propelling—in sequence—the events that are related to the destiny of the tribe."[15] The American search for the democratic epic—not fully realized in Whitman—comes to fruition, I would argue, in the Caribbean.[16] The sacred "process of renaming" is that of "finding new metaphors."[17] It is not facile, but testing, exhausting, a "translation" of the world into art that is intrinsically metaphoric. Speaking of his starting *Omeros* in French Creole and running out of vocabulary, he continued: "What happens in translation is, if you work in rhyme, you create new metaphors." It is an "evolution."[18] The exigency of the task, the difficulty of finding shapely expression, is itself a generator of new imagery.

Walcott's epic method merits examination in some detail. There is in particular a recurrent icon in his work that goes right back to a childhood memory, the development of which gives, I think, a particular insight into his method. He has devised an integrated system of epic metaphor, providing a developing symbolism capable of carrying the meaning of the whole as the living bone gives shape to the flesh. He has described how as a young child he watched the unloading of coal from the ships, a scene that was to become for him one of those "reduced, race-containing" symbols. With its large harbor, Castries was chosen as the coaling station of the region by the British, shiploads of the fuel being offloaded onto the wharf until trans-shipped. The St. Lucian contribution was badly paid hard labor—no machinery was used—something that not only men but also women of the poverty-stricken colonial community had no choice but to accept. Writing in his mid-thirties about his late school days, he reminisced about the way the town had changed: "Down by the wharf, past the coal dunes near by grandfather's house, I had watched during childhood the crossing friezes of erect, singing women carrying huge panniers of anthracite coal, each weighing a hundredweight, but the port was no longer a coaling station. That had gone too."[19] In "The Glory Trumpeter," also published, like this account, in 1965, a jazz trumpeter reawakens the scene for Walcott:

Now, as the eyes sealed in the ashen flesh,
And Eddie, like a deacon at his prayer,
Rose, tilting the bright horn, I saw a flash
Of gulls and pigeons from the dunes of coal
Near my grandmother's barracks on the wharves, . . .[20]

Here the view of the coal heaps already has its monochromatic schema, of hills of coal ("dunes" in both early accounts) with their black shape offset by wheeling white birds. The poem, although it lacks the "frieze" of laden, singing women, which was later to come to the fore, relates the image to an enlarged human dimension, that of the whole abused black race in the Americas. The sense of an appeal to his personal moral commitment is already deeply rooted in this poem.

In *Another Life,* from 1973, the scene from his grandmother's window, on the Sunday visits, is revisioned with a new clarity:

From the canted barracks of the City of Refuge,
from his grandmother's tea shop, he would watch
on black hills of imported anthracite
the frieze of coal-black carriers, *charbonniers,*
erect, repetitive as hieroglyphs
descending and ascending the steep ramps,
building the pyramids,
songs of Egyptian bondage,
 when they sang,
the burden of the panniered anthracite,
one hundredweight to every woman
tautened, like cable, the hawsers in their necks.
There was disease inhaled in the coal dust.
Silicosis. Herring gulls
white as the uniforms of tally clerks,
screeching, numbered and tagged the loads.[21]

Now the image (ancillary in "The Glory Trumpeter") has been given full expression, with the historical, moral, and social contexts of the earlier poem's wider narrative revealed within the image itself. The monochrome of the image is sharply delineated via the color words, the social signifier of race in imperialism brought to consciousness via the symbolic color composition of the landscape. The Caribbean bondage is given a biblical resonance through the term "Egyptian," so that the hallowed parallel between the exile of the Israelites in Egypt and the enslaving of Africans in the New World leads the image back to another Judeo-Christian mythic icon: the endless chain of coal-carriers "descending and ascending the steep ramps" suggests an infernal inversion of Jacob's ladder. In this supposedly paradisal New World, Walcott exposes a diametrically opposed reality that bears the stamp of damnation.

The mythic strength of this icon is demonstrated by his subsequent development of it in *Omeros*, where it is enlarged with variations to become a visual symbol of the entire Caribbean experience, a symbolic representation of history that charts the collective suffering, the collective achievement, and the collective heroism. In the later epic, Walcott suggests once more the heroic pyramidal ascent of the coal-carrying women but overlays it with two other images, one from a different, peopled scene, of mounting a liner's gangplank, and the other from the natural world, of ants scaling a flower-pot. The sign, carried over from the earlier work, of the pyramid mounted by a frieze of tiny figures is given a new incarnation early in the poem. Ma Kilman, faced with Philoctete's pain, ponders how to help:

> "It have a flower somewhere, a medicine, and ways
> my grandmother would boil it. I used to watch ants
> climbing her white flower-pot. But, God, in which place?"[22]

There is no overt link at this point with the coal-carriers image, only the similarity of "silhouette"—the color value and verticality of the pyramid are inverted, the scale is reduced, and the human figures become insects. The context embeds the image in the idea of nature's healing power. In this shift, the basis is laid for a major development of its associative meanings.

About a quarter of the way into the poem, the image is given an extended presentation, the ants now being matched explicitly to the coal-carriers, here introduced to this work for the first time:

> From here, in his boyhood, he had seen women climb
> like ants up a white flower-pot, baskets of coal
> balanced on their torchoned heads, without touching them,
>
> up the black pyramids, each spine straight as a pole,
> and with a strength that never altered its rhythm.
> He spoke for those Helens from an earlier time. . . .[23]

The color value of the pyramid up which the figures climb is now problematized, with a binary alternation flicking from white to black in the reader's imagination. The metaphor is restless. The application to the women of the ants' climb has the effect of reducing the emotional load implicit in the human story. Our experience of ant behavior suggests an almost abstract progress that transcends the fate of the individual. Walcott is moving his trope into a different sphere—from history into natural history—a strategy that paradoxically returns it to its human value. By adducing the "law of nature" idea, what transpires is a sense of history making positive progress. In the Darwinian view, the natural world is governed by progressive adaptation to circumstance, so that obstacles are inexorably and inevitably overcome, but on such a vast temporal scale that it is nearly imperceptible. When this reading of the natural world is applied as a metaphor to human society—which is, of course, part of nature—the natural phenomenon reads as imaginative "proof" of the inevitability of social progress (a central thesis of socialism). This lends a moral authority to the image of the heroically persevering ants and introduces a subtle note of optimism to the portrayal of human suffering.

This conceptual development is enlarged in the other transformation of the image in this poem. Here the whiteness of the flower-pot "version" is taken up and varied. The coal-women and the ants are revisioned as the ascent of tiny figures up a steep gangplank to the sheer prow of a white cruise liner. Its "immaculate hull insulted the tin roofs / beneath it": "'in their ascending // the narrow wooden ramp built steeply to the hull /of a liner tall as a cloud, the unending / line crossing like ants without touching for the whole // day.'"[24] Here, prompted by the flower-pot image, the imagination substitutes for the black pyramids of coal the "white" liner introduced a little earlier: "'a city to itself, / taller than the Fire Station, and much finer . . . than anything Castries could ever hope to build.'" The liner was named as "Fame." Now, the image is reconnected to its old form, of the "silhouettes" seen from the grandmother's house against the "infernal anthracite hills."

A new schema of the scene is emerging. The repeated association of the wharf's level with hell and the "cloud" metaphor for the height of the liner introduces a Dantean metaphysical variant on the icon of Jacob's ladder:

> "Hell was built on those hills. In that country of coal
> without fire, that inferno the same colour
> as their skins and shadows, every labouring soul
>
> climbed with her hundredweight basket, every load for
> one copper penny, balanced erect on their necks
> that were taught as a liner's hawsers from the weight."[25]

The women's heroic self-elevation is matched to the poet's through the instruction by his father's ghost: "'Kneel to your load, then balance your staggering feet / and walk up that coal ladder.'"[26] The two kinds of action are paired: "'They walk, you write,'" but the second derives from the first and owes it a debt:

> "your own work owes them
> because the couplet of those multiplying feet
> made your first rhymes. Look, they climb and no one knows
> them;
> they take their copper pittances, and your duty
>
> from the time you watched them from your grandmother's house
> as a child wounded by their power and beauty
> is the chance you now have, to give those feet a voice."[27]

It is a moment of great significance, within the poem and beyond it, in that it asserts that a simple iambic rhythm is as much a part of the Caribbean experience—as the natural rhythm of laden feet—as are the rhythms claimed as more distinctively Caribbean in a Caribbean discourse of aesthetics.[28] In fact, the poem traces the education of the poet to that first lesson in rhythm. An aspect of the image that had been part of the memory of the childhood scene, the women's song, is thus projected onto the poet's role. They had had real voices, of course, but the world had not listened—they had been silenced by a history that ignored them. It is the poet's task to bring them to collective memory by giving them public "voice," through his epic, to match their heroic "feet"—to make of them a myth.

From this point in the poem the "ants" aspect of the meaning cluster becomes dominant. In carefully mirrored accounts, the line of ants becomes a chain of human figures, diminished by distance and by abuse, in North America and Africa; the distant view becomes an expressive signifier of the lack of regard (of seeing and valuing), of their abusers, in whose minds they have less than human significance. During his dream journey to African history, Achille watches a slave raid:

> Achille climbed a ridge. He counted the chain of men
> linked by their wrists with vines; he watched until
> the line was a line of ants. He let out a soft moan
> as the last ant disappeared. Then he went downhill[29]

Now the connected ideas of ants and coal-carriers have been linked to Africa, the endless line of black figures signifies with new meaning as an expression of the Middle Passage. The "pyramid" is now reformulated as the oceanic triangle of the Atlantic slave trade. Achille, as the poem says, "died again" thinking of:

> the ants arriving at the sea's rim,
> or climbing the pyramids of coal and entering inside
> the dark hold, far from this river and the griot's hymn.[30]

The endless line of black figures now crosses from east to west along the base of the triangle, with its two "white" sides above.

But the sufferers of the past are shown to be the ministers of relief in the present. The ant-like, anonymous hieroglyph of the slaves undergoes a metamorphosis to the poem's "frieze" of black figures, each with her or his own particularity and individuality. The ant-like forced migrations of history are exchanged for the Caribbean present, where a line of ants beckons and leads Ma Kilman to epiphany on the mountain. Ma Kilman howls at her discovery of the healing herb, Philoctete's pain is eased, and the first person narration resumes to mark the moment's importance:

> See her there, my mother, my grandmother, my great-great-
> grandmother. See the black ants of their sons,
> their coal-carrying mothers. Feel the shame, the self-hate
> draining from all our bodies[31]

This initial stage of healing signals its ultimate stage, although the narration of the healing ritual as drama is still to come. It is placed in the context of the centuries of pain, looking back to an ancestral past but forward to a relieved future for the race (the first person singular migrating significantly to a first person plural). The legacy of that history, the trauma of self-loathing, which is still real, can be cured by a perception that the history was not one of shame—that any shame belongs to the oppressors—but that, on the contrary, it is a history of heroic survival through that moral and spiritual strength without which physical strength collapses.

Thus the geometric and kinetic sign, the hieroglyph of the coal-carrying women, forms part of a pattern traversing Walcott's poetry but illustrates in particular his remodeling of the traditional epic simile. Instead of using allusions from outside, he valorizes his work internally: the core of *Omeros* is disclosed through this "race-containing" image, which condenses shape, color, and movement, and extends them in variations through the linear time of the work, delivering finally the epic grandeur in terms of heroic ascent. The quasi-organic life and growth of the specific incarnations of the compressed sign produce a sum of meaning that expresses in one symbol the complex premise of the whole.

In his Nobel lecture, he returned to the theme of "the grace of effort" and to the process of translating that truth, of real people's lives, to literature:

> That is what I have read around me from boyhood, from the beginnings of poetry, the grace of effort. In the hard mahogany of woodcutters' faces, resinous men, charcoal burners; in a man with a cutlass cradled across his forearm, who stands on the verge with the usual anonymous khaki dog . . . not to mention the fishermen, the footmen on trucks, groaning up mornes, all fragments of Africa originally but shaped and hardened and rooted now in the island's life, illiterate in the way leaves are illiterate; they do not read, they are there to be read, and if they are properly read, they create their own literature.[32]

This is not patronizing but derives from a profound respect and humility. Like the African griot, the poet is charged with the responsibility of voicing the people's story into the world of discourse, but ultimately the world of discourse is secondary to their lived reality.

The mythopoeic project to narrate the Caribbean story, an intrinsically epic story, is doubled by the project to deconstruct the North's culture of dominance. Hence Walcott's dialectical engagement with Homer, which is a major signifier in the Western tradition and specifically the American tradition, the classics being naturalized to North American culture in a unique way. As the narrator of *Omeros* points out, now "Homer and Virg are New England farmers, / and the winged horse guards their gas-station."[33] Homer has been of huge cultural importance in the anglophone world: the most frequently translated texts in the English language, according to George Steiner.[34] For Walcott, the Homeric offers a rich language of symbolic signifiers, in whose terms he now inscribes his own people's story. He asserts that Homer is just as much his, as a St. Lucian, as anyone's, although he is careful to avoid the language of takeover: "to make it Caribbean, or to do it in dialect, is to get very nationalistic and I'm not interested in that, because it's like trying to claim Homer in the same way that the British try to claim Homer. The English think Homer belongs to them . . . the attitude will be, yes, basically it's an English poem that has been translated into Greek."[35] In a sense, he is doing what Joyce did with *Ulysses:* he is mapping his own place to the world using a Greek atlas as palimpsest. But in another sense, his is very remote from Joyce's project.

Here there are no programmatic parallels. *Omeros* reads more as a critique of or an answer to the Homeric than an imitation or version.

In *Omeros,* in fact, he not only deconstructs the hegemonic myth, he also reconstructs Homer by giving us, subtly, four Homers, revealing the demotic alongside the patrician. By replacing the one with the many, his assertion of the pluralism of the tradition (suppressed under the monoculture of imperialism) is made graphic. This multiplicity of the Homeric symbolizes both the actual pluralism of the human condition and the goal of cultural pluralism. It is a distinctively New World phenomenon he uncovers, yet one which, as he shows, is firmly rooted in the old.

The myth of the ancient world is represented in the poem by the bust of Homer. It is white, it is hard, it is cold, and it is blind; and it is a familiar icon of Western culture, the artifact of Greek sculpture, expropriated from the Mediterranean, often in the eighteenth century, by north-west Europeans and exported as the keystone of imperialist culture around the world—but particularly to the New World, where the claim to status became habitually couched in terms of the Attic ideals of democracy and art. Walcott ironizes it as "the Athenian *demos* / its *demos* demonic and its *ocracy* crass," where "ideals went cold / in the heat of its hate."[36] The bust of Homer became an icon, recognized in all corners of the European empires. It became one of the earliest targets of art-object mass production and has gone on to find a niche in all sorts of establishments associated with the dominant culture and with power, from the grand edifices of government to those on a socially aspirant domestic scale. The marble bust that accompanies the narrator in his spiritual voyage is partly this Homer, who issues commands and speaks a "marble tongue."[37]

But this is also a Homer who can break into demotic song, a calypsonian of the Aegean, Omeros: "I heard his own / Greek calypso coming from the marble trunk."[38] In opposition to the hegemonic voice, Walcott creates a plebeian other, its revolutionary twin. Homer is now revealed to include his "shadow," his tanist (to borrow Graves's term for mythic twin), Omeros, "Homer" revoiced in vernacular Greek, the centuries of anglicanization and the accretions of social status swept away. Walcott suggests that this persona was always present within Homer but has been suppressed by millennia of mythologizing: "Homer could only have written in a demotic language . . ." he has said, "what we would call a dialect because of its regionality and concentration."[39] The Homeric figure, to him, is the folk artist, rooted in the oral tradition, like the blues singers and calypsonians of the modern Americas and their equivalents elsewhere, who express their people's story. He has spoken of:

> the emblematic figure of Homer as an itinerant person, poet, moving around the islands and to different cities, singing these songs that he picked up and making them one big epic poem . . . the emblematic idea of Homer and that story-teller, or that singer, who contains the history of the race. . . . There've been great blind blues singers—and the same thing is true of the calypsonian, who . . . contains the history of the race, who is a vessel for that. And I see absolutely no difference. . . . Because who is there you can say in England who would be a Homeric singer of songs: a rock star or an opera singer, who? Because the whole tribal sense has gone; in these cities you have no tribal sense. And the tribal sense is unified in the black man, in the blues singer, and it's true in other cultures, where that is more Homeric than having somebody with a harp up there, and a beard, you know, plucking away at a lyre.[40]

This exposition of the other Homer makes clear how revolutionary Walcott's view is. By reinventing Homer as Omeros, he shows how, through black culture (which transcends national boundaries), the world's competitive hegemonies can be replaced with a unified "tribe" of humanity: the "international consciousness" of which Frantz Fanon speaks,[41] Rex Nettleford's "new international cultural order."[42] Though shadowy, Walcott's Omeros is very much alive—dark, and warm, where the bust of Homer is cold and white. He is a figure of independence, a solitary, living on the margins without reference to the power structures of organized society; he is the tramp, crouched over his fire in the forest, the wanderer who calls no man master—a figure Walcott has used from his early years, the "most reduced, race-containing" figure of the woodsman.[43]

Given the nickname of Seven Seas, which (as the classical term for the known world's oceans) suggests his global range but also links him, via the name of a modern pharmaceutical company, to the poem's theme of healing, he reappears in all locations and epochs, observing the fate of mankind as history unfolds, participating as watcher, and engaging as narrator. What the eponymous Omeros brings is a demotic alternative to the hegemonic view of the Homeric. His is a counterdiscourse, voiced from the margins, by the one whose story has always been suppressed, the cultural and racial other. The implication is that the corrupt center cannot reform itself, therefore deliverance can be looked for only from the margins. America was once "marginal" to the Old World but has now, in Walcott's formulation, fallen under the malign spell of a neoimperial myth of itself and has therefore become as degenerate as the Old World. What this poem delivers, from America's "backyard," is the old American dream of the democratic epic, with its plebeian heroes.

Just as the poem constructs a binary dialectics through the twin poet-personas of Homer and Omeros, so another two Homers, both artists in the visual arts, mirror a similar antithesis. These both belong in the New World, one a nineteenth-century white American, the other a living black St. Lucian. Both are painters, one bearing the anglicized form of the ancient Greek's name, Homer, the other a name that reads like a francophone, Christianized form of the name, St. Omer, which is also Homer "St. Lucianized," reflecting the French patois and dominant Catholic faith of the island.[44] Winslow Homer is aligned in the poem with what Homer stands for, the hegemonic tradition with its monumental culture—he is even ironically linked with Boston's Marblehead coastal resort[45]—but Walcott's friend Dunstan St. Omer, who plays a prominent part in *Another Life,* resists that dominant with his own demotic, as Omeros challenges the received view of Homer, the ancient poet.

One work by each artist is given prominence in the poem, one overtly, the other covertly: in Winslow Homer's case an allegorical painting in a naturalistic idiom; in Dunstan St. Omer's an abstract and symbolic design. The first is Homer's painting *The Gulf Stream,* of 1899, which appears in the poem, recognized by the narrator as an image of its protagonist, Achille.[46] Homer's painting portrays a young, strong African man helplessly adrift on a mastless and rudderless raft, on a shark-infested ocean with a storm brewing. It gives a tragic reading of the black American experience, doomed and comfortless. This Achille is "circled by chain-sawing sharks; the ropes in his neck turned his head towards Africa." He is forever becalmed, displaced "forever, between our island // and the coast of Guinea." The sharks "always circle / his craft and mine." The second is the St. Lucian flag, designed by St. Omer for St. Lucia's independence, which provides the poem, I think, with a symbolic design.[47] It is both a symbol of the island itself and an idealistic statement of faith in the possibility of a pluralist society. Its triangles—white as if "overlaid" with black, which is "overlaid" with a gold triangle, so that it appears rimmed with black and white, all on a surrounding blue ground—represent the island's social identity (of racial pluralism) in relation to its existence as part of nature (the gold of the sun and the blue of sea and sky), with the triangles representing the conical heights of the volcanic island. The natural world provides the greater part, and the social pattern imprinted between sun and sea is in harmony with its form and beauty.

The different artistic codes that these two works deploy also bear a symbolic relationship to the design of the poem. The construction of meaning via a naturalistic representation, as in Homer's painting, is bound by the world's limitations. Abstract symbolism, on the other hand, is liberated to construct a New World, a world of artistic meaning that can draw the limited world after it. The flag, explained to generations of St. Lucian children, can help to bring about the ideal society it portrays. Homer's painting is essentially an act of voyeurism, with the artist constructing an image of an exotic other who confirms the dominance of the voyeur. St. Omer's design, however, is democratic art of the highest kind, in which the artist, from his special skill, makes an image of itself for the community of which he is part. St. Omer defines his society's identity through a design that has no more valuable "original" but can be available to all its members by being reproduced any number of times in any number of ways. Homer's painting, on the other hand, is an elite object, codified as of value by being placed in a museum, with any reproduction regarded as radically inferior. Walcott has been blunt about the symbolic and political difference between literature and the fine arts: "There's one painting: anything else is a reproduction . . . whereas a novel or a poem can be held, and shared. There's not a single object."[48] The paradox is, of course, that realism has been historically regarded as the sine qua non of socialist art, while symbolism and other modes of abstraction have tended to be disparaged as bourgeois and elitist. But the design for a national flag to mark a newly independent nation is a reminder that symbolism is only elitist if it is obscure. By adopting a symbolic method, Walcott, from a premise close to socialism, is able to revision the world, bringing to our ears and inner eye an image of the healing of historic wounds and of the possibility of renewal. The fact that it should be "saint" Homer who shows the way to this epiphany is significant. The name St. Omer (derived from the French saint and founder of an abbey, after whom the town of Saint-Omer in the Pas-de-Calais is named) seems to canonize Homer, to bring the pre-Christian art of the Greek poet within the realm of Christianity, as Walcott does in *Omeros,* where the classical elements of the narrative are combined with a Christian symbolism. Dunstan St. Omer was Walcott's soul mate from childhood, as described in *Another Life*. He was also his alter ego as artist, the tanist or twin who completes the whole. St. Omer's symbol of St. Lucian hope counters Winslow Homer's image of despair, of the tragic reading of blackness, just as the figure of Omeros re-democratizes the Homeric.

The four Homers—Homer and Omeros, Winslow Homer and Dunstan St. Omer—thus pair both across and down: two poets are balanced by two painters, but more importantly, two key figures of Western hegemony are opposed by two resisting artists who challenge the center's reading of the world. Homer's epic world is full of violent conflict, and Winslow Homer can see only a tragic doom for the African American. But St. Omer has given his people a flag of faith in pluralism, and Walcott, who like the demotic Omeros is one of the poem's several poet-personas, uses that flag as symbolic structure for a poem that eschews violence, and celebrates hope, despite history, and faith in both racial and cultural pluralism.

Like the blue of sea and sky, the yellow triangle of the flag can be "read" in the poem as the yellow dress, which passes from Maud, the ageing Irish woman, to Helen, the young black woman, and is finally used to robe Achille androgynously for his Jon Konnu dance, twinned with Philoctete, celebrating their healing. Its shape is emphasized, that of a double triangle like a yellow butterfly—or as if reflected in water. The flag's triangles, black "overlaid" on white and topped with yellow, so that just a rim of white and black can be seen, symbolizes, I think, the figures of coal pyramid, liner, and flower-pot, as well as representing the social makeup of the island. The portrait of the elderly white couple, the Plunketts, which Stuart Hall, a Jamaican, characterized as "extraordinarily generous,"[49] is thus seen to be crucial to the poem's dialectics. The pluralism is authoritative from a man who is himself of mixed race and diverse cultural heritage, and a twin, who recognizes the sharedness of difference. To have omitted the white part of the island story would have betrayed Dunstan St. Omer's image and its symbolic meaning. And in that it would represent a failure to assimilate the features of one of the ancestors (not just his own personal ancestors, but the society's), it would indicate, according to Walcott's code, a lack of maturity. As he says, maturity is the assimilation of the features of *every* ancestor.[50]

By taking the myth of Homer and not only providing a revolutionary counterdiscourse through the voice of Omeros but actually opening it up several ways so that it can be revisioned as truly plural, Walcott gives his poem both the strength of a four-square structure, like a "good box,"[51] and the reversible heterogeneity and reciprocal flexibility of an image reflected in water. The iconography uses the flag's geometry in an entirely original way; the triangles of the butterfly yellow dress replicate and alter those of the coal-dunes, the liner, the flower-pot, and the Jacob's ladder image; while the frieze of ants matched with human figures—of ant-like people—descending and rising against the gradients of landscapes and artifacts, models the epic fact of human perseverance, the simple miracle of Caribbean survival.

Heroic imagery serves the project to counter the pain of history and ongoing racism and exploitation. As Dunstan St. Omer said on hearing the news of Walcott's Nobel Prize, "Derek . . . is like a Moses of his nation. He actually brought the people into the promised literary land."[52] He has uplifted those whom the centers of power conspire to construct as lowly, by demonstrating their heroism. But he also addresses the privileged North, calling on those who have power, to wield it with compassion to deliver a more humane world. If, therefore, the North's ultimate statement of existential dissociation is Rimbaud's "*Je* est un autre," the culture of the Caribbean (which both shapes and is shaped by its artists) offers a radically different understanding of the human condition. There are understandable concerns about the romance of "all a we is one" becoming no more than empty rhetoric. Rhonda Cobham-Sander, for instance, says, "You should be careful not to romanticize what's happening in the Caribbean. There's lots of tensions between different ethnic groups, between people of different classes, people of different ideological persuasion, and islands are very small, so those clashes can be at your doorstep in all sorts of uncomfortable ways."[53] The perception of Fanon (not one to underestimate the negatives of the Caribbean), however, is that the Caribbean struggle "aims at a fundamentally different set of relations between men. . . . This new humanity cannot do otherwise than define a new humanism both for itself and for others."[54] In *Omeros*, Walcott gives voice as never before to the pain of the Caribbean experience but makes just one thing greater than it: his faith in its capacity to be healed. The language bears simultaneously "its cure, / its radiant affliction."[55] He focuses his epic on the plural "Helens" of all St. Lucia's women, including the coal-carriers, on the healed dance of Achille and Philoctete, and ends with the restored couple, Helen and Achille, expecting a child, a future. In epic there is no closure: only the open-ended present tense of survival, with the sea "still going on."[56] And for the people's shaman, the natural vehicle for epic is metaphor: "In tribal, elemental poetry, the epic experience of the race is compressed in metaphor."[57] By its mythopoeic construction of a system of symbolic signs, the language can lead the world.

7

Appropriating Heirlooms

The Fortunate Traveler's Intertext

> *Gonzalo:* . . . our garments, being, as they were, drenched in the sea, hold notwithstanding their freshness and glosses; being rather new-dyed than stain'd with salt water.
>
> ***The Tempest*, II.i.65–68**

Intertextuality as method is a distinctive mark not only of Walcott's aesthetics but of his politics—of his art as act of political engagement. It has, however, been persistently misunderstood, particularly in the North, where there has been a tendency to co-opt it to a conventional politics of assimilation. Robert Hamner cites Walcott's resentment at the double standards of metropolitan critics, who approve what they call "acquisition" from colonial cultures but judge the colonial writer "'imitative' when he reciprocates."[1] It is not a case of the secondhand or salt-stained but, as in Gonzalo's perception, of the "new-dyed." Walcott's own view is quite clear:

> I once called myself a sponge . . . not that I sponge *off* people—but something that I think can absorb whatever it likes. And if the holes in the sponge suck in whatever they want, you may call it parasitic if you want. But I think that I have never let myself feel original in that sense. I've never vaunted about originality. I don't think originality is a quality in poetry. I don't think that trying to identify yourself, and being different, and trying to separate yourself from the ancestry of the language, I think that's just a career move, really.

The sense of the presence of predecessors is part of "the intensity with which you work on the craft": "you have shadows of other people in the room. If you have any kind of awe or humility, if you can induce the image of Ovid looking and laughing at the absurdity you've just written, that's a sacred thing, I think."[2] This particularity of Walcott's attitude to past poets modifies his "writing back" (in Salman Rushdie's phrase) to the canonical texts of colonial discourse, which has been a characteristic feature of postcolonial literatures. The dialectical impetus, the desire for a counterdiscourse, remains, but it is not undertaken in a spirit of antagonism. Instead it is driven by the twin desires to honor aesthetically and simultaneously to contest politically, which result in an epic ambition, the daunting imperative of the attempt to be as good, because anything less would be unworthy.

Walcott quite often engages intertextually with canonical works, not only Homer, but Defoe (*Pantomime*) or Shakespeare (*A Branch of the Blue Nile*) for instance, but "The Fortunate Traveller" is selected for discussion here because it represents an extreme case of Walcott's intertextual method—some would say, its test to destruction. The poem is elaborately and widely allusive, often cryptically so, and yet its topic is urgently political. In general, the critics have steered clear of its deep waters. The volume of which it is the title poem has been criticized by Helen Vendler for "ventriloquism," displaying a "learnedness" that "might be the death of him" in work that is "peculiarly at the mercy of influence," yet Seamus Heaney understands that although Walcott has had the capacity to "make himself a ventriloquist's doll to the English tradition which he inherited," he has in fact been making "himself a romantic tongue, indigenous and awash in the prophetic."[3] Gerald Moore regards him as a "neoclassical writer," for whom "it has never been a problem . . . to strike echoes from . . . that whole living tradition of poetry," but this makes its emphasis retrospective and nostalgic.[4] Rei Terada observes that Walcott's is "a poetry that knows there are no first times,"[5] which is only a part-truth. Mervyn Morris, however, discerns in it the dynamic of the new: "Walcott often seeks to make us actively aware of the varying cultural elements he pulls together, or of the transfiguring lens of history, literature or myth through which he views the present."[6] The emphasis is rightly on the transfiguring, the difference of the vision, which creates new meanings precisely through its historical and cultural self-location. We must learn to read as Gonzalo does and see the fresh meanings that intertextuality makes possible. Walcott's work is not "stain'd with salt water" but "new-dyed." For him, great poets are those whose "originality emerges only when they have absorbed all the poetry which they have read, entire. . . ."Far from being "at the mercy of influence," "The Fortunate Traveller" quite deliberately constructs its meanings in and through the context of literary tradition. The ethical interface of art and life is its subject. Walcott looks to his readers to recognize his allusions and mocks those who track them in a spirit of finding him out: "Some critics thought, 'Ho-ho, I know where you get that from!' So do I! I took it from. . . ."[7] At the same time the compressed allusiveness of such poems as "The Fortunate Traveller" can alienate readers. There is, I think, a place for such exegesis as is offered here. It is made in the hope of perhaps elucidating a fine work that, although striking, is arcane enough, it seems, to have frightened off critics, and probably to have distanced readers from the "frisson" of direct response to an impassioned and important poem for our time. Its signifying practice exemplifies once again the "I-an-I" pairing of difference in similitude. It is itself paired here with the poem that follows it, the final work of the volume, "The Season of Phantasmal Peace," without which the significance of "The Fortunate Traveller" cannot be fully read. Accordingly, that poem too is included in this analysis, which does not follow the poetic sequence but proceeds intertext by intertext.

Walcott's "The Fortunate Traveller" is the Third World's "J'accuse" addressed to the affluent, an angry cry on behalf of the world's starving (to Calvin Bedient a "brilliant scary Third World political cartoon"),[8] which moves powerfully to figure both the right to justice and the claim for vengeance. At the same time, it inverts the dynamic of cultural colonialism, addressing itself, as mission, to the "soul" of its others, the neoimperialists, hoping to effect a moral transformation. "The Fortunate Traveller" is a poem about the guilt of empire, spoken primarily from the South to the North. It discloses a binary world, split between haves and have-nots, distinguished by race as well as geography, and it anatomizes the betrayal of the one by the other. But it does not just point an accusing finger; it appeals to the privileged to reform themselves and the world over which they wield power—in other words, it directs them to redemption rather than damnation. To do this it dramatizes the experience of the privileged through the allegorical figure of the "fortunate traveller," revealed to be the traitor who betrays the people of the South for personal gain. But in espousing this subjectivity, it becomes also a self-projection for the poet, honest enough to recognize his own privilege and his own guilt. The volume in which this poem is published was the first to appear after Walcott had moved to the United States, abandoning (as it must have seemed to him) his long-standing and much-publicized commitment to remaining in the Caribbean. The sense of the poem's fictional persona presenting a generalized address gradually yields to a sense that the poet in describing his tussle with his own conscience is reaching out directly to the reader. The reader by definition is one of the privileged who is being invited to consider his or her complicity with the unjust world order, in step with the poet. Reading, like traveling, is deconstructed as not innocent, not ideologically apart from the world of sociopolitical reality. Thus in locating itself in the cultural tradition of the West, the poem sets up allusiveness as central to its project—an acutely original one.

Crucially, it shows the Western tradition as dominated by a culture of tragedy, expressed through a mythification of sacrifice that empowers destructive relations at the social level. In the North, it suggests, the redemptive message of Christianity has been upstaged by a godless culture of apocalyptic power, with the Nietzschean superman as hero, glorifying the triumph of individual will, which we have come to call fascist. Lois Zamora argues that the apocalyptic—"the end of the world . . . described from the point of view of a narrator who is radically opposed to existing spiritual and political practices . . . awaiting God's intervention in human history, when the corrupt world of the present will be supplanted by a new and transcendent realm"—has a particular relevance to artists of the Americas: "Because the myth of apocalypse insists on the inevitable link between individual and collective fate, it is precisely those writers prone to apocalyptic visions who are most likely to concern themselves with essential relations between the self and its surroundings, between autonomy and solidarity."[9] Through the story of his fortunate traveler, Walcott is aiming to lead a whole culture to self-knowledge and moral responsibility, showing those pathologically accultured to isolationist autonomy the imperatives—and the rewards—of solidarity. He belongs with the writers Zamora describes, who are "aware of humanity's propensity for communal self-destruction" and of "the effects of crisis, for both good and evil, on the individual." The thriller-like momentum of the poem toward a closure in suspended apocalypse is an attempt to create crisis for the good, to deliver an awesome warning in the name of prompting change in the social order. It is thus urgently political. As Zamora concludes, "This concern with the outcome of our individual and communal histories, coupled with the conviction that literature may yet influence the outcome, has never been more necessary."[10] Yet as well as modeling holy terror, the poem points beyond an eschatology of judgment and vengeance to the possibility of benign closure, offering to teach the northern world of pathological power the way of the South, where cultures are based on the affirmation of life rather than death, and where ways of communal living have been developed, based on respect rather than competition—where the other tends to be seen as an equal, not an inferior. It is a multiply epic project (through its breadth of "canvas," its Brechtian political signifying, and in the sense located in this volume, exploring a public-private continuum)—an ambition which the poem simultaneously ironizes in a postmodern way with its deprecating self-awareness. But its self-location against some key canonical texts of the Western tradition is the focus of its signifying. At a superficial political level, these texts are where the problem is located, but at a more profound level of thought, they are also the site at which it can be solved. The double relationship to tradition is thus not a sign of confusion or of ambiguous loyalties; it is the core paradox where meaning is to be found.

Walcott has never hidden his conscious self-affiliation as artist. Asked about his awareness, as a young poet, of working within a tradition, that of canonical English literature, Walcott replied,

> I remember the Faber Auden and the Faber Eliot . . . and just the physical thing of holding these books. . . . What I used to do is, almost every day, or as often as I could, I had an exercise book, or exercise books, in which I would model a poem directly . . . almost like an overlay, down to the rhyme and the metre, but out of my own background and family and landscape, and so on. . . . It was just to me a complete apprenticeship, a complete surrender to modelling, because I knew that I was in a landscape that didn't have pylons and trains and autumn, or whatever. . . .[11]

This self-apprenticeship, arising from an acknowledgment of difference and marking deliberate self-affiliation to a literary tradition, has matured into a dialectical self-location within the canon, the affiliative mode doubled and countered by the revisionary and the revolutionary. As Walcott says in *Another Life,* on the one hand there is the constant injunction "faites vos hommages" [pay your respects], and on the other: "I had entered the house of literature as a houseboy, / filched as the slum child stole, / as the young slave appropriated / those heirlooms temptingly left / with the Victorian homilies of *Noli tangere.*"[12] The impetus toward affiliation is like that of the just inheritor asserting the legitimacy of his claim; the impetus toward revolution is like that of the inheritor denied. These patterns are the basis of Walcott's aesthetic, as they are the basis of black politics. In Spike Lee's famous conclusion to his 1989 film *Do the Right Thing,* the different stances of Martin Luther King and Malcolm X are stated, returning the viewer to the imperative of the title, "Do the right thing!"—which leaves it to each to invest "right" with meaning in accordance with individual conscience. "The Fortunate Traveller," the title poem of Walcott's 1981 collection, is also about the projection of meanings—about the freedom to invest signifiers with new signifieds, and therefore about the open-endedness of both culture and history—and about moral responsibility, personal and collective. Its intertextual method establishes the extent of the field on which this innovative creed can be enacted, nothing less than the whole tradition from which the contemporary language practice has sprung—a world of prior texts against which and through which new meanings can be created. History is locked in to chronicity, but textuality is radically open.

If *Another Life* writes back to Wordsworth's *Prelude, Pantomime* to Defoe's *Robinson Crusoe,* and *Omeros* to Joyce's *Ulysses* (not to mention Homer), then "The Fortunate Traveller" is particularly an engagement with Conrad's *Heart of Darkness,* but a dialectical engagement in which aesthetics are exposed as a political field. Moral responsibility is the poem's quest, as it is of *Heart of Darkness,* a primary intertext, among a large number either referred to or implicit in it. As well as by the Conrad, however, the poem was evidently also directly inspired by Chinua Achebe's famous attack on *Heart of Darkness* and on Conrad as a "bloody racist." Achebe's essay "An Image of Africa" was published in 1977 and the poem in 1981, so the poem may have been prompted by the Achebe piece rather than the Conrad work, which, like the Achebe, it interrogates.

First, however, the Conrad/Walcott parallels need to be examined. Where Conrad, at one level at least, wishes to promote awareness of the moral complicity of Europeans at home, in the wrongs of late-nineteenth-century empire, Walcott is likewise raising consciousness among the privileged readers of the North of their (our) complicity in the great wrong of the global economic (dis)order in the late twentieth century. The implicit presence of the Conrad in the poem thus extends beyond the passage in which it first becomes overt—"Through Kurtz's teeth, white skull in elephant grass, / the imperial fiction sings"—which proceeds to an investigation of Conrad's title. The poem has in fact been mirroring Conrad's story in its broad outline from the beginning: its British protagonist visits French speakers in continental Europe for a business agreement at the beginning, returns to London, then sets off on a (neo)colonial journey to the tropics. Conrad's "imperial fiction" still in Kurtz's teeth is that Africa is the "heart of darkness," but the poem's revolutionary revelation is that the home of moral benightedness is the North, the source of exploitative power: "The heart of darkness is not Africa. / The heart of darkness is the core of fire / in the white center of the holocaust." Crucially, it reinvests Conrad's now mythified title with contrary meaning, not once but twice.

The Marlow/Kurtz binary pair that gives the Conrad its dynamic is now collapsed to a single figure, the fortunate traveler. The poem's persona is like Conrad's Marlow in that his journey proves to be a quest for spiritual enlightenment, but as a figure of guilt he is more like the Faustian Kurtz. The Conradian imperialist voyager of the late nineteenth century is now the air traveler from the neoimperialist world of privilege. As the Everyman whose conscience has slept, he is taken through a series of experiences that uncover his own state of moral turpitude. The way in which culture relates to political reality is Walcott's target as it was Conrad's. But where Conrad's ending has proved itself prone to a century of partial readings, Walcott has made sure that his ending delivers a forceful and unmistakable warning. In place of ivory, the poem has, as its symbolic commodity, food. Its target is the global power structure that keeps the people of the South hungry so that the people of the North can indulge their greed, but it does more than locate guilt. It delivers a revelation of its own: that it is to the cultures of the South that the world should look for alternatives to the tragic model of the human condition. Its morality coincides with the Christian ethic, in which the Old Testament's harsh logic of justice is replaced by the New Testament's gift of mercy. The guilty, the northern "fortunate travelers" who enjoy privilege at others' expense, stand accused. But, as Marlow finds when he commits the great sin of complicity by lying to the Intended, the divine justice he expects to strike him down does not follow; he is spared. Walcott's poem too spares those it accuses. It eschews vengeance, which Christian theology reserves to God, and closes with the apocalypse threatened, not delivered.

There are a number of parallels between the two works, as well as significant differences. Like Conrad's novella, the poem charts a journey that begins in the North and moves to the South. Both works open in Europe, evoking a plural Europeanness by setting a text in English in a "continental" context: as Conrad's story says of Kurtz, all Europe went to his making. Where Conrad has an unspecified "sepulchral city" to which Marlow travels from London (on whose river the whole story is narrated) to secure the commission that takes him to an unspecified river in Africa, Walcott opens with an unspecified northern European city in winter, with a frozen river, and an encounter between the protagonist and two men from francophone Africa. The atmosphere is reminiscent of a "film noir" Europe and the spy thrillers of the Cold War period. In fact, it is not only *Heart of Darkness* itself that the poem evokes but other works with an intertextual relationship with it, particularly films, their influence seen in the poem's aesthetics of strongly visual and dynamic imagery.

In particular, the opening evokes Carol Reed's 1948 film from Graham Greene's story *The Third Man,* a powerful mythification of a physically and morally torn Vienna in the immediate postwar period, shot in black and white. If seen in the light of this (also an intertext with *Heart of Darkness*), it is clear that Europe is now occupying the Gothic role Africa is given in the Conrad (appropriately since Europe is the place of origin of the Gothic). The collective psychology of displacement, which produces cultural phenomena such as the representation of Africa in Gothic terms as a feature of colonial discourse (an off-loading of guilt by projection), is here, in effect, brought to closure, enabling the "truth" of the collective guilt to be identified. Instead of Conrad's nightmarish African grotesque, Walcott makes *Europe* a chamber of horrors. The North is evoked as a claustrophobic, sinister space, a lidded landscape like a cave, replete with religious symbols translated into horrific associations, as in the Gothic tradition of popular culture—to be contrasted later in the poem with the innocent symbols of religion in the South. The color composition of the scene is symbolic, as so often in Walcott's work (his painter's eye informing his poetry)—a monochromatic scene of a city under snow, in which gray predominates. The harshness of the physical climate becomes an expressionist signifier (as it often does in Walcott's work) of inhumanity—of the harshness of social conditions for the black immigrants whose skins are "gray" not only from lack of sun and the threat of the "hooked worm" of intestinal parasites but implicitly also from the struggle to survive in a climate of racist marginalization, in which a mythified coldness has entered the hearts of white people. In this claustrophobic landscape, muffled with snow, the protagonist provides the only splash of color with a crimson carnation in his buttonhole "for the cold ecstasy of the assassin." Although a flower is evoked, the red becomes an expressionist signifier of the blood from an imagined bullet wound. Where Conrad makes a riddle of Marlow's first sight of Kurtz—by having him remote, but brought up "close" through binoculars, and rotating him to a recumbent position, marked enigmatically by his seeming extremely long—Walcott does the reverse: the first sight of its protagonist the poem offers is of a marked man, as if in the sights of a rifle. The red denotes the repressed guilt of the protagonist as exemplary northerner, now made visible, as in the Freudian concept of the "uncanny," in which, as Fredric Jameson describes, an "archaic fantasy" irrupts into consciousness, making itself felt "by the garish and technicolor representation of what is given as an essentially black-and-white reality."[13] The poem's whole project can be interpreted as to effect the return of the repressed. But (as with *Heart of Darkness*) to bring to consciousness the guilt of empire, so well buried under complacent self-esteem, is no easy task. The relationship evoked between the poem's "I" and the reader is clearly crucial.

The poem's opening group of three figures—the pair of Africans and the protagonist with whom they rendezvous—echoes *The Third Man.* The film has a character called Kurtz, an Austrian aristocrat, but its principal Kurtz figure is an American (an Englishman in Greene's original version). The prosperity of the poem's man with the buttonhole is like that of Harry Lime (as played by Orson Welles) with his elegant attire, and he can be seen as the elusive emblem of guilt, like Lime. The poem's opening positions the protagonist as its "third man," illicit trader and traitor to humanity, like Graham Greene's Lime, with the secret deal about tractors rather than penicillin. Both give expression to the moral crux, the failure of compassion that results from a denial of equivalent value to all others. Lime argues from the top of the famous Vienna Ferris wheel that it is not important if a few more of the human dots below stop moving, while the fortunate traveler asks, "who cares how many million starve?" But where Greene's story opens and closes with death (the "false" funeral of Lime and finally his "real" one), Walcott's poem opens and closes with only a threat of death. The assassin-avenger's presence is implied at start and finish, the elusiveness of Lime replaced with a clear sense of the fortunate traveler's exposure—that he is in the target position—but the poem does not enact his nemesis. Instead of leading his reader to a revelation of the "horror" of another's guilt through an observing Marlow figure (Holly Martins in the film), Walcott centers his poem directly on his protagonist's guilt, giving not an external but an internal perspective on the experience of a "Kurtz." By removing the "Marlow" distanciation from the Kurtzian "horror," Walcott prevents the easy reader-identification with a benign polarity against a demonized one, which has enabled generations of Conrad readers to evade his text's moral challenge. Walcott encourages every reader to examine his or her own conscience and moral ambivalence.

The geography mapped in the poem moves from a frozen river of north-central Europe—a mythic setting, unlocated—to Britain. There an evocation of London and the Thames, as in the Conrad, is paired with the Severn and Bristol, which shared with Liverpool the dubious distinction of forming the northern apex of the three-cornered traffic of the British slave trade.[14] The third point of the triangle, Africa, is represented in the poem in several ways: by the two French-speaking Africans from the "dark river," which by implication is Conrad's "Congo"; by Albert Schweitzer, whose mission was in West Africa; by Arthur Rimbaud, who became a colonial trader in the upper Nile region; and by the "Sahara," which features in the poem's symbolic discussion of food. The doubleness of Conrad's northern locations—London and the sepulchral city—is here mirrored not only within Europe (London and the city of the frozen river) but in the South, with its two points of the Black Atlantic compass, African and Caribbean.[15]

The anonymous protagonist waits in London in a rented room for the call instructing him to go to Bristol. From there he takes a ship, leaving England by the Severn estuary, bound for the West Indies and the island of Walcott's birth, St. Lucia, identifiable by the place-name Canaries (pronounced "Ca-na-wi"). The journey thus reverses that of the slave trade. The relatively few slaves who were brought on to Bristol—a city with street names that still echo that history—experienced the Severn voyage upriver with the rising tide, not the downriver journey on the ebb, which Walcott so powerfully evokes and which resonates with Conrad's account of waiting for the Thames ebb. The sense of the tidal cycles of rise and fall is to become an expressionist movement in the sequence's moral odyssey. The route Walcott describes is that of the Europeans rather than of the Africans, but for his protagonist, as for the slaves of the past, the Caribbean island is the destination, the place from which there is no moving on. The rest of the poem is based on the tourist-like experience of being in a hotel room in St. Lucia, regarded as a refuge in which to hide from a coming nemesis. The poem ends in a gathering sense of impending doom: the protagonist, the betrayer, a Judas, cannot hide from justice. The language and tone of the spy thriller with its mystery and tension create a heightened atmosphere that affects the reader, giving access to the idea of guilt.

The feminine is set up, in line with the Conrad, in a special relationship to idealism. Walcott's protagonist is, on the one hand, a person of conscience who tells Margo[16] that he "cannot bear to watch the nations cry." As in *Heart of Darkness,* the masculine self addresses its compassionate persona to woman (the vaunted sensibility undercut by narcissism). On the other hand, it is evident that the protagonist has done something others regard as reprehensible, for which they will take revenge. There seems to be a gap between the self-image he cherishes and the reality of his behavior—which is putatively double-crossing, selfish, and exploitative.

The sense of a filmic aesthetic is not evident only in the parallels with *The Third Man.* The poem also invites a reading against Francis Ford Coppola's 1979 film, *Apocalypse Now,* another *Heart of Darkness* intertext, then quite new, in which Conrad's story of colonial Africa is adapted to the Vietnam War. Walcott's eloquent image uniting nature with culture, "Treble clef of the snail on the scored leaf," is a revision and a moral inversion of the recorded voice of Col. Walter E. Kurtz at the start of the film, saying, "I watched a snail crawl along the edge of a straight razor. That's my dream. It's my nightmare."[17] Walcott takes the Kurtzian "horror" out of the image, redeeming it, an emblem of the poem's metaphysical project. The idea of a sacrificed natural world is remote from the poem though central to the film. The film dangles a "sacred cow" below a helicopter near its beginning and climaxes in the sacrificial beheading of another as image of the killing of its Kurtz, but the poem's bias is against violence and death, opposed to the tragic premise of sacrifice or vengeful justice. The "bright water" remains water, not blood, and its Kurtz figure is left alive. The film dwells on the idea of apocalypse in adapting the colonial Conradian scenario to one of war, but as Laurence Coupe points out, Coppola's film, while "already in the now of crisis and catastrophe," is also radically in process: "it forces the viewer to inhabit a moment of endless traumatic transition, in which Babylon is continually about to fall and Armageddon about to be fought. Justice is absent, but the viewer is forced to confront that absence."[18] This account could have been written for the closure of "The Fortunate Traveller." In fact, Coppola released his film in alternative versions, one ending with the apocalyptic air strike on Kurtz's compound, the other calling it off. Walcott likewise hesitates: he withholds nemesis at the end of "The Fortunate Traveller" and moves to a benign closure in the following poem, which ends the book.

The Conradian chiaroscuro, inverting the cultural locations of darkness and light, in the poem is given significant development. Not only is the Conrad title's deployment of "darkness" interrogated and redeployed, but the South is made the place of a culture of light, in which the votive lights of Hinduism and Catholicism in the Caribbean (the local culture's "deya" and "lampion") are set against the secular bedside lamp of the tourist hotel room (representing the outsider's experience of the region, like that of the returning poet, now a resident of the North). The natural light of sunset over water seems to the narrator an expressionist image of his guilt, but the poem reminds the reader that nature itself is not guilty: the guilt is a cultural projection. Similarly in line with Conrad's rhetoric of ironization by inversion, the poem uses the word "savages" of Europeans. In *Heart of Darkness,* the Roman conquest of Britain is recalled as a device to prompt identification with the victims of contemporary imperialism. Walcott goes further back, to prehistory, when, the fortunate traveler says of his European ancestors, "we savages dyed our pale dead with ochre, /

and bordered our temples with the ceremonial vulva of the conch." It is evoked as a time when culture was the product of plenty, imagination thriving when people had enough to eat (illustrated by "fat"), and is in implicit ironic contrast with the Third World's modernity, of starvation.

Now to return to Achebe's critique of the Conrad. Walcott reverses the Conrad scenario, in which, according to Achebe, Africa is "a metaphysical battlefield devoid of all recognizable humanity, into which the wandering European enters at his peril," to an inverted binarism, also metaphysical, in which the North produces inhumanity, while the South produces the humane. However, the distinctive references in Achebe's discussion to Albert Schweitzer, Nazism, Arthur Rimbaud, and Haiti, all of which Walcott incorporates in his poem, warrant a firm assertion of intertextual genealogy. The West has a psychological problem, Achebe argues, of "deep anxieties about the precariousness of its civilization," from which it seeks reassurance by comparing itself favorably with Africa.[19] This is very much in line with Octave Mannoni's perception that many Europeans "project upon the colonial peoples the obscurities of their own unconscious—obscurities they would rather not penetrate. . . . In any such act of projection the subject's purpose is to recover his own innocence by accusing someone else of what he considers to be a fault in himself."[20] Achebe goes on to argue, however, that racism disqualifies a work from being regarded as great art: "For poetry surely can only be on the side of man's deliverance and not his enslavement; for the brotherhood and unity of all mankind and against the doctrines of Hitler's master races or Conrad's 'rudimentary souls.'" For Achebe, *Heart of Darkness* is "a story in which the very humanity of black people is called in question." It is, he says, "inconceivable that great art or even good art could possibly reside in such unwholesome surroundings." Achebe's assertion about the individual, Conrad, and his racist psychology, is thus developed to a point about the collective culture of Europe and the West, and to an issue of aesthetics, a large claim as to the moral purpose of art. The canon is Achebe's ultimate target. He wants *Heart of Darkness* to be dropped from syllabuses, rather than taught as an exemplary text.

In taking the argument forward in a new literary work, Walcott might be regarded, paradoxically, as entrenching the Conrad further in its canonical position. The conjunction of the two works, however, enables us to read the Conrad with a sharper awareness than was possible earlier. Even though, in my view, Achebe underestimated Conrad's project to ironize colonial discourse, his attack was a needed counter to a culture of myopia, and it was productive not just in raising consciousness generally but in inspiring this further work of engaged art. It would be difficult to refute Walcott's polemic. Achebe is chiefly concerned with the misrepresentation of Africa, its peoples, and its cultures, his intention being to "teach my readers that their past—with all its imperfections—was not one long night of savagery."[21] From the beginning, Georg Gugelberger argues, modern African literature "could not but be *reactive,*" since it used "the 'weapons of words' for the *légitime défense* of the African heritage. The consciousness which dominated this reaction was one of African *affirmation.*"[22]

The need to combat the negative effect on Africans of racist representations is, however, only half of the problem. There is also a need to combat the originating culture of that racism, the white supremacist culture of Europe and the West. Achebe's essay identifies the binarisms deployed in Conrad's story and relates them to the hypocrisy of white liberalism, so adept at sidestepping "the ultimate question of equality between white people and black people."[23] He then uses as an illustrative case Albert Schweitzer, missionary and doctor at Lambaréné in Gabon, who was at that date still held up as an exemplar of the benign face of imperialism. He was awarded the Nobel Peace Prize in 1952 for his work in Africa, but Achebe reminds his readers of the racism on which his apparent philanthropy was founded. He quotes Schweitzer's dictum (revising the emancipation slogan) that "the African is indeed my brother but my junior brother," and he explains that this philosophy was enacted in an inferior standard of medical care, such as would not have been acceptable in the North. From the Schweitzer case he proceeds to Nazism, the generally agreed worst case, arguing that the censure of Nazi talents applied "to the service of virulent racism whether in science, philosophy or the arts" should be extended to other creative artists who "apply their talents, alas often considerable as in the case of Conrad, to set people against people." Achebe then cites Russian poet Yevgeny Yevtushenko (who had achieved fame in the West at this time), who says "that a poet cannot be a slave trader at the same time, and gives the striking example of Arthur Rimbaud who was fortunately honest enough to give up any pretenses to poetry when he opted for slave trading." Achebe then supports his assertion of Conrad's racism by quoting his first fictional portrait of a black person, an "enormous buck nigger" in Haiti.[24] Each of these elements of Achebe's argument reappears in Walcott's poem, though deployed in different configurations. In its second section, the white priest enters his St. Lucian church "as Albert Schweitzer moves to the harmonium / of morning, and to the pluming chimneys, / the groundswell lifts *Lebensraum, Lebensraum.*"

But before this, Achebe presides over the first section's reference to Haiti, which becomes, as it were, Walcott's prompt to reorient a revisionist reply to *Heart of Darkness* via the Caribbean. He offsets a Europe now reunited with its own Gothic (which colonial discourse had displaced onto Africa) against the tourist experience of the Caribbean. In the poem's first section, the fortunate traveler inside his Haitian hotel is watched by a gecko, like a starving child at the window, Haiti having long been one of the poorest countries of the region and one in which naked exploitative power politics have been most in evidence. The traveler has the privileged lifestyle of the international jet-setter, which the poem contrasts with the lives of those trapped in poverty. The fish-tank world of the international hotel, with its cozy exoticism, has the starving pressed to its glass in frustrated desire. The word "Mercy" puns between two languages: it is the plea for pity in English (and the plea for divine compassion—a meaning that is recalled later in the poem, as the Duchess of Malfi dies with that word on her lips) and the word for thanks in French, "merci," uttered as a plea for a gift that has not yet been made and therefore carrying a pathetic irony. There is an echo here of Aimé Césaire's famous prototype of postcolonial modernism, *Cahier d'un Retour au Pays Natal,* in which the poverty of Caribbean people is eloquently conveyed through a description of his grandmother's makeshift bed: "above the bed in a pot full of oil a candle-end whose flame looks like a fat turnip, and on the side of the pot, in letters of gold: MERCI." Frantz Fanon cites this passage as proof that the poor "do not complain."[25] Its archetypal scene, in which the imagery of material deprivation is linked with a notion of spiritual grace through a lamp flame, metaphorized as food, resonates closely with Walcott's poem, which also interweaves extended tropes of light and food. But where Fanon shows a Marxist impatience with the patience exhibited by the oppressed, Walcott tends to stress the goodness of the Caribbean personality, so ready to give thanks to its creator.

The reality of political power and privilege is brought into the poem through its economic and statistical discourse, but, like Kurtz's report in *Heart of Darkness* with its official decorum, the data of the supposedly liberal project is undercut with subversive graffiti—not inviting apocalypse (Kurtz's injunction to exterminate) but calling for compassion. Walcott's narrator, whose guilty complicity the reader will be led to share, begins as a liberal who has "scrawled" on the World Bank documents, which maintain the Third World in poverty, "the one word, MERCI." The poem underlines the chasm between First and Third Worlds, the one in safety and control, the other inheriting only suffering, with the figure of the fortunate traveler, who operates in both worlds, used to disclose the truth of the relationship: that it is based on immorality. The symbolic role of the fortunate traveler is evident in his use of "we." The group he identifies with is that of the world's power brokers, presented, in the first of the poem's insect images, as cockroaches, who scuttle back to safety when their "cabinets crack." His is a world of rampant self-seeking, devoid of true pity.

The gecko[26] is the first of a chain of images in the poem in which creatures commonly regarded as vermin are used as ambivalent access points to both abjection and compassion. The strategy is first to enlist the reader's antipathy, and then, by exposing the "vermin" as a figure for the fellow human being, to awaken compassion, and, finally, guilt. The poem is less about Achebe's project of raising black consciousness and self-esteem than about raising white consciousness of guilt. Guilt is a tricky target, so well defended by all kinds of psychological mechanisms, carefully programmed into culture. Walcott's strategy is not naive. First, he centers a protagonist and part-narrator who can function as a figure of identification for white northern readers, to lead them to awareness of their complicity. The antipathetic image of the "roaches" scattering when the (neatly punning) "cabinets" crack is meant as a paradoxical hook to reader identification, resonating as it does with Jean Rhys's famous portrayal of former slave owners as "white cockroaches" in *Wide Sargasso Sea*.[27] Those who know they would return to the northern metropolises if their lives of privilege in the South took a downturn are positioned to question their ethical position. The evocation of Schweitzer also introduces a novel perspective on the European: as the lines unfold, the hero figure of the white liberal project is exposed as demonic. The organ-playing patriarch (he used to raise money for his mission by organ recitals in Europe) is associated with the ideology of Nazism. The poem relates the "organ pipes of coconuts" to his harmonium and to the wave's "groundswell" of "*Lebensraum, Lebensraum.*" Nazism is offered as a negative polarity, the rhythm suggesting the Teutonic sentiment of the song "Edelweiss" but "Lebensraum" being the Nazi catchword to justify genocide in the name of expansion, "room for living," the ideology not only of the Jewish Holocaust within Europe but that on which Europe's overseas empires were constructed. Thus Nazism is used to access related European oppression, and its universally deplored racism is held up as an image of the deeply entrenched racism still widely sanctioned in white culture. As Chinweizu says, "White power gave birth to white racism, and white racism serves white power. It is that simple."[28]

Although the paralleling of the New World black experience with that of Jews in the Holocaust had been a long-standing theme of Walcott's, the theme of Nazi atrocities takes on a fresh prominence in this collection, as he develops the North/South binarism. The smoking chimneys of the concentration camps from "North and South," earlier in *The Fortunate Traveller,* are here reprised. The images of Third World famine are overlaid with those of the camps and found to be identical: the gecko like a starving child has a "concentrating" head. The godless era of genocide is still going on, as Anno Domini is reconceived with bitter irony as After Dachau. Behind Conrad's mythification of Africa as "heart of darkness," a racist projection in Achebe's view, Walcott discloses the hidden truth, that if "darkness" means immorality and the failure of compassion, then it can be found in the horrors of Nazism. The "Jacob" figure suggests Max Jacob, an early surrealist writer and painter, a Parisian Jew, who died in a concentration camp in 1944. He is here imagined as expressing the horror of what was happening in appropriately surreal terms, in which the effort to imagine a negative is couched in firmly positive terms: "'Think of a God who doesn't lose His sleep / if trees burst into tears or glaciers weep.'" The idea of an expressionist natural world, sentient and compassionate, is what leaps from the page, not that of an uncaring divinity. The collapse of time, of the death camps' "then" into the Third World's "now" is accompanied by the collapse of geographical difference. The globe is used to provide an emblem of hunger, as the earth "shows its rib cage" and the moon "goggles with the eyes of children." By bringing Third World starvation into an imaginative relationship with the hunger and suffering at camps such as Dachau, a moral relativism is implied: that it is not right to look for guilt in relation to one event (the Holocaust) but not the other (Third World deprivation). The sinister use of science, which has replaced religion, with its "tinkling nickel instruments on the white altar," is part of the pattern: the North is the abode of scientific rationalism, which, to Walcott's mind, undermines our capacity to feel and care. In this volume, his first collection published since his new residence in the North, he seems to have sharpened his perspective of the particularity of his own region, the Caribbean, conscious of the values he misses, while reaching out to a wide-ranging engagement with what he sees as specifically northern problems.

Fanon as well as Achebe may have inspired this address to racism through the case of Nazism. In *Black Skin, White Masks,* Fanon states the egalitarian ideology: "Colonial racism is no different from any other racism. / Anti-Semitism hits me head on: I am enraged, I am bled white by an appalling battle, I am deprived of the possibility of being a man. I cannot dissociate myself from the future that is proposed for my brother." He follows this with an assertion of moral responsibility: "Every one of my acts commits me as a man. Every one of my silences, every one of my cowardices reveals me as a man."[29] Fanon's footnote relates this to the ideas of Karl Jaspers as to collective guilt, linked specifically to the case of Germany. Jaspers argues that "each shares responsibility for every injustice and every wrong committed in the world, and especially for crimes that are committed in his presence or of which he cannot be ignorant. If I do not do whatever I can to prevent them, I am an accomplice in them." Fanon repudiates Jaspers's religious concept of morality but allies himself with his idea of responsibility, in that "the least of my actions involves all mankind." He then cites Jung as saying that, "confronted by an Asiatic or a Hindu, every European has equally to answer for the crimes perpetrated by Nazi savagery."[30] Walcott, on the other hand, reconnects the humanitarian responsibility directly to divine ordinance, showing Nazism as specifically a failure of the religious spirit in a godless age (derived from Voltaire and Nietzsche, as noted above) and ending with a biblical mantra, "*and have not charity.*"

The poem's cryptic Rimbaud allusion falls into place in the light of the Achebe. Famous for giving up poetry in favor of a colonial life on the upper Nile, he is shown as caring "less for one human face / than for the scrolls in Alexandria's ashes." The scrolls are both commodities and culture, both of which are overvalued if they are put above the precious individual person. Walcott portrays Rimbaud as the possessor of the cynical knowledge that people do "turn away to read," insulating themselves from others' suffering by taking refuge in culture, narrowly defined. The world traveler, in particular, is willfully blind. The sunset scene on the Nile is redolent of the Severn embarkation earlier in the poem and recalls the twinned rivers of *Heart of Darkness,* the Thames and the "Congo," with their different lessons as to the consequences of imperialism. The setting also recalls Walcott's own distinction in "Origins" between the great rivers associated with continental scenarios of abuse of power and the innocent seas and little rivers of his own region.[31] Rimbaud, in Africa, never took up his pen creatively again but in his querulous correspondence revealed his scorn of his own predicament and of the societies in which he had put himself—"des déserts peuplés de nègres stupides."[32] In embracing the goals of a materialist and racist empire, he found only misery, not compassion, and not guilt.

With typical deftness of suggestion, in "the bright water could not dye his hand," Walcott reveals also an intertextual relationship with Auden's essay *The Dyer's Hand,* which explores the function of poetry. Auden, whom Walcott met and admired, also refers to Rimbaud in a discussion to which he offers the preamble, "I am always interested in hearing what a poet has to say about the nature of poetry."[33] He examines the "modern" compulsion of the poet "to justify his writing poetry at all." This is followed immediately by a compressed reference to Rimbaud: "The Rimbaud Myth—the tale of a great poet who ceases writing, not because, like Coleridge, he has nothing more to say, but because he chooses to stop—may not be true, I am pretty sure it is not, but as a myth it haunts the artistic conscience of this century."[34] The point is a subtle one. Auden proceeds, by reference to different cultures' understanding of the sacred and the profane, to an analysis of what he describes, adapting Coleridge, as the sacred and profane kinds of imagination, and of the role of art:

> The impulse to create a work of art is felt when, in certain persons, the passive awe provoked by sacred beings or events is transformed into a desire to express that awe in a rite of worship or homage, and to be fit homage, this rite must be beautiful. This rite has no magical or idolatrous intention; nothing is expected in return. Nor is it, in a Christian sense, an act of devotion. If it praises the Creator, it does so indirectly by praising His creatures—among which may be human notions of the Divine Nature. With God as Redeemer, it has, so far as I can see, little if anything to do. . . . In poetry the rite is verbal; it pays homage by naming.[35]

This passage could stand as epigraph to Walcott's works. His sensibility is very much in this mold, seeing the act of naming as a rite for the race, undertaken by a few (Auden's "certain persons") and motivated by homage: the aspiration, as he puts it in *Omeros,* to "give those feet a voice."[36] The claiming of special status that the assumption of the mantle of artist entails is counterbalanced by the self-abasement of homage, the dedication of the self to the rite. The artist can thus defend him/herself against charges of self-overvaluation. Auden's title *The Dyer's Hand* suggests both a high valuation of poetry as a craft that "colors" the world and the way in which its practitioners are "marked" by their craft. Walcott, however, writes, "the bright water could not dye his hand / any more than poetry." There is an implicit allusion here also to Shakespeare's *Macbeth,* with its symbolic idea of indelible blood-guilt staining the murderer's hand.[37] The idea of an expressionist nature, accusing the guilty by demonstrating to them the "horror" of what they are responsible for—the imagined reddening of the water with the blood of Africans, sacrificed to the colonial project—is revealed as just a fantasy. But the poem ironizes its own project in parallel, with an acknowledgment that it too is incapable of marking the guilty (echoing Auden's sentiment in "In Memory of W. B. Yeats" that "poetry makes nothing happen"). The complex implication would seem to be that the only guilt that is morally productive is not that which is allocated but that which is self-assumed. In Christian ethics, only the sinner can say "mea culpa." The progress of the poem's agonistic thought is inexorably toward the fortunate traveler's self-accusation and implicitly toward the poet's "mea culpa," inviting that of the reader.

"The Fortunate Traveller" is also intertextual in other ways. In particular it is, as it were, Walcott's *Waste Land,* responding to the form, the cultural pluralism, and the apocalyptic metaphysics of Eliot's poem (itself a response to the Conrad).[38] The relationship with the Conrad is explicit; that with the Eliot implicit, though profound. Like the earlier works, Walcott's poem addresses the great ethical questions of social and personal responsibility, but it shifts the ground of social critique from Conrad's imperialism and Eliot's materialism to the neocolonialism of global capitalism, the system that ensures that in the latter part of the twentieth century the majority of the world's people stay hungry. It resembles the Eliot also as a philosophical exploration of the modern condition, perceived as atheistic, to which the poet posits a reaffirmation of spiritual values. The shape and scope of both narratives is broadly similar, although there are major differences of style and treatment. Both are small-scale epic poems, in the epyllion tradition, subdivided into unequal sections. Eliot begins, like Walcott, with a season (spring becomes winter in the Walcott), in a different language milieu in Europe, and moves to England. Each poem juxtaposes the English imperial center of London and the Thames, where a history of empire is remembered (as in the Conrad), with other rivers and other warmer climates. In both, a desert landscape is evoked, but in the Eliot there is a turning east to a different river, the Ganges, and to different spiritual traditions, those of Hinduism and Buddhism (a development of the Conradian presentation of Marlow as a Buddha figure). Walcott's equivalent is to suggest the archaic religious practices of early European communities, of "savages [who] dyed our pale dead with ochre." Both use a range of narrators, and both make extensive intertextual allusions, including quotations, the most prominent being from ancient sacred texts. Each poem evidently intends the newness of its meanings to be inserted into a grand narrative, the intricate, extensive, and diverse discourse of Western culture. Eliot's equivalent of apocalypse is couched in orientalist terms (with its Sanskrit invocations), but Walcott keeps the religious resonances of his poem firmly within the Christian tradition. Most significantly, however, he follows Eliot in going beyond the Conrad's threat of apocalypse to a promise of peace.

This is delivered not in "The Fortunate Traveller" itself but in the volume's concluding poem, which parallels the development of Eliot's to a closure in the mantra "shantih," the Vedic invocation of peace. The movement to resolve the negative in the positive is powerfully realized in *The Waste Land.* When "The Fortunate Traveller" is read in sequence with its following poem it displays a similar movement, "The Season of Phantasmal Peace" seeming to complete the preceding poem's radically unconcluded thought. Walcott's lead poem, extending Eliot's references to a literature of revenge tragedy, ends on a minatory apocalyptic note, addressed to the world's fortunate travelers but not enacted. Where it concludes with the threat of vengeance on the guilty, "The Season of Phantasmal Peace," however, functions as a coda enacting redemptive relief. Because the two poems unfold such a close dynamic relationship, they will be considered here in tandem, as if a diptych.

Like Eliot's, Walcott's poem is enigmatic and intricately allusive, and, like his, its surface delivers images strong enough to support that burden of intellectualism. Walcott, like Eliot, anatomizes the soul of Europe in his time (a project that demands complexity) and finds great guilt, but where Eliot's concern at a godless age is explored particularly through allegories of problematic personal relationships, Walcott (while hinting at the narrator's relationship with the Margo figure) moves the moral issue from individual guilt to the collective failure to distribute resources equably and to recognize the full humanity of others (these are also the Conradian twin targets, the political wrong enabled by the cultural error). Walcott's Kurtz figure is alive and well and traveling first class. In a radical revision of *Heart of Darkness,* this "Kurtz" brings his northern guilt to the South for sanctuary among the innocent. Conrad's focus on the discourses that mythify power as benign is adapted by Walcott to a revolutionary reading of the power of language. As the poem unfolds, he invests the phrase "the heart of darkness" with different meaning not once but twice, demonstrating the renewability of culture, which could lead the transformation of social relations. Eliot offers "the heart of light" as counter to the Conradian phrase, but Walcott takes on the much more radical project of disclosing the arbitrariness of the bond between signifier and signified, and the open-endedness of language, always open to metamorphosis.

Like Eliot, Walcott is drawn to the early modern period of English literature, that of the Elizabethans and Jacobeans. Walcott's poem foregrounds its title, "The Fortunate Traveller," voicing a class-privileged variant with obvious irony: "One flies first-class, one is so fortunate." The reader is distanced from the speaker's clearly evoked class-signifying orality in the same way that Eliot distances his reader from his aristocratic reader-traveler, Marie, by the tone of her speaking voice: "I read, much of the night, and go south in the winter." Walcott's title is, however, an ironization of Thomas Nashe's *The Unfortunate Traveller,* published in 1594, which uses a fictional journey to convey in satiric vein a loveless and godless approach to life through the persona of Jack Wilton, its anarchic hero.[39] Walcott exposes the moral subterfuge of Nashe's title: the details of the story show that rather than being subject to misfortune, Wilton is as much oppressor as oppressed. It may be, too, that Walcott has particularly in mind H. F. B. Brett-Smith's 1927 edition of the narrative, which compares Nashe's picaresque hero with "the little Spaniard of Tejares, the first *picaro* of literature," emphasizing their difference, but in terms that resonate with the themes of "The Fortunate Traveller." The prototype, Lazaro, "servant in turn to many masters and starved by them all, spends the earlier part of his life in a miserable conflict with hunger, and the latter in a replete and greasy satisfaction." Nashe's protagonist, however, is different, suffering cash-flow problems rather than poverty.[40] Like Walcott's protagonist, Nashe's is, in fact, "fortunate," particularly when set against those in real misfortune. By using Nashe in this way, Walcott displays how the Western elite has for at least four centuries appropriated the rest of the world as cultural tour and has indulged in self-pity when it should have been showing pity to others.

Where Conrad evokes the Elizabethan age at the start of *Heart of Darkness* as an age of adventurers, Walcott, more like Eliot, revisits less its history than its culture—in particular, its theater of tragedy. Eliot alludes in *The Waste Land* to Shakespeare's Cleopatra, to Webster (several times), to Middleton, and to Kyd. Walcott, in parallel, implies Shakespeare's Macbeth (in the idea of the guilt-reddened hand) and several times invokes Webster; Walcott's fortunate traveler is not just the person with the privilege of the plane ticket but is also the generic figure of the intellectual voyager, the artist and the scholar. He is the "Sussex don" whose subject is Jacobean drama with its "anxieties," a man who would know Nashe's *Unfortunate Traveller.*[41] The freedom to enjoy such tragedies as Webster's is, the poem suggests, a luxury.

A culture of tragedy can, however, produce a collective pathology. The poem invites a comparison of the enacted cruelty of such drama with the acted-out barbarism of Nazism, which it links to the atheistic heroics of Nietzschean tragic philosophy. Webster's plays' accelerating movement toward tragic closure, with its cathartic effect, is implicit in the poem's climax: "The drawn end comes in strides." The poem in fact mimics the drama: the mood of existential dread at its conclusion is modeled on Webster's, and its address to white guilt seems an implicit echo of his title, *The White Devil,* a revision of Conrad's redeployment of European culture's traditional association of devils with blackness. The polarities of Webster's moral landscape—the unscrupulous ambition of Flamineo in *The White Devil* at the opposite end from the Duchess in *The Duchess of Malfi,* who wished only to love without class and was sacrificed to power—make for a drama of exquisite pathos at the prospect of damnation. It is also a theater of revenge. In the Italian tradition, honor demands that the individual wreak vengeance on the one who has done him wrong, and the Italianate plays of Webster take what we might with hindsight call a Gothic satisfaction in pursuing the logic of this imperative to its bloody conclusion. Importantly, however, Walcott's poem stages the Two-Thirds World's demand for justice and for vengeance against the rich world but closes with the nemesis threatened rather than enacted. It thus defers to the biblical injunction that vengeance is a divine prerogative, although it uses the moral terror that its threat creates. Here, once more, nature is the force outraged by human immorality, and implicitly the potential avenger: the "drawn sword" along the length of the beach is a figure for the gleaming length of a breaking wave, but it does not destroy, its apocalypse deferred. The refusal to incorporate revenge in the poem, however, has major implications for its ethical exploration of justice as against mercy, privileging the latter.

The Madonna figure of Webster's duchess ("I loved my Duchess" says Walcott's narrator) is a beacon of love in the morally benighted landscape of *The Duchess of Malfi,* murdered with a plea for mercy on her lips.[42] The poem's evocation of this pathos in the Haitian gecko/child's plea, "Mercy, monsieur. Mercy," is recalled in the line about the Duchess, the indulgence implicit in the Webster's mood of high tragedy exposed by the flatness of Walcott's following sentence: "Then I saw children pounce / on green meat with a rat's ferocity." Webster's duchess begs her murderer not to forget her son's "syrup for his cold," but Haiti's children, scandalously, four centuries later, have no access even to food fit for consumption, much less medicine. Can tragedy be entertaining as fiction to those who are alert to the real tragedy in the world, the poem seems to ask.[43] The crux of the poem is thus enlarged. It becomes clear that it is not only about the conjunction of money and morality but about the conjunction of the world and art. The attention is pinned to the difficult question of the responsibility of art: if it makes possible a world in which pity is exercised in response to fictional tragedy, rather than life—in which the privileged are moved more by Webster than by real suffering, and pity is another titillation rather than a spur to action—it must be changed. The aestheticization of tragedy that has characterized European culture since ancient times is identified as a key moral problem, conditioning Western minds to an acceptance, even a glorification, of suffering. Western culture sees the tragic hero as noble, and courageous sacrificial death is exalted. Walcott's poem questions this aesthetic, exposing its historical role as enabler of atrocities and oppression and raising instead the exemplar of the southern cultures, based not on tragic but on comedic relations between people, where myths of redemption and healing prove of stronger appeal than myths of violent sacrifice.

Finally, by situating his poem against such texts, Walcott secures and validates an aesthetic, enabling himself to match the high-flown tone of their metaphysical and poetic drama. He attempts the "high style," disregarding "the prevailing conviction among poets and readers that eloquence is no longer possible," says James Atlas, while Denis Donoghue characterizes Walcott's tone here as "dangerously high for nearly every purpose except that of Jacobean tragedy."[44] The irony of such comments being intended as criticisms will not have been lost on Walcott, but it remains a difficulty that the poem is complicit in the aestheticization of suffering, which at another level is its target. In other words, the poem repeats the conflicted morality of the Conrad, in which the aesthetic undercuts the avowed politics.

The poem also has an implicit intertextuality with one by Robert Lowell, whom Walcott knew and admired, and whose death in 1977 is commemorated in his preceding volume, *The Star-Apple Kingdom*. Lowell's poem "Where the Rainbow Ends" has a related theme, cast also in an apocalyptic mold.[45] The spiritual quest of the narrator, an "exile," is for faith in love, "the dove of Jesus," in a world dominated by commercial exploitation. Boston is depicted ironically as a counterimage of the holy city, its materialism rampant. Walcott cues his poem as a kind of response to Lowell's by echoing Lowell's presentation of "the scythers, Time and Death" as "helmed locusts," saving his own death-bringing locust till the end of "The Fortunate Traveller." Lowell has several apocalyptic "Beasts"; as well as Time and Death, he gives "Hunger" a capital letter, and the "Scales, the pans of judgement rising and descending." The apocalyptic tone is resolved in the final image of redemption: the threat of justice, from which none can escape damnation, is replaced by the image from Genesis of the dove with the olive branch of forgiveness—the move from Revelation to Genesis (from last book of the Bible to first) enacting the redemption that enables the Christian to "begin again." Walcott places a "leather-helmed locust" at the end but follows it with another poem, "The Season of Phantasmal Peace," which corresponds to Lowell's ending. Lowell's use of standard Christian iconography in his resolution, however, is transformed by Walcott. The bird idea is common to both, but Walcott, prompted perhaps by Lowell's opening in a threatening, visionary image, "I saw the sky descending, black and white, / Not blue," inverts it in a great positive, of ascent. Walcott's two poems open out Lowell's in a (now partly secular) meditation that considers the prospect of justice as apocalyptic destruction—as it approaches at the end of "The Fortunate Traveller"—but then follows it with a separate proposition, of a redemption couched in untraditional imagery that transcends the particularities of religion. The figure of the fortunate traveler as flier has resonances in relation to both the bodily and the spiritual worlds. Like Joyce's figure of Dedalus, Walcott, whose earlier persona of Shabine had embarked in the vessel *Flight,* reverses Lowell's image of the earth-bound pilgrim to whom the dove descends, with one, not only of the modern air-traveler, but of the spiritual voyager, who eventually rises up to bliss.

The intertext presiding over the poem as a whole is, however, the Bible, which provides it with an epigraph from Revelation, the final book of the New Testament, also known as the Book of the Apocalypse (the term Coppola foregrounded in his film's title). Lois Zamora argues that apocalypse has a particular relevance to artists of the Americas, concerned to dramatize "the integral relation between private and social destiny"—the relation denoting epic, exemplified by the poem's concerns.[46] Walcott, however, turns to the Bible not only for apocalypse—the dramatization of judgment through imagery of violent destruction—but also for the parallel epiphany of paradise. In addition, "The Fortunate Traveller" quotes the well-known biblical letter of Paul to the Corinthians as part of its figuring of the opposition of justice to mercy and thwarts its movement toward vengeance with an assertion of its antithesis, love. The moral concerns of its politics thus mirror its metaphysical concerns. The persona of the fortunate traveler is an allegorical figure of particular social relations, but it is the state of his soul that exercises the poem, as much as the state of the world.

The part of the poem set in the Caribbean maps a locus of spirituality: it is "where the phantoms live." St. Lucia is characterized as a place of animist faith, perceived to be full of not (Germanic) ghosts but (French-inflected) phantoms. Conrad, who spoke French before he spoke English, also uses the word "phantom," of the starving Africans. The term links Walcott's longer poem with its sequel, which foregrounds in its title the unusual word "phantasmal" as part of the developing emphasis on questions of spiritual grace. The fortunate traveler is at first in dread of secular vengeance: "Now I have come to where the phantoms live, / I have no fear of phantoms, but of the real." The Caribbean is characterized as the abode of friendly spirits, as opposed to the scientific rationalism of the North. But the nocturnal meditation becomes a spiritual odyssey, addressing the dread of death, "thanatos." It is conceived in specifically Christian terms. The Jonah myth of the Old Testament has long been read as proleptic of the death and resurrection of Christ: in this exegesis, the whale is the engulfing death, from which Jonah, like Christ, is later disgorged. But the poem takes a different line: "Cetus," the word for the whale in the Latin of the Vulgate Bible (as expounded by Melville in his chapter on the mythology of the whale), "was Christ." The poem's firm statement echoes particularly Melville's American myth. The story of the urge to kill the great white whale, Moby Dick, is often read as a spiritual parable, reenacting the crucifixion. Walcott makes it seem also a political fable, in which (as in his play *Dream on Monkey Mountain*) the authority figure of whiteness—of white culture's hold on the self-image of black people—has to be sacrificed. In the poem, the blood-red sunset before the narrator's eyes expresses the ancient guilt, as if once more mankind has killed its god. But the spiritual exploration does not end there.

The sequence enacts the mythic pattern of renewal. The sentence that begins "[s]ince God is dead . . ." appears to be about to confirm atheism, but as it unfolds it achieves the opposite. The "heart of darkness," now, as it were, redeemed from the negative significance given it earlier in the poem, is given new, positive meaning, referring to the heart (as center of compassion) of dark-skinned people, construed from centers of power as "benighted" in ignorance. It is in those hearts that a more profound knowledge persists and that faith is kept alive—"it's in the heart of darkness of this earth / that backward tribes keep vigil of His Body." The image is of the watch over the newly dead, but the force of it is as in the Bible's story of the two dead witnesses of the apocalypse, whom the people will not allow to be buried.[47] In effect, by refusing to allow the idea of God's death, they keep him alive. Walcott's capitalization of "His Body" conveys his respect, in a traditional Christian way, but the inclusion of "deya" with "lampion," the little lamps of faith, in Hinduism and Catholicism respectively (both now naturalized to the Caribbean), shows the inclusiveness of his faith. Even the narrator (and by implication the poet), writing by the tourist hotel's "bedside lamp," is engaged in a rite that helps to keep God alive. What began as an apparent confirmation of atheism thus turns out to be a statement of faith. The "news" that is to be kept from the "blissful ignorance" of the watchers is the report, now glossed as a lie, that God is dead. The "backward" tribes' vigil over the divine body is thus the poem's central image of hope, and faith, the other two qualities (with charity) marked out in the Sermon on the Mount.[48] It occupies the place that in the Conrad delivers Kurtz's revelation of "the horror," followed by his death. The scene provides the final remaking of the Conradian phrase "heart of darkness," which is now invested with benign meaning: it is among the races victimized by white racism—who are the true "heart" of "darkness"—that faith and hope are to be found in abundance, and where miracles such as the exchange of death for life may be looked for.

Now the poem enacts a rising movement, like a resurrection. In a Dantesque vision, the climax of the poem's vermin imagery, famine's millions are imagined swarming toward the tree of life, as they would if they had wings. The sequence begins in a deliberately alienatory way, crawling, with "lice," moves on to the rain flies (which shed their wings), and then reverses the wing-shedding image in the agonizingly acute figure of human beings growing "from sharp shoulder blades their brittle vans" and flying to the object of their desire. This swarming of the starving to the tree of life gains meaning in the light of Revelation's description of the tree as provider of everlasting fruit to feed the faithful,[49] although another Caribbean text may also be implicit in the image of the rain flies (as with the Jean Rhys echo in the "roaches" figure), in that it seems to echo and invert a climactic trope in V. S. Naipaul's *In a Free State*. However, where the crushing of a cloud of white butterflies on a car windscreen in the Naipaul symbolizes the pointless waste of human life,[50] Walcott once again reinvests a similar signifier with an opposite signified: he changes it from tragedy to divine comedy, from death to life, although it remains a figure of desire, unrealized. This is not paradise, and the tree of life is not that in the holy city, but life in this world, denied the poor by starvation. The poem voices the call for justice, but in an elegiac tone: "ah, Justice! But fires / drench them like vermin, quotas / prevent them." The insect imagery is explained: this is a world where people are really killed like vermin by greed, elevated to a global system. The poem brings not only the fortunate traveler but its reader to self-disgust, in the acknowledgment that wherever there is real suffering, "we," the fortunate travelers, "turn away to read." The error, or sin, of valuing art above life is the subtlest target for a work of art. At the climax of the poem's quest to get the guilty to whisper their "mea culpa," it recognizes its impotence: "the bright water could not dye his hand / any more than poetry." The passage ends with a riddle. The "ordinary secret" that the river conceals at every sunset "until we pay one debt" is deliberately enigmatic. It hints, in association with "shroud," that the debt we must eventually pay is death, but the language is redolent of Christian metaphor, to do with the ransom of death by the divine sacrifice. If that is so, then the "ordinary secret" will be the proof of resurrection, the apparent extinction of the sun being always followed by its reappearance. This is perhaps confirmed by the scenario being linked to Rimbaud on the Nile, the home of the ancient Egyptian myth that the sun was swallowed every night by the sky goddess Nut, to be reborn from her in the morning. Even in articulating the tragic, the poem's encompassing philosophy refuses tragedy.

The final, fourth section of the poem, however, revisits the avenger's tone, with the threat of death paramount. Walcott leads the reader through this night of agonized meditation with his narrator, to a dawn like the last dawn of the condemned. It is evident that the moral self-examination of the night is central to the whole poem. In the manner of the Jacobean revenge play, the moment of death approaches, bringing with it the nemesis of divine judgment. The "spy" persona, who, using his superior vantage point, "screws down the individual sorrow," is no different from the poet or any other enjoyer of privilege: the poem reminds its readers that we should all fear the accusation that we have failed the Third World. The epigraph, with which the poem's intertextual relationship with the apocalypse was initiated, introduced the running trope of food through which the poem has addressed its political target, the global order of injustice. Now it returns as the third of the four horsemen of the apocalypse—famine—uniting the beginning with the end. Famine rides on a black horse, with scales for weighing grain and for justice, combining the twin concerns of the poem, material and ethical. The poem's "drawn sword" recalls the swords wielded in the biblical account by the second and fourth of the four horsemen of the apocalypse, war and death (although the sword is only one of the many kinds of death envisioned).[51] The emphasis on the sword, through its matching with the gleam of a breaking wave, enables the sense of an action always imminent, like the sword of Damocles as figure of divine vengeance, suspended, never falling. It models the radically unfinished chronicity of epic, as at the end of *Omeros,* with the sea "still going on." The poem thus withholds the threatened apocalypse.[52]

The third horseman finally proves to be the locust, an appropriate image of the ultimate threat of global famine. While being the creature most associated with famine in real life and in the Bible generally, the locust is also present in Revelation as one of the woes sent in divine vengeance after the opening of the seventh seal. Loosed from the abyss by the fifth angel, these are not like earthly locusts but are warhorses with human faces and women's hair. Led by a king known in Hebrew, Greek, and Latin as Abaddon, Apollyon, or Exterminator, they are to attack those without God's mark on their foreheads. The poem, however, clearly intends nature's "grasshopper," which brings famine, rather than the gold-crowned mythical locust of the apocalypse, which brings pain.[53] In the middle of the poem, empire was shown as locust, a multilayered figure of the terrible triple imperial abuses of political conquest, hypocrisy, and rape, committed symbolically on the female body of the land, a New World named after its flowers, by the also appropriately named conquistador, Ponce:

> I saw them far off, kneeling on hot sand
> in the pious genuflections of the locust,
> as Ponce's armoured knees crush Florida
> to the funereal fragrance of white lilies.

The act of love is here deformed into an act of death. The nexus between the poem's twin themes of empire and hunger is exposed: the imperialist strips both land and people as does the locust. The "darker" people are being cast in the role of sacrificial victims by the consuming whites who wish to play cannibal. The final locust is an inversion of this, suggesting nature may turn the tables by inflicting famine on the greedy, a figure of what is ironically often called "poetic" justice.

The overarching discourse of the dialectics of justice as against mercy is central to Christian thought. The book of Revelation gives terrifying images of justice as punishment for sin, clearing away the old corrupt order, as preparation for its delivery of the image of the City of God. But the poem's concluding lines quote also one of the best-known Christian texts of all, St. Paul's letter to the Corinthians, here in unfamiliar tone as a threatening chorus. The repeated phrase "and have not charity" reads as an urgent imperative (the tense that has its existence somewhere between present and future)—"and if you have not charity" taking on the force of "have charity!" What the biblical text teaches (and it follows after a reminder of apocalyptic judgment) is not only the core of Christian theology but a commonly held secular gospel, that love is paramount. Today the continuum of meaning in English usage between "love" and "charity" is increasingly weakening. In the poem, "charity" is used, as in the King James Bible, for "love," with an eye on its popular meaning, the giving of alms to the less fortunate. The world the poem describes, divided between the haves and the have-nots, is the product of a failure of "charity" in the strong sense, of love.

The poem's closing apocalyptic tone thus proves to be secular as well as religious, the threat of divine retribution represented in terms of the threat of starvation for all. Walcott now revisits Revelation for its particular chronotope, that of eschatology, in which the ending of everything is articulated. An accelerating sense of the fortunate traveler's impending personal end in death is staged, but it is clear that this is an allegory, that the real drama is collective and symbolic. The poem ends on the brink of an apocalypse in which the whole of history will be judged and in which the individual may be condemned for ever. It is a threatening ending, which haunts the imagination, as it is intended to do. The present tense, word order, assonance and repetition, and deliberate, leaping rhythm of "stalks / grasshopper: third horseman / leather-helmed locust" are meant to terrify. This political and metaphysical threat brings the poem-as-story to an end, demonstrating that there will be no hiding place for the greed-driven privileged. As the fortunate traveler has his refuge in the islands "found out," so the northern fortresses of Western and Eastern power blocks are also vulnerable. The threat the poem articulates is in terms of food shortages, caused by "natural" disasters such as the final "locust," but its representation of the "soft teeth" of pests destroying crops is not only a warning about the environmental impact of industrialized food production. The moral warning is Bible-inspired, that as you sow, so shall you also reap. The "invasion" by vermin, a running metaphor, is therefore a political allegory: the starving millions who are likened to rain flies swarming to the tree of life are here the eaters, who threaten the North's supplies. The world economy, in which the producers maintain prices by destroying food rather than distributing it to the hungry, is condemned in ringing tones: for "though you fire oceans of surplus grain" (now spoken in direct second-person address from the Third World to the rich world), the present economic order is unsustainable, both practically and morally.

"The Season of Phantasmal Peace," which follows "The Fortunate Traveller" and concludes the volume, also has its roots in a text of Revelation, but Walcott completely reconceives it. Revelation speaks of all the birds of the air being summoned by the angel of the sun to feast on the carrion of the armies of Satan (defeated by the first horseman).[54] Walcott assembles the birds for quite another purpose. In remaking the apocalyptic story, he also remodels the image in "The Fortunate Traveller" through which the persona expresses the most sinister yet seductively aesthetic philosophy: "I thought, who cares how many million starve? / Their rising souls will lighten the world's weight / and level its gull-glittering waterline." In the following poem, however, the essence of this image of rising and lightening is given exquisite expression in a new mode, as blessing, instead of damnable callousness. As in the reconstruction of the phrase "the heart of darkness" from a negative to a positive meaning, so here the negative expression of lack of pity is remade into an expression of great and tender concern, which expresses the central tenet of Walcott's philosophy, a belief in love. Although "The Fortunate Traveller" ends with the threat of divine vengeance, "The Season of Phantasmal Peace" models a benign paradisal vision.[55] It seems intended to be taken in tandem with "The Fortunate Traveller," since it carries forward the apocalyptic drama, using the biblical silence that follows the opening of the seventh seal, and ushers in the redeemed order of heaven. The relief offered in the sequel is profound. The darkness of the earth is contrasted with the upper realm of light, revising Conrad's schema one last time. The poem's lifting movement is an extraordinarily physical evocation of flight, and of transformation to weightlessness, figuring a visionary translation from body to spirit. The Bible's image of the heavenly realm as city is here translated into natural terms, as birds (not angels) lift the "wingless" up to the sky, leaving behind the perhaps irredeemable world beneath, with its urban "dark holes." In this poem, the previous poem's dialectics of justice and mercy are reconceived as "Love" (the capital letter indicating the Christian concept of divine love), the only thing "brighter than pity." The binary symbolism of climate in "The Fortunate Traveller" is now transformed, the world's mutability translated to divine changelessness, "Love, made seasonless," an elevation of the tropical climate to metaphysical symbol.

But the poem offers only a glimpse of this possibility. The epiphany lasts for "one moment" of apocalyptic time, in which things are held, not reeled back as in "The Star-Apple Kingdom" (Walcott's earlier engagement with a poetics of apocalypse).[56] The poem and the volume end on an exquisitely judged note of balance, between the depressing truth of degenerate human nature and the hopeful, encompassing truth of a greater compassion, in the acknowledgment that "for such as our earth is now, it lasted long." It thus returns its reader to the world of injustice and suffering, the "now" recording an acutely contemporary chronicity, as in Coppola's title, *Apocalypse Now.* It seems that like the previous poem this too is a response to Nietzsche, who declared that mankind had killed God, and wrote, "God is dead; but considering the state the species Man is in, there will perhaps be caves, for ages yet, in which his shadow will be shown."[57] Walcott includes the "dark holes" of human habitation but lifts away the Nietzschean "shadows" to reveal a realm of "phantasmal light," before reinscribing the world's degenerate reality. The poem therefore concludes its Dantesque vision (redolent of Canto XXXIII of the *Paradiso*) in a resumption of the ethical project of the preceding poem, its impetus of desire for bliss reconnected to sociopolitical reality. The unspoken admonition haunting the symbolic silence is that to realize the vision we must first change the world.

This brings my argument back to the start of "The Fortunate Traveller" and its dedication to Susan Sontag, referring, I think, to her essay "The Death of Tragedy."[58] In the late-twentieth-century world, she says, the "modern dilemmas of feeling, action, and belief are argued out on a field of literary masterpieces." Walcott's poem seems to take this as its prompt. Reflecting on the relations between tragedy and a Christian philosophy, Sontag argues that the "moral adequacy of the world asserted by Christianity is precisely what tragedy denies." She notes Brecht's didacticism, as we may note Walcott's. Exposing how we turn away to read is Walcott's didactic strategy to make his reader aware of the moral evasions art (particularly tragic art) can foster: "modern man lives with an increasing burden of subjectivity, at the expense of his sense of the reality of the world," says Sontag. This could have been written "for" the poem, rather than the other way around. The paradox is that Walcott can attempt his moral consciousness-raising only in the very form that is deeply implicated in the problem: literature. The challenge is to make the self-absorbed act of reading so moving an experience that it returns the reader to reality with a new commitment to respond to such "tragedy" as the Third World's starving. Walcott would probably take issue with Sontag's making the "moral adequacy of the world" a tenet of Christian faith. For the politically and ethically engaged artist who is also a believer, the task is to deconstruct the world's moral *in*adequacy at the same time as honoring the promise of redemption. The resulting ambivalence need not be a mark of inner contradiction: Walcott's crystal of ambiguities denotes a both/and situation, not an either/or incompatibility.

It is as if "The Fortunate Traveller" represented a kind of extremity for Walcott. With its quasi-dramatic sequence and the intense reductiveness of its web of cultural reference, it is the culmination of his experiments, since the completion of *Another Life,* to find a new form of extended poem. Although all the longer poems of the volume use literary allusion, the intertextual method reaches a *ne plus ultra* here, an arcane sophistication that might seem counterproductive but that on reflection delivers a condensed signifying reachable no other way. He counters the critics' tendency to co-opt him, pejoratively, to a politics of mimicry by pointing out, "mimicry is an act of imagination, and in some animals and insects, endemic cunning."[59] The almost Machiavellian strategy in this poem could perhaps be described as a version of shibboleth: only cultural insiders will be able to decode the message, but by the same token they identify themselves as the guilty. It is a high-risk strategy. Even those who "understand" at one level may remain blind at another, for there is still a tendency to read works with a high degree of aesthetic elaboration and self-awareness as necessarily apolitical. "The Fortunate Traveller," if read aright, demonstrates the untenability of this assumption. Yet it would be wrong to imply that the poem is impenetrable, when its surface is constantly hauntingly memorable. But for Walcott, a simple statement of pathos—as in James Berry's contemporary poem on the theme of Third World starvation, "Fantasy of an African Boy," which won the British National Poetry Competition in 1981 (and Walcott often deploys intertextuality with other Caribbean texts)—is no longer enough, a tougher stance seeming necessary to jolt the complacency of the privileged reader.[60]

His new theme of exile in this volume, conveyed through the persona of the fortunate traveler, is tinged with guilt and grief at the loss of a better place, for Walcott, in self-imposed exile, does not shed the Caribbean as poetic subject, despite the *congé* tone of formal leave-taking characterizing "The Schooner *Flight*" but is, if anything, closer to the shamanic responsibility: "The tribe requires of its poets the highest language and more than predictable sentiment."[61] More self-consciously its spokesman, he shoulders the task of pricking the moral conscience of the fortunate, coming nearer than ever in "The Fortunate Traveller" to righteous anger—"saeva indignatio"—on behalf of the Third World, but his moral quest to cry "J'accuse" to the North on behalf of the South cannot in the end escape reinscribing the Christian imperative of mercy, and the personal odyssey that leads him to a tormented acknowledgment of complicity in guilt leads him also to the hope of grace. The revelation delivered at the core of the poem, the inversion of Kurtz's "horror" to the act of faith in keeping God alive, alters the poem's apocalyptic project, its impetus toward vengeance. The faith the poem shows still surviving in the "heart of darkness" (now remade as a positive) is, above all, a faith in divine mercy, extended, of course, to the guilty. The equivalent of Marlow's "lie" to the Intended in *Heart of Darkness* is the poem's great final "truth": that its threat of revenge can be no more than a threat, for ultimately redemption is available to all, whether of South or North. Finally, the threat of nemesis has to be translated into nature's terms, the ecological disaster of global famine, because the greedy materialists of the North (significantly the USSR[62] as well as the United States), the fortunate travelers whose moral self-examination it seeks, would mostly repudiate any transcendental notions of theocratic justice. The poem makes an angry protest at injustice and at the failure of compassion. In Walcott's near despair, art remains the last hope:

> I'm saying that what we absorb daily as human beings in the twentieth century is that we absorb massacres, we absorb earthquakes, we absorb genocide. And we absorb it through the media. It isn't that one is more callous, but there is some kind of terrible indifference that goes on. . . . We invent a language that covers the idea of pity. We have an absolutely Orwellian condition now of language . . . what we say about famine in Ethiopia is "My God, weren't they starving last year? You mean they're starving again this year? Does that mean another benefit?" . . . "l'homme moyen"—the average man or average woman—just takes that as part of daily life, and that is terrifying . . . art is perhaps the only chance we still have left to find that compassion.[63]

Once more, a problem constituted and perpetuated in a discourse is seen as best addressed in a counterdiscourse. The intertextual method is a mythopoeic engagement with the world of language. But again, Walcott's ideological strategy is double. He not only deconstructs the prevalent failed discourse with his ironizing narrative, he makes the gift of a positive image, as something to aspire to,[64] for the other abiding figure of the poem is of the good people of the South, who, despite their material poverty, are rich in the things that matter most and can teach the mean-spirited and tragedy-oriented North about the value of faith, hope, and love.

8

"The Theatre of Our Lives"

Founding an Epic Drama

Antonio: His word is more than the miraculous harp.
The Tempest, II.i.90

From his earliest days as an artist, Walcott's vision of a Caribbean aesthetic led him not just to epic poetry but to epic drama, the topic of this study's final chapters. First it may be useful to pause on the thinking behind his theater practice (revisiting some questions of ideology mapped in the first half of the book). That practice has much in common with Brecht's concept of epic theater (investing the term with a deliberately antiheroic meaning), but Walcott has developed Brechtian ideas in his own personal and particularly Caribbean way. As a term from classical literature, epic is associated first with poetry; in the Western tradition it has not been usual to apply it to drama. The plays of Shakespeare, for instance, are usually classified as comedies, tragedies, and some hybrids between these two categories variously known as romances, tragicomedies, and histories, not epics, although a number of the plays might be called epic. The way plays such as *Antony and Cleopatra* or *Coriolanus,* for instance, deal with the connection between the individual and the collective invites such a term (Cleopatra's private desires, for instance, are carefully shown drawing her country's political fortunes in their wake). Adaptations, such as that of the Antony and Cleopatra story, to the modern technology of film, adaptations that invite a populist label of "epic," underline the complex relationship between epic and romance. Both tend to be concerned with nonmimetic representation—with narrative remote from everyday life—but for different ends: where the objective of romance is escape from reality, the objective of epic is the reintegration of the reader-spectator into the real political world. The unusual combinations of effect Walcott has sought in some of his plays have led them sometimes to be regarded—and dismissed—as romance, when, if they had been understood as epic in intent, they might have earned a different kind of attention and respect.

Where epic poetry, associated with the classics, had, in the European tradition, acquired an aura of remoteness from the ordinary people, the term "epic" in this century has been repopularized through its application to the new art of film. From the earliest days of cinema, the designation of epic was attached to certain kinds of drama with an ambitious scope of representation, usually of events regarded as originating the contemporary nation or cultural group, such as Griffith's *Birth of a Nation* made in 1915, which Woodrow Wilson likened to "writing history with lightning,"[1] or the films of Eisenstein, narrating the key events of the Russian Revolution. The term "epic" was subsequently applied to the stage: Brecht promoted the idea of an epic theater,[2] borrowing Eisenstein's concept of the new style of representation—his montage approach, in which each episode could signify independently, and his provocation of the audience to think and act rather than to empathize.[3] After reading Marx's *Capital* in 1926, Brecht saw him as the ideal audience for his drama.[4] He rejected the aesthetic of psychology, demanding an intellectual response more in tune with sociology and philosophy: "The sociologist is the man for us," he wrote; "This is a world and a kind of drama where the philosopher can find his way about better than the psychologist."[5] In an early attempt to summarize his concept of epic theater, Brecht wrote:

> The essential point of the epic theatre is perhaps that it appeals less to the feelings than to the spectator's reason. Instead of sharing an experience the spectator must come to grips with things. At the same time it would be quite wrong to try and deny emotion to this kind of theatre. It would be much the same thing as trying to deny emotion to modern science.[6]

This is a crucial qualification: Brecht's idea of epic is not anti-emotion, but against unthinking emotion, the kind that bolsters the status quo by suppressing critical thought. The emotion that results from full political consciousness—the kind, for instance, that Brecht seeks to provoke with Mother Courage's silent scream—he saw as altogether different.[7]

Brecht's "anti-metaphysical, materialistic, non-Aristotelian drama," which sought to teach the spectator a new "practical attitude, directed towards changing the world," was much discussed in the 1950s when Walcott was grounding himself as a dramatist and director.[8] The anti-mimetic stance was one that Walcott's early drama reflected, although some of his more recent plays have returned to a more conventional Aristotelian approach. In Brecht's phrase, "the Aristotelian play is essentially static; its task is to show the world as it is. The learning-play ["Lehrstück"] is essentially dynamic; its task is to show the world as it changes (and also how it may be changed)."[9] From his early plays on, Walcott explored different models of didactic theater, ranging from the dialectical materialist episodes of *Drums and Colours* to the generic and symbolic approach of the folk morality play in *Ti-Jean and His Brothers*. His objective has certainly been to change the world, but where Brecht's notion of change is pinned firmly to the relations of production in the materialist world—to the political order—Walcott's has always been concerned primarily with the symbolic order that validates the political order. He has identified the most pernicious injustice suffered by his people as one of cultural representation, of which material injustice is a product. To address the latter without the former would be pointless. He therefore, while in exemplary Brechtian manner drawing attention to the means and control of production (for instance, by writing the cocoa-dancers into the story of *The Last Carnival*), focuses on key moments of cultural production, transmission, and interaction. Walcott's equivalent to a Brechtian symbolic moment—such as that in *Mann ist Mann*, in which a spurious "elephant" is marketed as a commodity—is perhaps a scene such as that in *The Last Carnival*, in which a mimetic Eurocentric tableau re-presents the past hegemony of European art in a deconstruction of the indigenous creole culture of Trinidad in 1970. Where Brecht lays bare the bones of materialism, Walcott exposes first the skeletons of *culture*.

Walcott has never sought a theater of elaborate mimetic effect, and even when representing what Brecht would have called bourgeois drama (in some of his musicals or in plays such as *Remembrance* or *Viva Detroit*), he does so for political ends, as Brecht does in *The Threepenny Opera*.[10] As with the public response to this play, the tendency of some spectators to read his plays within a dominant type rather than as an anti-type is a problem common to much ironic representation. Like Brecht, Walcott typically gives trenchant exposure to the materialist causes of action, taking on capitalism principally in its imperialist manifestation, and he is less interested in the Freudian psychology of his characters as individuals than in their interaction with society, both as products of the social order and as transmitters of it. However, in a theatrical tradition still largely wedded to mimesis, the unconventional nature of the effects sought can be alienatory without being productively so, as Brecht intended. As Brecht was acutely aware, to appreciate epic theater, the spectator needs to become an "expert," schooled in "complex seeing," a perceptiveness blunted by the linear manipulation of the spectator in conventional theater, who is led through a carefully controlled sequence of responses.[11]

Walcott parts company with Brecht, however, and with the modern Western tradition in general, over his metaphysical strategy. Brecht's antimetaphysical position reflects the scientific rationalism of the modern West, but for Walcott the refusal of mimesis as method entails its replacement with a symbolic method drawing on myth. Like Brecht, he draws on mythic forms such as the folk fable, but unlike Brecht he does not just use them dialectically but takes the metaphysical seriously. In the act of disenchantment, he re-enchants, with the fundamental mythic gest (to borrow Brecht's term) of the refusal of death in a return to life, enacted as a recurrent motif in his drama. As a result, his drama is ultimately not Brechtian, although it draws on Brecht's ideas, nor is it traditionally mimetic. It offers a new model: a postcolonial theater that is politically oriented but reconnects to drama's ancient root in sacred ritual in order to reach its ideological objective.

Although Brecht subsequently replaced the term "epic" with "dialectical," in response to persistent misunderstandings, he did not significantly alter his meanings. Elizabeth Wright sums up what his epic theater signified:

> By "epic," Brecht is broaching a definition which transcends the traditional concept of the genre. The epic (*das Epische*) is not only not tied to a particular genre, but it can also be found in other genres, taking with it its connotations of narrative distance. The drama thereby surrenders the old characteristic quality of suspense, together with its concomitant effect of luring the audience into purely subjective identifications and the final granting of emotional release. Instead the stage begins not only to narrate but also to comment and criticize from a viewpoint not necessarily tied to the immediate action.[12]

The theater of illusion was to be replaced by a new relation between drama and audience, the distance of "Verfremdungseffekt" [alienation or estrangement] provoking the audience to think rather than feel, and in particular to think historically in order to make informed choices about action in the future. The past, particularly as conceived post-Foucault, becomes a primary subject: in Wright's phrase, "the re-writability of the text of history offers a model for the theatre."[13] Brecht regards the author not as originator but simply as someone who "produces from the materials of history."[14] Walcott, too, is concerned with representing history not only in his poems but also in his plays. Proceeding from a lively awareness of the role of the grand narratives, which ignored the existence of communities like his own and portrayed the past in order to maintain the hegemonic center, he began from his earliest days as a dramatist to write alternative histories for his own people, reflecting different starting points, choices, and assumptions. This takes place within a developing critique challenging the value of history as discourse; he deconstructs the dominant account, replacing the grand narrative with a socially aware local alternative—but then affirms that history is not as important as it claims to be. The apparent ambivalence is a dialectical strategy resulting in the mythic approach: to overemphasize history would be to lock the present to a tragic past and, disastrously, the future to revenge, when what he wishes to assert is the possibility of renewal and of fresh beginnings. In Christian terms, it connects with the difference between the ethic of justice in the Old Testament and the ethic of redemption in the New. While it invests in the ideal, it does not repeat the old utopianism of the bourgeois theater of illusion.

Myth and history have gone hand in hand in Walcott's dramatic works. Where some of his early drama, most notably *Drums and Colours,* shows a very Brechtian approach to history, Walcott was already developing his own style with the mythic folk play: both *Ti-Jean and His Brothers* and *Drums and Colours* were first performed in 1958. As his career has progressed, he has never entirely abandoned the history play, his most recent one, *The Ghost Dance,* integrating the two dimensions of history and myth to an unprecedented degree. Walcott has gone beyond Brecht in understanding the role of myth in society and its radical potential in art. Walcott, like Brecht, believes in the transformative power of art, but unlike Brecht he regards that power as essentially metaphysical.

This has implications for kind and form. Brecht used comedy for social change: for him, according to Wright, the "target of comedy is the historical irrelevance and inauthentic modes of living of a society stuck with an outworn set of beliefs long after history has moved on."[15] His perception that the comic process could be introduced anywhere led to his refusal of comedy and tragedy as absolute categories of narrative. In his own practice as a playwright, he blurred the genres, as Wright explains, allowing the historical context to determine whether a sequence of events was to be regarded as comic or tragic. The categories, in Wright's terms, "are not to be regarded as mutually exclusive, as essences which can be reconciled, as in tragicomedy, but as something intertwined in an ambivalent way: the comic combines with the serious when their connection with social and historical realities is revealed. The literary separation of them into two genres is itself an ideological act."[16] This is particularly helpful in an evaluation of Walcott's practice as dramatist. He, too, typically intertwines comic and tragic elements in an ambivalent way, for ideological reasons, as the plays considered below demonstrate. He identifies the predominance of comedy as a feature of his cultural milieu. His 1970 essay "What the Twilight Says," which delineates a marked sense of his separation from the actors and the mass of the people, explores his relationship with his company and through them with the culture of his community, describing how his actors were "humanists" whose "genius is not violent, it is comic." Rehearsing Genet's *The Blacks,* they "cannot enjoy its mincing catamite dances of death," because "their minds refuse to be disfigured." Yet Walcott as their director wishes to lead them into a "truly tragic joy."[17] But he differs from Brecht in that his ideological position is not tied to the materialist world. For him, the world of "reality" matters not "in vacuo" but because of its connection to a transcendent metaphysical "reality." Philosophically, then, Brecht's works of skeptical rationalism are remote from the metafiction informed by Walcott's faith; but both, as artists and socialists, use a similar practice in devising theater pieces that will, they hope, help to transform the world.

Brecht's lasting importance, according to Wright, derives from his diversification of theatrical language, using folk forms and language to dialectical ends: he "de-literalized the language of the stage, drawing upon the dialects of his own region in order to create a new language of the theatre that was neither purely regional nor purely classical."[18] The terms could be applied to Walcott's forging of a new language for Caribbean theater, which draws on the Creole continuum as well as on the whole literary tradition in English. His signal contribution has been to explore ways in which textuality can deliver simultaneously in the theater both the accessibility of informal language and the depth of poetry.

The founding of a theater is an act not only of great vision but of great willpower. As children, Derek and his twin brother, Roderick, had, like most children, been play-makers; as adults both became dramatists.[19] In a very small island, with a tiny, fragmented community and little access to formal theater, it would be difficult to overestimate the originality of such choices. What formal theater there was in the region was dominated by the Western tradition, with an indigenous regional theater barely budding. In the 1930s and 1940s, Marcus Garvey, C. L. R. James, and Roger Mais, among others, had initiated local drama with an ideological objective, as part of the anticolonial movement, but to two boys growing up in St.

Lucia in the 1930s and 1940s, these must have seemed remote, with films (mainly American) providing their only regular exposure to formal drama. But by 1994, according to Errol Hill, Derek had written thirty-eight dramas, Roderick twenty-six, with both of them writing musicals and screenplays alongside their stage plays.[20] Walcott, looking back from middle age, has written, "When one began twenty years ago it was in the faith that one was creating not merely a play, but a theatre, and not merely a theatre, but its environment."[21] The dream was that the theater was to build the society it would serve and which would sustain it.

The lead from the older generation had been crucial. The boys' mother, Alix Walcott, was a keen amateur actor who recited Shakespeare about the house.[22] The family's commitment to art had been beleaguered from the start, because it had to be asserted defensively against the island's disapproving Catholic majority:

> My mother's friends, those who had survived my father, had been members of an amateur dramatic group, some cultural club which had performed Shakespeare and given musical concerts, when my father was their "moving spirit.". . . Their existence, since most of them were from a religious minority, Anglican, Methodist, or lapsed Catholic, had a defensive, doomed frailty in that steamy, narrow-minded climate. Perhaps because of this they believed in "the better things of life" with a defiant intensity, which drew them closely together. Their efforts, since the pattern would be repeated for my brother and me, must have been secretly victimized.[23]

Where the lead of the parental generation is often resisted in the antiauthoritarian phase of adolescence, the boys were able to follow in their seniors' theatrical footsteps perhaps partly because these were already in an antiauthoritarian mode. Both twins went on to find themselves with early plays, selected to represent St. Lucia in the 1958 festivities for federation, banned by the Catholic Church: Derek's *The Sea at Dauphin* was considered antireligious, and Roderick's *Banjo Man* immoral. As a result, the St. Lucia Arts Guild withdrew from the festival, although Derek's play *Drums and Colours* became its centerpiece.[24]

But more importantly, as well as being surrounded by a small group of educated people committed to active drama and knowledgeable about world theater, the boys identified with the island majority, who in their daily lives engaged in informal drama, in their storytelling, their entertainments, and their community rituals: "being poor," said Walcott, "we already had the theatre of our lives."[25] A band of evangelists surrounded on a street corner were "the shadows of his first theatre," as was the Christmas masquerade of the devil and his imps who "would perform an elaborate Black Mass of resurrection at the street corners."[26] This is where Brecht said his theater was to begin: "The epic theatre wants to establish its basic model at the street corner, i.e. to return to the very simplest 'natural' theatre, a social enterprise whose origins, means and ends are practical and earthly"; but that street life in Walcott's experience was from the outset not just earthly but myth-inflected, bound up with his community's expression of spirituality, as his choice of examples demonstrates.[27]

St. Lucians lived a theatrical life, with "everything performed in public": "The theatre was about us, in the streets, at lampfall in the kitchen doorway, but nothing was solemnised into cultural significance."[28] Walcott has described it as a "simple schizophrenic boyhood" with its two lives, "the interior life of poetry, the outward life of action and dialect."[29] What the oral tradition offered was the example of spontaneous creativity to set against the literary tradition's notion of text. Narration exhibited a primary formalism, a primary theatricality:

> Best of all, in the lamplit doorway at the creaking hour, the stories sung by old Sidone, a strange croaking of Christian and African songs. The songs, mainly about lost children, were sung in a terrible whine. They sang of children lost in the middle of a forest, where the leaves' ears pricked at the rustling of devils, and one did not know whether to weep for the first two brothers of every legend, one strong, the other foolish. All these sank like a stain. And taught us symmetry. The true folk tale concealed a structure as universal as the skeleton, the one armature from Br'er Anancy to King Lear. It kept the same digital rhythm of three movements, three acts, three moral revelations, whether it was the tale of three sons or of three bears, whether it ended in tragedy or happily ever after. It had sprung from hearthside or lamplit hut door in an age when the night outside was a force, inimical, infested with devils, wood demons, a country for the journey of the soul, and any child who has heard its symmetry chanted would want to retell it when he was his own storyteller, with the same respect for its shape. The apparent conservatism of West Indian fiction, whether in fiction or in theatre, is not an imitative respect for moulds but a memory of that form.[30]

To a young dramatist with "a mind drenched in Elizabethan literature," to whom "the Jacobean style, its cynical, aristocratic flourish came naturally," the long-refined graces of the oral tradition with its simple, effective formalism offered a vital example.[31]

Fired by this twin heritage and the independence movement's politics, the young Derek Walcott saw the need for founding a local theater—first island-based and then regional—and from the outset conceived of his own role not only as a poet but as an initiator of drama. In 1950, he and his brother established the St. Lucia Arts Guild, which performed both canonical plays of world theater and new local drama by themselves and others. Derek was active with the undergraduate drama group while at Mona, the Jamaica campus of the then University College of the West Indies,[32] and in 1959 he founded the Trinidad Theatre Workshop, a group that met and rehearsed for seven years before making its first public performance.[33] Walcott remained dedicated to this group for twenty years. It was only after a personal crisis that he decided to make the move that most contemporaries with literary ambitions had made years before, the migration to a northern metropolis. After settling in Boston, he continued to involve himself regularly with playmaking, not only as a dramatist but as a director, both in America (for *The Ghost Dance,* for instance) and in the Caribbean, and he has made an occasional foray elsewhere to assist in the rehearsal of his work, for instance, residing at Stratford-on-Avon while *The Odyssey* was in rehearsal.

His life as a man of the theater has thus been central to his aesthetic project. Although it has rarely been his only activity (he has continually written nondramatic poetry and necessarily been involved in other activities such as his journalism for the *Trinidad Guardian* to support his family), it has been a crucial determinant on where the middle decades of his life were lived, and it came to represent a symbolic choice. Walcott's name became a byword among Caribbean artists for the possibility of remaining at home and becoming an artist. He was the living proof that to stay in the region did not have to mean sacrificing the chance of a wider reputation—although at the time there must often have been doubts as to whether, if he had gone to London or stayed in New York in the 1950s, his worldwide reputation might not have got under way earlier. He was ambitious, but from the beginning he was clear that his primary ambition was to create for the Caribbean. What he secured for himself by staying there was the continual renewal of his aesthetic commitment to the region, and to his epic project to create an art worthy of it. His sustained involvement in theater was vital to his staying in touch with the community at large; it prevented him from becoming a remote and mannered poet. He came to see the pathos of actors of his company who strove for what they called "better speech when theirs had vigour that was going out of English."[34]

Drama was central to Walcott's idea of a Caribbean aesthetic for several reasons. First, where written poetry required not only literacy but literary awareness and was an art that few would appreciate, drama could appeal to all the people regardless of educational opportunities, excluding no one. It could be a genuinely popular art form, which poetry in print would never be. The immediacy of shared performance—the orality of the language, the scope for sound of other kinds, particularly song, and the expressive potential of the visual element, via the human figure as actor, dancer, and musician in the milieu of setting and lighting—attracted Walcott as idealist and visual artist as well as wordsmith. The scenic design invited a dramatist with a highly developed visual sense to conceive of the staging as a vital signifier, intrinsic to the action. It lent itself naturally to symbolic expression. The text came into being with its role as visual sign part of the conception, not applied later by a design team, as in so much metropolitan theater. In addition, the cooperation of the performers and their presentation to a responding audience in the shared space of performance (whether in the open air or an enclosed space) offered a model of community, the kind of community which art itself could help to build. Even the creation of the drama's backbone, the text, participated in this collectivity, as the company of players developed the playwright's initial draft with him in rehearsal. The theater offered the experience of a shared (and radically unclosed) art, unparalleled in any other art form; only the theater united all the arts in a collectively produced display. It was also local and particular, made for the home community in a sense that the poetry was not. The poetry was an outreach art, a means of communicating first with the Caribbean community, isolated across the region, but also potentially with a worldwide readership, wherever English was understood, but the drama was conceived essentially for the Caribbean, couched in a verbal, visual, and symbolic language directed primarily to the insider.

This drama was to be epic in two senses. First, it was, in the Brechtian sense, to use nonmimetic methods to raise political awareness. Secondly, it was to perform the social role of epic poetry. The events of a cruel history and the discourse of imperialism had conspired to produce a people with low self-esteem and little regard for either their individual or collective identity; the task for the new art was to remedy that lack. As Walcott wrote: "Colonials, we began with this malarial enervation: that nothing could ever be built among these rotting shacks, barefooted back yards and moulting shingles; that being poor, we already had the theatre of our lives. . . . If there was nothing, there was everything to be made. With this prodigious ambition one began."[35] Epic poetry had been the worldwide form through which a people sustained a sense of their identity, but in the absence of a continuing ancient tradition of oral poetic performance, drama was the most crucial art form precisely because of its popular appeal. Walcott's focus, in his Nobel lecture, on the *Ramleela*—doubly epic as "the epic dramatization of the Hindu epic the *Ramayana*"[36]—draws the world's attention to a miraculous cultural survival from India to Trinidad of a community ritual, creolized and vigorous in its new location: "The performance was like a dialect, a branch of its original language, an abridgement of it, but not a distortion or even a reduction of its epic scale. Here in Trinidad I had discovered that one of the greatest epics of the world was seasonally performed, not with that desperate resignation of preserving a culture, but with an openness of belief that was as steady as the wind bending the cane lances of the Caroni plain."[37] It was a case not for nostalgia or elegy but for "celebrations of a real presence."[38] Walcott intends irony, of course, in his use of the phrase "I had discovered . . ."; discovery in the "New" World is an indication of prior ignorance rather than of innovation. The *Ramleela* had always been there, since the East Indians had come to Trinidad, just as the Americas were there before Columbus. He develops the irony: "I had recently adapted the *Odyssey* for a theatre in England, presuming that the audience knew the trials of Odysseus, hero of another, Asia Minor epic, while nobody in Trinidad knew any more than I did about Rama, Kali, Shiva, Vishnu, apart from the Indians, a phrase I use pervertedly because that is the kind of remark you can still hear in Trinidad: 'apart from the Indians.'"[39] It is a judicious reminder that the Western literary tradition has its roots in just such orally transmitted folk rituals and that the "European" tradition should be traced beyond Europe, to Asia. It is also a tart reminder that marginalization of one group by another is not confined to the old dominant cultures. What it shows above all is that the Antillean culture of today is a composite of anciently diverging cultures coming together once more.

There were other folk forms on which to draw. The folktales about Ti-Jean, which are part of the eastern Caribbean patois heritage, are adapted to the stage in Walcott's early play, *Ti-Jean and His Brothers*. His brother Roderick has used the St. Lucian festivals of the Rose and Marguerite rival groups in his drama.[40] The Trinidadian carnival is another public theatrical ritual that Derek Walcott has used on stage, but for him it is problematized by commercialization and state exploitation, resulting in commodification and debasement. In his intention as dramatist and director to "transform the theatrical into theatre,"[41] carnival is the prime example of Caribbean society's theatricality and has been accepted by many artists as the starting point for indigenous drama, but Walcott pinpoints carnival as a symbol of the rule of illusion that the Brechtian artist aims to destroy: "this was a society fed on an hysterical hallucination, that believed only the elaborate frenzy now controlled by the state. But Carnival was as meaningless as the art of the actor confined to mimicry."[42] He identifies the consequences for their theater: "as their society avoids truths, as their Carnival is a noise that fears everything, too many of the actors avoid the anguish of self-creation."[43]

As the basic figure for his study of Caribbean drama, Kole Omotoso juxtaposes Walcott's strictures about carnival with Errol Hill's claim that carnival offers the basis of a national theater, although with the disclaimer, "The history of Caribbean drama and theatre, and consequently its future, cannot be predicated on the opposite views of Errol Hill and Derek Walcott."[44] He contextualizes Hill's claim in relation to Eric Williams's rise to power in Trinidad and sets Walcott's remarks on carnival against the background of the then new phenomenon of ministers of culture supporting the "folk" arts (seen as entertainment) to the exclusion of the "serious" arts (such as Walcott's theater). He not only suggests that Walcott's position set out in the essay is a "bitter poetic lamentation" at the lack of official support—which is to reduce a serious discussion to a materialist level—he misrepresents Walcott's position as positing "the Caribbean-colonial condition which underlines its incapacity to create anything for itself."[45] Walcott in fact quotes the now notorious passage from Froude, which claims of the West Indies that there are "no people there in the true sense of the word, with a character and purpose of their own," in order to demonstrate the cultural hegemony of imperialism, which can shake the confidence of those trying to be the region's artists.[46] Caricaturing Walcott's argument, Omotoso concludes that it is "an extreme position which cannot be validated without doing grave injustice to the *oral* history of the Caribbean" and goes on to characterize Walcott's Trinidad Theatre Workshop as a "failure, in spite of what looks like a heroic effort," because it was "transplanting theatre as it was understood in the West into the Caribbean" and "ignores some important aspects of the expression of the play-consciousness of the Caribbean."[47] Hill's position is clear and straightforward and is well understood; Walcott's is complex, though not inconsistent, and is often misrepresented, though not often as seriously as here.

His remarks in "What the Twilight Says," far from being a repudiation of folk culture, come out of a lifelong commitment to its value. It is the appropriation by government of folk culture and its commercialization in the name of tourist attraction that Walcott so strenuously opposes; what then passes for folk culture he sees as essentially folk culture traduced. He addresses himself in a kind of meditation:

> You despise the banal vigour of a future, where the folk art, the language, the music, like the economy, will accommodate itself to the center of power, which is foreign, where people will simplify themselves to be clear, to be immediately apprehensible to the transient. The lean, sinewy strength of the folk dance has been fattened and sucked into the limbo of the nightclub, the hotel cabaret, and all the other prostitutions of a tourist culture: before you is the vision of a hundred Havanas and mini-Miamis, and who dares tell their Tourism Boards and Cultural Development Committees that the blacks in bondage at least had the resilience of their dignity, a knowledge of their degradation, while their descendants have gone both flaccid and colourful, covering their suffering with artificial rage or commercial elation?[48]

His grief for the lost integrity of the folk forms drives the attack: "Their commercialization is now beyond anger, for they have become part of the climate, the art of the brochure."[49] The hypocrisy of intellectuals who now "found values in [carnival] that they had formerly despised" and "apotheosised the folk form, insisting that calypsos were poems," is attacked for the dishonesty of the position espoused, not because the position itself is untenable. The "[W]itch doctors of the new left with imported totems" are opportunists, anathema to one who has a long track record in building art out of folk forms.[50]

Walcott's use of the term "hallucination" is part of a chain of recurrence designed to dominate the essay. "Hallucination" describes a way not only of seeing but of experiencing the world: it is a trope of transformation, but negatively coded, the "reality" that we infer from it, as its opposite, being presumed preferable. It is a dangerous illusion of the kind Brecht set out to destroy, bearing a complex relation to imagination and to art, as in Walcott's opening exploration of the twilight-transformed ghetto as "the gilded hallucinations of poverty . . . as if . . . poverty were not a condition but an art. Deprivation is made lyrical, and twilight, with the patience of alchemy, almost transmutes despair into virtue."[51] In such a context, the attack on carnival comes to seem very different from the polar opposite of Hill's faith in it. Motivated by a belief very close to Hill's, Walcott is in fact protesting against the appropriation of the folk forms to support the new hegemonies, as he makes clear:

> In these new nations art is a luxury, and the theatre the most superfluous of amenities. Every state sees its image in those forms which have the mass appeal of sport, seasonal and amateurish. Stamped on that image is the old colonial grimace of the laughing nigger, steelbandsman, carnival masker, calypsonian, and limbo dancer. These popular artists are trapped in the state's concept of the folk form, for they preserve the colonial demeanour and threaten nothing. The folk arts have become the symbol of a carefree, accommodating culture, an adjunct to tourism, since the state is impatient with anything which it cannot trade.[52]

Walcott saw that what was needed was a revolutionary art, not one that perpetuated the old illusions. If folk forms were used to prop up the colonial subservience, they had failed. If they were to meet Brecht's criteria, they must be used in ways that recovered their original energy. In using carnival in *Drums and Colours* and *The Last Carnival,* and in using the characters and forms of the folktale in *Ti-Jean and His Brothers,* Walcott was not using the folk arts for bourgeois ends; on the contrary, he was entering into their essence in order to make them signify as new.

With such folk elements, epic drama could also establish a popular mythology and could reconnect the people to self-knowledge and to pride by modeling history as not just a site of humiliation but as the locus of dignity, survival, and heroism. As John Berger observes, "A people or a class which is cut off from its own past is far less free to choose and to act as a people or class than one that has been able to situate itself in history."[53] But as Walcott saw it, for Caribbean people the past was a double-edged sword that could wound in unexpected ways and had to be handled with care.

Walcott's first choice of a subject for historical drama, suggested to him by his brother, was *Henri Christophe,*[54] written in 1949, which drew on the story of heroic revolution in the francophone Caribbean—which was in a sense his history directly as a St. Lucian—and which the Marxist writer and philosopher C. L. R. James had introduced as drama to the region. His choice also indicated a vision of a regional identity that embraced the whole geographical area, extending across linguistic and political boundaries. It signaled that the symbolic moments of the region's history belonged to all of its inhabitants, regardless of their ethnic, cultural, or political identity. Also, by focusing on the region's direct legacy of the French Revolution, Walcott was in a sense sidestepping British rule, at that date still firmly entrenched in his homeland, thus subtly marginalizing the British history in the region, although of course his use of English as his artistic vehicle was an acknowledgment of that history. France, however, was not his topic; his subject was the heroic antislavery revolution of Haiti that resulted in the Americas' first republic. He has described how at the age of nineteen he was "drawn . . . to the Manichean conflicts of Haiti's history" out of a sense of identification and envy from his prerevolutionary St. Lucia: "The parallels were there in my own island, but not the heroes: a black French island somnolent in its Catholicism and black magic, blind faith and blinder overbreeding, a society which triangulated itself medievally into land baron, serf, and cleric, with a vapid, high-brown bourgeoisie."[55] The heroes were tragic figures to him then, in the mold of Webster's heroes with their magnificent decadence. Dessalines and Christophe were "men who had structured their own despair": "Their tragic bulk was massive as a citadel at twilight. They were our only noble ruins." They enacted a revolution against the plantocracy which was like a heresy, contaminated with the sin of pride. In a crucial parallelism, the forty-year-old Walcott describes himself as a young poet matching two tropes of power, secular and divine:

> He believed then that the moral of tragedy could only be Christian, that their fate was the debt exacted by the sin of pride, that they were punished by a white God as masters punished servants for presumption. He saw history as hierarchy, and to him these heroes, despite their meteoric passages, were damned to the old darkness because they had challenged an ordered universe. . . . Those first heroes of the Haitian Revolution, to me, their tragedy lay in their blackness. . . . Now one may see such heroes as squalid fascists who chained their own people, but they had size, mania, the fire of great heretics.[56]

If they failed, because of divine intervention to destroy their presumption, as he saw it then, they were heroes, though tragic ones. The later gloss on their fascism—"the corruption of slaves into tyrants"—was not how the nineteen-year-old saw it: if they had defied the old order, they deserved his admiration. His was a revolutionary desire; by modeling in his play the heroism of the Haitian Jacobins, to use James's term, he hoped to stir his own somnolent people to similar vision and courage. He tells how he apprenticed himself to the contemporary revolutionaries of French Caribbean origin: "the young Frantz Fanon and the already ripe and bitter Césaire were manufacturing the homemade bombs of their prose poems, their drafts for revolution."[57] But they were both "blacker" and "poorer," and he envied the clarity of their position, seeing his own as complicated, even compromised, by a bourgeois and mixed-race heritage. *Henri Christophe* was an important play, for Walcott and for the Caribbean. With its high style, its blank verse, and its history-given tragic closure, it demonstrated that the region's history could provide the theater with subjects of a high seriousness, a grandeur that was unfamiliar. The fact that the heroes in question were slaves who became statesmen meant that they subverted the usual (Aristotelian) notion of the "great" man as the focus for tragedy. Walcott chooses to quote from his play in the later essay; the passage he selects is that in which Christophe answers the Archbishop's imputation of his guilt before God with a statement of pride, ending: "I am proud, I have worked and grown / This country to its stature, tell Him that."[58] The evident admiration for the courage of the defier of authority is fundamentally metaphysical. As he says, "The theme has remained: one race's quarrel with another's God." Christophe's surviving citadel clinches it with a symbol: "a monument to egomania, more than a strategic castle; an effort to reach God's height. It was the summit of the slave's emergence from bondage. Even if the slave had surrendered one Egyptian darkness for another, that darkness was his will, that structure an image of the inaccessible achieved. To put it plainer, it was something we could look up to. It was all we had."[59] Christophe's moral stature is like that of Faust, or Milton's Satan. Although the Walcott of 1970 distances himself from the revolutionary power of the vision, it remains with him as the core epic struggle, of man against God, which, for Walcott, courts atheism but always returns to faith. Christophe prefigures a range of antiauthoritarian heroes in his plays, heretical challengers, culminating in Odysseus.

The Haitian Revolution was revisited by Walcott in his play for the inauguration of the West Indies Federation in 1958, *Drums and Colours*. It was, according to Omotoso, a "major achievement" particularly "given the time it was written": "The scope and leadership which this epic gives to the direction of West Indian theatre has not been equalled by another historical play from the West Indies."[60] Although written in the early 1980s, the substance of the claim is still valid. This was a play with a given historical program, commissioned to represent the region's past. Gordon K. Lewis has identified the peculiar difficulty of this: "There is no first principle of reference, no great martyrology to inspire the new generations. When therefore the West Indian playwright is asked, as in the Federal Festival of 1958, to produce a pageant-play on the region's history he has no one great single event, like the Haitian war of liberation or the Cuban Ten Years War, to use as the central *motif* of his production."[61] That the region should be characterized by an absence of martyrs may seem a particularly tragic irony, given its history, and Lewis's comment indicates another obtuseness that Walcott's solution to the "problem" shows up. Why, after all, desire to represent four hundred years of history by a monolithic image? Although the federation was made up of former British colonies only, Walcott declined the narrow political definition of the region and its history (always geographically absurd) by including the Spanish and French empires as well. This play has an obviously epic scope (in the conventional sense), broader than that of *Henri Christophe,* its approach to history not nostalgic but representing the past for the sake of the future. In John Berger's phrase, the past "is not for living in; it is a well of conclusions from which to draw in order to act."[62] The play was clearly motivated by an ideology of racial and cultural pluralism, and by egalitarianism: at the originary moment of the new community symbolized by federation, art, it promised, could help to bring about the transformed society. This was a Brechtian position. Brecht's project is "to provoke the audience to want to change the social reality that goes on producing distorted objects, including persons," according to Wright: "For Brecht knowledge is that which results in a process of continual transformation of the world as we know it."[63] Walcott proceeds by selecting examples from history that hold up to the light the dystopian image of the world as it has been. The drama follows the Brechtian epic principle by demystifying the exploitative social relations of the past, determined by imperialism, but it also models the kind of egalitarian pluralism that a collective society can deliver. In a development of Brecht typical of Walcott, it also flirts with a comedic utopianism, offering an image of the desired world in the hope that life, on the mimetic principle, may eventually mirror the aesthetically represented ideal.

Epic's need for heroes would seem to be at odds with egalitarianism. The Western epic with its roll-call of "great" men has been deeply implicated in art's co-option to the perpetuation of oppression; one might ask, for example, whether the notion of revolutionary heroes is incompatible with egalitarian objectives. After citing Froude's assertion that "[t]here has been no saint in the West Indies since Las Casas, no hero unless philo-Negro enthusiasm can make one out of Toussaint," Walcott writes of his own generation's experience of the revision of history: "My generation since its colonial childhood had no true pride but awe. We had not yet provided ourselves with heroes, and when the older heroes went out of fashion, or were stripped, few of us had any choice but to withdraw into a cave where we could scorn those who struggled in the heat . . . [I]t is this fever for heroic examples that can produce the glorification of revenge. Yet revenge is a kind of vision."[64] Walcott mentions his play *Henri Christophe* in "What the Twilight Says" but not the play that most tested his and the region's ability to provide historic examples of the hero, *Drums and Colours. Drums and Colours* focuses on four protagonists who were prime movers in history; two were the heroes of imperialism and are shown in decline, and two were martyrs to the anti-imperial struggle: one seeing the integrity of the cause destroyed by the instinct for revenge, the other making the nonviolent stand of heroic self-sacrifice. Alongside these historic heroes, the play reflects Walcott's lifelong preoccupation with other kinds of hero. His particular contribution to epic has been the exploration of the Everyman hero, a plebeian who is a kind of antihero in that he models an anarchic, antiauthoritarian stance.

Walcott's initial position is an anti-imperialist stance, which he explores in anticapitalist and antiwar terms in accordance with Marxist thinking. But in that a Marxist ideology has been claimed by regimes just as authoritarian and repressive as those of Western capitalist imperialism, Walcott's position is also interrogative of such abuses. Hegemony of the right or the left is challenged in the name of the individual—the ethical test always comes down to what one individual does to another as manifest of a system—but what might seem a very American focus on individualism is tempered by a very Caribbean sense of community. In aesthetic terms, this moves the focus away from a single protagonist, the hero, toward the group. Here the drama leads the poetry; long before he defined the group focus of *Omeros,* for example, or even the "alphabet of the emaciated" in *Another Life,* Walcott created the multicultural group of interventionist carnival maskers, symbolizing the ordinary people of the Caribbean, who preside over *Drums and Colours*. Later plays, such as *The Last Carnival* and *The Ghost Dance,* avoid giving prominence to a single hero but explore the interwoven stories of a number of individuals. There is a focus on ordinary people's relations with the "great" events recorded in the history books and an awareness of the small-scale situations in which political decisions are commonly executed. Power is shown in its effects on the people, the anonymous ones exposed to the world's gaze by their re-creation in the drama. The stoicism, and faith in goodness, of the sufferer becomes a heroic subject. As noted, in *Dream on Monkey Mountain* the history of racist contempt that lies behind the naming of Makak (macaque) of "Monkey" mountain is turned back on itself, as the scorned "Nobody," the old, poor charcoal-burner, rediscovers his real name, Felix Hobain ("Felix" meaning "happy"). The trickster-hero, surviving by his wits and his compassion, whether Anansi or Ulysses, is a recurrent figure in the plays, long before Walcott's dramatization of the *Odyssey* itself. Odysseus founds the reversal of negative identity: by naming himself to the Cyclops as "Nobody," he secures his heroic survival and return to his own.

As well as pioneering the revisioning of a tragic history as heroic, and the presentation of the "little man" as revolutionary emblem of the collective egalitarian experience, Walcott has also initiated another approach to epic with his focus on the artist. In "What the Twilight Says," he models the artist as hero, writing of his company of actors as "heroes . . . because they have kept the sacred urge of actors everywhere: to record the anguish of the race."[65] He also projects himself as a heroic figure, as one of the company of artists who began as "new Adams" and,[66] with irony, as a sacrificial, godlike figure, one of the "self-appointed schizoid saints," confessing, in 1970, to having been guilty of an "egotism which can pass for genius."[67] Although the self-projection of the creator in the work can serve Brecht's purpose of reminding the audience of the fictionality of the representation, Walcott's preoccupation with the artist as figure is Romantic as well as Brechtian. In fact, the artist as fictional persona participates equally powerfully in both dimensions, the individual and the collective, drawing on the inner self for his art but doing so for the sake of and with the help of the community, the "I-an-I" group. In the drama, the representation of the artist as persona in a shared performance gives trenchant symbolic meaning to this Janus-like role. In *The Last Carnival*, for example, Victor (named significantly to indicate the power of art, the "fountain" of his surname) is the artist as inspired solitary—in the post-Romantic Western tradition—but his art is developing toward community, as in his tableau for carnival, while the son who succeeds him dedicates himself to the collective art of carnival design, creolizing the family tradition.

As the artist exemplifies the way in which the individual and the community in an ideal society can unite, so sexual love demonstrates in a different dimension how two can be one. The creative encounter of difference is at the root of creolization, both in Caribbean art and personal relationships. In his concern to hold up the hope of the "republic of love"[68] (which is essentially egalitarian, available to all), Walcott tends to incorporate in his dramas a narrative element of sexual romance that may seem populist in a rather naive way if its symbolic function is not appreciated. The appeal of the Don Juan myth to Walcott is that it embodies just that hope, as his play adapting Tirso de Molina, *The Joker of Seville,* demonstrates. The epic poems of the Renaissance, by Tasso or Spenser or Ariosto, led by Dante, use earthly love as a figure of its divine equivalent, in accordance with Christian Platonic thought. For Walcott, too, sexual love is an epic subject that can serve as metaphysical allegory.

Both art and sexuality are transformative. They represent a creative response to the world and can deliver the magic of metamorphosis, capable of reinventing as positive that which appeared locked in to a tragic negative. As already noted, the tone of epic is usually composed of a blend of the tragic and the comic. (Brecht's revision of the genres is something rather different.) Traditional epic often sets up an "eros"/"thanatos" opposition—love, symbolizing the comedic, against war, symbolizing the tragic. Heroism can be shown in either field. Walcott's epic work tends toward open-ended closures, in *The Last Carnival,* for example. *The Ghost Dance* has an apparently tragic ending of a Brechtian ambivalence. A festive play such as *Drums and Colours* weaves comedy and tragedy in a tense web, conjuring an upbeat ending, yet the late plays of Shakespeare that evince a similar pattern are known as his "romances," in a literary discourse in which "romance" has come to be used faintly pejoratively. Since "romance" in this context is applied to comedy, and since it is normally characterized as in opposition to realism, this would seem to associate tragedy with mimesis. A complex question of philosophy underlies the distinction. Walcott, writing from within a mythic tradition—that of redemption—which is essentially comedic, is challenging, by his art, the modern Western rationalist skepticism, which is characterized by a nihilistic perception of the human condition, finding its artistic manifestation in tragedy. Several of his plays present a mythic action, of apparent death followed by a return to life. In such refusals of tragic closure, Walcott is most conspicuously at odds with mainstream metropolitan tradition. This is culturally derived; it is in the name of his people's habit of faith that he addresses any audiences who wish to hear. Even the terrible history of the Native Americans as narrated in *The Ghost Dance* is placed in a strongly positive context.

This metaphysical optimism, unfamiliar as it is in "serious" metropolitan drama, can be an obstacle to the appreciation of his plays by northern audiences. In the Caribbean, ironically, the pattern is reversed: many of the plays have tended not, after all, to reach a broad popular audience because of their high seriousness. In response, Walcott has sought to avoid the high-brow label by populist devices, sometimes risking the integrity of his piece by his concern for its entertainment value. As a result, some of his least Brechtian plays have been some of the weakest. Yet there is a growing list of popular successes, not least—surprisingly perhaps, given the modern disregard for the classics—*The Odyssey*. Also, although most of the plays were devised with a Caribbean audience in mind, they increasingly find international audiences. Some originally staged in the Caribbean are being performed not only in diverse anglophone communities but also in places such as Sweden and Italy.[69]

It may be that epic is most popular when closest to romance, as the success of *The Odyssey* may indicate, both as Homer's poem and as Walcott's play. Although superficially one of his least Brechtian plays, it is actually a skillful politicization of the mythic story. Brecht might have been surprised at the part Walcott has made myth play in his dialectical theater. Some of his most memorable gests (the Brechtian term) are those which signify mythically. Also, to the three levels of language that Brecht identifies—"plain speech, heightened speech and singing"[70]—Walcott adds from the inception of each drama as text a concept of visual representation, reciprocal to the verbal sign, and commonly symbolic in function. The dramatist who is also a painter has this advantage, but both Brecht and Walcott bring their experience as poets to their theatrical writing. Brecht, after listing six of his own plays as involving the "application of music to the epic theatre," said, "music made possible something which we had long since ceased to take for granted, namely the 'poetic theatre.'"[71] Walcott has from the beginning regularly used music and song in his plays and has written a number of musicals. He has also made prominent calls for the restoration of poetry to the theater. His own practice, which began with quasi-Jacobean verse, has moved on to combine the fluidity of colloquial speech with profound poetry often of an inspired simplicity, in a way that has become the hallmark of his epic theater. It is particularly Walcott's use of poetry in the theater that carries the dramatic experience over into widely different cultural milieux.

Brecht found the audience of his time frustrating, saying it "hangs its brains up in the cloakroom along with its coat,"[72] but while Walcott may be disappointed at the lack of response, to date, to much of his dramatic work, he would probably not be much concerned, unlike Brecht, at audiences being unaware of his political subtleties, confident that, if anything, in performance (and securing that objective is the first hurdle) the language and the mythic patterns work their "magic" directly on the unconscious.

9

"All You Stick Together"

The Epic Federation Dream

Miranda: What foul play had we that we came from thence?
Or blessed was't we did?

Prospero: Both, both, my girl.
The Tempest, I.ii.60–61

Walcott's early play *Drums and Colours* is the most Brechtian of his dramas, epic in Brecht's sense but also epic in the popular sense. It has a particular relationship to history in that it not only chronicles the history of the Caribbean dialectically but was written for a historic moment, the opening of the first parliament of the Federation of the West Indies. It therefore not only represents but makes history. In addition, in its forging of a language and a style for a distinctively Caribbean drama it marks a high peak right at the start of the region's theater. It demonstrates how aspects of folk culture as various as carnival and calaloo can be charged with symbolic significance in an essentially serious art, and it explores the rich contrariety of theatrical episodes designed to be simultaneously both tragic and comic. As the epigraph suggests, it marks the tragedy of Caribbean history, the "foul play" by which its people were displaced, but also the comedic "blessing" of arrival. Most occasional pieces become curiosities once their moment has passed, but this, remarkably, remains a fine play, which deserves to be restaged.

After agreement that a drama should be created for the occasion "depicting the four hundred years of West Indian history," and after sampling scripts by a Trinidadian and two Jamaican authors, Philip Sherlock of the University College of the West Indies' Department of Extra-Mural Studies commissioned Walcott in August 1957 to write not a pageant but a serious, cohesive drama.[1] The conception, of "a dramatic text with a linked sequence, a saga told by a poet with concern and insight," was soon being referred to as the "Epic."[2] Directed by Noel Vaz, then staff tutor in drama at St. Augustine, the Trinidad campus, it was premiered at the Royal Botanical Gardens, Port of Spain, Trinidad, on April 25, 1958.[3] Walcott was twenty-eight and already acknowledged within the region as a man of exceptional talents.

Walcott's first move to address his sense that his culture denied itself heroes had been his focus on Christophe, as dramatic a hero of the Americas' first republican revolution as any of the famous names were of the French Revolution. His first play, *Henri Christophe,* broadcast on the BBC's Caribbean service when he was twenty, had used the idiom of the English Jacobean drama to explore this core subject of Caribbean history. By using the form and verse style of the drama of the English Renaissance, he was laying claim to serious attention, asserting, in effect, to the wider world that his region's history and heroes were as remarkable as those of any other. Now, in the commission for the federation festivities, he was faced with some difficult choices. Those whom empire had regarded as heroes had become negative symbols to the mass of the people, yet their historic importance could not be denied. Would it be possible to represent a figure such as Columbus productively, not just conventionally or reductively, so as to extend the understanding and usefulness of history? Such questions were serious and required a thoughtful response.

In the event, Walcott's drama more than fulfilled its brief. The practical task of representing four hundred years of history is executed with imaginative and technical ingenuity, the weighty style devised for *Henri Christophe* now leavened with local speech and comedy, in the name of raising the dialectical awareness that the future would need. He uses a Shakespearean blend of iambic pentameter and colloquial prose, comic and poetic, juxtaposing the "high" and "low" styles to good effect. By using Brecht's method of showing history from the underside by means of invented episodes involving ordinary people, Walcott liberates himself from the grand narratives that had marginalized and reified the Caribbean. Instead he gives optimistic, though not naive, expression to what it means to be Caribbean, overturning the damaging negative evaluations of the past. Many of the concerns and hopes of the later work are already in evidence: the faith in pluralism, the antimaterialism, the repudiation of violence and of revenge, and the focus on the "little" man. The title chosen for the play, which evokes the military ritual so evident in the maintenance of extensive empires, takes on, as the play unfolds, a different meaning. As the historical narration proceeds chronologically from Columbus to the present, it gradually transforms the initial meaning of the title, represented by the opening stage set focused on "regimental and African drums, with the flags of Britain, France, Spain and Holland in the background," to a signifier of the "colors" of racial pluralism and the "drum" of a soup cauldron. History, whether of Africa or Europe, with its imposed hierarchies, is gradually translated to a local epic present of creolization, and the drama's title with its imperial overtones emerges as a pun, with a new meaning in the demotic. At this early stage in his career, Walcott already had the technique of troping on difference and similitude as his aesthetic for an intercultural, still creolizing community.

Although it is a kind of history play, it begins, again in a way that has become typical of Walcott, by drawing attention (pre-Foucault) to the fictionality of all historical discourse, and by refusing its claimed authority by framing it in mythopoeic fiction. The drama starts from the premise that the whole thing is a carnival presentation, the central group of characters intervening to "ambush the roadmarch" and change the performance to "a serious play." The conventional expectation that the historical inserts would be the meat of the sandwich is inverted in a deft move: the seriously nourishing part here is the "bread" of the plebeian group's antics. Carnival, of course, is a unique and symbolic Caribbean art form, distinguished by its origins in antiauthoritarian role reversal and by the collective nature of its rite, as much as by its free-associating iconography and performance. History translated as carnival is redeemed as comedy or epic, however tragic the reality might have been, its chronicity collapsed in a calaloo [soup] of intermingling period and place. History is reduced—or elevated—to style. As when Brecht uses folk forms such as fable, Walcott here does not simply reproduce carnival—which would be mimesis—but uses it to bear a dialectical significance: "We changing the march now to War and Rebellion!" The representation of history is thus offered as play: the drama is self-aware, a metadrama, the audience is reminded that it is an "act." This functions in textbook Brechtian manner:

> *Verfremdung* is a mode of critical seeing that goes on within a process by which man identifies his objects. It goes beyond the concept "defamiliarization": it sets up a series of social, political, and ideological interruptions that remind us that representations are not given but produced. Contrary to popular belief, *Verfremdung* does not do away with identification but examines it critically, using the technique of montage which shows that no representation is fixed and final.[4]

The audience is not lulled by an illusion of reality but is made conscious of the provisionality of the narration. At the same time, the representation of war and rebellion as "serious" is, of course, immediately ironized by its presentation as masquerade: the focus falls on the ludic and exemplary nature of the show, as the group of ordinary characters around Pompey the shoemaker—reminiscent of the group around Bottom the weaver in Shakespeare's *A Midsummer Night's Dream*—come in to "rummage among set properties and dress."

This group then presents the scenes that follow, from the Columbus era to the ringing out of bells for federation, the "present." First, as the road-march passes, Mano, one of the group, picks out of the parade maskers dressed as Columbus, Raleigh, Toussaint, and Gordon to join them. In an important sense, these heroes are the givens of the narration, who were always already there, as their appropriation as mythic icons in the popular culture of carnival demonstrates. In fact, they have long been naturalized to Caribbean culture in the performative present. The composition of the "nonheroic" group is symbolic: Pompey, Mano, Yette, Ram, and Yu represent the racial and cultural pluralism of the communities of the Caribbean. Yu is Chinese (and later takes the conventional generic role of cook). Ram is East Indian. Mano is implicitly African-Caribbean: in one of the intermediate scenes, the African king taken into slavery is named Mano. Yette is his woman, of mixed race, who appears in one of the intermediate scenes as a concubine being thrown out of the "great house." Pompey the shoemaker becomes "Pompey the warrior starting from today." The tone of militancy is simultaneously ludic and deeply serious. Walcott is setting up a drama in which to expose the real workings of power, through the control of money and people, and the manipulation of war, in the hope that such consciousness-raising will have real consequences for the emerging nation. Pompey as the epitome of the small craftsman, the play shows, has within him the capacity to be Pompey the militant, the political activist. The politicization of the folk is the Brechtian message, telling ordinary people that they can take control of their political situation, at the same time as warning them of the pitfalls of power.

Walcott cleverly avoids the stuffiness of most shows designed to celebrate historic occasions, in which, typically, the power structure reinforces its imaginative hold on the mass of the people. Instead he anchors his drama on this diverse plebeian group and shows their imaginative and moral strength as well as their physical energy as good omens for the future of the community. They are poor and chaotic, but they are well motivated and deal with adversity with wit and wisdom. Although the bulk of the play's history scenes are in Standard English and blank verse, this group uses prose and an expressive Caribbean vernacular, incorporating elements of specifically Trinidadian, Jamaican, Barbadian, Chinese, and French Creole-inflected idiom. Mano and Yette seem to be Jamaican,

Pompey and Ram Trinidadian, Yu uses his own Chinese version of Caribbean English, and, to keep the balance, Walcott creates as interlude a vignette of carnival "picong" in which an indignant steward, who calls shame on a drunken British sailor for letting down his empire, is centrally defined as a Barbadian.

The tone of the group's scenes is basically comic, with the healthy anarchy of comedy. Their prime concern is to eat rather than to fight, with Yu's calaloo tureen the focus of their Maroon camp. Their identification as Maroons gives them a clearly heroic anarchic status, as the Maroons were the community of escaped slaves who succeeded in evading recapture in the heart of Jamaica. They are thus symbolic outsiders, refusers of authority and of historically prescribed roles. Pompey's fierce talk of war and revenge, carefully undermined by absurdity and described as carnival "robber talk" rather than serious threat, is met with Ram's soothing, "Pompey, pal, eat your eat and don't worry." Yette—a dominant figure more in the mold of Nanny, resistance hero of the Maroons, than gangster's moll—rounds up the planter, Calico, and Pompey with his bugle and delivers them to the camp, saying, "I bring you more recruits. We got a Chinese cook, an East Indian tactician, now we have a preacher and a ruined planter." As in his play *Ti-Jean and His Brothers,* which belongs to the same period, a group of generic characters is being assembled for symbolic purposes. Walcott allows no one, not even the hated planter class, to be excluded from the new federal consciousness.

When Mano asks Pompey "what make you fight for the cause of emancipation and constitutional progress?" he replies in surprise, "You never heard of me?" and then answers Ram's question "You is a soldier?" with the splendid "robber talk" reply, "I is a calypsoldier. I bugles, I incites violence, I tread the burning zones of Arabia. I was a meek and mild nigger, a pacific man, but now. . . ." At the heart of the jokiness—and the idea of the "pacific" man is a running joke throughout the play—there is great seriousness; at an earlier point, the "pacific" temperament is contrasted with the "rough Atlantic," in an ironic comment on the history of the Middle Passage as occasion for vengeance; but having looked hard at the ethics of revenge, the play comes down firmly against it. America, faced with the choices symbolized by its flanking oceans, is encouraged to look west to pacificism and the dream of egalitarian island communities rather than east to the bitternesses of the Old World. The "calypsoldier" is the way out. To be active through art is the only form of retaliation, the only way to secure justice, that does not repeat the destructive errors of the past. Walcott accepts no distinction between the comic and the serious, the comedy typically being most serious when it is most funny. For example, when the Maroons are ambushed, their strategy is to use Yette as a decoy, "singing a local song" and showing a leg to halt the advancing troops. Puns on the "interesting flank movement" as she displays the "artillery" of her leg lead to Yu's observation, "sex being a great republic. . . ."[5] The flippancy masks a serious philosophical point, central to Walcott's work, that it is in our ability to respond to one another across racial and cultural boundaries (in which "eros" leads the way) that hope lies. The "I-an-I" model comes to mind once more.

But the play is not all in a comic vein. Within the fiction of carnival, a series of episodes is enacted by the four heroic figures picked out of the roadmarch and the shoemaker's group, who eventually appear playing themselves in the Maroon story. Since the Maroons of Jamaica were historically the region's earliest anticolonial independent society, it is apt that the Pompey group should represent them. The Pompey scenes frame a chronological sequence of historical dramas, predominantly tragic in tone, although even here a plebeian spirit is in evidence, disrupting the tragic closures with the irruption of "low"-life comedy. The whole drama is conceived spatially as manifest of the relationship between tragedy and comedy. The four historic "heroes" around whom the scenes revolve are all given tragic representation: Christopher Columbus, the Italian on a Spanish mission, whose hopes are betrayed and whose impact was tragic; Walter Raleigh, the English courtier, poet, and adventurer in Guiana, later executed by Elizabeth I; Toussaint L'Ouverture, Haitian revolutionary and founder of the Americas' first republic, later dying in a French prison; and George William Gordon, a Jamaican Christian rebel, executed by the British, and now, like Nanny, one of the national heroes of Jamaica.

The first two are the most strikingly different from their conventional representation; these are revolutionary portrayals, particularly for the 1950s. The glorification of the history of "discovery" is devastatingly demystified. Columbus is shown being clapped in irons to be returned to Spain; on the voyage he becomes a figure of pathos, weak, old, and disillusioned. Raleigh, shown first as a boy in a beach scene that sets up an ironic tableau of the famous painting of *The Boyhood of Raleigh,* is then shown off Guiana, first initiating action that results in the death of his son and the suicide of Keymis, and finally facing execution in the Tower. Those demarcated for centuries in imperialist discourse as heroes are exposed as men of petty passions and shown in all their human vulnerability as their fortunes turn. Each is portrayed in decline. Columbus is in disgrace on his third voyage. Raleigh, released after years of imprisonment in the Tower with the commission to find El Dorado, knows he must succeed or die.[6] The perfidy of imperial power in relation to its principal emissaries—those who risk all in its name—is very clearly demonstrated. Not honor but disgrace and death are shown awaiting in the capitals of Europe. Significantly, most of the scenes in the first half of the chronicle (the Columbus and Raleigh stories) are either on board ship or in Europe: the first part of the play, titled "Conquest," declines to legitimate the presence of the imperialists in the New World by showing them on Caribbean soil.

By contrast, in the second half, "Rebellion," all of the scenes take place on the Caribbean islands. Death, however, is still in the hands of the imperialists. Toussaint, the text reminds us, although it does not show it, met his end in a French jail, and Gordon was executed by the British in Jamaica in the aftermath of the Morant Bay rebellion, although the play leaves this implicit, his part ending when he leaves to give himself up.[7] If Columbus and Raleigh are a type of antihero, these two are Caribbean heroes proper, historic figures whose stand against imperialism cost them their lives. In choosing these two figures, the play is also making an intertextual point. It indirectly acknowledges its two great history-play predecessors, founding texts of anglophone Caribbean drama, C.L.R. James's *Toussaint L'Ouverture,* which had blazed the trail as early as 1936, and Roger Mais's *George William Gordon.* The treatment of these historic episodes is very Brechtian. Each scene can be looked at independently as a signifier of dialectical relationships. Walcott in fact designed it with Brecht's principle of montage in mind, as his author's note makes clear: "the scenes are so arranged that interested producers can excise shorter, self-contained plays from the main work, for example, the story of Paco, the El Dorado theme in the Raleigh scenes, the betrayal of Toussaint and the relationship with M. Calixte (in which the young Anton becomes the central figure) and the escapades of Pompey."[8] It should be noted also that this was a practical device. The original concept of the play was to enable different theater groups in different islands to rehearse separately, coming together in Trinidad just for the final rehearsals. "A primary goal of the festival," notes Bruce King, "was to show that the many local governments and peoples of the Federation could work together."[9]

The structure of the play thus reflects Caribbean reality—of diverse communities with shared interests—and symbolically represents the archipelago, in that there are small "islands" of plays within a play, to which the group of plebeian characters supplies the connecting "sea." It becomes an expressionist work. Each of the four inner plays contextualizes its hero and its socially elevated characters in a society that includes people of all social groups, the ordinary sailors, soldiers, workers, and beggars of the time. It thus becomes a counterdiscourse to hegemonic history with its focus only on figures of power, and the chronological progress from Columbus to Gordon emerges as a symbol of the struggle for independence. The stand of a single man of courage against the juggernaut of empire, however tragic the closure for him personally, becomes the true moment of independence, in that it shows an independent mind and the will to defend it.

The drama's class dialectics are carefully worked out. To balance the spotlight on the familiar "great" heroes, Walcott creates a "little" hero through whom to provide an interrogative focus. The mythopoeic chronicling of Paco's story from boy to old man is an effective device for exposing the consequences of the first stage of European imperialism in the New World. As a *mestizo,* with an Amerindian mother and Spanish father, he represents the process of creolization on which the American societies were to be built. He crucially introduces to the story the Amerindian tragedy that the European empires caused. Walcott powerfully evokes not just the anglophone Caribbean community but the pan-Caribbean world, which includes those territories with French and Spanish colonial histories. For him, the federal dream was, and remains, for a truly pan-Caribbean political cooperation. Paco is tragically displaced from his homeland to become a wanderer living by his wits in Europe. It thus stands not only for real history of the time (such as is narrated in Naipaul's "A Parcel of Papers, a Roll of Tobacco, a Tortoise,"[10] which traces the story of an Amerindian who returned to England with Raleigh, based on historical events) but for a contemporary history, then in full swing, of West Indian emigration to Britain, as wittily ironized in Louise Bennett's poem "Colonization in Reverse."[11] When asked later if he wishes to return, Paco says he does not, since there would be nothing to return to, the advent of the Europeans having destroyed his people. The work aligns itself with dialectical materialism by bringing the whole monetarist system into sharp focus. One of the Spaniards who has been guilty of wanton cruelty against Indians tries to salve his conscience by giving Paco a coin; from the story of this coin, the whole history of capitalism is shown. Later, pimping on the wharves of Lisbon, Paco meets his mirror image, a Jew displaced by prejudice from his homeland in Europe and seeking a better life in the New World, who tries to rescue him by offering to buy him. Paco avoids slavery but not the selling of flesh, that of others in his role as pimp, his own in the intra-European wars he goes off to fight in as a mercenary. Walcott does not romanticize his heroes.

At the same wharf, Paco meets his people's successors, the Africans being taken into slavery, their total commodification exposed in the way they are referred to by the Europeans as just another cargo. The development of their story by the later scenes on the Middle Passage sets against their savage treatment their heroic resilience in suffering. The moment of landfall in the New World, so familiar from the European grand narrative and its icons, is wrested out of the hands of the imperialists and given to the Africans. Columbus and Raleigh are shown offshore and sailing for Europe, which remains their home. It is the Africans whom Walcott shows landing in the New World.

Walcott links his first two sections by showing Paco, now old, as a vagrant on an English beach, shipwrecked from the Armada, who encounters the boy Raleigh. The idea of a Native American's life spanning encounters with both Columbus and Raleigh is an ingenious and plausible connection of a sort which in reality was probably more common than we tend to think. It also enables Walcott to make a witty and trenchant reference to Millais's iconic painting *The Boyhood of Raleigh,* painted in 1870 and widely reproduced, of huge cultural power in the valorizing of empire at the peak of its nineteenth-century expansion. Walcott was already interested in using visual "quotation" in the theater as a means to a richly signifying icon in the Brechtian manner. Instead of a nameless old man, with his back to the viewer, pointing the young Raleigh to far horizons, Walcott makes us see an individual, Paco, a Native American cast away forever on the margins of Europe. Significantly, what he offers the boy is stories; he has become the narrator of the story of empire to the imperialists. The visual quotation—"a sort of cliché but I wanted it," said Walcott[12]—also functions to extend the episode's range by enabling the historical reference to be doubled: the scene is to stand not only for the phase of Elizabethan adventure, the looting followed by primary settlement of the Americas, but also for the later worldwide expansion of the British empire, set in train by men such as Raleigh. The reference to the red on the world map, by which their empire was represented to the British, clinches the connection in a powerful metaphor:

> The blood that jets from Raleigh's severed head
> Lopped like a rose when England's strength was green
> Spreads on the map its bright imperial red
> To close the stain of conquest on our scene.

The blood-guilt of empire, even in its treatment of its own, is made memorably clear; Europe is exposed as tyranny and a place of self-predation.

The second half of the drama, headed "Rebellion," shows how the violence that founded the mixed societies of the Caribbean was returned and resisted. Again, Walcott presents intricately calculated scenes to show the material processes and the collective psychology behind the events recorded in the history books. The inverted racism of the Haitian revolution, for instance, is seen in the light of the ingenious tortures casually inflicted on slaves by the plantocracy for their amusement. We are brought to understand that the will to revenge was an inevitable consequence of such treatment, but the play is not content simply with explanation. It makes a moral stand also, coming down firmly against the revenge ethic. The heroism of Gordon, who gives himself up knowing that he will be killed, is held up as the difficult alternative. A violent stand against the abuse of power involves the perpetrator in further abuse of power, but the nonviolent stand can achieve more, the play suggests, by its heroic self-sacrifice. The continuation of the Gordon episode in Pompey's flight back to the Maroon camp develops the theme. The "little" man's equivalent of Gordon's noble self-sacrificial pacificism is the simple nonviolence of one whose main concern is the next meal, and whose principal notion of military defense is the decoy. The parallelism invites the audience to see the comic group as a key alternative to the "high" drama of violence and suffering on the upper level of political power. It is a similar strategy to Shakespeare's in *A Midsummer Night's Dream,* where the assertion in the inner play (nominally a tragedy) that "the wall is down that parted their fathers" lays down a profound anti-tragic marker.

Thus the four tragic stories in the heart of the play, to which the plebeian characters serve as encompassing frame, provide a symbolic structure, the meaning of which is manifest in the spatial design of the performance, just as in the masques of the Elizabethan and Jacobean court. But where the comic Renaissance anti-masque had been subordinate to the story of the "great" persons represented for the entertainment of the nobility, in Walcott's drama that hierarchical dynamic is reversed. In *Drums and Colours,* the "great" men's stories are subordinated to the "anti-masque" story of the "little" people, which surrounds, penetrates, and actually presents their stories to view, via the fiction of the carnival roadmarch. The knowledge that the tragic stories are in what Homi Bhabha calls the performative produces a Brechtian "Verfremdung" that ironizes the tragedy and transforms it to epic.

Walcott also uses a Chorus—a Shakespearean rather than classical one reminiscent particularly of the Chorus's role in *Henry V*—to introduce the chronicle scenes. The terms in which this Chorus explains the stage's symbolic locations are highly significant:

> This barren height towards which the steps ascend
> Is that fixed point round which some issue wheeled,
> There our four heroes meet their common end,
> There in harsh light, each age must be revealed.
> *(Steps down)*
>
> Below them, on this level of the stage
> The spokes of normal action turn their course,
> *(Enter SPANISH SAILORS)*
>
> Just as these sailors, fished from a drowned age
> Were simple men, obscure, anonymous.
> And where the stage achieves its widest arc
> The violence of large action shall take place,
> Each sphere within the other leaves its mark,
> As one man's dying represents the race.

There is thus a profound philosophy behind the hierarchy of position: the conventional model of dominance is deconstructed in favor of one of interaction. The stage's dominant position is shown to be a "barren height" and becomes the site of tragedy and death of the "heroes" as the play unfolds. The level of the stage, in hierarchical terms "below," is to display "normal" action, that of the unremembered "anonymous" individuals who were as much a part of history as the "heroes." The outer limit of the stage (presumably its interface with the audience) is to exhibit the "violence of large action," the whole coordinated in the concept of concentric spheres, as in the ancient cosmology. In the concluding image, not only is the symbolic nature of the stage representation alluded to—one actor performing in the name of the countless numbers of history—but the death of the ordinary person, at the lower level, is shown to be just as meaningful as the death of the elevated "heroes." The continuum between the individual and the community is given powerful linguistic expression in this introductory speech and performed symbolically in the episodes that follow.

The crest of tragedy keeps surfacing in the play but is constantly undermined by the undertow of comedy. Again, this is signaled at the outset by Mano setting up on a staff two masks, of comedy and tragedy, which he hands to the Chorus "[a]s the figure of time and the sea." His gesture embraces the whole audience: "every blest soul going act the history of this nation." The involvement of the audience is another of Brecht's objectives for epic theater; if the audience is passive, the project fails. Mano's remark, however, is also a "double entendre" addressing the future: in their lives to come all those present, a metonymy for the whole population, will enact the unfolding history of the nation. It is a way of summoning both national pride and responsibility. And the time symbolism is made clear: "as the sun been on his roadmarch all day cooling his crack sole in the basin of the sea, we starting from sunset, through night to the dawn of this nation." The symbolic moment of the birth of the nation is expressed through the diurnal cycle, as in so many independence celebrations when the flag of empire is hauled down at midnight to be replaced by the banner (or colors) of the new nation. The idea of the "dawn" of the new era is given literal as well as symbolic meaning as the night scenes give way to daylight.

The repeated pattern of closure in tragic death, enacted on the upper stage, a "central balcony with steps leading up to it from either side," and mirrored in the fate of many of the humble characters below, is also used to give symbolic meaning to the arc of the play. In the midst of the extended comic scene with the Maroon band, supposedly contemporary with the death of Gordon—the point at which the language and rituals of Christian faith enter the play—to the audience's consternation, Pompey falls in the fighting and dies. In the following moments of the play, all of the anguish of the centuries of suffering, for Native Americans and Africans, which the play has vividly evoked, the tension of the Toussaint scenes with their moral dilemmas and the grief of betrayed idealism, and the awesome courage of Gordon, choosing martyrdom, come to bear down on the sense of loss that the death of Pompey brings. In a death scene of great pathos as well as comedy, Pompey's last words resonate as first words of advice to the new nation, a creed:

> It ain't water I want, Yette. I want all you boys stick together, you hear? All you stick together and don't hate nobody for what they is or what they do. This is all we land, all we country, and let we live in peace. I want all you hold hands there near me, and live like brothers, Calico, dont buse coolie, coolie dont buse Mano, give the boys a break sometimes because this is confusion time.

As John Thieme comments, the play "promotes federalism not only as a union of nations, but also as an ideal of inter-racial harmony."[13] The audience resists Pompey's death as gratuitous, as if all of the other deaths could be accepted, but not his. It is a crucial stage in the Brechtian dramatic experience Walcott has planned. By making the audience refuse the death of Pompey, he enacts the hope for the future.

After the extremely painful, delicately handled scenes of Pompey's death and burial, which are funny as well as acutely sad and serious—full of the contradictions Brecht regarded as such an important stimulus—Yette swings the play around with her, "All you taking this too serious, is only a play. / Pompey boy, get off the ground, before you catch cold." The mood breaks, although the tension is held for a delicious moment longer by Pompey's failure to stir, until stung into action by an insult. As he springs up, he enacts the great myth of the defeat of death. Relief is almost tangible. In the drama's mimetic pattern, in Pompey's "resurrection" we are all enabled to wake from the nightmare of history into the "dawn" of a new, hopeful era. It is as if our resistance to his death has brought about his ability to surmount it: his defiance of a tragic closure is closely linked to our own. The multicultural discussion over Pompey's body as to what sort of funeral rite would be appropriate is replaced by imagery informed by the Christian faith, as elsewhere in Walcott's drama and poetry, where the portrayal of a return to life is given far-reaching symbolic resonance. The notion of hero is remodeled as Everyman. Pompey is the quintessential little man, an absurd figure like Shakespeare's Pompey with the surname of Bum in *Measure for Measure,* rather than eminent Pompey, the triumvir, of *Antony and Cleopatra.* As Mano says as Pompey runs to find the man who hit him, "Lord trouble again, trouble again. Thank God the little men of this world will never keep still."

It is Pompey who introduces the final Chorus, a figure of both time and memory as we were told at the beginning, saying "The man nearly mash up me memory. / But I feel it coming back." History, the text suggests, must not be forgotten, as it can teach us how best to enter the future. This is where the epic spirit lies, in the usefulness of revisiting the past, compounded as it is of comedy and tragedy mixed:

> Return again, where buried actions lie,
> For time is such, alternate joy and pain,
> Those dead I raised have left us vows to keep,
> Look, a new age breaks in the east again.

Since the prevalent modern view of Caribbean history is of a long night of suffering and grief, it would seem that Walcott's positivism might risk banality, but far from denying the force of the great negatives he gives them moving representation. Paco leads us through the tragedy of the

Native Americans from an unfamiliar perspective, his story leading to the story of African slavery, first on the Middle Passage and then in the abuses of the New World, and the courageous acts of rebellion are shown in all their problematic tragedy.

But against the fully tested weight of the suffering and anguish, Walcott sets up the heroism of survival, which is rooted in defiance and the comic instinct. The Maroons' banter round the symbolic calaloo pot—calaloo itself being a creolization, born of necessity, a versatile recipe for cooking available ingredients—is the play's abiding image of benign community, of the sacramental domestic hearth, naturalized to the open air. Later a related yoking of the trickster spirit to iconic domestic intimacies was to find equally memorable expression in Walcott's *Odyssey,* where Odysseus mirrors the Pompey ethos. The spirit of Autolycus, of Ulysses, and particularly of Anansi, in the end triumphs simply by not giving in, whatever the odds. It is this that makes the play revolutionary. As Ram says, trying to patch his impossibly ragged trousers, in an ironic counterpoint to Calico's repeated cry that "the bottom fell out of the sugar market," "You think any man have a right to dead in this pants?" Like the robber Barnardine in Shakespeare's *Measure for Measure* who thwarts death by refusing to go to his execution because after a night's drinking he is not "fitt'd" for it, Ram says in effect that he cannot die because his trousers are not dignified enough.

In the end, the myth of comedy always comes down to the defeat of death, and the spirited refusal of the plebeian hero to be dignified enough to die can be modeled as a mechanism of survival. But the articulation of grief needs to be set alongside the heroic defiance; even Brecht's Mother Courage makes eventually her silent scream over her children. Ram's funeral speech over the "body" of Pompey is a memorable poetic assertion of the epic spirit:

> We only a poor barefoot nation, small, a sprinkling of islands, with a canoe navy, a John Crow air force, and a fete father philosophy, but in the past we was forged, Mano, and, Oh I can't talk enough to tell you, but for this Pompey dead, stupid as he did seem, I wish I could talk. Oh where the fellar with the language to explain to this man?

As Judy Stone notes, "*Drums and Colours* proved that an integrated regional theatre company creating West Indian theatre is not only possible, but capable of outstanding achievement." It had been a tremendous production in every sense, performed by two hundred actors, dancers, and singers, before audiences of up to fifteen hundred, despite the rain, which led to its being dubbed with characteristic irreverence "Drums and Water-colours." Above all, it "kindled in both participants and spectators a lasting pride in their West Indianness."[14] In the same year in which he had written the powerful play *Ti-Jean and His Brothers,* it clinched the point that the young Walcott was capable of outstanding achievement as a dramatist as well as a poet—and specifically as the poet of an epic theater, using all the non-naturalistic resources of visual symbolism, movement, collective involvement, and heterogeneous juxtaposition for a total, political theater.

10

"The Moment of Stillness"

The Arrivants' Last Carnival

> *Prospero:* Our revels now are ended. These our actors,
> As I foretold you, were all spirits and
> Are melted into air, into thin air.
> *The Tempest,* IV.i.148–50

The ephemeral nature of performance is part of its magic. In Trinidad, elaborate costumes representing many months' hard work are trashed the day after carnival, without regret. The impetus for the ephemeral is in opposition to that for the museum, and it is the former that Walcott celebrates as characteristically Caribbean, American, and implicitly revolutionary in its drive for change and for the new. The provisionality of art—its status as radically unclosed—is his accompanying aesthetic philosophy. His play *The Last Carnival,* first performed in Trinidad in 1982 with the author as director, is a reworking of a play from a decade earlier, *In a Fine Castle,* itself derived from the earlier *The Wine of the Country.*[1] In 1986, a revised version was published as *The Last Carnival* with two other plays.[2] Judy Stone examines these early adaptations, including one for television, which was not produced.[3] In 1992, it was reworked again for a production in Birmingham, England, which Walcott was able to see in rehearsal, as it coincided with his residence in Stratford-on-Avon while *The Odyssey* was in rehearsal.[4] *The Last Carnival* seems therefore to be a play that matters considerably to Walcott, yet with which he remains restlessly unsatisfied. It illustrates his habit of reworking material over many years, in different idioms, and his refusal to give up revising even after publication. Stone explains how *In a Fine Castle,* which he had had on the stocks for some years, became Walcott's engagement with a revolutionary moment in Trinidadian history, while it was unfolding:

> In 1970 Trinidad was shaken by a brief Black Power revolution. Walcott was inspired by the event to a fresh perspective on a subject

> that had long preoccupied him: the validity in the West Indies of European culture, and the rightful place there, if any, of the colonial descendents. Walcott spent his curfew hours working on a play in which, by alternating his scenes between the black and the white milieux, he contrasted the militant extremism of the Black Power movement with the gentle decadence of a French creole enclave.[5]

Walcott had been settled in Port of Spain since 1959, when the Trinidad Theatre Workshop was founded. The revised *In a Fine Castle* was premiered by Walcott's workshop later in 1970, but in Jamaica, not Trinidad. Walcott's program note indicated that the play was conceptualized as television and that it grew from an outline "proposed by an actor who worked with Bergman." Bruce King paraphrases Walcott's introduction: "he tried to keep in its style the 'fluent impartiality' of a camera. Only after facing the madness of the world and accepting his own flaws can a person find 'true peace, which is separate, personal.'"[6] The play revisits some themes dealing with changing power and culture in the Caribbean, which have recurred in both his drama and his poetry. Epic in its historical sense of national identity and its reading of the individual in the context of history, it also has elements of epic theater in the Brechtian sense, with its episodic structure and its dialectical approach to action. The Jamaican production initiated Walcott's professional partnership with the design team of Richard and Sally Montgomery (then Sally Thompson), who brought out the Brechtian politics of the piece in their design, using, among other things, "Brechtian slides."[7] The play poses difficulties similar to those that *Drums and Colours* solves with such panache, but the integrity of purpose, which makes an electrical exchange of the earlier play's contrasts, seems to be lacking here. There is a real ambivalence, it seems, at the heart of the play, not just a chosen dialectical strategy.

Set in Trinidad, it takes place against a carefully defined epic history, narrating Trinidad's colonial past, its independence, and its revolutionary present. Although it makes play with the idea of stopping the clock in its opening sequence, this is a drama in which time becomes a protagonist. Walcott, as ever, is interested in the paradox of yoked difference: the urgent upheavals of social change are in a sense its center, and yet the stage is made a contrasting arena of stasis—of reflection, of language, and of art—which relegates the political to the margins. If this is understood in the light of Bergman's influence (his films were becoming increasingly reflective and static, in a style that culminates in the television drama *Scenes from a Marriage*), its aesthetic purpose becomes clearer. Agatha, newly arrived in Trinidad from Britain in 1948 to take up a post as governess, is met by her employer, an artist who insists that she take off her watch, as symbol of having stepped out of linear time into a kind of paradisal limbo. In its 1992 version (the version discussed here except where indicated otherwise), virtually the whole drama is framed as a series of flashbacks narrated to a local journalist reporting on the artist, Victor DeLaFontaine, who has killed himself.[8] Agatha, who tells how she went on to become Victor's partner, is the narrator. Brown, the journalist, listens. His is a difficult role to play because it is so passive, and Earl Lovelace's criticism of Brown's part in the earlier version remains apt: the play "deserves a more comprehensive and comprehensible Brown; like the play itself, Brown contains too much potential to be so limp."[9] Brown is, of course, a symbolic name for the mixed-race individual who represents the crux at which the two cultural dynamics, of the black community and the white, collide and creolize. His stasis is therefore symbolic, as the still point between equal and opposed forces. Walcott addresses what he sees as the pitfalls of Black Power in "What the Twilight Says," the essay written in the same year as the revolution and the drama's inception:

> Once we have lost our wish to be white, we develop a longing to become black, and those two may be different, but are still careers. "The status of native is a nervous condition introduced and maintained by the settler among colonised people *with their consent,*" says Sartre, introducing Fanon, and the new black continues that condition. . . . Slaves, the children of slaves, colonials, then pathetic, unpunctual nationalists, what have we to celebrate?[10]

The drama's play of stopping the clock is thus both a satiric point about the society's failure to take itself seriously enough, which results even in revolution being compromised, before it is begun, by inadequate organization, and simultaneously an acknowledgment that an efficient revolution would be worse, since it would involve the terrorism of a fascistic approach to time and history, which—fortunately, he seems to suggest—is alien to the Caribbean. But the essay's criticism of both "careers," its refusal of the reactive binary racial politics in which black was henceforth to be privileged and white to be repudiated, was deemed reactionary under the dominant politics of the time. Likewise the play's courageous focus on the right of whites long-established in the Caribbean to be accepted as part of the new nations was not likely to find favor with militant factions. The subtler point, that the revolutionary spirit betrayed socialism if it practiced a reverse racism (indicating only that the trauma caused to black people by colonial history was not yet healed), was too hard to see from vantage points of engagement in the urgently unfolding political drama. The quietism of Brown derives from his (and Walcott's) acceptance of both halves of his heritage, the only route, as Walcott sees it, to healing. That it should be the mulatto who understands this and reaches inner peace first is perhaps not surprising. But the play's controversial message for black Carribeans (as in so much of Walcott's work) is that the acceptance of the European heritage is also necessary for the healthily integrated black identity. European culture, he repeatedly reminds us, is an integral part of Caribbeanness, the point being that it need no longer imply deference to Europe, because it is fully assimilated, naturalized, and creolized in Caribbean culture, which is its own resplendent self.

A series of retrospective episodes fills out the play, which concludes with a sequence of events contemporary with the journalist's visit. Once again, the fictionality of the narration—its status within its own text as one version of events among many, and beyond that as fiction anchored in historical epochs open to many possible interpretations—is brought to the audience's attention, as Brecht suggests. The location in history of the retrospective "narrated" episodes is significant. From 1948 and the years following, the time jumps to 1962, then on to 1970. The first represents the postwar phase of new immigration from Europe to the colonies, imperialism's last fling, as it were, before the independence movements got under way. The other two dates are important to Trinidad specifically: 1962 is the date of independence, following the failure of federation; 1970 is the date of the armed uprising in Trinidad in which a substantial takeover of the country by the Left was maintained for some time before being crushed. The play's present, of the narration to Brown, is the time both of the historical revolutionary uprising, which in reality coincided with carnival, and of DeLaFontaine's (fictional) suicide. The rest of what is presented comes to read as an account of how the 1970 moment was produced. The play is therefore in part about the origins of revolution. But the drama investigates the 1970 moment also by giving it parallel significance in terms of the artist's suicide. There are thus two principal fields, politics and art, through which the racial theme is exhibited; it is the dialectical relationship between these that the play examines.

The climax of the Trinidadian cultural year, carnival, with its origins in a purgatory religious festival in which conventional power relations were inverted—the master playing the servant and the servant the master—is matched to the crisis of Trinidad's historical development, the overturning of the social order by revolution, in a series of dramatic parallelisms and inversions. The irony of carnival's revolutionary inversions, however, is that they are ludic and temporary and function in fact to reinforce the hold of the ruling class by allowing the underclass to let off steam. The irony of Walcott's focusing of his play about the Trinidad uprising on the metaphor of carnival therefore bears down on the fact that the uprising eventually failed (a fact not represented in the play but naturally adduced by its audience from their knowledge of what was recent history when the play was first written), and in failing, reestablished the old order in a stronger position than before. By calling his play not just "carnival," however, but the "last" carnival, Walcott seems to be exploring a Marxist view of the ultimate inevitability of change: one reading of the historical events is that the ruling class—in which old colonials reemerge as neocolonialists—may remain in place after this uprising, but their position is essentially doomed. Their "carnival" of misrule cannot last forever, and this may be their last fling. The apocalyptic nature of carnival thus comes to the fore: the festivity on the eve of the season of sober abstinence derives its energy from a temporal imperative, that of the last chance. What emerges is a desperate gaiety, doomed, with its beauty raddled. As in the paintings of Watteau that give the play its key visual images, the delicate idyll is febrile, diseased, and unsustainable. In *Midsummer,* his collection of sonnet-like short poems published in 1984 and therefore arising from the same period as the first production of *The Last Carnival,* Walcott characterizes Watteau as "malaria's laureate."[11]

His method is to focus on a French Creole Trinidadian family, the DeLaFontaines, whose ancestors sought refuge there at the time of the French Revolution. This is an epic part of Trinidad's history. The island was opened substantially to European settlement by Haitian-French landowners, fleeing Toussaint L'Ouverture's slave revolution in Haiti (a direct consequence of that in France), which led to the first republic in the Americas. Walcott is indirectly revisiting the topic of his first play, *Henri Christophe,* and his epic for federation, *Drums and Colours.* Essentially, then, the Trinidad revolution of 1970 is being traced back to Haiti and then to the great revolutionary moment of 1789, while its immediate antecedent is the near revolutionary events in France in 1968, which sparked similar protest in the Americas. As Tony says cynically but significantly to Brown, "All our ideas in Trinidad are imported. / The Black Power March began with students abroad." A complex relationship is therefore being postulated between the politics of France and those of Trinidad, between Europe and the Caribbean. At the same time, a complex relationship is being posited between the arts of France and the arts of Trinidad. The notion of mimemis, of Trinidadian politics or art as copies of a European original, is thus put forward for discussion. The audience, as in Brecht's epic theater, is invited to consider a range of contradictory propositions: opposite the possibility of the mimetic reading of Trinidadian politics and culture the play suggests the contrary, their distinctiveness and originality. A great deal depends on this, because if Trinidadian culture is only mimetic, it ceases to exist as a phenomenon in its own right. But if a Trinidadian cultural identity exists in and of itself, defined by its difference, it must be able to demonstrate something distinctive and culturally unique. Since it cannot be denied that there are historical links between the Trinidadian culture of today and that of France in the past, the question of difference has to be carefully tested.

The play's dialectical approach to the narrative by which these propositions can be investigated is essentially binary. First, the society of the 1970 "present" is divided by class and race, reflecting the historic divisions of Caribbean societies. The white DeLaFontaines, with their plantations, their great houses, and their privileged lifestyle, inherit one side of history; the black servants and the estate laborers, represented by the women who "dance the cocoa," turning the beans with their feet while singing, inherit the other.[12] Walcott also gives the family two brothers, carefully differentiated on dialectical lines. The artist Victor identifies so closely with his European French cultural heritage that he eventually goes mad and thinks he is Watteau. His brother Oswald is the planter, the son of the soil with no cultural pretensions, only pride in his family's history as nurturers of the land. The one harks back to Europe, tragically; the other is at home in Trinidad and survives. Victor's children, Clodia and Tony, whose mother's death occasions the need for a governess, mirror the difference between the brothers, but with a crucial variation. Tony is to become the artist and Clodia the un-intellectual lover of the island and all it stands for, but with this generation both are fully Caribbean, both rooted, one in the local culture of carnival, the other in her love of the island. The sense of the continuity and yet difference of generations can be brought out in the casting: as Judy Stone notes, "Walcott has written *The Last Carnival* in such a way that the leading actress plays the young Agatha in the first act, and Clodia in the second, in which the older Agatha is played by a supporting actress. In the same way, the leading actor plays Victor in the first act, and in the second Victor's son, Tony."[13] Such a practice, used also in *The Odyssey,* is not only an economical device: it is symbolic of theater as a shared activity, in which membership of the group is as important as individuality (a theater company is a good example of the "I-an-I" community). The family is served by the devout George, who invests heavily in the status quo, and the young maid Jean who resists it. The play is in two halves, with a brief scene marking independence at its hinge; it therefore invites comparison of the portrayal of the society before independence with the postindependence society. In this way, the audience is led through a very Brechtian intellectual experience of comparing and contrasting the items of the play's textual evidence. We are made to think.

From the beginning, the play introduces an agent of change. The irruption of Agatha, a Marxist, into the family's virtually feudal system in 1948 disturbs its carefully maintained calm. Agatha is working class, a cockney who (rather implausibly for the time) is a graduate of the London School of Economics. With her red hair she symbolizes revolution. She it is who protests at the exploitation of the cocoa-dancing women, raising awareness of the real economic relationship on which the seductive luxury of the family's lifestyle is based. And it is she who starts a veranda school for the young servants to teach them, among other things, their rights. She is thus a catalyst: her disruption of the status quo circa 1950 initiates the chain of events that deliver a real exchange of power. But to show an English outsider, a relatively recent arrival, as the source of demands for social justice, which produce first, independence, and later, near revolution, is to be quite controversial.

Not only does this relate to the issue of mimesis, it also becomes part of a dialectic of French as against British colonialism that the play puts forward. The 1962 moment of independence is portrayed via the essentially English image of a cricket match. Agatha is almost absurdly shown as a chirpy "cockney sparrow," with memories of the blitz, of evacuation and wartime songs, and with a battered suitcase that has seen service in the Indian empire, and which she addresses as "missis Boggs." In trying to fix a character's social milieu by her/his tone of voice (in itself good dramatic practice), Walcott does not always avoid cliché. In good Brechtian manner, however, Agatha links her pleasure at the smell of cocoa beans on the Port of Spain wharf to the smell of cocoa she knew as a child and wonders whether what she drank in Britain came from Trinidad: the workings of empire and of international capitalism are emblematically exposed through this reminder of the Third World countries' role as agricultural primary producers, laid down by imperialism but sustained by the postindependence neocolonial system. Agatha's complicity in the imperial project is inescapable, for all her Marxist ideas. This accords with Brecht's concern to show that "objects, including people, are produced via the relations of production in which they are engaged."[14] For Brecht, "Whatever props are used, they are there not just as realistic background but as something to be acted upon."[15] The suitcase, however absurdly, is intended as a complex signifier. This suitcase that Agatha drags round the world with her has an imperialist past: she is burdened with empire whether she approves it or not. But it is not a French but a British suitcase, and the imperial story of the British is shown as relatively honorable. In a long speech, Tony launches a diatribe beginning with martyrdom as "so French!"[16] He despises the British, except Agatha, hates the French, and goes on to attack French assimilationist imperialism:

> I detest anything French that shows in me and I suppose, although I admired my father, I detested him. He made us cherish taste and it was the wrong taste for this country, and that makes us useless. The French are shitty colonizers. They create this longing for the metropole in their colonials. . . . But what's worse is that they also create this longing for paradise in *their* metropole, and when the intellectualizing bastards get there, the way they fucked up Indochina, Algeria, Tahiti, Martinique, Africa, their whole empire, and that's their other deceit, they never called it an empire like the British; they called it simply an extension of the metropole, which was a lie; the bastards get so cynical and disappointed about these native paradises, they turn them into hell. And that's the Empire that victimised your hero. Papa. Mon pere.

As a St. Lucian who grew up on a British island with a francophone culture and French territory just across the water, Walcott is making an important distinction between the different colonial policies of the French and the British empires, which have resulted in radically different political status in the Caribbean for former French and British colonies. The first are now legally part of France and therefore the European Union, while the second are mostly independent countries. He is in fact opening a debate rarely evident in anglophone Caribbean writing, and potentially of considerable importance in discussions of the nature of creole culture and of its future.

Tony goes on to describe Victor's suicide as the product of a moment of truth in a demented life of delusion: "once he knew that he was Watteau, he didn't have to paint anymore, you see. He had done it all already. Well, after many doctors, he had one of his lucid periods, and in one of these rational periods, he did the rational thing. No more illusions. No more *Embarquement Pour Cythère*! He killed Antoine Watteau." In one sense, the suicide is absurd; in another it is heroic, in that Victor recognized the falseness of his identification with Watteau and Frenchness and "killed" it. His death is symbolic, as is that of the "white goddess" is in *Dream on Monkey Mountain.* Tony's perception that the French way is "the wrong taste for this culture" makes an important contribution to the play's dialectics about mimesis. The British are approved both culturally and politically: for not mythologizing their imperial project with complex projections of symbolic desire, and for not making their Caribbean territories part of metropolitan France as the French have done. The play makes us reflect that if Trinidad had been under French control, 1962 would probably not have seen independence. More probably, Trinidad would have been, like Martinique and Guadeloupe, an overseas department of metropolitan France, a state of affairs that Tony (and, implicitly, Walcott) regards as a betrayal of its identity and integrity. Once federation had failed (to Walcott's regret), the independence of the principal anglophone Caribbean territories, among them Trinidad, was rapidly implemented. In 1970, Trinidad had autonomy, which meant that revolution could be performed locally, in terms of control of the government building, the Red House (the equivalent in the French Antilles would have to take on metropolitan France). In cultural terms, Trinidad could encourage the particularity of its art to develop, without being tied to metropolitan objectives. The result of the different colonial histories is that Martinique and Guadeloupe resemble France much more than the former British West Indies do Britain. Carnival is the central symbol of this: it has come to stand for Trinidadian cultural identity as difference, which, as *Drums and Colours* shows, can be extended as a pan-Caribbean cultural icon. *The Last Carnival* is itself an example of independent contemporary culture, as a Caribbean dramatist resident in Trinidad develops a form of folk art (carnival) as signifier in a complex investigation of national identity. Again, the dialectical process that the text invites is epic in the Brechtian sense. Audiences used to a supposedly apolitical theater that proceeds by psychological characterization and empathy are likely to balk at Walcott's approach, which places the individual as symbol within a dialectical investigation.

The cocoa dancers offer a provocative image of the creation of an indigenous culture. At the heart of the slavery system, which denied the value of the individual and repressed independent expressions of community, the imposed act of physical drudgery was turned by the oppressed into an act of cultural self-expression by making it a dance and accompanying it with song. The difficult corollary to this is that the working practices maintained on the DeLaFontaines' estate after independence, and long after abolition, mimic the social structures of slavery sufficiently for that practice to survive: the white family still enjoys its privileges in the big house at the expense of its black workers who are still fulfilling the role of cheap labor in the international commodity market. That they still sing is at one level miraculous, at another tragic: a central Brechtian ambivalence. The dance of carnival is thus reflected in the cocoa dance with its political skeleton exposed. Although the play does not engage openly with the danger of carnival being altered to a servile inscription of neocolonialism by its commercial debasement to an adjunct of the tourism industry, as Walcott fears in "What the Twilight Says," the tracing of carnival back to its roots in French culture, which the play foregrounds, implicitly raises these issues, to which the end position of the play offers no easy resolution.

The culture of France is given focal representation in the play; its classical painting, literature, and music are all deployed as symbols of what is available to Trinidadians as a cultural "origin," should they wish to affiliate themselves to it. The binaries of culture, "high" and "low," are tied to those of class and race. The DeLaFontaines' "great house," the beautifully crafted rural estate house, and their town house, which (like Robinson Crusoe) they call their castle, are symbols with a complex meaning. The title of the first version of the play, *In a Fine Castle,* is an ironic reference to this, using a phrase from a Trinidadian children's song, therefore invested with great folk significance and important in the debate about the specificity of Trinidadian cultural identity. George Lamming with his title *In the Castle of My Skin* ironizes a Walcott phrase, signifying on the folksong to address a white girl's remoteness (in his poem it is "your" skin) from her young black admirer; Lamming's inversion centers the black youth, placing him in the "castle" of his racial identity, a place both of strength and isolation.[17] The play's centering of the "great house" as symbol of social relations is thus linked to the whole question of race through the folksong as signifier, developed through the region's literature. It is a fine example of the interaction of "high" and "low" traditions that to Walcott is typically Caribbean.

As the play unfolds, it becomes evident that it is particularly interested in the racial attitudes that accompany the revolutionary politics. Clodia, secure in her Trinidadian identity, expressed textually by her use of Trinidadian English, finds herself when "jumping up" at carnival singled out as an outsider by a black militant because of her race. As a white person, she is defined by some as irredeemably not Trinidadian. The way this is introduced invites the audience to sympathize with Clodia's sense of injustice. But the reading of such an episode will vary according to the audience: Clodia's narration to a predominantly black Trinidadian audience, particularly one contemporary to the social upheaval portrayed, will have invited the majority community to consider the implications of its actions and attitudes in the name of a racially inclusive concept of community; but played to a predominantly white northern audience, it will read very differently, tending to entrench negative racial stereotypes and social divisions. This difficulty affects the reading of the whole play: it could be regarded as either a plea for a long-established minority to be accepted as insiders under the new order, or as a pro-white defense of the old order. The former is, I think, what is intended, but to northern audiences not versed in Caribbean history and social attitudes, the latter reading may tend to dominate. This has serious implications for how Walcott is seen, as there is a misleading tendency for him to be co-opted to a reactionary standpoint, characterized by nostalgia.

Walcott clearly signals the inadequacy of Victor's mimetic approach to art. He shows tableaux reproducing Watteau's imagery to be a static, dead art characterized by nostalgia, locking the Trinidadians of the twentieth century into the roles of the past. His son, Tony, however, is a carnival designer in the Trinidadian style, making images for the mass of people to move to, not carefully composed myths of a frozen order. The essence of creolization is change; a creole culture is one that continues to change, characterized by an ongoing process of creative transformation, of which carnival is the great symbol. Just as Victor's art is locked in to an old doomed concept, so are Agatha's politics. Her Marxism is shown as skin-deep (ironically). As soon as she finds herself in a colonial situation, her socialism, important as the catalyst of political change, is compromised by her readiness to adopt the ways of the white mistress. Brown, the journalist, characterizes her as a neoimperialist in her manipulation of the 1970s Trinidad that she has taken as her home: it is a case of "[r]emote control of the colonies," in which her narration of a myth of Victor's art is part of an attempt to "present this family in a golden light / as if it were some Impressionist masterpiece." She is pulling political strings. Of her manipulation of the government minister, Brown says, "she moves Jean Beauxchamps any way she likes."

As the two senior white personas are problematized as moral signifiers, the two white children, Tony and Clodia, are moved into sharper focus as relatively uncomplicated positive signifiers of the new nationalism. Clodia is coded with her love of the island, its people, its natural landscapes, and its culture, as honorably Trinidadian; as is Tony, by his commitment to the artistic potential of carnival. The generations represent history: time is the factor that can transform the expatriate to the native, the cultural metropolitan to the indigenous creole. But the test of nationality is not how long an individual or a family has been resident but what their attitude to their place of residence is. Once it has been embraced fully as "home," the location "belongs" to the resident, of whatever history; and that embrace necessarily involves a commitment to the indigenous culture. However, the "high-low" scheme of culture complicates this, because Walcott is also pleading that the indigenous art forms should not be confined to a "low" model of mass appeal. He wants his own exploration of the potential extension of popular forms into "high" art (as exemplified in this play) accepted to be just as Trinidadian as carnival itself. The play needs to be seen against another argument from "What the Twilight Says" about the cultural policies of the newly independent Caribbean nations, with their "prostitutions of a tourist culture."[18] The commercial debasement of what had been dignified folk forms is attacked for its own sake but also as the root position from which Walcott's own artistic contribution to the national culture is marginalized. What the official policy sidelines as elitist is, to Walcott, the route to growth and a crucial tug against the seemingly relentless convergence of popularity with commercial vacuity. He honors folk forms by using them in new art, not debasing them with new commercialism.

Ironically, however, it is in its representation of racial roles in power and culture that the play eventually fails. It problematizes both the white attitudes of Victor and Agatha and the black attitudes of the revolutionaries, in a way that would require a carefully calculated balance if the dialectics represented are to provoke thought by their inner contradictions, as Brecht wanted. But in the event there is no contest, as the imagery associated with Victor's art dominates the art of the drama. The relationships between the white characters are also more important to the play than those of the black characters, who tend to remain symbolic in their roles. Sydney, the nephew of the loyal George, who lives and plays with the DeLaFontaine children as a boy, grows up to become a revolutionary who calls himself Colonel Daga and ends up a sacrifice to the restoration of order. He objects, as an adult, to the way Victor had made him play the servant role in the past: "Dressing me up like I was some pappyshow. / That was the last Carnival I ever play." Jean, the maid, becomes Minister for Housing in the postindependence government. Both, however, are marginal to the main action as practical design, although not dialectically marginal.

Although the play begins by mapping the island as a place apart—Cythera, a paradise outside time (but awkwardly reminiscent of the Hollywood period romance with its rather phony governess and its upstairs/downstairs division crossed but not disrupted)—it shows the romance to be illusory, as history irrupts to destroy the "great house" idyll. As history unfolds, the class barriers are breached, with the new order taking on working-class people like Jean as government ministers. The reciprocal movement is the toppling of the ruling class. As the social unrest of 1970 develops offstage, news is brought to the DeLaFontaines' town house "castle" of their beautiful old estate house being burnt down. The establishment fights back. A helicopter circles overhead and the military forces catch Sydney and bring back his body. To Agatha, time is the real enemy. The play articulates a powerful desire for a place apart from history, with its cataclysms, its misguided idealisms. It still feels like something created under curfew. But for all the initial ludic "suspension" of time, time is in fact the dimension that makes possible not only the revolutionary history but the creole culture.

The DeLaFontaine children are also involved in change. Clodia, educated in England but passionately Trinidadian, is persuaded to leave the island at the end of the play. She makes a powerful speech to the journalist about her love of the island:

> I really not smart enough for your kind, you see. I don't know what I want. Ah can't paint. I don't read no poetry, my head is pure sawdust, but I know one thing. I know I stupid. But leave me stupid, because if is stupidness to love this country, the mountains, the flowers, black people, the savannah, the sea, then I proud of my stupidness! And now they wouldn't let me love it because I'm white. And I can't stand all you intellectuals who keep changing your mind and your skin, because maybe my father was no great shakes as an artist, but he wasn't no damn lizard to change when colours changed. He loved this place, and what hurt him was how he couldn't express that love of it beautifully enough.

This is a significant defense of Victor, in keeping with Walcott's consistent privileging of the benign discourse of art over the dangerous one of politics, and a powerful exposition of his belief that a sincere love of a country should be the only test of national identity. The pressures on Clodia expose in the Brechtian manner the consequences of ideology. Because of her love for Sydney and her wish to aid the cause, she consents to leave: "if I'm in the way of their winning, let me go away, then." Her willingness to sacrifice her own happiness for what she loves makes her the key to the latter part of the play, lending her a heroic stature. Her departure closes the play, in a scene made consciously to echo the first, of Agatha's arrival, by Clodia narrating it to Brown, who comes to see her off. The play is thus patterned on a reciprocal migration; the white woman of one generation who arrives, opportunistically, replaced by the white woman of the next who leaves, self-sacrificially. The audience is invited to reflect on which is the better Trinidadian.

The story of Clodia's brother is a different matter. As noted, where his father Victor was involved in a mimetic art—copying Watteau both in his paintings and by organizing the family into eighteenth-century tableaux—Tony (Watteau's name Antoine anglicized and familiarized) becomes a designer for carnival. Victor's colonial affiliation to a European art implicated in the old power relations is therefore replaced by the next generation's commitment to the local and indigenous culture: carnival in Trinidad is a syncretist art form that is specifically Trinidadian. Tony does not intend to leave. He and Clodia go opposite ways. His sister finally contradicts his assertion that "we can't move" by her departure: the twin possibilities are offered for comparison—on the one hand, the continuing presence of white people in the Caribbean; on the other, the forcing out of whites by the demand for racial revenge.

Walcott thus opens up a dialectical view of history through his portrayal of the fortunes of the "great house" microcosm. He chooses to disrupt imperialist assumptions from the outset, focusing not on a conventional encounter between an upper-class European and a lower-class colonial, but on an upper-class colonial (Victor) and a lower-class European (Agatha). But this is the white story. His presentation of the black story begins with the upwardly mobile mixed-race journalist of 1970 and then revisits the past with its history of black servitude. But the early scenes show the essential lack of difference between the servants and those whom they serve: George is a man of as fine a sensibility as Victor, and Sydney is a better horseman than the DeLaFontaine children and is otherwise indistinguishable from them—indeed he loves Clodia and she him—except by his skin and the social position to which it confines him at that point of history. The later scenes showing a society in which the talented young black person is not limited by a glass ceiling (Sydney as a boy could only aspire to becoming a jockey) model a social justice that is nonetheless still complicated by the continuance of the "great house" phenomenon. The burning down of Santa Rosa is to Sydney an important symbol of the need to attack neocolonialism: if families like the DeLaFontaines retain past feudal privileges, then independence has little meaning.

The emotional center of the play is ambivalent, however. The binary thematics of stasis and action requires that carnival be kept marginal, like the revolution, in order to allow the stage to be appropriated as the ideal zone outside time, the play's Cythera, but its consequence, the absence of vigor at the center, remains a weakness. It is intended perhaps as a Bergmanesque reflection on psychology, not that of the individual but of cultural groups, in the quest to define not a personal subjectivity but a collective identity. For all its implicit targeting of the European-oriented colonial elite (as opposed to their thoroughly Trinidadian children), it seems seduced by their style and by Victor's artistic premise, of the desirability of a filial art. Visually, the intellectualized re-creation of Watteau dominates the play's iconography rather than Trinidadian carnival in all its heterogeneity. Victor insists on seeing Agatha as a Watteau shepherdess and organizes the whole family into the Watteau tableau. The dominant image is that of Watteau's famous painting *The Embarkation for Cythera,* which is referred to in the 1992 text and formed the basis for the stage design in the Birmingham production. Speaking in 1981, Walcott acknowledged his method of deploying painting in his plays:

> All directors, all scenic artists—and I do paint—say to themselves, well, this is like X or Y, after all it's no different to film. You have an image using human beings and backdrops and . . . dark and light. You are painting, really. Whenever there has been an echo, I have chosen that echo—like in *Drums and Colours* an imitation of "The Boyhood of Raleigh," which is a sort of cliché but I wanted it. Then in *Marie Laveau* I wanted something impressionistic like Manet in the beginning . . . I used the "*Déjeuner sur l'Herbe. . . .*" You just do that there because you want the audience there to get that echo deliberately. That's your choice, it might be a cliché and corney but you do it.[19]

Stage directions for *The Last Carnival* specify direct replications of Watteau's imagery. In the 1992 Birmingham production, an enormous suspended cloth like a sail, painted with the "Embarkation" image, dominated the otherwise minimally dressed stage, and the color and composition of the human tableau that Victor arranges was immediately evocative of Watteau.

In addition, the carnival tableau is not just visual but is to be accompanied by recitation of Baudelaire's post-Watteau poem "Un Voyage à Cythère" (which is given a reprise later in the play in the 1992 version), as well as by Oswald on his knees as an absurd representation of Toulouse-Lautrec, and Agatha dressed as Jane Avril. The text thus moves the erotic to center stage. But Cythera as the locus of desire is always remote, never achieved. The whole idea of embarkation frames the play, with Agatha's arrival in Trinidad signifying her leaving of her native Britain in quest of some kind of fulfillment, in ironic counterpoint with the leaving of Clodia at the end from the same wharf. Morally, the crucial difference is that the European is serving her own desire, while the Trinidadian is serving another's. The play shows different dreams bringing the characters to different points of departure. The dream of social justice is set up in opposition to Victor's dream of the great tradition of art. Victor is drawn into the Watteauesque illusion until it kills him. Sydney is drawn into a different dream, which faith in his own heroism turns into a dangerous nightmare, killing him too. Agatha, with her dream of a fairer society, is seduced by materialism to betray her ideals, and she ends up living a lie. The wisdom of Baudelaire's poem is that the dream-isle of love, "Cythère," is no paradise but a barren and gloomy place—"cette île triste et noire"—where the poet projects a self-image as a tortured figure: "Dans ton île, ô Vénus! je n'ai trouvé debout / Qu'un gibet symbolique où pendait mon image."[20] Such metropolitan exotic nihilism is alien to Caribbean culture, as Walcott sees it.

The exoticism of fevered Watteau and self-tortured Baudelaire are aligned also with the metropolitan dream of paradise in French nineteenth-century opera. The play refers to the tenor aria "O paradis," from the scene in Meyerbeer's opera *L'Africaine* when Vasco da Gama discovers the long-sought new land. In the 1992 text of Walcott's play, the aria is introduced nostalgically as a song the brothers' mother sang long ago. The play loads these manifestations of French culture heavily with superficial nostalgia, later strongly coded negative, and alien to the local culture.

Walcott, in his poem about Watteau (and particularly about his *Embarkation*), speaks of "the hollow at / the heart of all embarkations," the urge to move on being "that prodigious urging toward twilight." Watteau's Cythera he perceives is "far and feverish," a kind of "nowhere," an exoticism, the hopeless dream of the unattainable. The form of the dream is determined by the waking consciousness, is its reverse: it is the "mirror of what is." A bleak rationale is left at the end, a nihilism of endlessly inverting opposed images, "mises en abîme," suggesting a postmodern evacuation of meaning: "Paradise is life repeated spectrally, / an empty chair echoing the emptiness."[21] If the dream can only reflect the real, there is little hope. Analogously, in political terms, if the revolution is doomed to repeat the errors of what it replaces, to mirror what was, there can never be progress. In the play, if Trinidad's carnival is just a mirror of its European origin, symbolized by Watteau, nothing has changed. But the corollary to this is that if Trinidad's revolution is the mirror of the Haitian revolution, which was a transatlantic "creolization" of the French Revolution, applied to a different society in a new way, then the possibilities remain open-ended.

As the play unfolds, however, so does its ambivalence. The "last" carnival, of the play's title, signifies in part the last blaze of glory—part of the "sunset" imagery of "What the Twilight Says" and of *Another Life* (from the same period)—of an anachronistic planter class before succumbing to history. But in the play's aesthetic, the perception of the beauty which that class symbolizes introduces a powerful nostalgia, with which the rise of the black underclass—shown as morally just, but swiftly and mechanistically—cannot compete. In the end, the play fails because it fails to integrate its ideological and its aesthetic tendencies: the attempt to contribute to an epic history is undermined by the play's loving fascination with the Watteau aesthetic and what it stands for. Its courageous and potentially powerful project to interrogate the racial exclusivism of Black Power politics is undercut by its parading of European elite culture, the subtleties of the aesthetic point about assimilation into Trinidadian culture obscured. Victor's abuse of Trinidad as a society of Philistines who "came to this paradise, this Cythera, / and with your Calypsoes turn into swine!" resonates without irony or rejoinder, as he tells them, "This is your last Carnival! You hear me?" The chance that the plot offers, of enacting the alignment of the twin energies in the Trinidadian carnival art of Tony, is not realized in the script (although in production greater emphasis might be made to fall on this). Although the dialogue refers to the extraordinary fact that carnival is continuing despite the collapse of the social order, the intrinsically revolutionary nature of carnival itself is unstated. The live carnival of the streets is outside the play: Clodia comes in from participating, but that is as near as the drama itself gets. The significant early scene in which a dancer masked as an African jumps out at Agatha offered a line of approach that is rapidly passed over. It is co-opted only to the characterization of Agatha, her abrupt reaction representing the worst kind of elitism, and giving an early indication that her role is to be problematized. Her shift from flaming revolutionary to colonial memsahib is crucial to the play's dialectics yet somehow fails to convince. It seems that once privilege is accepted, commitment to the cause of the oppressed is fatally compromised.

Unfortunately, the play delivers its resolution crudely. Perhaps because of time constraints caused by the complex plot, the return of Sydney and Jean as agents of the new political order is presented almost as a *deus ex machina* and therefore risks seeming contrived and unreal. It may be that Walcott, who focuses on the white story, wishes to surprise his audience as he surprises the DeLaFontaines and Agatha with the sudden realization that the revolution is already under way—that the old order that secured their privilege is already, and inevitably, crumbling. A late detail almost redeems the situation: the Major's pride in returning the DeLaFontaines' horse, on which Sydney was fleeing, the horse unscathed in his killing. An ironic target is momentarily revealed—the corruption of the new power moguls, intent not on reform but on securing privilege for themselves. As Walcott says in his satiric poem "The Spoiler's Return," "nothing ain't change but colour and attire."[22] But again, the moment soon passes. His wish to expose the corruptions of power risks decentering the play as moral project: if in the end the tone is cynical, the idealism vanishes, and with it the serious interest in the staged debates and any serious hope of change for the better.

In a passage cut from the 1992 revision, as the revolution begins, Tony refuses to abandon his carnival plans, explaining that this year's designs, in tribute to his father, are based on Watteau: "Now, with this light like the fire, orange, and the silks, the sunset, I see the moment of stillness Victor wanted. Because we are here, we can't move. Just like the people in the painting. Motionless. . . ." Ultimately, this version suggests, art is not history, and Watteau can still be beautiful. Above all, art can transcend time by locating itself in myth's "place apart." But the play's meaning as myth is that the epic story of migrations and arrivals, shared by all Trinidad's diverse peoples, including the whites, can be concluded in growing rooted there, in achieving the stasis of painting. The stage, like the Watteau iconography, is thus a metonymic signifier of Trinidadian society as a place of cessation of motion, of "home." But the dialectical construction of this myth in opposition to the myth of Trinidad, as typified by the restless energy of carnival or revolution, manipulates both carnival and revolution into rhetorically negative positions. The intended privileging of

Trinidadian assimilation and creolization of foreign models is then powerless against the iconographic authority of the stasis. The play is divided against itself. It needs to allocate a lot of its space/time to the establishment of the thesis about stasis (which is intrinsically anti-dramatic), thus relegating to the margins the energized Trinidad, but these logistics destroy the balance necessary for the Brechtian dialectics to work.

Brechtian epic drama needs and uses ambivalence. What flaws this play is its failure to show clearly enough how its yoking of the heterogeneous worlds of art and politics works as a single project. The play itself is an enactment of the thesis that art itself is a political practice, but its internal dynamic is unclear. It remains nonetheless a courageous play, a landmark in the history of racial politics, and a work of great ambition and achievement that may yet find its ideal form.

11

"The Joy of the Ghost Dance"

The American Epic

> *Caliban:* This island's mine, by Sycorax my mother,
> Which thou tak'st from me.
> ***The Tempest,* I.ii.331–32**

> *Chief Sitting Bull:* If a man loses anything and goes back and looks carefully for it he will find it and that is what the Indians are doing now.
> **Brown, *Bury My Heart at Wounded Knee,* 415.**

Walcott's as yet unpublished play *The Ghost Dance,* which has an intertextual relationship with its contemporary, *Omeros,* visits, like *Henri Christophe* and *Drums and Colours,* a historical subject. Here Walcott moves on, however, from Caribbean history to that of North America, but once again the topic chosen is epic: the play presents from an unfamiliar angle a key episode in the colonization of America. Already recognized in the discourse of history as a moment of symbolic significance whose meaning extends beyond its immediate time frame, it is the final phase of the suppression of the Native American population of the Great Plains to which Walcott turns his attention. The events that led up to the massacre at Wounded Knee have, in recent decades, been subject to revisionist historiography: that which in the first half of the century was regarded as illustrating the heroism of the white man's conquest of the Great Plains has been reevaluated from an Indian-centered perspective, to give a tragic reading. A long chapter of oppression amounting to genocide reached a closure in that winter of 1890. As in *The Last Carnival,* there is in this play an apocalyptic momentum to the events to be narrated: the tone is one of closure and doom. But the historic pain of loss—like Caliban's—is contextualized (as so often in Walcott) in a mythic perception that encompasses and transcends it. Sitting Bull's faith in the possibility of recovery will seem tragic to some, but to Walcott the sacred dance which the Sioux performed in the faith that they could redeem their losses does not signify tragic illusion but a superior truth.

The Ghost Dance is also like *The Last Carnival* in that Walcott chooses to double the spiraling of the apocalyptic with a narrative of romance. This raises a problem of audience response. Just as the love affairs of *The Last Carnival* can seem to obscure the dialectical meaning of that play, so the love themes of *The Ghost Dance* can seem to chafe against the tragedy of the Indian story. If, however, the reasons for the inclusion of the romance element are carefully examined, it will be seen that both plays deploy sexual love dialectically as part of the reading of history, and that it is therefore central and vital to the meaning, not a trite extraneous concession to popular taste. Walcott's method in *The Ghost Dance* is Brechtian in that he proposes contradictory signs to encourage dialectical thought, but in other ways it builds on the mythic theater he has developed, in which symbolism is used to deliver a metaphysical meaning.

First, however, a consideration of the play as history helps to account for its origin and intention. The history that gives rise to Walcott's creativity is a particularly shameful chapter in the destructive history of white power in North America, one that put the final nail in the coffin of Native American hopes by breaking the power of the Sioux nation. Two connected events wielded the hammer: the killing of the revered chief, Sitting Bull, then the notorious massacre at Wounded Knee at which another chief, Big Foot, died. Walcott explores the first of these events in the play. The main events were as follows. When forty-three Indian police under Lieutenant Bull Head surrounded Sitting Bull's log cabin on December 15, 1890, to arrest him, they were opposed by four times as many Indian warriors. When shooting broke out, in which Sitting Bull fell, the American cavalry who had been held in reserve, with their superior fire power, were brought up, and a full-scale battle resulted.[1] The survivors of Sitting Bull's people fled and joined Big Foot's group heading for the gathering of the remaining clans at Pine Ridge. On December 30, two hundred miles to the south of where Sitting Bull died, the chapter was closed in the Wounded Knee massacre, in which Big Foot and more than two hundred of his people, mostly women and children, already prisoners of the military, were killed. The independence of the indigenous Americans was effectively over.

Retrieval is one of the projects of counterdiscourse. As Michel Foucault says, "The manifest discourse . . . is really no more than the repressive presence of what it does not say." Although history cannot be relived or altered, the discourse of history can be reconceived, there being no privileging of "authenticity" in Foucault's formulation: "We must be ready to receive every moment of discourse in its sudden irruption. . . . Discourse must not be referred to the distant presence of the origin, but treated as and when it occurs."[2] The re-narration of the Native American story in the last quarter of the twentieth century is conspicuous because of that history's role in popular Western culture, with a number of popular American films revisiting the Indian story from a revisionist standpoint. The aporia of the dominant discourse can be filled with narrations of recovery—the recovery and dissemination of lost texts, but also re-creations, imaginative mappings of lost experience. Walcott's play is an act of recovery, but it proceeds by a method that is easily misapprehended, an epic method that shoulders a particular responsibility in relation to the future as well as the past. In that sense, it is intensely political: it engages with America's dream of itself by both raising awareness of the past and by leaving the door open to a more benign future—modeling the possibility of hope. "Recovery" is a term that has meaning in the sense of retrieval but also in the sense of restoration to health.

Walcott's perception of himself as a St. Lucian Caribbean has always been informed by his sense of identity as an American, as a member of that cross-fertilization of cultures that Columbus initiated in the Americas. His move to Boston in the late 1970s led to an increasingly direct creative involvement with the United States, addressing, principally in his poetry, not only the fantasy of the glamorized American present and its compassionless reality but also the American past. In *Omeros,* the narrator tells how

> . . . Manifest Destiny was behind me now.
> My face frozen in the ice-cream paradiso
> of the American dream, like the Sioux in the snow.[3]

As well as using the same approach as to his island geography, reading both rural and urban landscapes as historic texts, Walcott focuses on what could be called epic moments in that history, when symbolic events exhibit in microcosm the essential meaning of the sweeps and confusions of history's macro-scale. As noted above, his focus has frequently fallen on the great absence from the American present, that of the Native Americans, in all but a very few enclaves. In his writing, he makes them present, refusing oblivion. Their ghosts people his fiction, from the Sauteurs of *Another Life* to the Ghost Dancers of *Omeros*. While he was working on *Omeros,* however, he was also working on *The Ghost Dance,* written for an upstate New York college. It arose from the intention to re-create the history of the epic moment of the Indian tragedy. This play presents a surface that can, I think, be misleading, if it is not seen in the context of its symbolic meaning. The problem is that it *appears* to be interested predominantly in the white experience of that phase of the subduing of the West, when, rather, it is attempting to understand and mark what happened to the Sioux by giving a dialectical account of the origin of history's givens, and to create meaning for the future.

The Sioux's Ghost Dance has a special place in the history of the Americas, coming as it did at the final crisis for Native Americans, in the autumn of 1890, the historic point of irreversible loss. Just as the political oppressors in the name of white America were abandoning all scruples to achieve "whiteout" on the remaining Indian communities of the Great Plains, Indian culture reached into its own creativity to produce a new myth. The myth promised the return of the dead and of the land with its buffalo—of all that had been lost to the white man—which would come with the spring if the Ghost Dance was performed all winter, a dance performed in a special shirt that rendered its wearer invulnerable. In the words of the disseminator of the new myth, Wovoka, known as the Paiute Messiah,

> All Indians must dance, everywhere, keep on dancing. Pretty soon in next spring Great Spirit come. He bring back all game of every kind. The game be thick everywhere. All dead Indians come back and live again. They all be strong, just like young men, be young again . . . medicine man tell Indians to send word to all Indians to keep up dancing and the good time will come.[4]

In terms of the linear time of history, it can be argued that this resort to myth precipitated the final political collapse of the tribes. As Dee Brown reads the fatal events of December 1890, "Had it not been for the sustaining force of the Ghost Dance religion, the Sioux in their grief and anger over the assassination of Sitting Bull might have risen up against the guns of the soldiers. So prevalent was their belief that the white men would soon disappear and that with the next greening of the grass their dead relatives and friends would return, they made no retaliations."[5] Yet for Walcott, the Ghost Dance is not a negative signifier. For him its appeal is rather that it shows the creativity of faith as a way of resisting a tragic history.

The background to the terrible events of December 1890 that concluded the Native American tragedy—specifically the murder of Sitting Bull—is given emotive exploration by Walcott, but he balances this bleak history by his attention to the Ghost Dance as cultural phenomenon, as resisting sign of redemptive faith. By focusing on the Ghost Dance, he does not diminish or mitigate the horror of the history but does suggest that the horror is not the only dimension of events. He offers, as it were, a politics of faith, which is not bound by time as history is but can continue to have an effect indefinitely by means of cultural rehearsal, repetition, and renewal. Thus although the events cannot be undone, and the individuals and society then lost cannot be recovered, the ideas they stood for can again become part of current thought and may even restore a later moribund society to life. For Walcott, the great dream of the Ghost Dance shamans, that if the people would dance through the winter they could defeat the destruction that the white men's history was bringing and dance their people to restoration, has the same creative potential today as it did in 1890.

Derek Walcott's concern is with art, but with art as a cultural phenomenon implicated at every level in how cultures see themselves and their others, and therefore with the resulting political realities. The Ghost Dance, as well as being regarded as a tragic enabler of the closure of Native American autonomy on the Great Plains, is also for Walcott irrevocably positive, in that it shows the human spirit triumphing over negative experience with its creativity—specifically a syncretist creativity, in its blend of traditional faiths with messianic Christianity—and with its faith in renewal. The fact that political reality may not (yet) deliver renewal does not, for Walcott, cancel the value of the faith. As Catherine Weldon says in the play, "When history wins it doesn't mean God has lost." The role of art, as he sees it, is to keep before us the images of potentiality, while demystifying the history.

In turning his own creative attention to the Ghost Dance, therefore, Walcott both deconstructs the historical events of 1890 and reconstructs the magic of faith in human potential. It relates to his symbolic use of dance as motif in *The Last Carnival,* where the meaning of "jumping-up" at the Trinidad carnival is related to the "dancing" of the cocoa. He has used the Ghost Dance twice, in different genres: to bring a pan-American dimension to the dance symbolism of his epic poem *Omeros,* and, while he was working on that poem, to focus an entire drama on it. The deployment of the story in *Omeros* is self-sufficient and does not require knowledge of the play, but the play enlarges understanding of the Ghost Dance's importance to Walcott, as well as being an important work of American literature in its own right.

It seems that the idea for the play led to the appearance of the Ghost Dance in the poem, rather than *vice versa.* The play was premiered by the

Cardboard Alley Players at Hartwick College, Oneonta, New York, on November 9, 1989, and the poem was published in 1990, but these dates by themselves are not conclusive. Duncan Smith, director of theatre at Hartwick College, has explained his own role in the genesis of the play:

> Thanks to the efforts of Dr. Robert Bensen, Mr. Walcott has been a regular visitor to Hartwick for some time. One of these visits was to a class in which I was planning to develop a script about the death of Sitting Bull. The historical material I showed him seemed to resonate deeply with some ideas he had long been dwelling on, and he announced he was going to write a play on the subject for us. . . . After two years of discussions and several workshop sessions, he delivered the script.[6]

It seems, therefore, that the presence of the Ghost Dance in *Omeros* can be traced to Duncan Smith. Robert Bensen notes that Walcott "began the script during a month-long residency in January 1987, while working on improvisations derived from accounts of the Sioux ghost dance and the death of Sitting Bull."[7] Smith notes the elements, marginal to the history, that appealed to Walcott: "He was particularly taken with the figure of Catherine Weldon, a minor figure in the accounts. He built her into a full character complete with a relationship with James McLaughlin, for whom he also supplied a fictional personality." The real Catherine Weldon was indeed a Bostonian who had lived with and been close to Sitting Bull, acting as his intermediary with the American authorities. Historically, as in the play, McLaughlin was an Indian agent, married to an Indian woman. He had a long history of contact with the Indians, and as the local agent charged with Indian affairs by the government, he played a key role in initiating the final events. The Indians in real life dubbed McLaughlin "White Hair."[8] Walcott does not refer to McLaughlin by this name, but he seems to have been prompted by it to give Catherine in his play the Indian name "Bright Hair Who Loves Us." From Smith's account, it is clear that the ideas for the play seeded the corresponding events in the poem: "Catherine Weldon did find her place in an even larger epic . . . when she found her way into *Omeros*." However, given the two-year genesis of the play and the three-year genesis of the poem, roughly coterminous, presumably, in 1989, when the *Omeros* manuscript would most probably have been delivered to Farrar, Straus and Giroux for publication in 1990, it is clear that after the starting point in Duncan Smith's idea for a drama about the death of Sitting Bull, Walcott worked up both his play and his poem in tandem.[9]

It is therefore not surprising that there should be a close match between some of the images of both, although in obvious ways they are so different. Both pair flour and snow metaphorically, for example, in exposing the way famine was used to suppress the indigenous people, and both use the chiaroscuro of a lantern in a frozen landscape. They are also complementary: the poem's selective representation, in which the most significant elements of the story are given symbolic resonance, enables the play to be read with a livelier awareness of its own symbolic structure, and the play enables some of the choices implicit in the poem to be better understood.

In the play, Walcott's foregrounding of historical figures such as Catherine Weldon and Major James McLaughlin, the Indian agent, is immediately striking. The play opens and closes with Kicking Bear, in real life a Minneconjou from the Cheyenne River, who had made a pilgrimage to Nevada to see the Messiah of the new religion, and who brought news of the Ghost Dance to Sitting Bull. There are other Indians in the play, most centrally Swift Running Deer, a Christian convert, given the name Lucy, whose tragedy is at the heart of the play as she commits suicide. But in terms of the balance of representation, the bulk of the dialogue is spoken by white people, and they are on stage significantly more of the time than the Indians, which raises the possibility that the play might be repeating the historic marginalization of the Indians.

In Duncan Smith's phrase, Walcott decided "to keep the agony of the Sioux as context not as the center of focus," but this may be misleading, as he was not betraying the importance of the Sioux's history. Although the white people's story, as Walcott re-creates it (and he may have had the ethnic composition of the group from whom he had to cast the play in mind), may seem to deflect attention away from the tragedy of the Sioux, reflection produces a different possibility. First, the concept of the play is founded on a third term between polarized binaries: the Native American story is in antithesis to the white story, but those who represent the synthesis of cultures take center stage. Then, Walcott perceived, I think, that if he was to represent usefully the disastrous phase of Native American history, which has come to symbolize the whole tragic history of their peoples, he would need to show the processes whereby power came to be used to make such terrible events happen. Revealing the ordinariness of history is a route to an understanding of responsibility. Revealing the mixed motives, and failure to see the consequences of their actions, in people like ourselves can alert us to our own complicity in political and human disaster. To avoid or combat oppression, it is necessary to understand the oppressor. By creating a story around Catherine Weldon and James

McLaughlin, Walcott has been able to show how even the well-intentioned—those who are liberal for their time—bear a direct responsibility for the tragic outcome.

It should also be borne in mind that production offers opportunities for bringing out certain aspects of the meaning, for creating a signifying dynamic, for instance by emphasizing symbolism. The whole significance of the land to the Indians was given imaginative expression in the Hartwick production, designed by Richard and Sally Montgomery, by making the natural world read as an Indian construct, people and their surroundings sharing one identity:

> With so rich a verbal setting as this verse play has, designer Richard Montgomery (who has designed eight premieres of Walcott's plays) enriched it further, making the set look as if Indians had made it; stripped trees lashed into an Indian burial scaffold, a dense forest of erosion cloth, a platform formed by tipi poles stage-right that served as a mound of earth, Weldon's cabin, the army's courtroom, and Dr. Beddoes' office. Sally Montgomery designed the costumes to play with the set, which made the army's fresh uniforms look incongruous and invasive, while the Indians and the set were costumed alike, as it were, in buckskin, feathers and paint, an effect enhanced by hanging fringed and feathered war shields (part of the Indian costume) on the trees as part of the scenery.[10]

With the action given visual representation of this order, the scenes between the white characters must have read quite clearly as subordinate to the Indian story, the purpose being to disclose the processes of history, but also the possibility of transcending it.

In Walcott's symbolic treatment, the dominance of white people and their culture is presented through the imagery of a white winter, both in the language of the play and in its action. This is appropriate also because the metaphor of whiteout for the political reality was central to the symbolic language of the Ghost Dance faith: as the spring would loosen the grip of the white winter and bring back life, so the Indians would be released from the grip of the whites and the vigor of the tribes would return. Although the play focuses on the positive hope of the Ghost Dance, it does not duck the tragedy. The main historical events take place offstage, but a carefully thought-out plot, which investigates those events' origin and consequences, is constructed for the main characters.

Walcott creates the part of Swift Running Deer, a Christian convert christened Lucy, to bring the pathos of the Indians' plight center stage. She is a part of the play's investigation of interculturalism. He builds on the historical fact of McLaughlin's marriage to an Indian by paralleling it with her story: she is about to marry a young white lieutenant. But after a key scene in which, wearing a symbolically white dress, she is humiliated by the white Christians by being made to dance, she is then drawn into Kicking Bear's Ghost Dance (wearing now her Sioux dress and with white markings only on her face), resuming her Indian identity. The first act ends with Kicking Bear at the end of the trance-like dance with "arms extended, crucified, transfixed," an image of sacrifice. Early in the second act, her father brings news that Lucy has killed herself. Catherine blames faith—"she paid the price of that difference"—and tells McLaughlin that his wife, another convert, is also spiritually dead: "Her heart is dead. She is among the lifeless. / They all are. They knew they were already ghosts." The idea of the dance of ghosts embraces all the doomed Indians. In the focus on those Indians who have the most direct contact with the white people and their culture, Walcott is able to show that assimilation is no protection, those who have adopted white ways remaining marginalized and threatened—psychologically made zombies.

The play's spatial language of inside and outside embodies the white Americans' annexation of centrality and their marginalization of everyone else. The dominant foreground, a hard interior world of army post, domestic kitchen, and courtroom, from which not only (inadequate) food and (infected) blankets but (Western) ideas are dispensed to the Indians, is set up in opposition to the natural world outside, across the stage and framing it, peopled with Indians who know how to inhabit a landscape without destroying it. The binarism is set out clearly in the opening stage directions, with stage right, Catherine baking in the ranch kitchen, and stage left, "A small stand of birches. An INDIAN, KICKING BEAR, in the birches. Light snow powdering his blanket, his hair, his face white."

The flour Catherine pours becomes an image of the snow, as in *Omeros,* in a symbolic representation of the policy to hold the Indians in reservations on starvation rations. The end of the play echoes the opening, with Catherine gathering her belongings and going out into the blizzard, followed by a final mime in which Kicking Bear is "whited-out" by the Christians:

> The Plain, snow, lightly. KICKING BEAR walks towards the hills, stops. He sits in the snow. He stays still. Snow thickens.
> The PARISHIONERS, in white, white faces, white veils, begin to circle him, each carrying a small sack of flour. Wind, howling.

> KICKING BEAR leans against a drift.
> The GHOST PARISHIONERS drift nearer.
> KICKING BEAR lies back. The GHOST CONGREGATION pour flour over his stiffening body, then they wait. Wind. KICKING BEAR, powdered with the flour, lying in the snow.
> The GHOST CONGREGATION unfurl a white sheet, but one which is made of net when held up in the light, and cover KICKING BEAR, who disappears.

The racial symbolism of this sequence is unmistakable, but its pathos is informed also by mimetic truth. For an impoverished people, cold is a great killer, and countless Indians did starve in the snow as a direct result of displacement, inadequate rations, and military action.[11]

A photograph of Big Foot's body, frozen as if about to rise from the snow with the new year, has become one of the indelible icons of a terrible history. Robert Bensen records that the final image in the play's first production was an allusion to that icon, although the accompanying mime appears to have lost some of Walcott's meaning:

> Kicking Bear freezes to death wandering in the mountains. He contorts in the rigor mortised posture of Big Foot in the well known photograph from Wounded Knee, while in a brief masque, four white Snow Maidens pull a stage-wide sheet of white gauze over him for the delicate blizzard foretold in imagery throughout.[12]

In Walcott's stage directions, not only the general symbolism but the political agency of the whiteout is clear (not Snow Maidens but ghostly parishioners, white demons with their deadly flour), allowing not only the tragedy but also the guilt to be represented.

That Walcott chooses to expand the historical material and this tragic framing story with a romance between his two white protagonists may at first glance seem odd, as if to trivialize a serious theme, or perhaps to popularize it. Walcott's placing of romantic love at the heart of the play is, however, crucial to its meaning, as it parallels with vivid dramatic representation the positive symbolism of the Ghost Dance myth. One of the other great dances of the tribes, the Sun Dance, is a celebration of life through sexual love, with its chant, "Look at that young man / He is feeling good / Because his sweetheart / Is watching him."[13] In the play's opening sequence, Catherine, alone at the Parkin ranch, goes to bed after picking up "a child's hobby horse, made of a carved horse's head on a stick," which she stands in a corner. Part of her story unfolds about her absent son, with his oedipally wounded foot, whose death is eventually narrated: at the level of naturalism, the hobbyhorse is his. But as the play develops, the toy is used as sexual symbol, when Catherine allows McLaughlin to be her lover after a playful scene in which they both ride the hobbyhorse.

The role of the horse in the history of the Great Plains, for transport and war, is thus counterpointed with the sexual "ride" at the heart of the play. Just as the Ghost Dance stands for the possibility of renewal, so the capacity of individuals to love one another stands for renewal of both body and spirit. In consequence, the seasonal cycle of death and rebirth allows the death phase of political history to be read as implicit signifier of restoration. The play closes in death, but in that its discourse establishes a meaning for death as precursor of renewal, that closure seeds the hope of restoration. The Ghost Dancers believed that if they embodied with sufficient faith the truth of death, both representing and by performance reanimating their dead, they would enable the dead to regain life. The complex exchange of identity that spiritual possession implies can be transferred imaginatively to the sociopolitical dimension: the play's implication is that if we could be "possessed" by a better world, we would enact it and could make that world literally come about.

By presenting two equal opposing forces balance is the product. In its twinning of the negative and the positive, offering optimistic myth as a counter to tragic history, the play achieves an epic tone and takes its place alongside Walcott's other epic works. In Duncan Smith's view, the play, in being worked up, overreached itself and them:

> The process of working with Derek was both exciting and difficult. It was wonderful to watch him explore the struggles of his central characters, and I appreciated his decision to keep the agony of the Sioux as context not as the center of focus. In the end, however, I felt that the play got away from him. From an early, tight concentration on Catherine—the cabin scene was the first one he wrote—the piece expanded toward a John Ford, big screen, western epic. Frankly, the script grew to overwhelm our production capacity.[14]

While sympathizing with the dilemmas of a director (and actor—Smith played Dr. Beddoes, "a role Derek claimed he wrote for me"),[15] it is possible to see the play as epic without accepting the implications of scale that the Ford reference suggests. Walcott has for many decades tested a simple theatrical style for its ability to achieve epic resonance. Like Brecht, from his early days as a director he was after an epic theater in which the epic quality was not in the technical or budget resources or the size of the company but in the signifying structure of the drama, and particularly in its text:

> One of the advantages that I think I had as a playwright was the advantage of being very poor; of being in a poor country, of being in countries where you could not afford changes of scenery and therefore what you had to do had to happen in the immediate environment of the actor, and that meant that the language really had to do the work of the set. And generally it has always been that wherever the set has been the least consequential thing the theatre has been at its most powerful. Wherever you get the set dominating the idea or the concept of what you are enacting then you have theatre (in terms of language) that is very thin, because the language dares not get bigger than the room it's in. It stays within that room.[16]

That Walcott has not abandoned the ideas expressed here at the end of his long directorship of the Trinidad Theatre Workshop is clear from the *Ghost Dance* script, which opens with an important note on the staging: "There are several changes of locale. These changes, and indeed more importantly than the changes, the play should be performed fluently and simply, as Indian theatre, with minimal props, with blankets, poles, flags to indicate locations, and with no furniture, which would make it Western theatre. Actors should squat instead of sitting on chairs." The epic quality is evident, for instance, in the announcement of the death of Lucy by her father, presented in a superficially low-key manner, reminiscent of Brecht's Mother Courage's reception of the news of her children's deaths, yet implicitly signifying also her silent howl. Catherine Weldon, too, gets news of the death of her child, a boy, news that the female bearer delays delivering, by chattering: as Catherine slowly realizes what has happened so does the audience.

Another fine epic moment is that in which a stock scene of white stereotyping of the Indian, that of the drunken Indian, is inverted by poetry to something heroic: the skeptical rationalist Dr. Beddoes and McLaughlin interrogate Kicking Bear by offering him whisky, regarding him as a "poor possessed sod," but he turns the scene on its head with his prophetic vision, voiced from within, of the future for the tribe:

> They will know the rapture of exaltation,
> the feathers in their hair will make them eagles
> over the broken mountains, the lakes will enter
> and prickle their cold skins like the fishes,

> they will tire like the salmon of a ladder of stones,
> and not only the Sioux, not only the Sioux,
> the Arapahoes, the Cheyennes, the Brules, the Ogalalas,
> the Minneconjus, the Sansaras, when the deathdance begins,
> to the drum in the heart, before the wide silence.

The Ghost Dance becomes a deathdance, but in a play that regards death differently from the typical Western attitude. In a culture of faith, time is cyclical, always containing the certainty of return. As Catherine says at the end of the play, about her dead husband who will not return in life:

> I have arrived at that natural acceptance,
> through nature, not through progress, I can stand now
> at the dead centre at the heart of time
> where time itself becomes a ghost dancer,
> and everything that seemed surely insubstantial
> returns, and that is the joy of the ghost dance,
> that they, the Sioux, if they believe in nature
> must first die to return. Just like the seasons.

The play is interested in what happens between cultures in the creation of new nations. Walcott shows the interaction of Native America with Europe because that models the kind of synthesis out of which modern America has emerged. He chooses historical characters in intermediate positions—Catherine with her relationship with Sitting Bull, McLaughlin with his Indian wife, Swift Running Deer with her lieutenant—because through them he can explore the opportunities history offered, whether seized or missed. Sexual attraction is the great motor of intercultural contact and exchange. Cross-fertilization is shown happening both biologically and culturally. But the hobbyhorse symbol on which the play centers is implicit at the end: one of the real opportunities for love and creative exchange that history offered—Lucy and Lieutenant Brandon—is broken, but McLaughlin, with Catherine's blessing, returns to his silent Indian wife. Catherine, who entrusted her sick child to Indian medicine rather than Dr. Beddoes's kind, does not regret that decision, only that she was not with him at his death. The great significance of her role lies in her acceptance of death, something she has learned from the Indians. The only way to live in harmony with nature, rather than rapaciously, is to do as they do and accept death as part of nature. We see Catherine creolizing, becoming more Indian. It is a lesson to white culture with its ideas of progress, science, and modernity.

Catherine understands the difference between herself and McLaughlin: she uses a sexual relationship to further her loyalty to the Indian cause by trying to persuade McLaughlin to reveal his orders in relation to Sitting Bull, while he acts to the Indians' advantage, showing her his sealed orders, not because he believes in the cause but for her sake, only to regret it later and to redeem himself in reasserting his American loyalties by an act of zeal: the action he initiates to arrest Sitting Bull is thus glossed by Walcott as the complex product of a moral dilemma between duty and sexual desire, overlaid with the irony of McLaughlin's patronizing attitude—his serious belief that he can thereby save the Indians from themselves. The three main white characters, Catherine Weldon, James McLaughlin, and Dr. Beddoes, present between them a carefully dialectical range of responses to the white dilemma. In the Brechtian manner, the spectator is invited to examine their predicaments, rather than to empathize. The doctor is the scientific rationalist, coded negatively in the play, who believes the Indians to be fundamentally different and inferior, although he is a humanist who deplores the suffering that violence causes, on both sides. He is also an atheist to whom death is the end. McLaughlin is in the intermediate position between two cultures with his Christian Indian wife and his position as Indian agent, in the front line of Indian affairs as negotiator, but ultimately an executive of the American government. He feels disgraced by his quasi court-martial and is moved to zeal in the final action, which, in his patronizing way, he justifies to himself as to the Indians' benefit, although his chief reason for undertaking it is to bring himself back into the favor of his military superiors.

Catherine is the text's moral touchstone: she has a culturally aware and continuing loyalty to the Indians, which neither her relationship with McLaughlin nor the death of her son compromises. As she tells Kicking Bear, "some white faces can keep their vows." She is the one who understands why Lucy kills herself; she is the only one who understands about sacrifice and who leaves, finally pulling her goods on a travois (the Indian sled). Her exit is ambiguous: at the naturalistic level, it seems from the opening of the scene that she is going back east, but when her exit comes, it seems to represent symbolically a rejoining of the Indians. Perhaps the ambiguity is a way of indicating that what matters is not location but rather an attitude of mind and a way of life. Early in the play, willingness to suffer for a cause is characterized as the test of loyalty: Kicking Bear says to Catherine, "if you say you love us, then suffer with us." Specifically, he invites her to "share in a famine to join all the ghosts."

The action of Sitting Bull with which the play opens, the return of

Catherine's gifts, which she rightly interprets as meaning that friendship is dead, comes to seem a prophetic wisdom. The nature of the gifts is significant: a portrait of Sitting Bull done by Catherine and a set of china crockery. Both could represent a way of life and a way of seeing that threaten the Indian identity. Sitting Bull, referred to disparagingly as a bullfrog and disliked by McLaughlin, is a figure of dignity to Catherine; her portrait is ambivalently either a tragic irony or the record of a cultural exchange symbolizing benign miscegenation, perhaps both. In contrast, the selling of the Indians' ghost shirts to the soldiers by Donelly, a stereotypical comic Irishman, clearly demonstrates exploitative power, as does the scene in which he humiliates Lucy by the dance he forces from her. The creation of Donelly's part is intriguing. It borders on the banal and the offensive by its use of stereotype and its part in the action—for instance in the comic interruptions to the trial scenes—but it is paradoxically also an important signifier of innocence: when told of Catherine's loss of her son, he immediately changes his tone and regretfully says he had no idea. The problem arises when intercultural contact becomes takeover, with the dominant suppressing its other rather than responding to it creatively. As Catherine poignantly puts it, "Why for that matter couldn't we become Indians? / Why do the Indians have to turn into us?" Catherine and the widow Quinn provide, in the heart of the play, an instance of what might have been. In their grief at the death of Catherine's boy—wounded in the foot by a rusty nail, in symmetry with the wounded protagonists of *Omeros*—they dance.[17] Sarah Quinn asks Catherine to teach her "a few delicate steps? For his sake?": "I thought how hard it had been for you, Kitty Weldon, with your husband lost to the Dakotas and now a son, and yet the river was lovely, and I thought, I said what do they do, the Crow and the Sioux when their loved ones go like a season? They dance. They dance!" The dance pervades the play as both image and act. From the opening scene in which Catherine speaks of "back East" in terms of "street lights and carriages, long white gloves and concerts," the white culture of dance balances the Indians' Ghost Dance. At the center of the play, the two come together in the person of Lucy, dancing first in the white dress, then in Indian dress as Swift Running Deer, but for her, they present schizophrenic choices that result in tragedy.

The unfolding plot brings the action nearer and nearer to the historical cataclysm. Toward the end of the play, the fighting is presented as distant sound effects to accompany McLaughlin's report of what happened. The tragic climax, the death of Sitting Bull, is not enacted but narrated, as in ancient Greek convention. It is a moment that achieves considerable tragic weight, intensified by the simple recitation of the names of the dead. In keeping with a culture in which naming is significant, the naming of the Indian dead on both sides—McLaughlin's Indian police as well as the Ghost Dancers, both groups with actual historical names—echoes with the countless unknown dead of the Indian nations. The audience responds with a Brechtian awareness of the irony that it was, according to Walcott, McLaughlin's desire to win back his honor in the eyes of the military—the honor he lost by confiding in Catherine for love—that initiated the tragedy.

But there is also a sense of inevitability; the text valorizes the view that life is inescapably tragic as well as always open to the possibility of metaphysical renewal. The spiritual hope is never easy. In the poem, Catherine faces the ubiquity of doubt. "Life is so fragile," she says in a voice that seems shadowed by Walcott's: "More and more we learn to do without / those we still love. With my father it was the same."[18] Walcott gives her an important wisdom:

> are not the Sioux as uncertain of paradise,
> when the grass darkens, as your corn-headed soldiers?
> Doubt isn't the privilege of one complexion.[19]

Yet the section ends with her reiteration of the reality of their belief. It is in such finely balanced profundities that the epic quality of both play and poem resides. In *Omeros,* Walcott explains how the story of Catherine Weldon appealed to him for use in the poem, in the context of his own pain:

> When one grief afflicts us we choose a sharper grief
> in hope that enormity will ease affliction,
> so Catherine Weldon rose in high relief
>
> through the thin page of a cloud, making a fiction
> of my own loss. I was searching for characters,
> and in her shawled voice I heard the snow that would be blown
>
> when the wind covered the tracks of the Dakotas,
> the Sioux, and the Crows; my sorrow had been replaced.[20]

The power of fiction to comfort is as real as it is miraculous. The consolation we find in tragic literature is a still unexplained mystery, despite Aristotle. In the poem, Walcott adds to the Catherine story an emblematic image: that of the familiar "snowstorm" toy, its glass globe containing a scene of cabin and pines, which when shaken are obliterated by a "blizzard" of white flakes. It is a powerful symbolic reference, an intertext with Orson Welles's famous American epic film *Citizen Kane,* in which the toy represents the lost innocence of childhood and the lost integrity of pre-Columbian America.[21] It is a totem that Kane cherishes throughout his meteoric career, which culminates in his "Xanadu," a preposterous jumbling of the world's cultures, finally consigned to the fire. The snow of the rural childhood, with its sleigh rides, symbolizes the purity of the American origin, for which there is a tragic sense of loss. As Kane (resonant with "Cain") progresses into degenerate materialism and the commodification of culture, hoarding treasures like a Bluebeard in his castle, freedom, like purity, is shown as past, a subject only for nostalgia. The story of Catherine Weldon and the Sioux may seem remote from this, but "Rosebud," the name that haunts Welles's film, and which is finally revealed as the name on the childhood sleigh as it burns, is the name of one of the Indian agencies near Wounded Knee, where the final chapter of the Plains Indians' independence was enacted. Welles, it seems, is equating the individual innocence of childhood with the innocence of that lost, ancient America, obliterated by imported materialism; it is a position very close to Walcott's. Both use symbolism to reach a Brechtian objective, making the spectator think dialectically about the meaning of history. In giving his Catherine a symbolic object like Kane's (a Brechtian prop), Walcott makes a subtle intertextual point, addressing both the American sociopolitical reality and the American aesthetic, in which the film has become a key signifier.

Walcott develops Welles's symbol, however. At the point in the poem when he narrates the historical tragedy, when the American cannon open up against the Indians' "useless shields,"[22] he returns to the toy as "globe," microcosm, in which the tragedy of the massacre is represented:

> The flour basting their corpses on the white fields.
> The absence that settled over the Dakotas
> was contained in the globe. Its pines, its tiny house.[23]

Finally, in the immemorial transformation of art, representation alleviates pain. It is "contained," framed by the child's globe, which isolates it from its power to hurt, as in the poem or the play, of which the globe is the symbol. The closure of *The Ghost Dance* is both tragic and uplifting, with an epic ambivalence that Brecht would have celebrated. The snow, which is the death-bringing blizzard, is also an image of the dance, part of humanity's artistic self-expression, which as shared rite can transmute tragedy to renewal. The blanket of snow signifies historically, as the tragedy of whiteout—the dominion of the white races, which imposed the loss of the indigenous people—but also mythically, as the possibility of restoration. Like human suffering, it will last only a season, and it will be followed by new growth. Once more, Walcott addresses history ultimately to expose its limitations as a way of explaining the world.

Walcott's play *The Ghost Dance* is thus a revealing indicator of his working method and of his philosophy. It is a reminder, once again, of his faith in language as the most hopeful sign of human potential, yet of his conviction that language is only a means to a greater end, a transcendent reality. It is, like so many of his plays, not only in verse; it is in every dimension poetic. Jean-Louis Barrault, the great artist of mime, says, "The theatre is the poetry of space," a perception that Walcott would understand, as painter and man of the theater, better than most dramatists.[24] But the particular referential power of theater, with its combination of arts—language, movement, music, dance, the visual—exhibits for Walcott an ideal that is essentially poetic. "Any play that works completely is a poem," he has said.[25] Through the play of *The Ghost Dance* with its special relationship to *Omeros,* Walcott confirms simultaneously the closeness of language to the visible world and the way in which this relationship signals transcendence. The immediacy of poetry, its ability to give dramatic expression to a narrative that is both intensely of the world and yet beyond it, is explored even more richly in his next play, *The Odyssey.*

12

"The Echo of the Shape"

Metamorphosis of the Homeric

> *Boatswain:* What cares these roarers for the name of king?
> *The Tempest,* I.i.18

It was the wisdom of the great classical scholar E. V. Rieu to perceive that "Homer invented drama before the theatre was invented to receive it."[1] Nearly half a century ago, he identified the *Iliad* as particularly dramatic in its idiom, but, as Walcott has now shown, the *Odyssey* is no less dramatic in its essence and not impossible to adapt to the stage. Its scope as epic, embracing the romance narrative, covering wide sweeps of both time and place, and presenting fragmented, episodic action, has for more than two millennia masked the fact that its core as fiction consists of compelling drama, and that this drama, far from being disastrously fragmented, has an overarching unity of theme and purpose. How else would such a long poem have retained such avid readers over the centuries, once its immediacy as performed epic had passed into history? Walcott, in creating a version of it for the stage, gives the world an *Odyssey* that is faithful to the original to an extraordinary degree, yet it is also a wholly new work. It is less a work of homage than another manifest of that process of assimilation discussed earlier: the energy is in the story, the "storm," which, in a profound sense, cares nothing for the Homeric "name of the king." Detail apart, two dimensions are innovatory: the dramatic form (the work now changing genres) and a shift of emphasis, which is used to disclose a radically different map of meaning within the ancient myth. Ancient Egypt is reinstated at the heart of the myth of ancient Greece as supplier of wisdom, culture, and labor, paralleled with Africa in the recent European empires. Just as Paul Gilroy has shown the black experience to be at the heart of modern Atlantic culture, so Walcott, "translating" Martin Bernal's historiography into imaginative terms, revises the Homeric to make visible the contribution of the racial other at the heart of ancient Greece—the Greece to which Western tradition looks for the "pure" origin of democracy, then defines as "European."[2] The Ulysses figure, with which Walcott has been preoccupied for so long, is given a representation in this drama that exposes its similarity to trickster-heroes such as Anansi, and the play of gender in the myth, so long used against women, is radically reinvented. The subversiveness of Odysseus is rediscovered along with the heroic role of the women, in an essentially postcolonial representation of gender, race, and power. Yet the play honors the great universal truths about love and loss, which have kept the Homer alive for so long, in its new-minted poetic dialogue, which adapts Shakespeare's combination of the symbolic with the colloquial in a language of stunning simplicity and depth. George Steiner asserts that the Homeric texts have been the most frequently translated texts in the English language, more so than the Bible or any other work originating in other languages.[3] Walcott's, however, is not a translation: "I wouldn't have had any fun," he has said, "in doing simply a transformation, or transliteration, of the *Odyssey*—because who needs it? Just read the book. But to do something that is theatrically exciting—and not just for the effect but because I felt vitally excited by it, genuinely excited, by the possibility of the theatre of the piece."[4] His drama is a creative reinterpretation, which brings to the fore the strengths of the original fiction and gives it new resonances as a text for our time. It is faithful to the Homer while revisioning it, and it offers valuable insights into his working method.

Walcott, fresh from the publication of his epic poem *Omeros,* which modifies and recombines Homeric elements in a metamorphic change to an intrinsically Caribbean—and specifically St. Lucian—poem, had been invited to give the Poetry Book Society's Ronald Duncan lecture for 1990. His choice of topic for the lecture, delivered in London in September, was "The Poet in the Theatre." His own history as a poetic dramatist made him well qualified to address the subject, which he had chosen in order to engage with current attitudes. He made an eloquent plea for the remobilization of poetry in modern drama. Identifying as grave error the prevalent view that "all sustained metre is now rejected as artifice and not life" and the consequent rejection of poetry in the theater as "literary nostalgia," he demonstrated that poetry and the liveliness of the speaking voice were not incompatible. Since, he said, "In literature the form that carries the greatest conviction is verse," it is to verse that we should look also for conviction in drama. The intensification process that yields poetry is evident even in prose: "The intention of prose theatre in comedy and tragedy, even of farce, whose metre contracts into the epigrammatic—the memorable—is that its greatest moments will be poetic." He ended with the rallying cry that "[m]odern poetry should reinvade the theatre, not hang out in the lobby shabbily like a second cousin."[5] When, therefore, an invitation came from the Royal Shakespeare Company to dramatize Homer's *Odyssey,* it must have seemed, as well as an enormous challenge, an opportunity to put his philosophy into practice in a particularly conspicuous way.

He described, just before the play opened, how the commission came about:

> the young director of the RSC, Greg Doran, had been asked what was it he wanted to direct, and he said *The Odyssey.* And then he got in touch with me and asked me if I wanted to do it. . . . I didn't want to do it because I didn't want to take on the idea of doing another—not a directly—Homeric thing like the book I'd just finished, but . . . I began to experiment with the idea of compressing some of the scenes into lines, and essentialising them, and then got excited about the shape of the poem, the stage poem, and it went pretty far down, and I showed them about fifteen pages, which they liked, and then I came over here and I worked with the workshop situation, with more pages, and a shape for the thing, and then they said go ahead—and now it's here.[6]

"Essentializing" was just the word for that process of condensing to epigrammatic memorability described in the lecture and demonstrated so unforgettably in the creative metamorphosis of the Homeric text to drama.

The play did not have a long gestation. Rehearsals began in earnest in May 1992, little more than seven months from the completion of the first draft. Walcott stayed in Stratford-on-Avon for several weeks prior to the premiere and was a direct participant in working the play up in performance, adding new lines or scenes, or rewriting, with great facility, as the need arose, according to the production's director, Greg Doran. Ironically, the published version does not record that the script was commissioned by the Royal Shakespeare Company, only that it was premiered by them in July 1992. All the drafts quote Robert Lowell as epigraph, "Pity the monsters," but this very Walcottian sentiment is omitted from the published text, in keeping perhaps with the cutting of a line in the early drafts about the power of pity: in the Cyclops episode, the Philosopher tells Odysseus, as one of his men is taken off to be killed, that the "real superiority" is "[t]o pity tyrants. Not the people they destroy."

The "terrific technical challenge" of making a play out of the *Odyssey* was to "try to compress and stay with the Homer over the arc of the story as much as possible, so it was like building a ship, that had to either sink or float—in that sense a technical challenge to construct a dramatic poem as close as possible to the original epic poem."[7] After his initial response of reluctance to revisit Homer, the technicalities of the project drew Walcott in: "It was like undertaking the building of a schooner or a ship: rig the thing out, and then plank it, and then hopefully launch it, you know. The carpentry was very exciting."[8] The metaphor resonates both with Odysseus's shipbuilding in Homer's Book 5 and with a line at the center of Walcott's play, where the response to Odysseus's storytelling is, "You can build a heavy-beamed poem out of this"—a line tongued and grooved with the play's (and the poem's) tree imagery, associated with moral strength. Eurycleia's assertion that "is strong-timbered virtues uphold this house" is one with the Homeric symbol of the rooted marriage bed: the sign of constancy to which Odysseus's flux aspires. In Walcott's hands, the ancient story emerges in fresh guise as a postcolonial "roots" narrative, as Odysseus reconnects himself to his origins.

On making a direct comparison of the Homeric poem to Walcott's play, it is immediately apparent that he has left out remarkably little of the plot. He has compressed a poem of more than twelve thousand lines to dramatic poetry of just under two thousand, but what is striking is that he has omitted almost nothing substantial or vital to the action. He was aware of the need to steer a course between the Scylla and Charybdis of the too long and the too short, which would verge on the sensational, saying as the first production was in rehearsal, "I didn't want to make it too long because your behind starts to get edgy. [Yet] you must have a sense of epic width. You know if you're going to see the *Odyssey* you're not going to see an hour and a half of boys' own comics—you are sitting down, going to look at something. And just from the fragments I've seen in rehearsal it is really very physical. I don't think it'll feel long."[9] His strategy was to essentialize it, experimenting by "compressing some of the scenes into lines," so that the challenge was not so much to select as to condense.[10] Greg Doran, the play's first director, was impressed with its compactness and speed: it has "quite a long first half, and the second half has a different kind of propulsion, but it still comes down under three hours, which is pretty good going. And why it plays so swiftly, it's the verse form that Derek has chosen to adopt. It's a flexible hexameter line but it's ordered in quatrains, but divided into individual people speaking, so that everybody only speaks a line at a time, and that really propels it forward. It keeps the company very much on their toes."[11] The rhythm of the language has none of the ponderousness that might be associated with hexameter in a literary culture more used to pentameter. The early choices about form were crucial. Walcott knew from the outset that he must do it in verse "because that's what the poem deserves—out of respect."[12] To have used pentameter would have located the play in an English tradition, as Walcott realized:

> I made up my mind I was not going to have any long speeches. I was not going to do it in pentameter, because that would have had Elizabethan echoes. I made up my mind I would do it in quatrains for the discipline of the containment of it, that I would do it in hexameters, and that what I was after was a huge poem. And I kept thinking of the shape—different images of lines, like lances laid down on racks, or perhaps a ship with its beams . . . so you had to build. It was great fun to build a poem which had to be launched and performed, and whose—not direct model—but the *echo* of whose shape was from the original itself.[13]

This project was different: it was an epic poem for performance, and it was filial, a reincarnation of Homer's poem, which should ghost its outline. In performance, it creates a special excitement by its blend of faithfulness, involving audience anticipation and the pleasure of recognition, and shifts of emphasis, which trump that process by surprising and making it new. The same doubleness is evident in the choice of verse form: to use hexameter mirrors the Homeric meter, but it becomes something quite new in English, a light and fluent line in Walcott's speech-influenced handling. The quatrains, rhymed *abab*—a scheme with a long history in English—offer an unobtrusive patterning (the rhyme less conspicuous than it would be with shorter lines), but the refusal of the long speech is wholly new, represented in neither Greek nor English tradition. The passing of the lines from one speaker to another, one to each voice (in rhetoric, "stichomythia"), gives the dialogue the athleticism of a basketball match. In this, Walcott was devising a form for drama: although he is aware of his play as in a sense a poem, it is theater first and foremost.

The choice of vehicle—the verse form—was the first and most crucial decision Walcott had to make, but there remained the technical problem of bringing such a long narrative into a shape that live drama could handle. His method is to select from each section of the Homer the essential features of the narrative. Obviously a great deal of the original is not represented directly in his drama, but the fact that his play both is faithful and runs for less than three hours shows that much of the Homer has a subordinate relationship to the main narrative. This is not an adaptation of the familiar kind, however, in which a complex and profound text is reduced to a sensationalist skeleton. The drama has just as much poetic depth as the Homer. Walcott wanted "to take the story the way he told it and to try to contain it—which is a huge arc of a story—starting as much as I could with the sequence of events, but leaving things out if you couldn't always put [them in] . . . the Oxen of the Sun and various other incidents that you just couldn't do in the given time . . . but to follow the narrative line of the story."[14] The most significant episode not enacted is that of the Oxen of the Sun, a relatively short section of the Homer for all its conceptual importance. It is, however, referred to in the play's dialogue, in much the same way as it features in the Homeric discussion between the gods, which means that the play does not lose the rationale of Homer's plot or his moral distinction between Odysseus and his crew (Odysseus is the only one allowed by the gods to reach home, as the divine favor was forfeited by his crew in their transgressive slaughter of the forbidden cattle). Other briefly narrated Homeric episodes, such as those of the Lotus-Eaters or the Lestrygones, which have a particular place in Western culture, may be missed by devotees, but in reality they play a very minor part in the epic and can be omitted without substantial loss. The poem's structural parallelism means that the Lotus-Eaters theme is mirrored in the Circe episode, for example, and the gigantism and cannibalism of the Lestrygonians is an echo of the Cyclops chapter. Such minor matters apart, a further significant structural difference of Walcott's version is his absorption of Calypso into Circe, with one persona and one episode, made possible by the symmetry of the Homeric episodes.

Certain structural freedoms, as Walcott is only too aware, are available to the epic poet, which are denied the dramatist:

> Because it's an epic and not a dramatic poem, it doesn't have to have—it does not have—a theatrical symmetry, because incidents can follow any way they want to, more like a novel than a play, so that you can progress from one episode to the other without any previous connection, losing characters progressively. Now, in a play, if you work on a character in Act 1 you presume that that character will return somehow in Act 2, or the theme of the character will be returned to. But that doesn't happen in an epic poem, because you can have one section dealing with Menelaus and Nestor—and there's no return to that; and so you progress from one section, one story, to another. And that's what the *Odyssey* is, from one story to the other.[15]

Others have called Homer's *Odyssey* a novel, among them its translators T. E. Lawrence and E. V. Rieu. For Lawrence, it is "the oldest book worth reading for its story and the first novel of Europe."[16] Rieu, who notes the likeness of the *Iliad* to tragedy, distinguishes it from the *Odyssey,* which, with "its well-knit plot, its psychological interest and its interplay of character, is the true ancestor of the long line of novels that have followed it."[17] To dramatize it is therefore not just a question of scale but of tone and structural method. Epic novel—or novelistic epic—is a very different genre from epic drama. As Walcott has long understood, the scale of meaning implicit in "epic" (leaving out of account the specific Brechtian sense) can be conveyed by other means than the physical scale of the work. The essentializing process results in a condensing of the energies of the Homeric, its most noticeable general effects being the absence of long colloquies (which grate on modern ears), the simplification of the narrative's convolutions, and the reduction in the role of the gods. With all these (alienatory) aspects of the Homer omitted, and the content reduced to the most telling detail of each incident represented, the irreducible myth reemerges naked in all its compelling immediacy and human appeal.

The requirements of dramatic form led Walcott to build in symbolic links to knit the episodic structure into an organic whole: "In a play you have to have a symmetry in terms of time, certainly, and certainly in terms of what kind of arc of a definition you have, and the concentration of keeping the arc of the story in the narrative form meant that some things are returned, so that in the second act what I do is to try and see that the people who return domestically are the equivalent of people who were there in [the first act], so that there is a theme of recurrence, a 'déjà vu' thing that happens in the stories."[18] The cycle of "eternal return" (to use Mircea Eliade's phrase)—the metamyth—is thus developed in the conceptualization of the play, as well as being intrinsic to its ancient narrative shape. Walcott uses the Homeric idea of parallelism dramatically, by linking incidents and characters across the sweep of the narrative. Arnaeus is shown as an image of the Cyclops, for example; Melantho is Nausicaa in a distorting glass.

A comparison of incident and sequence reveals a surprisingly tight match. Walcott follows Homer's broad pattern in moving from the state of affairs in Ithaca twenty years after Odysseus left, through the Telemachus story, to pick up Odysseus on his travels, although he omits Homer's opening glimpse of Odysseus yearning to get away from Calypso's island to return home. As in the Homer, the central episodes are presented as a retrospective narration: after being found shipwrecked on Scheria by

Nausicaa, he participates in the Phaeacian Games and narrates, to Alcinous, the episodes with the Cyclops, Circe, the underworld, the Sirens, and Scylla and Charybdis. Alcinous lends Odysseus a ship (implied in the play) to take him back to Ithaca, where the incidents unfold as in the Homer. The action of the frame story thus takes up a relatively short time, between Athena's spur to Telemachus to set out, contemporary with Odysseus's move to leave Calypso, and his return with his father. The Homeric Odysseus's ten years' journey home is thus narrated from a frame narrative that starts near its end. In that the Homer comes with the narrative loop in its center, typical of the oral tradition, Walcott wisely stayed with a structure that might have been devised, had it not existed, to tie the episodes into a tighter unit.

The extended retrospective narration does, however, pose dramatic problems of its own. Unlike Prospero's formal narration of his history to his daughter Miranda, which stiffens the second scene of *The Tempest,* Walcott's retrospective narration is given dramatic representation in flashback (to borrow a film term): the voice of the narrator, Odysseus, is exchanged for the voice of Odysseus as participant in the action, replayed before our eyes. While this makes the episodes dramatically compelling and is one of the great strengths of the drama, it is also true that it obscures the structural relationship of the central episodes to the frame story—their nature as subordinate narration, dramatized—so that relatively few of those seeing the play without knowing the Homer are likely to come away with a clear sense of the distinction. This is, however, a matter of minor concern, since the vivid dramatic narration of the central episodes maintains its own momentum, and the general sense that the opening phase of the story relates closely to the concluding phase, and that Odysseus's many adventures before returning home mean that his wife has waited for him a long time—all that it is necessary to know—is well established as a structural rationale. The device of the whirling vase, which Walcott inserts as signifier of the shift into inset narration in the Menelaus episode, for example, is an attempt to clarify the relationship between the parts, much as film convention uses a dissolve to introduce a flashback, but while it works in the printed text, it serves when staged (at least in the initial production) more to underline its redundancy as formal device than to deliver clarity.

The narrative's connective tissue is, however, modified effectively at this point. Where Homer gives Menelaus the protagonist's role in the story of the wrestling of Proteus, which he tells to Telemachus, Walcott substitutes Menelaus explaining a vase painting to Telemachus, showing Proteus wrestling not Menelaus, but Odysseus. By bringing Odysseus into the metamorphic scene with Proteus, who in Homer changes himself to lion, snake, panther, boar, water, and a tree, to elude capture, Walcott underlines the centrality of the idea of metamorphosis to his story. Not only is the story of Odysseus, with its sequence of magic challenges, an example of the myth of the sacred king who passes through different symbolic roles in the course of his rule (as Robert Graves and others have argued), but in Walcott's interpretation the language of disguise—of the person who adopts, in particular, a monstrous appearance—is given a precise critique: the mythic account of extrahuman agency is rejected in favor of an assumption of moral responsibility, which postulates that if we are monsters, it is as a result of self-construction. Walcott's reduction of the role of the gods in his drama is therefore not just practical, in order to focus on the human drama, but arises directly from the meaning. In terms of narrative sequence, the vase, like a crystal ball, enables Telemachus to "see" Odysseus on his ship, the scene that follows, as inset narration, implicitly contemporary with the scene in Menelaus's palace. The narration leads to the shipwreck, which leads to the Nausicaa episode, which in turn leads to further inset narration.

Lead scenes for the retrospective narration to Alcinous and Nausicaa in Scheria help to draw attention to the narration's status as story, told to entertain the court. Walcott deliberately raises our awareness of the episodes as fictions as much as reportage. While his storytelling skill is admired, Odysseus's veracity is questioned, and Nausicaa's demand for monster stories is met so transparently by the horrors of the Cyclops episode that the audience seems invited to regard it as more likely to be "fiction" than "fact." Placing the narration in the tradition of "old salts, sailors, [who] always have fish that got away," Walcott has talked of his intention to seed doubt: "Is this guy lying? Is he just jiving? Is this a fact? The figure in the Homer is somebody who exploits. . . . Because he tells his stories he gets rewarded, and so you say, 'This guy could be a helluva bullshitter!'—you know what I mean?"[19] Walcott's treatment thus draws attention to the "fiction" aspect while representing it with such imaginative power that the quasi-factual authority dominates. The ludic quality of this is reminiscent of Shakespeare's *Winter's Tale,* where the text's discourse about old wives' tales and the child's ghost story make the audience aware that they are witnessing "only" fiction, while forcing them to acknowledge its authority over mind and heart.

Walcott also reminds us repeatedly of the tales of old nurses. Eurycleia herself deprecates her own "Nancy stories me tell you and Hodysseus" (the Anansi-story reference planting the Caribbean firmly in the drama), but Telemachus's disparagement of Proteus's metamorphic powers as "my old nurse's tale" is capped by Menelaus with the rejoinder, "Then consider yourself forever in her debt." The idea of the story told to a child returns as the final phase is initiated, with Eurycleia's lullaby to "lickle Odysseus," brought sleeping to Ithaca in a symbolic act of rebirth. Fiction is analogous to both dream and madness, as the scene points out: "Are all of these monsters a child's imagination?" / "Or the madness of a mariner too long alone?"

The oral tradition with its stories is thus held up as a precious cultural resource. In Walcott's play, it is passed on particularly by those whose racial and cultural otherness is marked as Egyptian and therefore signaled as part of an African tradition that is still alive today in Africa and in the Americas. By coding Eurycleia and Billy Blue as both "Egyptian" and "Caribbean" or "African American," Walcott shows that the oral tradition from which the Homer sprang is not other and over, but here and now. Although the Homer comes down to us because it was written down, it bears the signs of its oral roots. Walcott has criticized as "scripsist" the presumption that it is too long and complex for oral transmission.[20] Indeed, the evidence of oral epic from many parts of the world demonstrates that length and complexity are frequently present in the extreme. In the play, he reinstates the orality of the Homer, which the many translations into formal literary English have obscured. His play is closer in that sense to the original: "the tone you get from the language of Homer is . . . colloquial . . . there are a lot of bad puns in Homer, for instance, so that you're starting from something that is already energised by a kind of vulgarity, not by a kind of pomposity. And by vulgarity I mean a theatrical thing: basically all storytelling is vulgar by its nature . . . it's not a remote language, removed in language."[21] Walcott sees the orality as part of a culture where the bard was "the evening's entertainment, . . . who probably was singing while people were having dinner, and had to be loud and clear, maybe be ignored while he was singing these stories . . . an itinerant person, poet, moving round the islands and to different cities."[22] In the play, this social function is recalled in the presentation of the Scherian court. Alcinous tells Odysseus, "The more outlandish your tales, the more they'll please us," to which Nausicaa adds, "My father loves stories, he rewards their singers." The need to entertain is vigorously met in the play, which is fast-moving and funny, as well as emotive and extraordinary, couched in language of wit and poetry in an informal colloquial idiom, one which is specifically American: Walcott speaks of "the fact that the real Homeric language now is not English but American, and that the inflexion of language is not English-accented but American-accented . . . we are all speaking American."[23] To the reader, the Americanness is particularly evident in the language of Eurycleia and, at times, Billy Blue. Otherwise, it is colloquial in a way that could be voiced with either an American or an English intonation. As well as giving the plebeian characters local and idiomatic speech (the ancient Egyptian identity is conveyed by modern Caribbean language, translating the Old World to the New), Walcott makes the socially elite characters speak in a modern vernacular idiom. Menelaus, for instance, sneers at Helen, "Your memory's fading like your hair dye, darling." The Noel Coward-like archness of this is in contrast with the elliptical speech of the cynic, Thersites: "Hate dogs. Slobberers. Dumb pain, dumb affection."

The transition to less naturalistic language, of metaphor and symbol, takes place within the continuum of orality. For instance, the lines following this of Thersites use the double caesura to maintain a colloquial rhythm, even when the content moves toward the metaphoric: "Open the gates of those locked teeth. Admit love, friend." / "I'll say it with grinding jaw. I loved you. Go on." The fresh tone of such dialogue, even when read, falls on the inner ear as if spoken. Even at its most poetic, the language is simple. The blend of simplicity and depth is everywhere, in lines such as "[t]he ship crawled like a fly up the wall of the sea." The metaphor is reified in the oral idiom by what follows: a joke about falling over the edge.

One part of this strategy of orality is the role created for Billy Blue, the blind singer, who is part Chorus in the Greek tradition and part griot or "djeli" in the African tradition—the two being, of course, branches of one cultural tree. Within the play's textuality, he figures the narrator, representing a quasi Homer, and by implication Walcott too, but with a name and in an idiom that connect him with a modern popular equivalent to the epic poet. It is clear from the role of poet-singers in the Homer that the court culture of ancient Greece had much in common with the court poets of the present century in many African communities and elsewhere in the world. The poets within Homer's narrative are storytellers who sing emotively of their people's epic past; Odysseus, whose eyes are described as "hard as horn or iron," is more than once moved to tears by their narration.[24] Phemius and Demodocus are poets of a type that would have been familiar to Homer. There may be no exact equivalent in the modern world, but Walcott makes the point that the advent of the electronic age makes possible a new kind of bard:

> here's the emblematic idea of Homer, and that story-teller, or that singer, who contains the history of the race: it's an oral history of the race that's being set, by this legend (or whether it's fact) . . . there've been great blind blues singers, and the same thing is true of the calypsonian, who is untouchable as a figure, who contains the history of the race, who is a vessel for that. And I see absolutely no difference. And since there's no equivalent now in Greece, I mean singing, and since there's no equivalent in any of the cities that we live in, and since it's not just a device, then the only reality is if this person is coming out of a context in which validly, and not just theatrically, that person is acceptable as a figure. Because who is there you can say in England who would be a Homeric singer of songs? A rock star or an opera singer, who? Because the whole tribal sense has gone. In these cities, you have no tribal sense. And the tribal sense is unified in the black man, in the blues-singer, and it's true in other cultures, where that is more Homeric than having somebody with a harp up there, and a beard, you know, plucking away at a lyre.[25]

Walcott's Billy Blue is a black blues singer in the African American tradition, who subsumes the Homeric roles of Demodocus and Phemius and goes further by his continuous reappearances to comment on the action. It is in his songs that the language becomes most poetic; he alone has extended utterances, based on multiples of the quatrain, but several times adapting this to a six-line conclusion to make a sonnet (although a hexametrical one), the lyricism all the more moving for its contrast with the rest of the play.

The Greek drama, which evolved after the Homeric texts, initiated, as far as we know, the group Chorus, but Walcott uses chiefly the single figure of Billy Blue, in occasional counterpoint with a group Chorus, as in the Circe and Cyclops episodes. In that the latter are used to give lyrical expression to the particular tone of the episode of which they are a part and are voiced by participants in the action, they are, however, more like the chorus in modern musical drama. Billy Blue's role is more like that of the classical Chorus in that he is both of the action and outside it, whereas it is to Shakespeare that we should look for a single choric figure with the character of a *dramatis persona*. Billy Blue first introduces the story, much like some of the Shakespearian figures—Gower in *Pericles,* or the Chorus in *Henry V*—but, unlike the Shakespearian figures, he also participates in the action, notably, for instance, in the RSC production, as the Ithacan musician, Demodocus, who recognizes Odysseus by his voice and height and refuses to be tricked, while in Hades he is a homeless beggar on the London Underground. In drafts of the Cyclops scene, he is also the Philosopher who becomes a victim, resisting tyranny with words of truth. As an outsider, an outcast, as well as ubiquitous poet and wise commentator, blind Billy Blue is reminiscent of the blind eponymous seer in *Omeros,* a figure of Homer rediscovered in the vernacular, who is also known as Seven Seas. In the play, Proteus, the Old Man of the Sea, billed in Homer as "Proteus of Egypt,"[26] is not overtly linked with Billy Blue, also Egyptian, although that designation is subordinate to the sense that both are of everywhere and nowhere. Such freedoms are classical too; Euripides' *Helen* places its eponymous protagonist unconventionally in Egypt and also includes Proteus among its characters.

Other passages recall the precise poetry of Homer, some playfully, others in a way that develops into something new. Helen's entry to the stage direction, "pushing a golden cart on silver wheels," mirrors her entry in the Homer with a workbasket "that ran on castors and was made of silver finished with gold,"[27] a gift from Egypt, which, in the RSC's realization came complete with the Homeric "deep blue wool." Details such as the fact that Ithaca is too stony for horses impart a sense of familiarity, but the poplars of Neriton are used in an inspired new way: where Homer has Odysseus recognize the landscape of his birth with his eyes when Athene disperses the mist, Walcott shows him realizing he is home because he recognizes the language of the trees, their sound in the breeze. Other adaptations raise a smile: Homer's "rosy-fingered dawn," for instance, is given fresh life in Walcott's opening account of Penelope, whose "rosy fingers at dawn unstitch the design." Walcott uses the famous phrase the "wine-dark sea" only once, but other less well known lines from the Homer acquire new prominence through their placing in the drama: for example, his "Men make weapons they intend to use" strikes as a fresh wisdom, although it is derived from the advice of the Homeric Odysseus to Telemachus, "the very presence of a weapon provokes a man to use it."[28]

Walcott makes the music of the Greek text present in his—"the whole idea of the context of the poem *is* Greek," as he says.[29] He has its opening line quoted by Billy Blue at the beginning and reminds ears used to English that the ancient Greek language was a seminal influence on present-day English: the rowers count their strokes with Greek numerals that are clearly cognate with many of their English counterparts. Walcott also plays with the sounds of some of the Greek names and provides some Homeric puns in English, as with the joke on his hero's name as an "odd Zeus." His humor is one of the salient qualities of Homer for Walcott:

> it's extremely funny; it is a humorous book, and Joyce knew that. [He] made his novel a comic novel because that is the tone of Homer—a very different tone from, say, the Greek tragedians, or the Shakespearian idea, even, of comedy—so that the book is funny. . . . I think the elan and the vigour of the book is humorous, that it comes out of this story in which a man goes through a hell of a bad time, but the essential drive is humour.[30]

The play is in fact funnier than the poem, in a witty and ironic but also a direct, physical way, but it contains great pathos too. One of the hardest scenes to adapt to the stage might have been the death of the old dog Argus, which could easily have become mawkish, but Walcott has it take place (classically) just offstage, watched by those on stage and narrated through their comments. The language carries the truth and the feeling of the moment, through to Billy Blue's memorable evocation of Odysseus's stoicism: "This man dare not weep. Though roads and nights can be wet." The lightness of Walcott's touch brings tears, however familiar the story. The poetry breaks down our defenses by making the story new.

In sum, the technical challenge of bringing such a diffuse narrative coherently within the confines of an evening's play-going is brilliantly met. At the point where Odysseus is returned to Ithaca by Nausicaa, the two narrative phases—of Telemachus's vase-gazing and the storytelling to the Scherians—are elided. The immediate precedent is the Scylla and Charybdis episode, after which Odysseus sleeps, with a lullaby from Eurycleia and Billy Blue's narration of nightmare, ending with the overturning of the raft. Odysseus's being carried ashore on Ithaca, asleep, which follows, thus functions as a logical outcome of this, from which it flows in natural sequence, and also implicitly as a loop back to the Nausicaa stage, in which the inset narration was prefaced with Nausicaa's question, "Is this just a dream?" The fluid nature of all fiction, all dream, and its power of restoration are what the text confirms. We have watched Telemachus watching his father, who narrates his past exploits to watching Scherians; in Act 2, Odysseus watches in disguise until the dénouement when action—destruction and reunion—replaces gaze. Athena watches all and we watch her. But as well as building his narrative like a telescope, Walcott gives his text a pattern of sound, as much as one preoccupied with vision. The play exists ultimately in its poetic music. The fact that the drama works as an imaginative sequence is in the end all that matters. It is appropriate to the text's self-consciousness of its own art that Billy Blue—both black American blues singer and ancient bard—should open the play and preside over its narration. He is the master-conjuror who summons up the whole story for us. His part anchors the episodic variousness of the action in a conceptual and linguistic tour de force. Typically, Walcott freshens the Homeric by shedding worn conventions and associations and rediscovers it in a language that is modern and at the same time closer to the original than the tradition to which we have become accustomed.

Walcott's faithfulness to the Homer, imaginative and true as it is, is not servile. He allows himself to bring out new meanings by his presentation, altering the detail of the incidents, shifting the emphasis, or drawing on post-Homeric tradition, as he sees fit. This is particularly evident in the treatment of Odysseus himself, who is both more real and more symbolic than his Homeric namesake. The story's mythic quality is moved on in the light of Dante and Tennyson. Menelaus's assertion that "[t]he gates of imagination never close" repudiates the equation of the fanciful with the childish, with a significant definition of adults as "[c]hildren who doubt." The blessing of faith is a recurrent theme of Walcott's work; in the play, those, like Thersites, who have "found no shore to believe" are pitied by those with direction in their lives. The Odysseus myth emerges as a metaphysical allegory, with the quest being for a spiritual home as much as for a physical one, but where Dante and Tennyson represent this by their hero's voyaging on alone to death, Walcott significantly allows his Odysseus to find, where he sought it, the spiritual union he seeks, figured through marital love. This has profound implications for the story's gender significance. Walcott offers a very different map of gender meaning from Homer and deconstructs the ancient story's implicit modeling of race. He also addresses with innovation some of the technical difficulties that the Homer presents and introduces new motifs to express his own vision of the story.

Like Homer, Walcott uses the patterning of imagery to create a symbolic structure to his narrative, but he drops some of Homer's ideas and introduces others of his own. In some cases, the smaller scale of his narrative requires the condensation of Homeric repetition. Homer's repeated anticipation of the routing of the suitors is an example; for the multiple references to an eagle killing geese, Walcott has only one, the most important, Penelope's narration of her dream for interpretation by Odysseus. In another instance, by exchanging the sharpened olive stake of the Homer for a skewer, as the implement by which the Cyclops is blinded, Walcott loses the symmetry between this episode and the final recognition scene, in which the bed built around an olive trunk is the means of reunion, Homer thus setting a destroying olive pole against a life-giving one—a trope related to the double olive tree under which Odysseus sleeps after his shipwreck on Scheria: a wild one with a fruiting one grafted on to it. The horror of Homer's vivid account of the blinding, however, which is partly derived from the scale of the weapon, introduces a tone that, it seems, Walcott prefers to avoid. On the other hand, the smallness of the skewer as weapon enables Walcott to introduce an ironic intimacy to the scene, and it is appropriate that the means by which the Cyclops makes a cannibal of Odysseus should be the means of his blinding. It also makes possible the highly symbolic ironic prostration of Odysseus, a piece of effective theater, to which attention is drawn by the Cyclops's furious "GET OFF YOUR KNEES!" Like Shakespeare, who was well aware of the symbolic potential of kneeling (as in *Coriolanus,* for example), Walcott makes Odysseus appear to humble himself as a prelude to striking. The incident models a very Caribbean understanding of subversion through ironized submission, a familiar strategy of Anansi, for instance. His playing of roles and his adoption of disguise has enabled Odysseus to survive: the theme of metamorphosis, now understood as the manipulation of identity as part of a strategy of adaptation and self-presentation—even to the point of self-naming as "Nobody"—is central to survival.

Another figure of Homer's narrative that Walcott develops differently is that of the pig. Homer introduces a range of animals as the product of Circe's magic (although it is to pigs that she changes Odysseus's men) and makes Eumaeus a swineherd, but Walcott skillfully extends the imagery of the pig, beginning with Telemachus's first assertion of his intention to rout the suitors: "Pigs! From today you will stop uprooting my house!" Via Eurycleia's assertion that "strong-timbered virtues hold up this house," the idea of home as a living tree, securely rooted, is established in antithesis to the "uprooting" tendencies of greed and lust, with punning on "boars" and "bores." The details of piglike appearance are negative tropes—the snout, the bristles, the proverbial greed and indiscriminacy—but Homer's "screw-horned" cattle seem to have suggested Walcott's coinage of the idea of the boar's "screw-prick," with its resonant satire of unrestrained sexuality.

A further symbolic addition is the introduction of the shield as emblem of portable protection, like the shell the turtle bears through the sea. As Odysseus finally reaches Ithaca, the symbol is recalled: "This turtle took ten years, Ajax, but it's ashore." The Homeric idea of the island as home is thus counterpointed with Walcott's idea of the traveling turtle with its home on its back, naturalizing the image of the wandering voyager. The recurrent use of such an image enables episodes to be linked poetically, strengthening what is in many ways an unpropitious structure for drama.

Although Odysseus is mentioned briefly in Homer's opening lines, full attention is turned to the protagonist late, in Book 5, where he is revealed tiring of Calypso's charms and longing for home. This late portrayal of the hero is a feature that could be fatal to a dramatic version. Walcott chooses to address this by opening differently. Before the portrayal of Ithaca in Odysseus's absence, he presents a scene from the Trojan tradition that is mentioned only briefly and late in the Homer, in the *Odyssey*'s epilogue: the funeral of Achilles. In the Homer, it is narrated by Agamemnon's shade as the ghosts of the newly dead suitors, killed by Odysseus, take up their places in Hades; it is followed by a summary of the poem's narrative, ending with praise of Penelope's constancy. By moving the funeral to the beginning of his play, Walcott shrewdly addresses a number of levels of meaning. First, it acts as a link to the *Iliad,* always implicit in the *Odyssey.* The first poem narrates the fall of one of its great pair of heroes, Hector, but at its end the other, Achilles, survives. Homer reveals in the central Hades episode of the *Odyssey* the shade of Achilles, reunited with Patroclus, a detail Walcott chooses to omit, making Achilles appear alone to Odysseus in his Underworld scene. The narration of Achilles' funeral rites at the very end of Homer's second poem, however, brings it into line with the first, in that it reinforces its negative closure in death. The positive movement toward the final securing of peace is given a marked counterpoint by Homer's treatment of the death of the suitors and the maids, and by the reception of the shades into Hades, which gives rise to the narration of Achilles' death rites.

Walcott constructs his play with a subtly different emphasis. By relocating the funeral of Achilles to the beginning, he initiates the centrifugal movement of his narration, as summed up in Billy Blue's prologue, "once Achilles was ashes things sure fell apart." The threats to Odysseus's return and to his wife's chastity represent that disintegrative phase, which is reversed in the centripetal movement that follows, brought to its conclusion in the dénouement's phase of reintegration. The whole pattern can be read as a critique of centrism. Yeats's famous assertion that "the centre cannot hold" seeded one of the founding texts of postcolonial writing. Achebe's novel *Things Fall Apart* uses Yeats's accompanying phrase as its title to signify both the destruction wrought by European empire in Africa and the historical inevitability of the eventual disintegration of that empire in

Africa and, by implication, elsewhere. By linking the story of Odysseus to that postcolonial signifier, Walcott models the fragmented narrative of scattering after the fall of Troy as a case of the center inevitably not holding but shows a new, previously marginal locus as the center of desire and fulfillment. The in-placeness of the colonial subject's secure identity derived from his cultural and affective home is ultimately what Walcott's *Odyssey* demonstrates.

Home is shown to be a constant, which everyone possesses. In a passage of fine irony, when father and son eventually meet up unknown to each other, after twenty years, Walcott gives them this exchange:

> ODYSSEUS: And where're you from, young man?
> (*Silence.*)
> TELEMACHUS: I'm from where everybody comes from. From my home.
> ODYSSEUS: And where's that? I said, "Where is that?"
> TELEMACHUS: Look, man, it's late.
> ODYSSEUS: It's never too late, youngster.
> (*Silence.*)
> TELEMACHUS: So, where are you from?
> ODYSSEUS: From home, as well.
> TELEMACHUS: Then we're both from the same place. Great.
> (*He exits.*)

Both are "from" home in the sense that they have been displaced from home, have been "away," both physically and symbolically. But both are also "from home" in the sense of being securely rooted in the identity their home gave them, wherever their subsequent lives might be lived. In these few lines, the whole tension between the "roots" movement and the exile's reality that has preoccupied postcolonial writers—and not least Walcott himself—is resolved. The play's eventual resting place is informed by this understanding. It begins in the aftermath of war and ends in celebration of peace—its centrifugal phase is balanced by its centripetal movement—but the peace it finds is one that was always already there: that of being mentally at home in the place in which childhood was spent, and which offers to old age the dream of a familiar bench in a familiar orchard.

Walcott's final line, as in the Homer, is an assertion of peace—"that peace, which, in their mercy, the gods allow men"—but the treatment of Odysseus's triumph alters the meaning of death. The exhilarating slaughter of the suitors is followed in the Walcott by the emotive censure of the women, first Eurycleia and then Penelope, who then thwart the threatened execution of the maid, Melantho, by their intervention. The mass hanging of the women, graphically narrated in the Homer, is thus dropped by Walcott, as is Homer's unproblematized glorying in bloody revenge. The scene of the suitors' shades being received into Hades likewise has no counterpart in the Walcott. By altering the Homeric in this way at the closure of his play, Walcott is able to place greater emphasis on the restorative drama of Odysseus's resumption of his role as husband, father, and patriarch, but he also creates a map of meaning in which matriarchy is on a par with patriarchy.

Concomitantly, by relocating the funeral to the beginning of his text, he is able not only to provide a neat implicit link with the *Iliad,* and most importantly to introduce his protagonist at the outset, but also to reinforce the symbolic structure implicit in the Homer: the play progresses from its start in death to a kind of rebirth, a conclusion that the Homer blurs with its re-presentation of closure-laden death rituals at the end. Odysseus, as a mythic figure of the sacred king, older than Homer, resists his own sacrificial death to reenter a further term of rule, the adventures of his voyage being myths of what Graves calls his "ninefold rejection of death."[31] The final phase represents the repulsing both of rivals—the suitors—and of the dynastic successor, Telemachus. This mythic reading goes, of course, beyond either the Homer or the Walcott, neither text foregrounding the negative implications of the dramatic structure for Telemachus. It is, however, fair to point out the differences between Walcott's presentation and Homer's. By giving stronger focus to the benign aspects of the story's closure, and by introducing a death ritual at the outset, Walcott sharpens the mythic symbolism of the structure. It is clear from his drafts, however, that Walcott's original intention was to introduce the scene of Achilles' funeral as a retrospective narration. The play was to open with Billy Blue singing for Penelope. Early in the Homer, she is pained by Phemius's song of Troy and comes down from her upper chamber to interrupt it. Walcott seems to have seen this as a good starting point, enlarging on it by borrowing the notion of Achilles' funeral from the end of the Homer to form his first inset scene, enacted as if Billy Blue narrates it. The accompanying of Billy Blue's prologue by a scene with Penelope weaving was only scrapped between the first preview night and the official opening night of the Royal Shakespeare Company production, which Walcott supervised—a late emendation which the printed text follows. This removal of Penelope from the opening moments of the play has profound implications for its representation of gender, as is discussed below.

Within the story, Homer's overall rationale for the action, the animosity of Poseidon, is played down by Walcott, and a new rationale is substituted. Walcott builds on an aspect of Odyssean legend not foregrounded by Homer although prominent in Ovid, the contest for the arms of Achilles (also implicit is Auden's "The Shield of Achilles," which may have prompted some of the play's imagery of totalitarianism). Moving the funeral of Achilles to the start of his narration not only articulates a link with the preceding Trojan story and enables a symbolic critique of centrism to be initiated, it also provides a new rationale for the ten years' journey home. Odysseus's rival for the arms of Achilles was Ajax. The two present competing claims, as in Ovid. The arms being awarded to Odysseus, Ajax in a rage, according to the tradition, slaughters a flock of sheep and then in shame commits suicide, the subject of a tragedy by Sophocles (in which Odysseus nobly intervenes to secure honorable funeral rites for him). Walcott presents a brief dispute over who should have Achilles' arms but develops it with a new idea. In resentment, Ajax curses Odysseus, as he is awarded the shield of Achilles, saying, "Bear it, you turtle! Take ten years to reach your coast." Walcott thus substitutes human rivalry for the divine malice of Poseidon, which drives the Homeric plot. Ajax, a part doubled with that of Antinous in the original conception, represents the secularization of the story; but Walcott, typically, is also careful to code atheism as error. Antinous, rival to Odysseus's sexual self as Ajax is to his martial persona, is given the line, just before the climactic scene of his routing, "There're no gods. We've thrown them out." The audience, which has seen Athena, knows this to be "wrong," and that divine as well as secular justice will be visited on Antinous.

As a result of Ajax's curse, the symbol of the wanderer is thus identified with the form of the turtle, the one who is naturally at home in the sea and who bears his house on his back, ultimately to return. The simplistic reading of Odysseus's quest, with the journeying coded as negative and the homecoming as a simple positive, is thus problematized. Odysseus is of course not a turtle; he is a man who, his rival knows, desires to get home—but the image tugs the other way, as does the ancient story's outline, with Odysseus's long stays with goddesses. Walcott balances the contrary movements: on the one hand the desire to return home to wife and family, to roots, on the other the desire for rootlessness, for the freedom of the wanderer, encoded particularly as a desire for sexual license. As Odysseus says, "At the back of all men's minds is a rented room."

It is largely because the opposing impulses are held in such finely tuned balance that the resolution has such dramatic tension. The encounter with Penelope, who almost withholds her acceptance of her husband, reminds us that desire, whether sexual or spiritual, is dependent on another for its fulfillment. The return of the aging hero to rout the young pretenders is a seductive story for all those past their youth, a story that has survived long beyond the faiths that gave rise to it, but powerful as its appeal is, it is its corollary—Walcott's addition in which the hero has to beg for forgiveness if he is to be readmitted to the desired intimacy, the position of favor—that really keeps the audience on the edge of its seat.

Walcott balances the discourse of vengeance that wounds—as in the ancient heroic code—with a discourse of forgiveness that heals. Scheria is "an isle known for healing," and Egypt is associated with curative herbs and nurture. The play brings to the fore the notion of Egypt as cultural other to the dominant of Greece, in Walcott's perception also its origin: as Eurycleia says, "Is Egypt who cradle Greece till Greece mature." It is an often ignored element of the Homer. When Telemachus visits Menelaus, for instance, Helen relieves the men of all painful recollection, with an anodyne drug from Egypt: "For the fertile soil of Egypt is most rich in herbs, many of which are wholesome in solution, though many are poisonous. And in medical knowledge the Egyptian leaves the rest of the world behind. He is a true son of Paeeon the Healer."[32] As mentioned, Homer designates Proteus an Egyptian deity, who herds seals and is visited by Menelaus, and has Odysseus land, on his return to Ithaca, at the cove sacred to Phorcys, in Homer another name for Proteus, the Old Man of the Sea.[33] Billy Blue in Walcott's version is made an Egyptian, and Eurycleia too is from Egypt.

By making these important personas Egyptian, in a socially subordinate but dramatically powerful relationship to the Greek central figures, Walcott models an often ignored aspect not only of the ancient world but of the modern world too, in which postcolonial communities are forced into serving the neoimperialists. His use of the Caribbean and African American vernaculars for the servants makes the class map of the society abundantly clear. It also enables him to assert the key role played in ancient Greek culture by its others in Africa and Asia (Bernal's theme)—and to imply its modern parallel, the vital role of the marginalized in developing Western thought—or, to put it another way, of the black contribution to the culture perceived as "white."[34] What the play offers, in fact, is a radically different worldview from that of Homer. The assumption of centrism is revised with a version in which the perspectives of the conventionally marginalized are given equal importance to those of the traditionally central figures. Circe, a figure of great power, here has, for instance, an "ebony arm."

In keeping with this shift of emphasis, Walcott makes more of the plebeian characters, whose impact in performance is even greater than that on the page as they tend to dominate the humor. Eurycleia, the old nurse, important at key moments in the Homer, is made more prominent in Walcott's version. She appears in more scenes and has a more central role in furthering the action: for instance, in the play she triggers the embrace of reunion between father and son, a scene from which she is absent in the Homer. Three details of the Homer are changed. Her assisting Odysseus with picking out the disloyal maids for punishment is dropped, and her willingness to wash the feet of Odysseus, disguised as a beggar, is replaced by Walcott with her indignation and reluctance, which is livelier and more satisfying dramatically. But most importantly, where Homer has her restrained by Odysseus from a yell of triumph at the slaughter of the suitors, Walcott completely reverses this, making her utter a terrible cry of grief. Where the Homer has toward the end a housekeeper named Eurynome, Walcott brings all the "old female servant" parts together in the memorable persona of Eurycleia, who is equally important at both the beginning and the end of his play.

To offset the benign, mature strength of his Eurycleia, Walcott develops the character of the young, rebellious maid, Melantho. Homer has two servant characters who react adversely to Odysseus, a man, Melanthus, and a girl, Melantho. Walcott rolls these into one, the maid Melantho, and brings her into the play from the outset, as an antithesis to Eurycleia. As the ambitious, sassy servant who is in no way servile but resists her servitude, she occupies an ambivalent place in the play's map of sympathies; on the one hand, she is constructed as an antipathetic character, as we identify with Eurycleia's censure and repudiate her insolence to Odysseus; but on the other hand, she is likeable for her spirit and becomes something of a hero of class resistance. When she is threatened with death by Odysseus at the end of the play, both Eurycleia and Penelope intervene to protect her, thus securing her position as a figure of sympathy.

Both Melantho and Eurycleia have a further dimension as a pair, in that they are implicitly black. It is clear from the text that Eurycleia is Egyptian, and she is mocked by Melantho in racially specific terms, while the "melan" root of the name suggests blackness. In putting Caribbean English in the old woman's mouth, Walcott both modernizes the story and reminds us that many of the servant class in ancient Greece would have been black. In moving these characters from the periphery, as in Homer's story, to the central ground of interest and entertainment, he revolutionizes the elitist assumptions of the Homeric treatment. Much of the richest comedy comes from the scenes with Eurycleia and Melantho, as does some of the most powerful emotion. Eurycleia in particular presides over the text's moral values. She it is who voices the central philosophy, "is strong-timbered virtues uphold this house," and who makes her great howl over the scene of carnage at the end. As Walcott's Penelope says, Eurycleia is "this house's foundation." After nursing two generations, she is the catalyst of their reunion, urging Odysseus and Telemachus, in their hesitancy, to embrace, her presence being an inspired addition to the Homeric version of the scene. In modeling Egypt as the nurse of Greece, as Eurycleia is the nurse of Odysseus and Telemachus, Walcott also implies a reading of history in which the benign, healing culture is older than the martial one, its wisdoms offering a means of tempering the violence of the new age and a route to the desired peace with which the play concludes. It reflects his presentation elsewhere—for example, in "The Fortunate Traveller"—of the often superior wisdom of the so-called primitive as compared with the self-styled "civilized."

The figure of Odysseus himself has a complex relationship to notions of civilization and civility. He has been viewed differently at different epochs, as W. B. Stanford so well demonstrates, along a continuum that ranges from the despised Machiavellian to the admired Romantic hero.[35] Walcott clearly stages the latter position, although he revises radically the characteristics by which Odysseus has been traditionally recognized. First, he brings him off the pedestal of the elite, to reveal him as ordinary, a kind of Everyman. The already noted re-vernacularization of Homer's story is achieved in part through the characterization of Odysseus himself. The tone of the opening scene, of Achilles' funeral, with the august Greek leaders paying tribute in formal language, is revolutionized at the entry, late, of Odysseus. He brings a pungent flavor of the plebeian with his irreverence: he comes to the funeral eating and brings only a small offering. His language is informal, and his philosophy is pragmatism: the show of honor to Achilles in death only reminds him that some were less than friends to him in life.

The character Walcott develops from this opening scene reveals an Odysseus who owes more to Shakespeare's Autolycus and to the Caribbean and African trickster-hero of folklore, Anansi, than to the Ulysses of post-Homeric European tradition with his courtly, silver-tongued duplicity. This is an acquisitive Odysseus, who "took his share" (of food and goods) and whose son, hearing Menelaus's account, comments that he sounds more like a "rug-seller." In Greek myth, Autolycus is the son of Hermes and the maternal grandfather of Odysseus, the one who names him and in whose company as a young man he receives the boar-wound in the thigh, by the mark of which he is recognized in his middle age. Shakespeare's Autolycus is an anarchic hero, a thief and a trickster but also a singer and a good fellow, associated with the play's assertion of the life force and of restoration. Anansi is also a rogue, but a hero too, with his antiestablishment tricks cheating the authority figure, Tiger, to put more food in his own belly.

Asked whether his concept of Odysseus was not informed by the figure of Anansi, Walcott said,

> Yes, very much . . . he is escaping, he has to go through certain labours . . . his thing is his wit, his evasiveness: the . . . zoological equivalent would be like a bear chasing a mouse . . . or some huge animal trying to catch another small one, and how does the animal evade, you know. Now if you transfer that into, say, a Cyclops and . . . anything you want, Anansi, a spider, whatever you want, it's the same thing. It's like the Tiger and Anansi. . . . All these stories come out of one imagination. There's only one imagination, and . . . there's always one figure in the folk imagination who is kind of a protestant figure, an elusive figure, who is not part of the cosmology and upsets the hierarchy somehow, either by defiance, or by wit, or by solving challenges . . . most of the West Indian jokes, which are based on African stories, are somebody always challenging Tiger, always making an idiot out of Tiger. . . . And in a sense the Tiger represents a kind of deity. And this person who is sceptical and smart and avoids the power of the Tiger is really a kind of protest . . . or query or scepticism [against] omniscience or power. And that's what he represents, I think.[36]

Both are essentially survivors, outsiders who live by their wits, and this quality is central to Walcott's Odysseus—a quality that is there in the Homer but that has become overlaid with a subsequent tradition in which Odysseus has become an antipathetic character. Walcott restores the likeableness to him and reveals a hero with much resonance for an age of democratic values. It is more important to the play that Odysseus is from a marginalized community than that he leads that community. He is heroic because he stands up for himself, demanding his fair share from a world that implicitly would not yield it up otherwise.

To Walcott, the challenging figure also has a metaphysical resonance, expressing an essentially positive spirit:

> I think Odysseus is in the largest sense of the word comedic, in that its comedy implies a questioning. If you stand up and ask god why, in the tone of voice [in which] he asks, it is comedic rather than tragic.... Odysseus is the first directly querulous figure that we have in the literature.[37]

The "querulous" Odysseus is a "little man" archetype and therefore a paradoxical hero. Walcott's Odysseus is a king because the story requires it, but he keeps reminding his audience that he is a little king, ruler of a small, stony island (too stony for horses, Walcott says, where the Homer says it is too steep for wheeled vehicles). The implication is that what he has is valued by himself, although it might not be by others. He manifests the particularity of value systems, an important lesson to those marginalized from the centrist imagery of desire. His dream of rule is in the domestic realm; his heroism lies in his personal qualities, for which Athena loves him and protects him. Walcott's Odysseus is heroic in his capacity for endurance and for his refusal to give up his dream of returning home. He denies the value of the military code and its definition of heroism. A pragmatist and a skeptic, he is suspicious of shows of emotion and resists the blandishments of poetry (though using eloquent language). He prefers peace to war, and making love, eating, and sleeping to derring-do. He is in essence a symbol of survival, with an eye on the main chance and a reluctance to ignore an opportunity for material gain. In putting such a figure at the center of his work, Walcott offers an implicit critique of the *Iliad*'s—and the subsequent tradition's—code of honor and its high and mighty heroes. He looks at the self-styled center and finds it hypocritical in its claims to virtue, and therefore dangerous. By making his hero a plain, practical man, of plebeian tastes and desires, an emblem of relative marginality in the stakes for social power, he probably restores Odysseus to his pre-Homeric significance. When such a man strings the impossible bow to rout his rivals, he carries the aspirations of all outsiders—those marginalized from the centers of power and those usurped from their own lives by others' interventions. In postcolonial terms, he symbolizes the colonized consciousness repudiating the myth of its marginalization to take charge of its own experience. Odysseus resumes control of his own.

Odysseus's counterpoint with Thersites, a new element in the story, provides an important clarification of his meaning. As a subversive figure, Odysseus might be taken for a cynic; Walcott, by showing him with Thersites as his foil, makes it clear that Odysseus's outlook is not to be confused with cynicism, which denies affective ties. This introduction of

Thersites flies in the face of the Homer, where Thersites the cynic is killed in the *Iliad* by Achilles for jeering at his show of emotion over Penthesilea's death. At Walcott's opening, it is Achilles who is dead, not Thersites. He is brought directly into the play's plot by speaking up for Odysseus in the contest for the arms of Achilles, which makes plausible the bantering exchange between the two of them that follows. Thersites serves to underline the masculinist philosophy of restlessness and violent action, implicit in the Trojan history and in Odysseus's journey, by introducing the idea of the sword as an alternative "wife." Thersites, the soldier of fortune, "married" only to his phallic sword, models a kind of masculinity opposed to that of Odysseus. Where Thersites illustrates the self-enclosed narcissism of the macho hero—however likeably—Odysseus's wisdom lies in the knowledge of his own incompleteness, which requires the feminine to make it whole.

Odysseus is thus the key to the play's revision of both gender and power relations. He needs the feminine. His masculinist triumph over the suitors, exciting though it is, is rapidly brought under a different value system and exposed as valueless by the women's condemnation, the only true value being not revenge but forgiveness. He realizes (as do we) that he is nothing unless he can persuade Penelope to value him. The wordplay of the name "Nobody" acquires a resonance beyond the Cyclops episode. The play's ethic is the Christian one of mercy; it concludes by valuing peace not just as a desirable interlude in a saga of heroic bloodshed but as a basis for existence. The ancient values have been turned on their head.

It would be surprising if this had not had implications for the representation of the divine. Homer's portrayal of Athene and Poseidon as controlling agents of human lives is subtly shifted by Walcott. It is not that he adopts a post-mythic modern skepticism, but that he introduces a Christian concept of benign deity, set against the idea of human responsibility, the protestant ethic that the individual has to earn grace. The malice of Homer's Poseidon is therefore marginal to the Walcott, and the occasional cruelty of Athene is not reflected in his Athena. Odysseus in Homer's story is a victim to divinity, at the mercy of the gods of sea and sky, the favor of Athene being shown as capricious. At the turning point of the narrative, at Odysseus's return to his own palace, Athene torments him a little longer, because she "wished the anguish to bite deeper."[38] Walcott, however, makes Athena a reliably benign divinity, appearing in a number of guises but always intervening to aid Odysseus's cause; she reflects the post-Homeric monotheisms, and particularly Christianity, and as the great goddess is a figure familiar from Walcott's work.

As well as her appearances as Captain Mentes and the Shepherd, followed from the Homer, Walcott introduces a new episode, her interruption of the lovemaking between Circe and Odysseus—a small scene worthy of Homer, in that it exposes her to be not just another mother goddess but one with feet of clay, capable of jealousy and having a more than platonic interest in Odysseus—in other words, a very classical divinity. A reciprocal shift is at work: as the divine partakes of human failings, so the human hero partakes of the divine.

Athena seems to be a force for aiding human beings to make the best of themselves; her antithesis is the godless state of the Cyclops's realm, which is portrayed in unequivocally negative terms (a fascistic portmanteau image meant to range from the world of the Greek colonels to that of George Grosz).[39] Circe, too, is divine, but hers is an influence that the text carefully defines: she does not make monsters of men, she simply persuades men to make monsters of themselves. Walcott gives the mythic concept of metamorphosis a particular significance. The idea of dissolving is a recurrent theme of the play, from Nausicaa's "soon I'll have the power to make grown men dissolve" to the "fluent" elusiveness of Proteus, central to the play's imaging of metamorphosis. Walcott's moral universe is different from Homer's, his central thesis being the power of the human imagination, to shape both ourselves and our image of the world. He asserts that the demonic is a figment of human imagination (Odysseus's final pronouncement on monsters is "we make them ourselves") and that we are not changed by divine intervention but by ourselves. As Odysseus says of Circe, "We create our own features. Not her. We change form." Metamorphosis here undergoes a particularly protestant sea change, more to do with the ethic of personal responsibility than the representation of the marvelous.

The mythic ritual used to explore these ideas is nominally classical but draws also on current religious usage. Circe's magic is presented through a mixed African and Caribbean terminology, alongside that of ancient Greece: Shango is paired with Zeus, Erzulie with Athena (a creolization evident also in *Omeros,* as noted above). The rites involving white-robed celebrants, drums, a sacrificial cock, and the marking out of sacred space by the sprinkling of powder, whether of flour or chalk (or soot, as in the RSC production's demarcation of the Underworld scene), can be paralleled today in both Caribbean and African rituals, which on the evidence of ancient texts apparently reflect similar ones of ancient times.

In contrast, no ritual invocations to Athena are represented in the drama, freeing her from culturally specific association. Her strong association with light in the Homer is adhered to by Walcott, but he changes her designation as "bright-eyed" to "green-eyed" and "sea-eyed," alongside "bright" and "shining," and to a family of epithets relating to her as skimming water with her feet, so that she is of the air, but only just, barely distinct from the realm of water. This Athena is "wet-heeled," perhaps suggested by Homer's portrayal of the sea-nymph Thetis, who comes to her son Achilles' funeral with her "silver feet,"[40] as much as by his early account of Athene's golden sandals that carried her "as surely and wind-swiftly over the waves as over the boundless earth."[41] Walcott identifies her with the African and Caribbean water divinity, *Maman de l'Eau,* who "hides in a waterfall's cascading curtain"; the closeness of the realms of water and air is encapsulated by Anticleia, who describes how "[a] breeze polishes the sea with Athena's feet." The sea then becomes a radically different signifier from that in the Homer, where Poseidon and his realm are implacably hostile and in antithesis to the desired land. Walcott has Anticleia assert, paradoxically, "Merciless Poseidon will grant you his mercy," thus constructing him as a kind of Old Testament divinity, paradoxically drawn closer to the milder, wholly "New Testament" ethos of Athena. He also sharpens the idea of home as object of desire, but he keeps this in tension with the pull of the sea. His Odysseus longs for his own shore, but at the moment when he exchanges it for a "surf of blossoms" in his orchard, he is allowed some nostalgia for what he is giving up, as he answers Penelope's question "Will you miss the sea?" with wistful lyricism.

The text sets the peace of home on land against the potentially destructive chaos of the sea, but it also acknowledges the value of the spiritual quest, the open-ended experience, of which the imagination offers an analogue; and although Walcott chooses not to make his Odysseus voyage on after just one night with his wife, he does incorporate in the body of the play a Dantesque or Tennysonian idea of the ongoing experience, of the spirit and of art. According to Nestor, the aged visionary, Odysseus the rationalist "defied the sea," disappearing "[t]hrough this world's pillars, the gate of human knowledge," a Dantean echo. The important shift in Walcott's presentation is that this dreamlike voyaging is concluded with Odysseus's resumption of his domestic role, whereas the onward journey signaled by Homer—and its realization by Dante and Tennyson—relegates the return to Penelope to nothing more than a temporary staging post in that great, endless quest.

The result of this is to make the feminine principle much stronger in the Walcott than in the Homer. Walcott's text reaches a true closure in Odysseus's homecoming to his "rock-steady woman" (a term from Caribbean popular music is here adapted to a new metaphorical significance, a characteristic Walcott move). By concentrating on the motif of homing, he produces a more satisfying whole than Homer, who defines the objective of return to the wife in terms of a one-night stand: immediately after their reunion, Odysseus tells Penelope of his "great and hazardous adventure" to come, and that just one night together was "what we desired."[42] Penelope herself is made more authoritative by Walcott; in the Homer, she is a less assertive character, ordered about by Telemachus, and, once convinced of her husband's identity, immediately accepting him back. Her outcry at the bloodbath Odysseus causes is Walcott's addition to the Homeric story, which gives her reluctance to accept the avenger as her husband further dramatic force. Finally, in accepting that he is truly Odysseus, she offers him a kind of absolution from the blood-guilt, "Oh God! I'll wash your hands with these tears."

Even the feminine in its most threatening form, as Circe the witch, is relatively benign (as in the Homer) in that it is through her agency that Odysseus is enabled to visit the Underworld. In addition, by interrupting the lovemaking with Athena's intervention (perhaps suggested by the scene in Homer in which Calypso is visited by Hermes), Walcott shows Circe's mischief to be at the mercy of a stronger, benign magic. Although his primary motive was probably practical, to do with length, Walcott's condensing of Calypso and Circe into one persona also serves to reduce the role of divine female obstruction to Odysseus's return home. It is counterbalanced by the much greater impact of the Sirens episode in the play than in the poem; the exquisite agony caused by the sensuous appeal of taboo women is given powerful dramatic expression, particularly as realized in the RSC production. The Nausicaa episode introduces an intermediate position: as quasi daughter, she is sexually taboo but available for passive titillation, her "freshness" able to "salt and cure" (a pleasing paradox) all the aging Odysseus's "sins." Significantly, Walcott introduces her as presiding figure over Odysseus's return to his homeland, as if the daughter figure has the power to redeem an errant parent.[43] Penelope's ability to silence the riotous suitors is a further instance of female power, while Walcott's enhancement of the roles of Eurycleia and Melantho enables Ithaca to be seen as a site of female domination, for all the suitors' noise.

In Walcott's hands, the fixed island becomes a metaphor of the desired female body, as in *Omeros* and elsewhere in his work. Odysseus answers Alcinous's question about Calypso's magic, "Was enchantment hidden in the island itself?" with "In her and the island. One cleft of flesh, one of stone," but her "happy grave" affords him no joy, as he "sank into a sadness no flesh could cure," out of longing for his own island. The wandering odyssey then becomes an image of masculinity, the quest for Ithaca a quest for the "right" sexual union. The counterpointing of Odysseus with Thersites, discussed above, functions as does Shakespeare's counterpointing of Coriolanus with Aufidius. Spurning affective ties, Thersites dedicates himself to unrest and war, although Odysseus wrings out of him a grudging admission that he loved him. His creed is the homelessness of the self alone, defined in terms of absence of faith—he has "found no shore to believe," married only to his sword—the opposite pole to that of home and love, represented by Penelope, his Ithaca.

Walcott's difference of approach is also conspicuous in the representation of Helen. The notion of home is problematized by irony in relation to her. Walcott revolutionizes the Homeric values in his presentation of Menelaus and Helen, disclosing the cruelty of male seizure of women as chattels. Where Homer blithely narrates Menelaus's pride in the marriage of his illegitimate son (his offspring with a slave girl once he realized he would have no more children with Helen) and poignantly implies the reunited couple's marital coldness—"the lady Helen lay in her long robe by his side"[44]—Walcott gives Menelaus some cutting and callous lines that bring the pain of Helen's experience center stage. His play suggests that Helen was a scapegoat, with the real cause of the war probably a new tax.

Just as he focuses on Helen's misery—and makes her part of the antiwar discourse of the play, with her spirited rejection of the idea that she misses Troy—Walcott also makes the suffering of Penelope imaginatively compelling. These iconic female figures whom post-Homeric history has tended to see as the catalysts of male action—Penelope, by her constancy, as evoker of heroism and consuming lust; Helen, by her "fickleness," as cause of war—are here given full and sympathetic attention and portrayed as powerful personae in their own right. Their mythologizing by men throughout history is devastatingly deconstructed. Instead, the women of the play are at least the equal of the men. It is no accident that the horrors of the Cyclops's realm lack female representation; there Walcott discloses the masculine impetus carried to its extreme. Elsewhere he edits out its worst excesses: Agamemnon's diatribe against women,[45] for instance, has no place in his play, nor has the hanging of the maids after the killing of the suitors. He stays with the Homer to the extent that he has Odysseus threaten Melantho with death, but this is subverted by the concerted action of the older women, Penelope and Eurycleia. The whole ethos of revenge, a masculine phenomenon here, is given a powerful critique in the reaction of these two to the slaughter. The dominant feminine principle in the play is nonviolent, nurturing, and strong to resist the morally reprehensible.

Penelope's quasi-divine role in promising absolution to Odysseus for his blood-guilt parallels his own quasi divinity. The last phases of the drama invite a reading of Odysseus as a Christ figure, as his decade of suffering culminates in the mock crucifixion jibes of the suitors—"Let's see if he's a god. Slip a spear in his side!" ". . . Make thorns his crown!" "Just nail KING O' BEGGARS over his bleeding head!"—but this godlike role is denied by Odysseus himself, who is reported as having refused offers of divinity and later says to Penelope, "I'm not a god. I'm Odysseus." It seems likely that Homer's mystical account of Odysseus as he tends the lamps, mockingly related by one of the suitors, may have seeded Walcott's passage: "some divine being must have guided this fellow to Odysseus's palace. At any rate it seems to me that the torch-light emanates from the man himself, in fact from that pate of his, innocent as it seems of the slightest vestige of hair."[46] Given the place of the concept of the "Light of the World" in Christian tradition, and specifically in the previous work of Walcott, the extension of Athene's brightness to a Christian idea of radiance, and thence to a matching of the suitors' mockery to the mockery of Christ, seems a natural step. The play gives Penelope too an emotive entrance with a beam of light.

The persona of Walcott's Odysseus balances the masculine with the feminine. He is both man of action and patient sufferer, of a Lear-like stoicism. The boar-wound in his thigh by which Eurycleia recognizes him is his symbol of suffering, linked to the play's discourse of sensuality as piggishness, the sexual libido bringing out the "beast" in man (Odysseus characterizes himself to Circe as "this pig-scarred adventurer"). From the feminist point of view there is, of course, irony in the representation of the sexual libido as the cause of suffering for the male. The story of Odysseus shows that it is not, however, a fatal condition. Odysseus's Homeric epithets as "sacker of cities" and "nimble-witted" are developed by Walcott to encompass a persona symbolizing survival: "What lasts is what's crooked. The devious man survives." Eumaeus gives him the ultimate description, as a "natural man," and Athena tells him he has earned the spoils he brings back with him. He is antiheroic relative to the conventional idiom of the grand narratives, without high-flown ideals or rhetorical posturing. He is "l'homme moyen sensuel," cautious, acquisitive, and clear as to his objectives, valuing his own home above all else. And unlike Homer's Odysseus, he is a man of passion, able to explain to the Cyclops the importance of the ability to weep.

In creating his play, Walcott makes something new of the Homer, while remaining faithful to it. The original is his Penelope, guiding his course yet not preventing innovatory experiences along the way. In matching the old story to newer histories and concerns, he has not betrayed it but, if anything, has revealed more clearly than ever the living root from which it springs. His poetic drama does not have the conventionally epic scale of Homer's poem, but it is truly epic in its imaginative power and the depth of its address to the collective experience, not of any nation, but of the human race. John Thieme sees it as a case of "reverse colonization" and "an iteration of the multicultural nature of contemporary British and European societies," but to my mind it goes beyond locale or the binarism of adversarial politics.[47] It has, in fact, the rich humanity, composed of many opposing strands of desire and experience, of Shakespeare's romances. Above all, it shows that poetry in the theater can once again be an intensifier of drama. Its great story of quest and homecoming now takes its place in the English language as never before, familiar but transformed to a new youth and vigor, as if by Athene's magic.

"To Praise Lovelong": Conclusion

Antonio: We all were sea-swallow'd, though some cast again,
And by that destiny to perform an act
Whereof what's past is prologue, what to come
In yours and my discharge.

Caliban: I'll be wise hereafter,
And seek for grace.

Prospero: And my ending is despair,
Unless I be reliev'd by prayer,
Which pierces so that it assaults
Mercy itself and frees all faults.
As you from crimes would pardon'd be,
Let your indulgence set me free.
***Tempest*, II.i.259–62; V.i.294; Epilogue 15–20**

Bob Marley: Won't you help to sing
these songs of freedom
cos all I ever have
redemption songs
redemption songs[1]

The Tempest closes not only with a commitment to taking responsibility for the future but with a movement toward grace, a strong word in Shakespeare, implying redemption. Bob Marley, who, like Walcott, has written Caribbean art into the hearts of countless people around the globe, made music of his own "redemption songs," a phrase that could also characterize Walcott's literary work. Walcott, who chose "Redemption Song" and "No Woman No Cry" as two of his eight records for the radio program *Desert Island Discs,* said of the first that "it's got the truth of Marley's belief in it": "the depth of it is very moving."[2] Marley uses Rastafarian language, his own speech, for his lyrics, which are also part of Caribbean poetry. Like Walcott's work, they have a triple strategy: to expose "Babylon" (the pernicious workings of the materialist world and the culture that powers it); to show compassion to those living under it; and to articulate the dream of "Zion," the ideal, spiritually oriented community of egalitarian brotherhood and sisterhood. Zion is both a politics and a faith. The Rastafarian "I-an-I" usage, which is threaded through this study, enshrines community in terms that do not erase individuality but allow it its difference, the rich resource it brings to the group. "I-an-I" also symbolizes the belief that even the solitary person is never truly alone, because s/he walks with spiritual companions.

It is significant, then, that at the end of Shakespeare's play, Caliban turns his attention to the state of his soul, whereas Prospero begs forgiveness from others, fellow humans. Of course, at one level, it is a neat way of inviting an audience to applaud at the end, but at another, there seems to be a recognition that Prospero needs first to be absolved in some kind of social rite—a rite of reparation, perhaps. The position at the end of empire, for Walcott, is clear: "It's good that everything's gone, except their language, / which is everything."[3] What language can offer is no little gift. Walcott has described it, speaking of Blake's work, as "going through experience and re-arriving at innocence."[4] The apple of Eden, the old order's taboo of forbidden knowledge, is remade, through culture, as the new order's apple of communication, the nourishing fruit, Gonzalo's gift. Such a transition is indeed enacted in the Bible, between the beginning of the Old Testament and the end of the New, for, central to the final vision of *Revelation,* is the tree of life, "which bare twelve manner of fruits, and yielded her fruit every month: and the leaves of the tree were for the healing of the nations. / And there shall be no more curse."[5] Caliban's part, as Shakespeare shaped it, was perhaps created with this text in mind. The language of the King James Bible has also shaped both Marley and Walcott as poets, its sonorous cadences imprinted in early life on the inner ear, as powerfully as was the distinctive speech of the islands, with what Walcott calls its "salt freshness."[6] The idea of the healing of nations endures, like Gonzalo's commonwealth, like Zion. Remote though it may be from sociopolitical actuality, it is in culture that it can be glimpsed.

Ali Mazrui expresses a related ideal: "full reciprocal international interpenetration is a precondition for a genuinely symmetrical world culture."[7] The current imbalance is here recognized, the neocolonial legacy with its devastating implications. The sense that the global social economic disorder—the abuse of power—must be tackled is acute. Walcott continually raises his voice in this essentially political and moral cause. His urgent objective is to "move the center," not geographically but emotionally, to move it to tears. Referring to Joseph Brodsky's Nobel speech, he said, "if tyrants read, really read, they wouldn't do what they did, because too much would be revealed, too much would touch them. I think we read now the way tyrants read: we read for information. We don't read to be touched. But what poetry does, and yes, that is the power of poetry—as Owen said, the power is in the pity—if that can touch, yes it has power."[8]

The Prosperos of the modern world, the fortunate travelers, are addressed by Walcott, who appeals to their compassion. Antonio Benitez-Rojo sees the Caribbean text as in quest of "routes that might lead, at least symbolically, to an extratextual point of social nonviolence and psychic reconstitution of the Self." This project disrupts with its pluralism the either/or structure of Western discourse: "The routes, iridescent and transitory as a rainbow, cross at all points the network of binary dynamics extended by the West. The result is a text that speaks of a critical coexistence of rhythms, a polyrhythmic ensemble whose central binary rhythm is decentred. . . ."[9] The going beyond binarism is also central to Walcott's rhetorical project. Likewise, to initiate a new discourse of the psychic reconstitution of the self is a large claim for the Caribbean text but, as has been argued here, may not be inordinate.

What a plural culture can offer is an alternative to the competitive model of the self and the other. Trinidadian writer Lawrence Scott affirms the particularity of a Trinidadian identity as geographically rooted and intrinsically heterogeneous: "The writer, and the literature, is speaking to the world from that place. . . . It isn't just that we hear all these different languages and we experience different dialects, and so on. It seems to me—and I feel this profoundly as a white writer, as a writer with European heritage—that there is something of Africa in me; I have to discover Africa; I have to discover India. And I think that is a profound thing, if people discover the other; you know, you discover yourself *in* the other."[10] This radical approach to identity is distinctively Caribbean but could be general. Its prerequisite is an acceptance of the full humanity of others, of their equivalence in value, remote from the dominant philosophy structured on different principles, regarding the other as alien and able to conceive of the plural self only in terms of alienation, the self without boundaries seen as pathology, not privilege.

Yet if the world's problems come down, as Walcott argues, to a failure of compassion, one of the projects of culture is to counter that failure. Art, in the end, seeks its aesthetic as part of a wider collective desire. The power is in the pity. The artist, therefore, has to be a challenger, a heretic, who is fearless in tackling orthodoxies. He has to be like Odysseus, as Walcott describes the archetype: it is the voice asking God why, the earliest "querulous" voice, but comedic rather than tragic.[11] To reject the tragic perception of the human condition is fundamental to his aesthetic.

It is not romance to suggest that the particular reality of Caribbean culture may provide a template for what is now a global phenomenon. Walcott is not alone in seeing the region as a kind of cultural ark for the world: "make of my heart an ark" is the invocation in *Another Life*.[12] The ideas of Maryse Condé, a writer from the francophone Caribbean, resonate with Walcott's: the world, she says, is "in a state of creolization, meaning that all the cultures are coming into contact . . . so a new image, a new diversity of the world is emerging." She uses as analogy the trope of the plantation, showing how it can be remade, redeemed from tragedy to comedy: "It is, as some years ago, in the plantation system, when so many people were forced to live together, and produced that Caribbean culture, that Creole culture. Now the world has a kind of plantation system—so many people coming to live together who were not supposed to know each other before; and in the forced contact they create a new form of culture where everybody would have something different to say, and to bring for the benefit of the other."[13] This is the "I-an-I" figure, the sharing of difference, and Walcott might qualify the remark by pointing out that it is not only forced contact that characterizes modernity. He offers his art (something different to say, for the benefit of the other), first, as St. Lucian; next, as West Indian (the anglophone community); then, as Caribbean—a pan-Caribbean concept, to which all the languages of the region contribute—then as Latin American, part of the group that is not North American; then as American, in the pan-American sense that embraces the North. In a very real sense, he is engaged in the quest for the American epic.

Finally, his work is offered to the language, to English and all those who speak it and use it, and to all the texts that exist in it. Distinctively, Walcott writes Caribbeanness into the language, doing so in ways that represent, perhaps, the next phase of Caribbean cultural history. He is already attuned to the plurality of languages in the region and was a pioneer of opening the West Indian consciousness to a sense of an enterprise shared with artists in the French, Spanish, or Dutch Antilles, and of opening black consciousness to the need to acknowledge a sharing of place and culture with groups of different, and differently mixed, ethnicities. His own ideology has much in common with the French Caribbean concept of "créolité," defined as "the *interactional or transactional aggregate* of Caribbean, European, African, Asian, and Levantine cultural elements, united on the same soil by the yoke of history." Jean Bernabé, Patrick Chamoiseau, and Raphaël Confiant also acknowledge, "We cannot reach Caribbeanness without interior vision," for it is "more a matter of vision than a concept."[14]

The first half of this study leads up to the idea of a mythopoeic art, which is the prerequisite of such vision; the second half examines that aesthetics in action. Necessarily, the works continually engage with their own status as art, in order to examine their relationship with the world. It is in that sense that the oeuvre, like Ariel, lays out a rich banquet for the postmodernists. The hall of mirrors in which Walcott's words are set in motion is not, however, a field of receding images fading into the spectral, but one in which dazzling new effects are continually sparked. The challenge is to use *all* of the resources—of language, of history, of particularity—to make something unforeseeable, something fresh as the dew as well as old as the hills. This means, of course, using such resources as the literary canon offers, including Shakespeare. Walcott's play of the early 1980s, *A Branch of the Blue Nile,* addresses the problematics of canonicity, of cultural "translation" to different historical and social contexts, and of performance. Yet it does so in a work that is not just reflexive, or even reflective, but constantly stages in front of those "hills" its own dew-spangled particularity; and through its prisms those hills take on a different outline. It challenges the centrist, racist presumption that (in the words of a poem of the same period that presents a parallel meditation, as so often in Walcott's use of genre) "'the blacks can't do Shakespeare,'" and demonstrates how Shakespeare must be done—differently. Crucially the play presents both the Shakespearean text and the Trinidadian reworking, interleaved, striking meanings off one another. Both are necessary. The primary imperative is to remedy the lack of cultural representation: "nutten in there had to do with my life, or the life of all them black people out in the hot sun on Frederick Street at twelve o'clock trying to hustle a living." To fill the gap, Walcott here chooses to mythify Trinidad through the Shakespearean prism, showing how a Cleopatra or an Antony, a Hamlet, an Othello, or a Lear's fool are on every corner. The awesome claim the artist makes is to expose such meanings, to make myth for his or her community, but as the holy fool—the madman who once was an artist—says, when art works, "is not you anymore, but the gift, the gift . . . something God lend you for a lickle while." Such a knowledge can only be recognized in humility, however large its claims. J. M. Coetzee, writing from his own sense of a postcolonial South African aesthetic, speaks of "that blinding moment of ascending meta-historical consciousness in which we begin to shape our own myths."[15]

The "we" here is a collective identification, a community, perceived at the moment when it emerges in the minds of its constituent members from the fragmented consciousness of isolated individuals with their own dreams and fears. The sense of pluralism is the determinant of the "we," the sense of a shared dimension to identity—not one that obliterates individuality but one that acknowledges what is referred to here as "the sharedness of difference." This "we" slides up and down a continuum from the simple pair to the global society. The ambiguous and sometimes unhelpful category of "nation" tends to come at the transition between cultural and regional community, perceived in a territorial dimension though flexible enough to embrace the concept of diaspora. Like many Caribbeans, Walcott has a clear knowledge of his Caribbean identity, which subsumes the nationality mentioned on his passport and which continues regardless of his geographical location (and which would have continued if he had proceeded to take out the American citizenship he once considered) because it has its existence chiefly in his culture. Conceived regionally, the idea of nation thus becomes mobile, not only sustainable but transmissible in locations remote from "home." Political nationality in the Caribbean, however, is a category of fragmentation. Since the demise of the Caribbean Federation there is no formal Caribbean nationality, but the reality of a cultural "nation" is lived by the region's diverse inhabitants and their diasporas. When Walcott mythifies St. Lucia or Trinidad, Jamaica or Guyana, Cuba, or Haiti, or the Virgin Islands, he does so as part of the overall project to render the region as myth.

The particularity of Caribbeanness, as Walcott sees it, is its cross-culturality: when he models distinctively Caribbean archetypes, he selects figures for whom every community could provide equivalents. Ultimately the "homing" persona is generic:

> the archipelago like a broken root,
> divided among tribes, while trees and men
> laboured assiduously, silently to become
>
> whatever their given sounds resembled,
> ironwood, logwood-heart, golden apples, cedars,
> and were nearly
>
> ironwood, logwood-heart, golden apples, cedars,
> men . . .[16]

Such recitation is not just "a naturalist's notebook"[17] but an identity-affirming incantation. Other communities could perform the same rite with different names.

Walcott's commitment to his home community has never wavered. "I'm lucky I didn't go abroad," he says: "I much prefer the route I took, to have been here, writing in a difficult but formative time."[18] In "Leaving School," he explains, "I had failed to win the Island Scholarship because of my poor mathematics."[19] In St. Lucia, it was awarded biennially on achievement in the London Matriculation and was part of a system of colonial education that lifted many of the most talented of his generation, such as Naipaul and Brathwaite, out of their home environment and into metropolitan universities at a still formative age, changing them forever. Again, in "The Muse of History" he wrote, "I felt, I knew, that if I went to England I would never become a poet, far more a West Indian, and that was the only thing I could see myself becoming, a West Indian poet."[20] This was more than just a choice of career; it was more like a mission: "the first duty of an artist is something beyond him (let's say him)—he's only the vessel of an expression of gratitude."[21] It has remained compelling, to the extent that he will admit, "I feel more responsible to my work than to my life."[22] In the end, the self evaporates in the creative act, which may not make for an easy personal life, but it can enable a phenomenal productivity of fine art. In the early poem "Roots," Walcott envisaged a future of West Indian art, made by "our Homer" with "truer perception," which would supersede the external cultural referents of the colonial era: as the poem observes wryly, "When they conquer you, you have to read their books."[23] It seems to have been Brodsky, however, who initiated the image of Walcott as that Caribbean "Homer," although the designation has since become something of an irritant to Walcott.[24] The Caribbean has been, says Brodsky, "immortalized by Walcott." At the same time, he has changed the map of the language: "his throbbing and relentless lines kept arriving in the English language like tidal waves, coagulating into an archipelago of poems without which the map of modern literature would effectively match wallpaper. He gives us more than himself or 'a world'; he gives us a sense of infinity embodied in the language."[25] This is powerful praise from an admired fellow craftsman as well as a friend.

Walcott modestly ironizes his own achievement. As a man commemorated even by a special issue of Swedish postage stamps, he speaks with mock horror of his sense of "turning into a very minor monument—you can feel the concrete coming over your skin."[26] Clearly the Nobel Prize awarded in the year of the five-hundredth anniversary of Columbus's first landfall in the Americas has special significance for Walcott's home community. St. Lucia, for instance, renamed the central square of Castries after him, jettisoning, symbolically, the old name of Columbus Square. The father of Andreuille, the beloved of his adolescence, who "had once prophesied that the name 'Walcott would blaze like a meteor across the black midnight sky of Saint Lucia,'" has had his perspicacity rewarded to a degree he may not have imagined.[27] Maya Jaggi records a significant glimpse of Walcott's meaning to Caribbean people: in St. Lucia, on the beach, "a young black Londoner 'from Crystal Palace' comes to shake his hand, saying: 'You mean as much to me as Nelson Mandela.'"[28]

But the man is one thing, the work another, for it is also true that a University of the West Indies academic, when asked in conversation how his literature students got on with Walcott's work, answered jokily "as little as possible." My own undergraduate students study two of the plays, *Ti-Jean and His Brothers* and *Pantomime,* as well as the demanding poem "The Fortunate Traveller," but it is only at Master's level that I have attempted to introduce *Another Life* or *Omeros.* Although much of the work is accessible, some is undoubtedly difficult, requiring an extensive intercultural knowledge—although no sooner is such a remark put down than an inner voice of protest raises itself. For even at its most erudite, the work is always compellingly musical, using the wit and easy rhythms of speech to deliver even its most complex thought. I am reminded of first reading T. S. Eliot's *The Waste Land* as a teenager, and the hypnotic effect of its closing sequence, which I found stunningly beautiful and memorable, although I didn't understand a word. In a very real sense, the power of Walcott's language, as music, is enough to carry us until we are able to reach other levels of meaning. There is a place for the reader as gleaner, picking up grains of significance as s/he works along the textual field. It doesn't matter if it isn't all gathered at one passing; there will be some left for next time. Reading is a labor of love, not a combine harvester, and texts are there for us to live with, like partners or relatives, in an unfolding relationship, with some easy times and some tricky.

I am very conscious that my own readings in Walcott's work are, in a sense, provisional, partial, and negotiable. People of our time, from our various perspectives, will read differently from subsequent generations, in all their heterogeneity. The great texts of the world are those that speak to readers or audiences across space and time—they are those which travel. For Walcott's work to "travel" in this way has involved choices as to presentation. Local language practice, for instance, is often suggested rather than rendered literally, or if the latter (as with his use of French Creole), followed by a translation into Standard English. Part of his skill as a poet derives from his reader-awareness; he is a mannerly writer, explaining that which, for some, needs explaining.[29] This courtesy is the "I-an-I" consciousness in action: the creative utterance that does not suppress awareness of the other but answers it. But although, like some reptiles, the works may have the miraculous ability to respond to different contexts, they remain distinctively themselves, with that strong lizard silhouette (like that of the island/iguana in *Omeros*), that extraordinary eye.

The aesthetic quest is not for universality, but for what the authors of *Eloge de la Créolité* call "diversality."[30] Walcott's works seem likely to transport their quiddity to coming generations, with all the particularity of their plural, independently swiveling gaze.

The story of the reception of Walcott's work at different times and in different social contexts remains to be told. Clearly the multiple strategies in evidence in any one text, as discussed above, invite plural readings. At a very obvious level, readers who are themselves Caribbeans are likely to bring a radically different perspective to bear than those from elsewhere. Those who are black will start from a different position than those who are white (ongoing racism invests these slippery signifiers with real meaning, however essentialist). People of the Americas will read differently from people of Europe. Those who have lived in more than one country or culture or who perceive themselves as heterogeneous will have an insight to the work that is different from those whose experience is limited to a monoculture. The great glory of art is that it can open us not only to a fresh or deeper vision of our own predicament but to that of others. Art is the field in which, above all, the other enters us—in which difference can be not only articulated but celebrated. Walcott has been an assiduous recorder of his own sense of difference, from metropolitan culture, from local orthodoxies, from the left, from the right, and so on. He has been an Odyssean challenger. But simultaneously and paradoxically, both in and through the project to name difference, he has also been a passionate articulator of his sense of sharing, his identification with the wider world, whether the plebeian life of the street passing the narrow wooden house in which he grew up, on Chaussée Road, Castries, St. Lucia, a life from which as a child he felt in some ways distanced by class, or the ultimate sense of connectedness with all that has been thought, felt, and expressed throughout human history. The phenomenal inclusiveness is not at odds with the individualism. Both are simultaneously and continuously present and necessary to Walcott's project.

There is a tendency, however, for his readers to take narrower perspectives—not surprisingly, perhaps, since such breadth of vision as his is by definition rare. As a result, as we reach the end of the twentieth century, the second half of which saw a steadily remarkable artistic contribution from Walcott, there are divergent views of its significance. Clearly the award of the Nobel Prize constitutes a seal of approval, but it comes from a particular group, which may not be as much the guardian of universal values as it perceives itself to be. *Omeros* in particular earned Walcott the Nobel Prize, and his poetry has so far won him most of his international fans. In contrast, he is relatively little known outside the Caribbean as a dramatist, although his prodigious output of plays, musicals, and screenplays would be an extraordinary oeuvre even without the poetry, and the increasing phenomenon of international productions of his plays—*Ti-Jean and His Brothers* in Italy, for instance, and *The Last Carnival* in Sweden—may be beginning to redress the balance (also, with publication of some of the work in translation, it is encountering new readers in global communities beyond the anglophone). With a characteristic refusal to take account of fashion, Walcott has stuck to his belief that the theater is a place for all kinds of expression, including poetry. After Eliot he has kept alive the idea of the verse play in English in the second half of the century (Tony Harrison is one of the few with a parallel commitment). His faith in the replicability of renaissance is a lived conviction; he refuses to subscribe to the current view that the elevated poetic drama that characterized the age of Shakespeare is no longer possible. Yet he has played hard for popularity in the theater, using wit, comedy, music, and dance as the vehicles for some thought-provoking scenarios and philosophic and social enquiry, and the elusiveness of success has been frustrating. Ironically the Royal Shakespeare Company's production of *The Odyssey* was a success, sold out in Stratford-on-Avon and London—ironically, because the decision was taken to stage it in the smallest performance space available, which resulted in an extraordinarily powerful, intimate theatrical experience for those lucky enough to get tickets, but excluded many. The story of Walcott's 1998 foray onto Broadway with *The Capeman* is a reminder that, even with the huge talents and resources of Paul Simon and others, there is no guarantee of success in a capricious market where taste tends to be determined by fashion, and by reviewers whose parameters of aesthetic evaluation are often preset.

It may be worth reflecting that if Shakespeare's friends had not seen fit to collect his plays into a posthumous folio edition in 1623, the story of their survival and dissemination to date might have been very different. Perhaps the dramas' Elizabethan and Jacobean audiences were sometimes unresponsive and critical. Certainly much of the verse would have gone over the heads of the uneducated. It remains true that the plays are fiendishly difficult to stage well, at the same time as famously worth performing again and again in different ways. It has also become true that many more people now know them from reading them as texts than from seeing them performed, although the video age has created huge new "live" audiences. And of course it would be difficult to overestimate the importance of pedagogy in fuelling the popularity of Shakespeare. If his name were dropped off all syllabuses tomorrow, how long would the Shakespeare industry last? How long would it be before annotated editions would be available only from secondhand bookshops, and before groups of enthusiasts met to foster their shared enthusiasm in the teeth of an indifferent society? Yet what we see at the moment is that people will learn English in order to read Shakespeare. Clearly the Shakespeare phenomenon is now so well established—and rightly so—that, like a modern oil tanker, it would be difficult to stop. The point I am after is that the "bubble reputation" and the quality of the art need not be in any direct relation (as the public relations profession understands so well). The latter, the quality, is always, in a profound sense, independent of the former, the popularity. Walcott would be as good a poet if he had *not* won the Nobel Prize.

Fashions, however, come and go—I remember being surprised in the early 1980s when I asked in a theater bookshop for Walcott's *Dream on Monkey Mountain* to be told airily that it was "finished," as if it were old hat, yesterday's play. The history of race politics in the second half of the century has had an impact on perceptions of Walcott (as of other artists) in ways that remain to be unpacked by social and cultural commentators.[31] Walcott is understandably infuriated by what he sees as the patronizing and subtle marginalization that being labeled a "black poet" can mean, even when he is being lauded. To him, it is a centrist refusal to accept him just as a poet, on an equal footing with any other, and is yet another sign that the old racist hegemony is alive and well. That this rage should cause some sectors of the black community to look at him quizzically is a poignant irony. His racial politics are actually more militant than they are perceived to be on either side of the Manichean divide. The white establishment tends to approve him as assimilated to Western elite culture, and the black constituency tends to disapprove him for the same reason. Both positions are based on misapprehensions. He is not assimilated to the Western hegemony but on the contrary has assimilated the Western tradition to his own revolutionary project, making it his own and investing it with new significance, as this study has aimed to show. His aesthetic project has much to offer us, not only as art but ideologically, as a tool to help us understand the world we share.

In the end, it is as rite of homage to a people and a language that Walcott-Anansi spins the web of his words. It is an epic project, on which his sights have been fixed since youth. In a poem written half a century ago, Walcott, aged eighteen, wrote an elegy to his father, which perceives death's gift, greater than death itself, as the power to "make us see the forgotten price of man / Shine from the perverse beauty of the dead."[32] In another poem of the same era, which links his decision to stay in the islands to the vision, recorded in *Revelation,* which St. John experienced on the island of Patmos, he made a commitment to "praise lovelong, the living and the brown dead."[33] The elegy for those dead has remained a lifetime's theme, producing that distinctive timbre of joy and grief simultaneously, the epic balance:

> From all that sorrow, beauty is our gain,
> Though it may not seem so
> To an old fisherman rowing home in the rain.[34]

The work in its entirety is really a praise-song for the islands, a rite of love. For him, "Heaven remains / Where it is, in the hearts of these people, . . ." and he himself exemplifies that which he has called "the miracle of possibility which every poet demonstrates."[35] He is grateful, he says, for his "gift" of poetry; he then goes on, self-deprecatingly:

> It sounds pompous because you say, who gave you the gift, and what is this gift? And the gift is where I am, the gift is what I have come out of, the people around me who, I think, are beautiful people. They are, because they have gone through so much, and their fortitude is tremendous, and their beauty is part of that fortitude, and the landscape they inhabit. Just recently a guy was playing a shac-shac in a band in St. Lucia and I was looking at that guy's face, and I was saying, *that's* why I'm here, that's what I want to do. I want to have that guy's face—a black guy, with beautiful creases in his face, you know, and wearing a hat, and a kind of serenity on his face, playing the shac-shac, and the creases on his face. Not to paint it, not just to say, "to paint it would be good," but to *feel* it. That's why I'm here. I'm here for this man's face.[36]

Walcott has spoken with admiration of Joyce's "extraordinary endeavour," in *Ulysses,* to "democratize the sublime by making it extremely ordinary."[37] His own unmistakably Caribbean aesthetic project could equally be described as democratizing the sublime. It is, again, inextricably a politics and a faith. Bob Marley would have understood.

Notes

The abbreviation C.P. is used throughout for Walcott, *Collected Poems 1948–1984*, New York: Farrar, Straus and Giroux, and London: Faber, 1986. For Derek Walcott's works in general, references are to London editions where these exist.

The Apple of His Island: Introduction

1. Hulme, *Colonial Encounters*, 110–11.

2. Benitez-Rojo claims King as someone who, because of his personality, was "able to be a Caribbean person without ceasing to be a North American, and vice versa." Benitez-Rojo, *The Repeating Island*, 24.

3. Walcott, "Muse of History," 63.

4. Ibid., 40–41.

5. Ibid., 64.

6. Walcott, "On Choosing Port of Spain," 16.

7. Ibid., 16–17.

8. Dabydeen, "On Not Being Milton," 73.

9. Walcott, "Muse of History," 36.

10. Drayton and Andaiye, eds., *Conversations with George Lamming*, 122.

11. Walcott, "Muse of History," 63.

12. Retamar, "Caliban," 99.

13. Walcott, *Antilles*, 79.

14. Shakespeare, *Tempest*, II.i.21.

15. Walcott, "What the Twilight Says," 9.

16. Froude, *The English in the West Indies*.

17. Naipaul, *The Middle Passage*, 29.

18. Drayton and Andaiye, eds., *Conversations with George Lamming*, 121.

19. Walcott, "Muse of History," 39.

20. Joseph, *Caliban in Exile*, 16.

21. Psalm 26.1. The whole verse is: "The Lord is my light, and my salvation; whom then shall I fear: the Lord is the strength of my life; of whom then shall I be afraid?"

22. Walcott, "Muse of History," 39.

23. Shakespeare, *Tempest*, V.i.275.

24. Lamming, "The Pleasures of Exile," in John Hearne, ed., 88.

25. Arnold, *Modernism and Negritude*, 270.

26. Brathwaite, "Caliban's Guarden," 2.

27. Joseph, *Caliban in Exile*, 127–29. Other conspicuous critical engagements with the myth are: Mannoni, *Prospero and Caliban;* Nixon, "Caribbean and African Appropriations of *The Tempest*"; Hulme, *Colonial Encounters;* and Zabus, "A Calibanic Tempest in Anglophone and Francophone New World Writing."

28. Lamming, "Pleasures of Exile," in John Hearne, ed., 87.

29. Walcott, *Arena,* BBC TV, February 20, 1993.

30. Walcott, "Roots," *In a Green Night,* 60; *Another Life,* 23.iii, C.P., 293. Edward Baugh notes that it is a quotation from Catullus (*Derek Walcott,* 19).

31. James, *Caribbean Literature in English,* 213.

32. Dabydeen, "On Not Being Milton," 73.

33. Rodney, *The Groundings with My Brothers,* 39.

34. Walcott, University of Milan, May 22, 1996.

35. Benitez-Rojo, *The Repeating Island,* 17.

36. Shakespeare, *Tempest,* II.iii.31–34.

37. Ibid., II.i.154–75.

38. Walcott, interview with Burnett, London, June 21, 1988.

39. Lamming, "Pleasures of Exile," 98.

1. "Becoming Home": Modeling the Caribbean Subject

1. Miller, ed., *The Seminar of Jacques Lacan,* 7.

2. Slemon, cited in Brydon and Tiffin, *Decolonising Fictions,* 45.

3. Harris, "Comedy and Modern Allegory," 137. Fred D'Aguiar distinguishes Walcott from Harris, arguing that only Harris goes beyond binarism to the pluralism of a "kaleidoscopic whole." "Ambiguity without a Crisis? Twin Traditions, the Individual and Community in Derek Walcott's Essays," in Stewart Brown, ed., *The Art of Derek Walcott,* 167.

4. Rimbaud, *Lettre du Voyant,* 1871; Miller, ed., *The Seminar of Jacques Lacan,* 7.

5. Kristeva, *Desire in Language,* 100.

6. "[S]ince boyhood I have delighted in criticism. I cherished the essays of Eliot not because of his perceptions but because of their quotations. They induced in me the truest humility: that is, the desire to imitate, to imprison myself within those margins. Since then a lot of dead fish have beached on the sand. Mostly the fish are French fish, and off their pages there is the reek of the fishmonger's hands. I have a horror, not of the stink, but of the intellectual veneration of rot . . . ," et seq. Walcott, "Caligula's Horse," 141.

7. Walcott, "Sainte Lucie," C.P., 314.

8. Walcott, *Arena,* BBC2, London, February 26, 1993.

9. Walcott, "As John to Patmos," and "North and South," C.P., 5, 405.

10. Krishnaswamy, "Mythologies of Migrancy," 128.

11. Walcott, *Omeros,* LVIII.ii, 291.

12. Brown, "The Century of Exile."

13. Jameson, *Postmodernism,* 372.

14. Kristeva, *Strangers to Ourselves,* 13–14.

15. Kristeva, "Foreign Body." Cf. Burnett, "The Ulyssean Crusoe and the Quest for Redemption in J. M. Coetzee's *Foe* and Derek Walcott's *Omeros.*"

16. Fanon, *Black Skin, White Masks,* 112.

17. Hawthorn, *Multiple Personality and the Disintegration of Literary Character,* 100.

18. Bhabha begins to address the ambiguity housed at the center of the construction of the subject position, responding to Fanon in terms of the "crucial splitting of the ego," in which the colonized subject is "primordially fixed and yet triply split between the congruent knowledges of body, race, ancestors," but he stops short of investigating the potential of the split to signify as positive marker. Bhabha, *The Location of Culture,* 80.

19. Cf. Walcott, "What the Twilight Says."

20. Deleuze and Guattari, *Anti-Oedipus,* 362.

21. Ibid., 359, 362, 361.

22. Ibid., 134.

23. Ibid., 133.

24. Bhabha, *The Location of Culture,* 251.

25. Said, *Culture and Imperialism,* 256.

26. Hawthorn, *Multiple Personality,* 106.

27. Young, *Colonial Desire,* 180.

28. White, *Carnival, Hysteria and Writing,* 166.

29. Walcott, C.P., 350.

30. Ibid.

31. Walcott, "Names," C.P., 306.

32. Walcott, "Muse of History," 36.

33. Walcott, *O Babylon!* in *The Joker of Seville and O Babylon!,* 216, 275. The final chorus relates faith that the individual consciousness will be reunited with God ("the great I / Am shall be one with I") and progresses from Aaron's repeated cry of "I-and-I-and-I-and-I" to the concluding statement of faith in the coming of the New Jerusalem, "Zion a' come, / Zion a' come someday."

34. Sherlock, *West Indies,* 13–14, quoted in Brydon and Tiffin, 37.

35. Ashcroft, Griffiths, and Tiffin, *The Empire Writes Back,* 26.

36. Ibid., 26–27.

37. Hearne, ed., *Carifesta Forum,* xi.

38. Walcott, "The Sea Is History," C.P., 366.

39. Walcott, *The Arkansas Testament,* 48. Terada adduces Rilke's version of the Orpheus and Eurydice myth in her analysis of this poem, with which her postmodern reading of Walcott's poetry concludes. Terada, *Derek Walcott's Poetry,* 216–26.

40. Walcott, C.P., 346, 350.

41. Rodman, *Tongues of Fallen Angels,* 255.

42. Walcott, "Muse of History," 63; "What the Twilight Says," 9.

43. Fanon, *The Wretched of the Earth,* 187, 198. Likewise at the end of chapter 3 of *Black Skin, White Masks,* he calls for a "restructuring of the world."

44. Nettleford, *Inward Stretch, Outward Reach,* x.

45. Ibid., 52.

46. Ibid., 53.
47. Bhabha, *The Location of Culture,* 235.
48. Benjamin, "The Task of the Translator," *Illuminations,* 79.
49. Deleuze and Guattari, *Anti-Oedipus,* 362.
50. Walcott, *Antilles,* 69.
51. "Derek Walcott: An Interview," with Scott, autumn 1993, 16.
52. Walcott, "What the Twilight Says," 16; *Antilles,* 69.
53. George Herbert, "Love," from *The Temple,* 142. An earlier poem of Walcott's may be regarded as a response to the same poem of Herbert's: "Love after Love," C.P., 328.
54. Walcott, *Omeros,* XXXIII.iii, 173–74.

2. "Is There That I Born": The Gift of Place

The quotation in the chapter title is from Walcott, "Sainte Lucie," C.P., 314.
1. Walcott, *Arena,* BBC2, London, February 20, 1993.
2. See "Introduction," n. 30.
3. Paul Brown, "'This Thing of Darkness I Acknowledge Mine,'" 65.
4. Walcott, "What the Twilight Says," 10, 19.
5. Ashcroft, Griffiths, and Tiffin, *The Empire Writes Back,* 8, 37.
6. Said, *The World, the Text and the Critic,* 8.
7. Walcott, *Arena,* BBC2, February 20, 1993.
8. Walcott, interview with Burnett, Stratford-on-Avon, July 1, 1992.
9. Hamner, "Conversation with Walcott," 412.
10. Walcott, *Omeros,* XLI.ii, 207–8.
11. Walcott, "Map of the New World," C.P., 413.
12. Brown, "The Century of Exile."
13. Walcott, "The Poet in the Theatre," 4.
14. Walcott, *Another Life,* 8.iii, C.P., 196.
15. "Le nègre possède une patrie, prend place dans une Union ou un Commonwealth. Toute description doit se situer sur le plan du phénomène, mais là encore nous sommes renvoyés à des perspectives infinies." Fanon, *Peau noire, masques blancs,* 140. My translation. The published English translation of the passage by Charles Lam Markmann loses the metaphor of the map. *Black Skin, White Masks,* 173.
16. Walcott, *South Bank Show,* London Weekend Television, January 15, 1989.
17. Burnett, ed., *Caribbean Verse in English,* 62.
18. Walcott, C.P., 17–18.
19. Walcott, "What the Twilight Says," 9.
20. Rodney, *Groundings with My Brothers*; Walcott, *Another Life,* 19.i, C.P., 270.
21. Walcott, "Muse of History," 57. This, of course, resonates with Wole Soy-

inka's famous rebuttal of the negritude movement, that the tiger does not need to proclaim its "tigritude."

22. Walcott, introducing a reading as part of the Brighton Festival, at the Royal Albion Hotel, Brighton, Sussex, May 16, 1991.

23. C.P., 314. "I am a St. Lucian. That's where I come from."

24. Walcott, *Arena,* BBC2, London, February 20, 1993.

25. Walcott, "Leaving School," 32.

26. Markham, ed., *Hinterland,* 18; Walcott, "What the Twilight Says," 14.

27. Walcott, interview with Burnett, London, June 21, 1988.

28. Walcott, *Sunday Guardian,* Trinidad, May 5, 1963, reprinted in Susheila Nasta, ed., *Critical Perspectives on Sam Selvon,* 125.

29. Walcott, "On Choosing Port of Spain," 15.

30. Walcott, "As John to Patmos," C.P., 5; "From This Far," C.P., 416.

31. Walcott, speaking at the Olivier Theatre, National Theatre, London, May 23, 1991.

32. Walcott, "Animals, Elemental Tales, and the Theater," 270.

33. Herbert, "The Price of Art," 24. The world represented in Dutch landscape painting is one of the "ancestral" milieux that Walcott, of part Dutch descent, includes in *Omeros.*

34. Walcott, *Arena,* BBC2, London, February 20, 1993.

35. Walcott, interview with Burnett, London, June 21, 1988.

36. Walcott, *Another Life,* 18.i, C.P., 261.

37. Brown, *West Indian Poetry,* 118, 121.

38. Taylor, *The Narrative of Liberation,* 189.

39. Walcott, interview with Burnett, Stratford-on-Avon, July 1, 1992.

40. Ibid.

41. Shakespeare, *Pericles,* IV.1.20.

42. Walcott, C.P., 415.

43. Walcott, *Midsummer,* XXXIII, C.P., 490.

44. Walcott, "Beautiful Translations," speaking at Tate Gallery, London, May 1, 1995.

45. Walcott, *Arena,* BBC2, February 20, 1993.

46. Ibid.

47. Walcott quotes from Carpentier's *The Lost Steps* as epigraph to Book Two of the poem, as well as citing it within the poem.

48. Walcott, C.P., 311.

49. Walcott, "Animals, Elemental Tales, and the Theater," 273–74.

50. Walcott, "Names," C.P., 308.

51. Baugh gives this spelling, which accords better with the word "iguana" than does Walcott's spelling in *Omeros.* "Iounalao," *Derek Walcott,* 49 n. 7.

52. Walcott, *Omeros,* LXIII.iii, 319.

53. Walcott, C.P., 383–95.

54. Allsopp, *Dictionary of Caribbean Usage.*

55. Walcott, C.P., 372.

56. In *Another Life,* for instance, the flocks of birds that visit the island on their seasonal migrations prefigure and naturalize the final departure of the protagonist.

57. In, for instance, "The Hurricane," *In a Green Night,* 69; "Hurucan," C.P., 423–26; *Omeros,* IX; or the extraordinarily physical evocation of heat in *Another Life,* 9.

58. "Leaving School," 24.

59. Benitez-Rojo, *The Repeating Island,* 2.

60. Walcott, *Another Life,* 6.ii, C.P., 180.

61. Walcott, *Omeros,* II.iii, 14.

62. Walcott, *Another Life,* 21.iv, C.P., 282.

63. Walcott, speaking at the Hay-on-Wye Literary Festival, May 30, 1993.

64. Brown, *West Indian Poetry,* 120.

65. Stratton, for instance, identifies its deployment within African literature as deriving both from colonial and indigenous traditions, calling it one of the "*defining* features" of the male literary tradition, which "reproduces in symbolic form the gender relations of patriarchal societies." Stratton, *Contemporary African Literature and the Politics of Gender,* 50–51.

66. Savory (Fido), "Value Judgements on Art and the Question of Macho Attitudes," 254. This is the most recent version of an essay published initially under the Fido name and widely reprinted. For the counterargument, see also my "Epic, a Woman's Place."

67. "Mother/lands," in Nasta, ed., *Motherlands,* 330–31.

68. Walcott, *Another Life,* 17.iv, C.P., 257.

69. Savory (Fido), "Value Judgements on Art and the Question of Macho Attitudes," 346.

70. Walcott, interview with Burnett, Stratford-on-Avon, July 1, 1992.

71. Walcott, "The Schooner *Flight,*" C.P., 350.

72. Walcott, *The Arkansas Testament,* 48.

73. Walcott, *Midsummer,* VII, C.P., 474.

74. Said, *The World, the Text and the Critic,* 8.

75. Walcott, "Sainte Lucie," C.P., 312.

76. Walcott, *Another Life,* 16.ii, C.P., 250.

77. Walcott, C.P., 321.

78. Walcott, *Antilles,* 72.

79. Walcott, C.P., 372–74.

80. "Leaving School," 26.

81. Walcott, *Another Life,* 6.i, C.P., 177.

82. Ibid., 6.ii, C.P., 179.

83. Walcott, at the National Theatre, London, for instance, on May 23, 1991.

84. Walcott, *Antilles,* 72.

85. Ibid., 76, 82.

86. Walcott, interview with Burnett, London, June 21, 1988.

87. Walcott, 74.

88. Benitez-Rojo, *The Repeating Island,* 211–12.

89. Walcott, *Antilles,* 76–77.

90. In the *Arena* program, Walcott remarks delightedly on the expectation of courtesy, which is still the norm in St. Lucia.

91. Walcott, speaking at the National Theatre, London, May 23, 1991.

92. Walcott, *Antilles,* 82.

93. Walcott, speaking at the National Theatre, London, May 23, 1991.

94. Walcott, *Another Life,* 23.ii, C.P., 292.

95. Walcott, interview in "Walcott Blasts Baron for Tourist Resort 'Greed,'" *Voice,* London, October 27, 1992.

96. Walcott, interview in Jaggi, "Paradise Fights Back," *Guardian,* December 13, 1997, 70.

97. Ibid., 68.

98. Walcott, interview in "Walcott Blasts Baron for Tourist Resort 'Greed,'" *Voice,* London, October 27, 1992.

99. Walcott, *Antilles,* 81.

100. Ibid., 68. Cf. "What the Twilight Says," 3–4.

101. Walcott, interview in Jaggi, "Paradise Fights Back," *Guardian,* December 13, 1997, 70. Plans for a casino at the Hyatt Hotel, St. Lucia, which opened in 2000, have not yet been determined, but if it is approved, it will be open only to hotel guests.

102. Walcott, *Antilles,* 82.

103. Walcott, interview in Jaggi, "Paradise Fights Back," *Guardian,* December 13, 1997, 69.

104. Walcott, interview in "And the Dish Ran Away with the Spoon," BBC2, London, May 21, 1992.

105. Fanon, *Black Skin, White Masks,* 140.

106. Rodney, *The Groundings with My Brothers,* 68.

107. Walcott in discussion session at the International Writers Conference, on the theme of "The Legacy of Europe," Dublin, June 20, 1991.

108. It should be pointed out, however, that Harris's philosophy incorporates the ideas of both science and progress in ways Walcott repudiates. Discussion with Wilson Harris, Milan, May 1996.

109. Lévi-Strauss has recently become the target of another Caribbean writer. Pauline Melville, the Guyanese novelist, brings a critical focus to bear on his appropriations of Amazonia in *The Ventriloquist's Tale.*

110. Walcott, *Another Life,* 6.ii, C.P., 180.

111. Walcott, C.P., 407.

112. Walcott, "Forest of Europe," C.P., 378.

113. Walcott in discussion session at the International Writers Conference, on the theme of "The Legacy of Europe," Dublin, June 20, 1991.

114. Walcott, *Omeros,* XXXVI.i, 184.

115. Walcott in discussion session at the International Writers Conference, on the theme of "The Legacy of Europe," Dublin, June 20, 1991.

116. Walcott, C.P., 405–6.

117. Ibid., 406.

118. Walcott, "What the Twilight Says," 9.

119. Walcott, *Antilles,* 72.

120. Walcott, "A Tribute to C.L.R. James," 1995, 44.

121. Walcott, *Omeros,* XLI.ii, 208; XLII.iii, 213.

122. Walcott, C.P., 409; *Antilles,* 72; C.P., 376.

123. "Rohlehr on Brathwaite," in Markham, ed., *Hinterland,* 111. "Greenwich Village, Winter" has "Each word, / Black footprints in the frightening snow" (*In a Green Night,* 50).

124. Walcott, interview with Burnett, London, June 21, 1988.

125. Walcott, *Antilles,* 77.

126. Ibid., 75.

127. Walcott, "The Garden Path: V. S. Naipaul," *What the Twilight Says: Essays,* 133.

3. "Where Else to Row, but Backward?" Dealing with History

The quotation in the chapter title is from Walcott, *Another Life,* 12.i, C.P., 217.

1. Walcott, "The Sea Is History," C.P., 364.

2. Hulme, *Colonial Encounters,* 124.

3. Shakespeare, *Tempest,* II.i.150–73.

4. Ibid., II.i.175.

5. Walcott, "Muse of History," 37.

6. Walcott, *Antilles,* 68.

7. Lamming quotes this as an epigraph for *The Pleasures of Exile.*

8. Walcott, *Another Life,* 21.iii, C.P., 281.

9. Juneja, *Caribbean Transactions,* 207.

10. Walcott, "Muse of History," 36.

11. Brodsky, "Laureate of the Supermarkets," 4.

12. Toohey, *Reading Epic,* 3–4, 19.

13. Hutcheon, "'Circling the Downspout of Empire,'" 170.

14. Toohey, *Reading Epic,* 19.

15. Walcott, *Omeros,* V.iii, 30.

16. Nettleford, *Inward Stretch, Outward Reach,* 53, 57.

17. Foucault, *The Archaeology of Knowledge,* 204–6.

18. Walcott, "Muse of History," 36, 39.

19. Ibid., 41.

20. Walcott, "The Caribbean: Culture or Mimicry?" 56 (hereafter "Culture or Mimicry?").

21. Walcott, interview with Burnett, London, June 21, 1988.

22. Walcott, "What the Twilight Says," 22.
23. Walcott, interview with Burnett, London, June 21, 1988.
24. Taylor, *The Narrative of Liberation,* 187, 189.
25. Hoegburg, "The Anarchist's Mirror."
26. Walcott, "Muse of History," 37.
27. Walcott, "A Colonial's-Eye View of the Empire," 73.
28. Said, *Culture and Imperialism,* 258.
29. Walcott, *Omeros,* IV.ii, 22.
30. See n. 103 below.
31. Walcott and Simon, *Songs from the Capeman.*
32. Lamming, "The Pleasures of Exile," in John Hearne, ed., 88–89.
33. Walcott, "Muse of History," 41.
34. Walcott, C.P., 460.
35. Ibid., 405.
36. Walcott, *Another Life,* 13.i, C.P., 225.
37. Ibid., 18.i, C.P., 261; 14.iii, C.P., 236.
38. Walcott, *Antilles,* 78.
39. Walcott, *Another Life,* 22.iii, C.P., 287.
40. Walcott, *Omeros,* L.i, 251.
41. Rushdie, *The Jaguar Smile,* 12.
42. Walcott, *Omeros,* XIX.iii, 104.
43. Ibid., VII.i, 92.
44. Ibid., V.iii, 31.
45. Ibid., VII.i, 38, 37.
46. Benitez-Rojo, *The Repeating Island,* 5.
47. Walcott, "Muse of History," 38.
48. Walcott, "The Schooner *Flight,*" C.P., 353.
49. Walcott, C.P., 88.
50. Walcott, "Muse of History," 37.
51. Walcott, *Another Life,* 19.i, C.P., 269–70.
52. Walcott, "Culture or Mimicry?" 57.
53. Walcott, *Another Life,* 22.i, C.P., 285.
54. Walcott, "What the Twilight Says," 9; "Muse of History," 42.
55. Walcott, "What the Twilight Says," 13; *Antilles,* 68.
56. Walcott, *Omeros,* XXXIX.iii, 204–5.
57. Ibid., XXIX.iii, 154.
58. Walcott, *Antilles,* 75.
59. Walcott, *Another Life,* 6.ii, C.P., 180; "What the Twilight Says," 31; *Antilles,* 76.
60. Thomas roundly challenges Froude's role as historian: "One last word on the crimes and blunders of Froude, not for his sake but for the sake of history. He perpetrated these falsifications because he started from a premise, the inferiority and instinctive barbarism of black people. This it was that shaped and twisted every historical fact." *Froudacity,* 43.

61. Walcott, "What the Twilight Says," 18.
62. Walcott, *Antilles,* 79.
63. Walcott, "Muse of History," 37.
64. Walcott, "Culture or Mimicry?" 57.
65. Walcott, "A Colonial's-Eye View of the Empire," 73.
66. Walcott, "Muse of History," 39.
67. Walcott, "Culture or Mimicry?" 53.
68. Ibid., 57.
69. Walcott, *Another Life,* 22.ii, C.P., 287.
70. Baugh, *Derek Walcott,* 48.
71. Walcott, *Another Life,* 22.vi, C.P., 290.
72. Ibid., 22.ii, C.P., 286.
73. Bhabha, "DissemiNation," 299.
74. Walcott, "Culture or Mimicry?" 55.
75. Walcott, interview with Burnett, London, June 21, 1988.
76. Walcott, "Muse of History," 41.
77. Nyerere, "Who Shall Inherit the Earth?"
78. Walcott, "Muse of History," 41; "The Schooner *Flight,*" C.P., 356.
79. Walcott, "Culture or Mimicry?" 52.
80. Ibid.
81. Ibid.
82. Walcott, "Muse of History," 41, 42.
83. Ibid., 41.
84. Walcott, "Culture or Mimicry?" 53.
85. Walcott, "Muse of History," 39.
86. Ibid., 40.
87. Ibid., 36.
88. Walcott, C.P., 350.
89. Walcott, "What the Twilight Says," 5.
90. Guillén, "Balada de los dos abuelos," *West Indies, Ltd.:* "los dos del mismo tamaño, / ansia negra y ansia blanca" [both the same size, black longing and white longing].
91. Walcott, "Muse of History," 64.
92. Ibid.
93. Ibid., 41.
94. "Cultural relativism (a European invention) has seemed plausible to our century because for the first time Europe found itself forced to confront non-European cultures in a serious way through the experience of colonialism and decolonization. Many of the developments of the past century—the decline of the moral self-confidence of European civilization, the rise of the Third World, and the emergence of new ideologies—tended to reinforce belief in relativism. But if, over time, more and more societies with diverse cultures and histories exhibit similar long-term patterns of development; if there is a continuing convergence in the

types of institutions governing most advanced societies; and if the homogenization of mankind continues as a result of economic development, then the idea of relativism may seem much stranger than it does now. For the apparent differences between peoples' 'languages of good and evil' will appear to be an artifact of their particular stage of historical development," Fukuyama, *The End of History and the Last Man,* 338. He does acknowledge that readings of the "recent worldwide liberal revolution" for the time being "must remain provisionally inconclusive," but this reads only as the correctness of the scientist formulating a conclusion within the limits of his experiment, when he is secretly confident that its implications will change the world.

95. Said, *Culture and Imperialism,* 264.

96. James, "Parties, Politics and Economics in the Caribbean," *Spheres of Existence,* 154.

97. Walcott, "A Colonial's-Eye View of the Empire," 73.

98. Ibid. Asked by Selden Rodman in 1974 whether Trinidadians felt they were being exploited by a new imperialism, Walcott expressed the view, "It's not a feeling. It's the truth. Burnham just took over the bauxite and gas companies in Guyana, with compensation. We should do the same. Not that we'd get the oil out more efficiently, but for our own self-respect. I'm neither a Marxist nor a fascist—and I don't deny there's an element of fascism in the way Fidel runs Cuba—but I wouldn't mind it at all if my son, Peter, was forced to work the land a couple of years here. I wouldn't even mind being forced to do it myself—if it helped Trinidadians feel this was truly *their* land." Rodman, *Tongues of Fallen Angels,* 243.

99. Walcott, C.P., 351.

100. Eagleton, *Walter Benjamin, or Towards a Revolutionary Criticism,* 161.

101. Baugh, who quotes the 1912 history narrating the Sauteurs story, an incident from 1651, notes that it was first inscribed into Caribbean literature in 1958 by Lamming in *Of Age and Innocence.* Baugh, *Derek Walcott,* 45, 48 n. 4. Walcott's use of it in his poem is therefore a case of intertextuality within Caribbean literary discourse, a typical engagement with and homage to a respected fellow writer.

102. Hearne, "An Introduction to Carifesta Forum," vii.

103. Carter, "For a Man Who Walked Sideways," in Burnett, ed., *Caribbean Verse,* 217.

104. Walcott, "Muse of History," 54.

105. Walcott, *Antilles,* 79.

106. Ibid., 81, 82.

107. Ibid., 68.

108. Young, *White Mythologies,* 66.

109. Chinweizu, *Decolonising the African Mind,* 88.

110. "Muse of History," 37.

111. Walcott, "Muse of History," 53.

4. "The Mind . . . Sees Its Mythopoeic Coast": Manipulating Myth

The quotation in the chapter title is from Walcott, "Origins," C.P., 14.

1. Shakespeare, *Tempest,* III.ii.155.
2. Walcott, interview in Jaggi, "No Trouble in Paradise," *Guardian*, July 12, 1997.
3. Barthes, *Mythologies,* 123, 138. Barthes points out that "culture itself is, in the last analysis, an ideology," 88.
4. Walcott, *Another Life,* 9.ii, C.P., 200.
5. Graves, *Greek Myths,* I.21.
6. Moretti, *Modern Epic,* 248–49.
7. Barthes, *Mythologies,* 147.
8. Walcott, interview with Burnett, London, November 2, 1998; Walcott, speaking at the Hay-on-Wye Literary Festival, May 30, 1993.
9. Walcott, speaking at the Hay-on-Wye Literary Festival, May 30, 1993.
10. Walcott, interview with Julian May, BBC, summer 1992.
11. Walcott with Schoenberger, *Threepenny Review,* 15, 16.
12. Walcott, "Culture or Mimicry?" 56.
13. Walcott, interview in Jaggi, "No Trouble in Paradise," *Guardian,* London, July 12, 1997.
14. "Derek Walcott on *Omeros*. Interview with Luigi Sampietro, *Caribana* 3, 1992–93, 37.
15. Anderson, *Imagined Communities,* 6–7.
16. Walcott, speaking at the University of Milan, May 22, 1996.
17. Soyinka, *Myth, Literature and the African World,* 2–3.
18. Walcott, interview with Burnett, Stratford-on-Avon, July 1, 1992.
19. Walcott, *Another Life,* 12.i, C.P., 217.
20. Walcott, speaking at the University of Milan, May 22, 1996.
21. Walcott, *Antilles,* 26.
22. Walcott, interview in Jaggi, "No Trouble in Paradise," *Guardian,* London, July 12, 1997.
23. Walcott, C.P., 99.
24. Walcott, "Forest of Europe," C.P., 377.
25. Walcott, interview in Jaggi, "No Trouble in Paradise," *Guardian,* London, July 12, 1997.
26. Coetzee, *Dusklands,* 24.
27. Soyinka, *Art, Dialogue and Outrage,* 105.
28. Bhabha, *The Location of Culture,* 233–35.
29. Soyinka, "The Critic and Society: Barthes, Leftocracy and Other Mythologies," *Art, Dialogue and Outrage,* 95–123.
30. Taylor, "Myth and Reality in Caribbean Narrative," 293.
31. Walcott, "Muse of History," 37.
32. Ibid., 38.
33. Walcott, "Muse of History," 37; "Culture or Mimicry?" 57.

34. Walcott, *Omeros,* XIII.iii, 75.

35. Walcott, interview in Jaggi, "No Trouble in Paradise," *Guardian,* July 12, 1997.

36. Frye, "Myth," 43.

37. Walcott, "Muse of History," 48.

38. Eliot, "*Ulysses,* Order and Myth."

39. Walcott, "Muse of History," 36.

40. Ibid., 38.

41. Fanon, *The Wretched of the Earth,* 43–45.

42. Barthes, *Mythologies,* 155.

43. Walcott, "Muse of History," 38.

44. Ibid., 37.

45. Ibid., 52–53.

46. Moretti, *Modern Epic,* 249.

47. Walcott, interview with Benitez-Rojo, *Night Waves,* BBC Radio 3, London, April 14, 1998.

48. "[M]ythology is certain to participate in the making of the world. Holding as a principle that man in a bourgeois society is at every turn plunged into a false Nature, as he attempts to find again, under the assumed innocence of the most unsophisticated relationships, the profound alienation which this innocence is meant to make one accept. The unveiling which it carries out is therefore a political act: founded on a responsible idea of language, mythology thereby postulates the freedom of the latter. It is certain that in this sense mythology *harmonizes* with the world, not as it is, but as it wants to create itself." Barthes, *Mythologies,* 170.

49. Walcott, "What the Twilight Says," 33.

50. Walcott, *Antilles,* 67, 76, 73, 69.

51. Walcott, "What the Twilight Says," 5.

52. Walcott, speaking at the Hay-on-Wye Literary Festival, May 30, 1993.

53. Walcott, speaking at the University of Milan, May 22, 1996.

54. Walcott in conversation with Burnett, Stratford-on-Avon, July 1, 1992.

55. Rodman, *Tongues of Fallen Angels,* 255.

56. Walcott, "Culture or Mimicry?" 56.

57. Ibid., 56–57.

58. "It is arguably only in the last few years that we have begun to elaborate 'other' ways of thinking that alterity which philosophy formerly consigned to the marginality of darkness. Probably one of the most unexpected results of this changed perspective has been to revive interest in those once-tabooed aspects of 'otherness' which can broadly be termed spiritual or religious." Berry and Wernick, eds., *Shadow of Spirit,* 2–3.

59. See, for instance, "The Light of the World," *The Arkansas Testament,* 48–51.

60. Walcott, "Origins," C.P., 11–16.

61. Walcott, "What the Twilight Says," 8.

62. Walcott, C.P., 414.
63. Walcott, "What the Twilight Says," 10.
64. Eliade, *The Myth of the Eternal Return.*
65. Walcott, "What the Twilight Says," 16.
66. Walcott, *Dream on Monkey Mountain,* 250, 263.
67. Walcott, *Antilles,* 66, 68–69.
68. Walcott, C.P., 425.
69. Walcott, *Malcochon, or The Six in the Rain*, in *Dream on Monkey Mountain,* 173. Cf. "Songs, II," noted in 1799, "One, two, tree, / All de same, / Black, white, brown, / All de same, / All de same. / One, two, etc." Burnett, ed., *Caribbean Verse in English,* 5.
70. Walcott, C.P., 372–74.
71. Walcott, *Another Life,* 21–22, C.P., 281–89.
72. Walcott, C.P., 424.
73. Walcott, *Omeros,* IX.III, 52–53.
74. Ibid., I.ii, 8.
75. "Derek Walcott on *Omeros.*" Interview with Luigi Sampietro, *Caribana* 3, 1992–93, 37.
76. Ibid., 41.
77. Walcott, "Muse of History," 48.
78. Walcott, *Another Life,* 4, C.P., 167.
79. Walcott, "Muse of History," 43.
80. Ibid., 48.
81. Ibid., 47.
82. Rodman, *Tongues of Fallen Angels,* 255.
83. Walcott, *The Arts Programme,* BBC Radio 2, London, June 26, 1992.
84. Walcott, *Another Life,* 4, C.P., 166–67.
85. Walcott, "Origins," C.P., 12.
86. Walcott, *Another Life,* 8.iii, C.P., 196.
87. Okri, interview with Melvyn Bragg on *Arts Review 1991,* ITV, London, December 29, 1991.
88. Condé, on *Night Waves,* BBC Radio 3, April 14, 1998.
89. Rodman, *Tongues of Fallen Angels,* 254.
90. Walcott, "Culture or Mimicry?" 56.
91. Eliade, *The Myth of the Eternal Return,* 208.
92. Walcott, interview in Jaggi, "No Trouble in Paradise," *Guardian,* July 12, 1997.
93. Heath, "Criticism in Art," 163.
94. Walcott, "Homecoming, i," *Bounty*, 31, and (wrongly in reprint as "Sensenne") *Antilles*, 80; "What the Twilight Says," 21. A photograph of Sesenne Descartes is included in Palmer, *Saint Lucia*, 75.
95. Walcott, *Midsummer*, XIV, C.P., 476.
96. Walcott, "Animals, Elemental Tales, and the Theater," 269.

97. Walcott, "What the Twilight Says," 21.

98. Walcott, "Animals, Elemental Tales, and the Theater," 274–75.

99. Walcott, *Ti-Jean and His Brothers* in *Dream on Monkey Mountain,* 165, 157, 164.

100. Rohlehr, "My Strangled City," 240.

101. Walcott, "Animals, Elemental Tales, and the Theater," 275–76.

102. Walcott, *Ti-Jean and His Brothers* in *Dream on Monkey Mountain,* 163.

103. Walcott, "Adam's Song," C.P., 302.

104. Lamming, "The Pleasures of Exile," in John Hearne, ed., 93.

105. Walcott, *Another Life,* 21.iii, C.P., 282.

106. Hartman, quoted by Helen Vendler in a review of his *Criticism in the Wilderness,* in *New Yorker,* May 3, 1982.

107. Walcott, *Another Life,* 12.i, C.P., 217.

108. Treves, *The Cradle of the Deep,* 109, quoted in Baugh, *Derek Walcott,* 12.

109. "Leaving School," 24. Walcott notes here also that his generation was taught that Columbus named the island, but John Robert Lee reports that historians have now proved that Columbus did not visit the island and that "St. Lucia" is, in fact, derived from the original French name "Sainte Alousie" (Lee, "Introduction," 12).

110. Graves, *The White Goddess* and *The Greek Myths,* passim, e.g., 24.1. Graves traces the historic connections between sub-Saharan African and Mediterranean myths of the moon as triple goddess in his Introduction, 22.

111. A fuller version of this argument is set out in Burnett, "The Ulyssean Crusoe and the Quest for Redemption in J. M. Coetzee's *Foe* and Derek Walcott's *Omeros,*" 239–55.

112. Harris, "Unfinished Genesis of the Imagination."

113. Walcott, *Omeros,* XIII.iii, 76.

114. Walcott, interview with Burnett, Stratford-on-Avon, July 1, 1992.

115. Macdonald, "College: ii. Achilles," *Jaffo the Calypsonian,* 64–65.

116. In place of the Fall's northern "apple," Walcott seems to use "pomme cythère," patois for "pomegranate," which links it to Cytherea (Venus), as the naturalized symbol. It is not just a classical allusion to the Judgment of Paris but seems to relate to the idea of original sin and its sexual overtones, as in Baudelaire's poem "Le Voyage," where the island of Cythère is a sexualized trope of physical suffering and spiritual destitution. In classical mythology, the pomegranate was associated with death.

117. Dante, *Paradiso,* XXXII.4.

118. A passage from Carpentier's *The Lost Steps* forms the epigraph to Book 2, "Homage to Gregorias," and is incorporated in the final paragraph of the work. The 1973 Jonathan Cape edition of *Another Life* printed this epigraph without the crucial final line and the attribution.

119. Lewis, *The American Adam,* 1955.

120. "[A] radically new personality, the hero of the new adventure: an indi-

vidual emancipated from history, happily bereft of ancestry, untouched and undefiled by the usual inheritances of family and race; an individual standing alone, self-reliant and self-propelling, ready to confront whatever awaited him with the aid of his own unique and inherent resources. It was not surprising, in a Bible-reading generation, that the new hero (in praise or disapproval) was most easily identified with Adam before the Fall. Adam was the first, the archetypal, man. His moral position was prior to experience, and in his very newness he was fundamentally innocent. The world and history lay all before him. And he was the type of creator, the poet par excellence, creating language itself by naming the elements of the scene about him. All this and more were contained in the image of the American as Adam." Lewis, *The American Adam,* 5.

121. Ibid., 6.

122. Ibid., 7–8.

123. Walcott, *Another Life,* 12.iii; 23.iv; C.P., 220, 294.

124. Walcott, "The Light of the World," *The Arkansas Testament,* 48.

125. Walcott, *Another Life,* 21.iii, C.P., 282.

126. Walcott, *The Arkansas Testament,* 104–17.

127. Walcott, C.P., 269.

128. Walcott dedicates the poem to (among others) his twin brother, Roderick.

129. Walcott, *Omeros,* XLVI.iii, 235.

130. Walcott, "The Figure of Crusoe," 35.

131. Ibid., 40.

132. Walcott, "Crusoe's Island," C.P., 69.

133. Walcott, C.P., 57; *Desert Island Discs,* BBC Radio 4, London, June 14, 1991.

134. Walcott, "Muse of History," 40; "Culture or Mimicry?" 57; *Antilles*, 83.

135. Jones, "With Crusoe the Slave and Friday the Boss," 236.

136. Harris, "Unfinished Genesis of the Imagination."

137. Walcott with O'Brien at the Hay-on-Wye Literary Festival, May 30, 1993.

138. Walcott, interview with Burnett, Stratford-on-Avon, July 1, 1992.

139. See Burnett, "The Ulyssean Crusoe and the Quest for Redemption in J. M. Coetzee's *Foe* and Derek Walcott's *Omeros.*"

140. Brown, *West Indian Poetry,* 133–34.

141. Walcott, *Another Life,* 8.ii, C.P., 195.

142. Walcott, *Omeros,* LVIII.ii, 291.

143. Walcott, *Antilles,* 77.

144. Walcott, *Malcochon, or The Six in the Rain,* in *Dream on Monkey Mountain,* 199.

145. Walcott, interview in Jaggi, "No Trouble in Paradise," *Guardian,* July 12, 1997. Since sugar is no longer grown in St. Lucia, the rum is manufactured from imports from Guyana: another kind of "creolization." See also Burnett, "Elegies at Ebb Tide from St. Lucia," *Independent,* July 12, 1997.

146. Walcott, speaking at the University of Milan, May 22, 1996.

147. Walcott, *The Bounty,* 16, 27, 35.

148. Ibid., 9.

149. Walcott, *Malcochon, or The Six in the Rain,* in *Dream on Monkey Mountain,* 205.

150. Walcott, "Muse of History," in *What the Twilight Says: Essays,* 46.

5. "The Smell of Our Own Speech": The Tool of Language

The quotation in the chapter title is from Walcott, *Another Life,* 12.i, C.P., 217.

1. Hulme opens his excellent book *Colonial Encounters* with, as epigraph, the Bishop of Avila's reply to Queen Isabella of Castille's question, on being presented with the first grammar of a modern European language, "What is it for?"

2. Walcott, *Omeros,* LXIV.ii, 323.

3. Moi, *Sexual Textual Politics,* 170.

4. T. S. Eliot, "Sweeney Agonistes," in Walcott, "The Poet in the Theatre," 4. Walcott also (mis)quotes the phrase in a 1964 review, "Necessity of Negritude," 20.

5. Walcott, *Omeros,* XIII.iii, 75.

6. Walcott, on *Start the Week,* BBC Radio 4, London, June 29, 1992.

7. Walcott, *Another Life,* 12.i, C.P., 217.

8. Ibid., 7.ii, C.P., 185.

9. Lamming, "The Pleasures of Exile," in John Hearne, ed., 97.

10. Walcott, interview with Frances Stoner-Saunders at Hay-on-Wye, BBC TV, London, June 1993.

11. Lamming, "The Pleasures of Exile," in John Hearne, ed., 95.

12. Benitez-Rojo, *The Repeating Island,* 138.

13. Naipaul, "East Indian."

14. Bedient, "Derek Walcott: Contemporary," 320.

15. Trinidadian usage from French "piquant," for sharp or satiric speech.

16. Walcott, interview with Burnett, London, June 21, 1988.

17. Brodsky, "The Sound of the Tide," 171.

18. Walcott, "Muse of History," 19.

19. Heaney, "The Murmur of Malvern," 26.

20. Walcott, interview with Burnett, London, June 21, 1988.

21. Brodsky, "The Sound of the Tide," 167.

22. Walcott, interview with Burnett, London, June 21, 1988.

23. Quoted on the cover of Walcott's *In a Green Night.*

24. Walcott, *Desert Island Discs,* BBC Radio 4, London, June 14, 1991.

25. Brodsky, "The Sound of the Tide," 166.

26. Walcott, *Another Life,* 1.i, C.P., 145.

27. Walcott, interview with Burnett, London, June 21, 1988.

28. Walcott, *Another Life,* 7.i, C.P., 183.

29. Joyce, *A Portrait of the Artist as a Young Man,* 189.

30. Walcott, "What the Twilight Says," 24.

31. Walcott with O'Brien at the Hay-on-Wye Literary Festival, May 30, 1993.

32. Walcott, "What the Twilight Says," 15–16. For all Terada's qualification of her book's title, *Derek Walcott's Poetry: American Mimicry* reaffirms a fundamental misconception.

33. Walcott, *Another Life,* 22.IV, C.P., 288.

34. Walcott, "What the Twilight Says," 10.

35. Walcott, *Another Life,* 7.1, C.P., 184.

36. Ashcroft, Griffiths, and Tiffin, *The Empire Writes Back.*

37. Walcott, "What the Twilight Says," 10.

38. Walcott, interview with Burnett, Stratford-on-Avon, July 1, 1992.

39. Walcott, *Midsummer,* XXXIII, C.P., 490.

40. Bakhtin, "Epic and Novel," *The Dialogic Imagination,* 29.

41. Ibid., 12.

42. Figueroa, "The Poetry of Derek Walcott."

43. Walcott, speaking at the University of Milan, May 22, 1996.

44. Walcott, interview with Burnett, London, June 21, 1988.

45. Ibid.

46. Walcott, *Antilles,* 69, 71.

47. Ibid., 70.

48. Ibid.; "What the Twilight Says," 9.

49. Quoted in Dwyer, "One Walcott, and He Would Be Master," in Hamner, ed., *Critical Perspectives on Walcott,* 326.

50. Walcott, *Antilles*, 80.

51. Walcott, *Another Life,* 23.i, C.P., 291.

52. Figueroa, "The Poetry of Derek Walcott."

53. Walcott, interview with Burnett, June 21, 1988.

54. Ibid.

55. Ibid.

56. Walcott, speaking at the University of Milan, May 22, 1996. This seems to confirm John Figueroa's assertion, mentioned above, that the *conte* in "Sainte Lucie" is in fact Walcott's composition, not the folk song it purports to be.

57. Walcott, "Animals, Elemental Tales, and the Theatre," 275.

58. Walcott, speaking at the University of Milan, May 22, 1996.

59. Walcott, "What the Twilight Says," 15.

60. Walcott, *Desert Island Discs,* BBC Radio 4, London, June 14, 1991.

61. Walcott, *Omeros,* III.iii, 18.

62. Terada, however, says that "[I]n *Omeros* poetic language, as a product of mimicry, begins in error" and follows her quotation of this passage with the comment that "Walcott's (mis)translation of '*blessé*' as 'blest' is play, not a mistake." Terada, *Derek Walcott's Poetry,* 211.

63. Walcott, speaking at the University of Milan, May 22, 1996. The process is a two-way one. In May 2000, Kendel Hippolyte told me that St. Lucians are beginning to say in English, "I have bless," for "I have pain."

64. English speakers may be surprised to realize that the game of "conkers" was originally played with shells, the word "conch" being originally applied to all shelled creatures, including snails.

65. Walcott, *Midsummer,* L, C.P., 504.

66. Walcott, "Sainte Lucie," C.P., 310.

67. Walcott, speaking at the University of Milan, May 22, 1996.

68. Walcott, Olivier Theatre, National Theatre, London, May 23, 1991.

69. Walcott, *Omeros,* VII.ii, 263.

70. Walcott, "Animals, Elemental Tales, and the Theatre," 274. Implicit in Walcott's remark here is a criticism of my anthology, *Caribbean Verse in English,* which is in two parts, separating the oral tradition from the literary tradition. As readers of the introduction will know, poets were allocated to one section or the other on the basis of the way they met the majority of their public, either as voice in the ear or words on the page. The point is clearly made that what is distinctive about the written poetry of the region is its acute evocation of orality in print. The reason the volume was structured in this way was in order to facilitate study of Caribbean orature, and because the literary establishment generally had no concept of there being a distinct and ancient oral tradition, and I felt it was about time it was drawn to their attention.

71. Walcott, speaking at the University of Milan, May 22, 1996.

72. Ibid.

73. "Leaving School," 31.

74. Brathwaite, *The History of the Voice,* 49. He calls the oral end of the continuum "nation language," which seems to me problematic in its use of "nation," whereas "vernacular" has a clear and appropriate meaning as the language of a people, as I argue in *Caribbean Verse.*

75. Brathwaite, *History of the Voice,* 49.

76. Alleyne, *Roots of Jamaican Culture,* 146.

77. Rohlehr, "A Carrion Time," 102.

78. Rohlehr, introduction to *Voiceprint,* 22.

79. Chamberlin, *Come Back to Me My Language,* 117.

80. Walcott, "What the Twilight Says," 8–9.

81. Ibid., 9.

82. Bakhtin, "Epic and Novel," 24.

83. Benitez-Rojo, *The Repeating Island,* 27.

84. Walcott, interview with Burnett, London, June 21, 1988.

85. Walcott, C.P., 432.

86. Walcott, *Omeros,* XXXVI.i, 184.

87. Ibid., XL.ii, 203.

88. Walcott, on *The Arts Programme,* BBC Radio 2, June 26, 1992.

89. Walcott, *Antilles,* 79.

90. Eliot, *The Waste Land,* 1.430.

91. It occurs twice in *Another Life,* 8.I, C.P., 194; 10.II, C.P., 207.

92. Ibid. 4.i, C.P., 165.

93. Walcott, *Desert Island Discs,* BBC Radio 4, June 14, 1991.

94. Walcott, *Another Life,* 10.ii, C.P., 207.

95. Benjamin, "The Work of Art in the Age of Mechanical Reproduction," [1936], in *Illuminations.*

96. Walcott, *Another Life,* 7.i, C.P., 183.

97. Ibid., 5.i, C.P., 172.

98. Walcott, *The Arkansas Testament,* 35.

99. Shakespeare, *Tempest,* I.ii.334.

100. Walcott, *The Arkansas Testament,* 34

101. Walcott, *Omeros,* XXXVIII.iii, 197.

102. Walcott, *Dream on Monkey Mountain,* 262.

103. Ibid., 267.

104. Ibid., 322.

105. Walcott, "Animals, Elemental Tales, and the Theater," 272.

106. Walcott, *Dream on Monkey Mountain.* Makak's "real" name is Felix Hobain.

107. Walcott, *Dream on Monkey Mountain,* 325.

108. Fox, "Big Night Music," 202.

109. Walcott, *Another Life,* 1.i, C.P., 146. This is also an intertextual homage, I think, to Burns and perhaps Yeats. In his essay "The Symbolism of Poetry," first published in 1900, Yeats quotes Burns's "The white moon is setting behind the white wave, / And Time is setting with me, O!" and comments, "these lines are perfectly symbolical." West, ed., *Symbolism: An Anthology,* 16.

110. Walcott, C.P., 341.

111. Walcott, *Omeros,* LVIII.ii, 291.

112. Walcott, "A Map of Europe," C.P., 66; John Berger, "The Infinity of Desire."

113. Walcott, interview with Burnett, London, June 21, 1988.

114. Walcott, *Midsummer,* XLIII, "Tropic Zone," v, C.P., 500; cf. *Midsummer,* VIII.

115. Walcott, *Another Life,* 23.i, C.P., 291.

116. Brodsky, *Watermark,* 134.

117. Walcott, *Omeros,* V.iii, 29–30. Cf. chap. 2, note 101.

118. Walcott, *Dream on Monkey Mountain,* 85.

119. Walcott, "Animals, Elemental Tales, and the Theater," 276.

120. Walcott, "Tales of the Islands," IV, C.P., 24; *Midsummer,* L, C.P., 504.

121. Walcott, *Dream on Monkey Mountain,* 297.

122. Walcott, interview with Burnett, Stratford-on-Avon, July 1, 1992.

123. Walcott, *Omeros,* XXIII.iii, 124–25.

124. Ibid., I.ii, 6.

125. Derek Walcott at the Olivier Theatre, National Theatre, London, May 23, 1991.

126. Walcott, C.P., 409.

127. Shelley, "Peter Bell the Third," part 3, "Hell," i.147.

128. Alleyne, *Roots of Jamaican Culture,* 147.

129. Walcott, "What the Twilight Says," 9.

130. Walcott, "'Name Him!' The priest intoned, 'Name! *Déparlez!*'" *Another Life,* 4, C.P., 170.

131. Walcott, *Another Life,* 22.iii, C.P., 288.

132. Walcott, "What the Twilight Says," 9.

133. Walcott, *Another Life,* 23.iv, C.P., 293.

134. Baugh, *Derek Walcott,* 78.

135. I am indebted for this information to Robin Hanford, who had it from Dunstan St. Omer on a visit to St. Lucia in January 1995.

136. Walcott, *Another Life,* 20.iv, C.P., 276.

137. Ibid., 20.iv, C.P., 276–77.

138. Baugh, *Derek Walcott,* 78.

139. Walcott, *Another Life,* 21.iii, C.P., 281. Implicit in the imagery are the distinctive round-bellied cooking pots made in southwest St. Lucia. Still made by women using traditional methods, these share a name with the west coast town Canaries, pronounced in Creole "Canawi." I am indebted to Patricia Fay's lecture given at the Caribbean Studies Association conference in St. Lucia on May 30, 2000, on "Bonfire Pottery in St. Lucia and the Commonwealth Caribbean."

140. Rohlehr, Introduction to *Voiceprint,* 11–12.

141. Studio discussion including Linton Kwesi Johnson, Channel 4 TV, London, 1983.

142. Walcott related in a workshop how Auden's line "poets have names for the sea" came back from the printer with "ports," which Auden kept because it was "better." Royal Festival Hall, London, June 18, 1988.

143. Walcott, speaking at the University of Milan, May 22, 1996.

144. Pantin, "Any Revolution Based on Race Is Suicidal," 14.

145. Walcott, *Desert Island Discs,* BBC Radio 4, London, June 14, 1991.

146. Walcott, on *The Arts Programme,* BBC Radio 2, London, June 26, 1992.

147. Walcott, *The Old Bard Teaches a New Spell,* BBC Radio 3, London, June 26, 1992.

148. Walcott, *Omeros,* XXVIII.ii, 150.

149. Walcott, workshop, Royal Festival Hall, London, June 18, 1988.

150. Doran in conversation with Burnett, Birmingham, July 10, 1992.

151. Walcott, on *The Arts Programme,* Radio 2, June 26, 1992.

152. Walcott, *Another Life,* 12.i, C.P., 216.

153. Walcott, "North and South," C.P., 407.

154. Walcott with O'Brien, Hay-on-Wye Literary Festival, May 30, 1993.

155. Ismond, "Walcott versus Brathwaite," 54–71; Brown, Morris, and Rohlehr, eds., *Voiceprint,* 10.

156. Walcott, "The Poet in the Theatre," 7.

157. Walcott, *Midsummer,* XXV, C.P., 484.
158. Walcott with O'Brien, Hay-on-Wye Literary Festival, May 30, 1993.
159. Walcott, on *Start the Week,* BBC Radio 4, London, June 29, 1992.
160. Walcott, interview with Burnett, June 21, 1988.
161. Walcott, workshop, Royal Festival Hall, London, June 18, 1988.
162. Walcott, "Forest of Europe," C.P., 377.
163. Walcott, *Midsummer,* XXXVI, C.P., 492.
164. Walcott, "Muse of History," 63.
165. Ashcroft, Griffiths, and Tiffin, *The Empire Writes Back*, 8; Walcott, *Midsummer,* LII, C.P., 506.
166. Walcott, "What the Twilight Says," 32.
167. Walcott, "Necessity of Negritude," 22.
168. Walcott, on BBC Radio 4, London, June 14, 1991.
169. Walcott, C.P., 510.
170. Heaney, "The Murmur of Malvern," 27.
171. Walcott, speaking at the University of Milan, May 22, 1996.

6. "A Crystal of Ambiguities": The Craft of Mythopoeic Imagery

The quotation in the chapter title is from Walcott, *Another Life,* 9.i, C.P., 200.
1. Walcott, "What the Twilight Says," 15.
2. King, "The *Collected Poems* and *Three Plays* of Walcott," 360.
3. Walcott, "A City's Death by Fire," C.P., 6.
4. Walcott, *Another Life,* 9.ii, C.P., 200.
5. *Bim,* 13, 1950, quoted in Baugh, 15.
6. Walcott, "Jackie Hinkson," 417.
7. Walcott, *Omeros,* IX.iii, 54.
8. Walcott, workshop, Royal Festival Hall, London, June 18, 1988.
9. Shakespeare, *Tempest,* II.i.90.
10. "Poetry—Enormously Complicated Art," cited in Hamner, *Walcott,* 164.
11. This is significantly different from the objective to purify the dialect of the tribe, in Mallarmé's famous phrase, adopted by James Joyce and T. S. Eliot. In *Four Quartets,* Eliot has: "Our concern was speech, and speech impelled us / To purify the dialect of the tribe / And urge the mind to aftersight and foresight" ("Little Gidding," 2).
12. Walcott, "Muse of History," 47.
13. Walcott, *Omeros,* XIII.iii, 76.
14. Walcott, interview with Luigi Sampietro, *Caribana,* 3, 1992–93, 34–35.
15. Ibid.
16. The epic label is one that belongs less conventionally to *Another Life* than to *Omeros,* yet even for *Omeros* it has been resisted: "much more a novel than an epic, while never losing its lyrical fire" is John Figueroa's judgment of the later poem, and others have taken similar positions. John Figueroa, "*Omeros,*" in Stewart Brown, ed., *The Art of Derek Walcott,* 197.

17. Walcott, *Antilles,* 70.
18. Walcott, speaking at the University of Milan, May 22, 1996.
19. "Leaving School," 27.
20. Walcott, C.P., 64.
21. Walcott, *Another Life,* 5.i, C.P., 171.
22. Walcott, *Omeros,* III.iii, 19.
23. Ibid., XIII.ii, 73.
24. Ibid., 74.
25. Ibid.
26. Ibid., XIII.iii, 75.
27. Ibid., 75–76.
28. See, for example, Brathwaite, *History of the Voice.*
29. Walcott, *Omeros,* XXVII.ii, 145.
30. Ibid., 146.
31. Ibid., XLVIII.iii, 245.
32. Walcott, *Antilles,* 81. The reprinted edition has "woodcutters:" which appears to be an error.
33. Walcott, *Omeros,* II.iii, 14.
34. Steiner, speaking at the Hay-on-Wye Literary Festival, May 30, 1993.
35. Walcott, interview with Burnett, Stratford-on-Avon, July 1, 1992.
36. Walcott, *Omeros,* XLI.i, 206.
37. Ibid., LVII.ii, 287.
38. Ibid., LVII.i, 286.
39. Walcott, interview with Burnett, Stratford-on-Avon, July 1, 1992.
40. Ibid.
41. Fanon, *The Wretched of the Earth,* 199.
42. Nettleford, *Inward Stretch, Outward Reach,* x.
43. For example, Makak in *Dream on Monkey Mountain,* or the figure "dressed like a tramp," in the Virginian woods in "North and South" (C.P., 409), or the castaway Crusoe figure of the early poetry and the essay "The Figure of Crusoe."
44. The poem refers to Omeros as "St. Omere." *Omeros,* III.ii, 17.
45. Ibid., XXXVI.iii, 186.
46. Ibid., XXXVI.i, 183. *The Gulf Stream,* an oil painting, hangs in the Metropolitan Museum of Art, New York. Walcott has written of his admiration of Homer as a watercolorist, and he compares him with J. M. W. Turner as a user of the medium: "Turner melts his subjects. Homer gives them a savage edge," "Jackie Hinkson," 417.
47. Dunstan St. Omer won a local competition to design the national flag for St. Lucia at its independence in 1979.
48. Walcott, interview with Burnett, London, June 21, 1988.
49. Hall, in "Derek Walcott," *Arena,* BBC TV, London.
50. Walcott, "Muse of History," 36.

51. Walcott, *Desert Island Discs,* BBC Radio 4, June 14, 1991.
52. *Caribbean Times,* October 13, 1992.
53. Cobham-Sander on *Night Waves*, BBC Radio 3, London, April 14, 1998.
54. Fanon, *Wretched of the Earth*, 198.
55. Walcott, *Omeros*, LXIV.ii, 323.
56. Ibid., LXIV.iii, 325.
57. Walcott, "Muse of History," 47.

7. Appropriating Heirlooms: The Fortunate Traveler's Intertext

Note to the chapter title: "I had entered the house of literature as a house boy, / filched as the slum child stole, / as the young slave appropriated / those heirlooms temptingly left / with the Victorian homilies of Noli tangere" (*Another Life,* 12.ii, C.P., 219). The subject of this chapter is "The Fortunate Traveller," *The Fortunate Traveller.* The London edition from Faber erroneously gives the date 1982 for the Farrar, Straus and Giroux New York edition as well as for itself. The American edition was published in 1981, as indicated in C.P.

1. Milne, "Derek Walcott," *Express,* March 14, 1982, 18, cited in Hamner, *Walcott,* 2nd. ed., 121.
2. Walcott, interview with Burnett, June 21, 1988.
3. Vendler, "Poet of Two Worlds"; Heaney, "The Murmur of Malvern," 24.
4. Moore, "Passion, Fire, and Music in Recent West Indian Poetry."
5. Terada, *Derek Walcott's Poetry,* 2.
6. Morris, "The Fortunate Traveller," in Stewart Brown, ed., *The Art of Derek Walcott,* 103.
7. Walcott, "Muse of History," 62; Walcott's address to "Caribana Milano," conference, University of Milan, May 22, 1996.
8. Bedient, review of *The Fortunate Traveller,* 40.
9. Zamora, *Writing the Apocalypse,* 2, 190.
10. Ibid., 192.
11. Walcott, *South Bank Show,* ITV, London, January 15, 1989.
12. Walcott, *Another Life,* 12.i-ii, C.P., 216, 219.
13. Jameson, *Signatures of the Visible,* 143.
14. Ships would sail down the Avon to the Severn carrying manufactured goods southward to Africa, then carry slaves to the New World across the equatorial Atlantic (the Middle Passage), and back from the Americas to Europe with plantation products such as sugar or cotton.
15. Gilroy exposes the modern culture of the West as informed by the Black Atlantic experience resulting from the historic slave trade, thus countering the North's tendency to construct the black experience as its other and thereby to marginalize it, in *The Black Atlantic: Modernity and Double Consciousness.*
16. This is presumably his partner—a name that resonates with Conrad's widowed "aunt," Marguerite Poradowska, to whom he wrote from Africa and who informed his portrait of the Intended, and perhaps with Walcott's wife, Margaret, from whom he had not long separated.

17. This is cited as evidence that Kurtz is mad, and it is used by the military establishment as justification of Willard's mission to murder him. *Apocalypse Now,* dir. Coppola.

18. Coupe, *Myth,* 87.

19. Achebe, "An Image of Africa."

20. Mannoni, *Prospero and Caliban,* 19–20.

21. Achebe, "The Novelist as Teacher."

22. Gugelberger, *Marxism and African Literature,* 23.

23. Achebe, "An Image of Africa," 787.

24. Ibid., 787–89.

25. Fanon, *Black Skin, White Masks,* 96.

26. "Gecko" is the spelling used in *Collected Poems 1948–1984*. The 1982 Faber edition uses the spelling "gekko."

27. Rhys, *Wide Sargasso Sea,* 20. The use of the word "cockroaches" rather than "roaches" is presumably in deference to metropolitan readers, since naturalism would demand that Tia use "roach," ubiquitous in the Caribbean. Walcott's "roaches" are also, by implication, an unnatural "white." This is one of a number of intertextual links with other works of Caribbean literature in the poem.

28. Chinweizu, *The West and the Rest of Us,* 403.

29. Fanon, *Black Skin, White Masks,* 88–89.

30. Ibid., 89. The references are to Karl Jaspers, *La culpabilité allemande,* and C. G. Jung, *Aspects du drame contemporain.*

31. Walcott, "Origins," C.P., 11.

32. "[D]eserts peopled with stupid negroes." Hackett, *Rimbaud,* 127.

33. Auden, *The Dyer's Hand and Other Essays,* 52.

34. Ibid., 53–54.

35. Ibid., 57.

36. Walcott, *Omeros,* XIII.iii.

37. Shakespeare, *Macbeth,* II.ii, and V.i.

38. Eliot, *The Waste Land,* 59.

39. Noted by Mervyn Morris in Stewart Brown, ed., *The Art of Derek Walcott,* 101.

40. "With such a rascal Jack Wilton has nothing in common but a varied and wandering existence, and whereas the Spaniard travelled only in Spain, and from necessity, the Englishman did it from a lively curiosity, and made the grand tour. His poverty in the opening scenes is not the gnawing hunger of the beggar, which drove Lazaro to steal loaves and small change, but the chronic impecuniosity of the undergraduate or the nobleman's page." Thomas Nashe, *The Unfortunate Traveller,* ed. H. F. B. Brett-Smith, viii.

41. Gerald Moore, who knew Walcott at this date—and who as an academic at the University of Sussex taught Elizabethan and Jacobean drama—acknowledges that he has been identified with the poem's persona. Conversation with Burnett, Milan, May 1996.

42. Webster, *Duchess of Malfi,* IV.ii.

43. Walcott explores the Caribbean culture's lack of interest in or response to tragedy in a number of works, e.g., "What the Twilight Says."

44. *New York Times Book Review,* January 3, 1982, 5; *New York Times Magazine,* May 23, 1982, 50. Both are cited by Mervyn Morris, in Stewart Brown ed., *The Art of Derek Walcott,* 102.

45. Lowell, *Poems 1938–1949.* It is particularly to Lowell's influence that critics labeling Walcott as derivative have turned, the best known attack being that of Helen Vendler.

46. Zamora, *Writing the Apocalypse,* 190.

47. Revelation 11.9. Cf. Walcott on Voltaire and Nietzsche, 109.

48. 1 Corinthians, 13.

49. Revelation 2.7 and 22.2.

50. Naipaul, *In a Free State,* 234–35.

51. Revelation 6.4–8. It is possible that Walcott had a painting in mind when writing this passage. Although there have been many representations of the horsemen of the apocalypse, among them Dürer's, an American painting seems to have a particular affinity to Walcott's use of the idea of the "drawn sword," which comes "in strides" as an emblem of death, the result of greed: Albert Pinkham Ryder's *The Race Track or Death on a Pale Horse,* 1895–1910 (Cleveland Museum of Art, Cleveland, Ohio). Ryder shows death naked on a pale horse, at full gallop around a deserted racecourse in the wrong direction, with the sword above his head. The dark landscape is featureless apart from a dead tree within the track's circle and a snake in the foreground below it. The subject arose from the suicide in Ryder's brother's hotel of a waiter who lost all his money on a bet on a horse and killed himself (Prown, *American Painting,* 98). Walcott's image suggests that the sword coming in strides, which stretches "the length of the empty beach," is also the sea; the natural world's expressionist sympathy with the protagonist's state of mind is part of the meaning.

52. Walcott's exclusion of the tragic in this way may be modeled on Rhys's closure of *Wide Sargasso Sea,* withholding the death of Antoinette/Bertha, so that it remains the prerogative of the intertext, Bronte's *Jane Eyre.*

53. Revelation 9.3–11.

54. Revelation 19.17–21.

55. The poem, much loved, has a special place in the Walcott canon and is often requested at readings. Paul Breslin confirms my supposition that the two poems form one aesthetic unit, by reporting that when giving a reading of them in Wisconsin in April 1989, Walcott read "The Fortunate Traveller" and went straight on to read 'The Season of Phantismal Peace," without a pause for applause.

56. Walcott, *The Star-Apple Kingdom.*

57. "Gott ist tot; aber so wie die Art der Menschen ist, wird es vielleicht noch jahrtausendlang Höhlen geben, in denen man seinen Schatten zeigt." Nietzsche, *Die Fröhliche Wissenschaft,* III.108.

58. Sontag, *Against Interpretation and Other Essays,* 132–39. The essay was

originally published in the *New York Review of Books* in 1963 as a review of Lionel Abel's *Metatheatre: A New View of Dramatic Form.*

59. Walcott, "Culture or Mimicry?" 55.

60. First published in *Poetry Review* 71.4.

61. Walcott, *The Star-Apple Kingdom,* 3; "Muse of History," 62.

62. Russia is also present in Achebe's "An Image of Africa" in the figure of the dissident poet Yevtushenko, who was well known in the West at that time.

63. Walcott, interview with Burnett, London, June 21, 1988.

64. Since this study was written, I find that T. J. Cribb comes to a related conclusion in his reading of this volume: "Walcott enters on any subject by a process of division, cleaving its apparent unity by his own double attitude as heir to both agent and patient, doer and sufferer. . . . It is in writing itself, then, that experience can be transformed and perhaps, in a fictive, potential sense, redeemed." Cribb, "Defining a Voice."

8. "The Theatre of Our Lives": Founding an Epic Drama

1. Rees, ed., *Dictionary of Modern Quotations,* 351.

2. Willett dates Brecht's first use of the term in print to May 1927 and cites a contemporary letter from Professor Fritz Steinberg: "It wasn't Marx who led you to speak of the decline of the drama and to talk of the epic theatre. It was you yourself. For, to put it gently, 'epic theatre'—that's you, Mr Brecht." Willett, ed., *Brecht on Theatre,* 22.

3. Brecht met Eisenstein on his visit to Berlin in 1929. Brecht's conception of the relation between early film and theater is instructive; in 1930 he wrote:

> It is conceivable that other kinds of writer, such as playwrights or novelists, may for the moment be able to work in a more cinematic way than the film people. Up to a point they depend less on means of production. But they still depend on the film, its progress or regress; and the film's means of production are wholly capitalist. . . . To the playwright what is interesting is its attitude to the person performing the action. It gives life to its people, whom it classes purely according to function, simply using available types that occur in given situations and are able to adopt given attitudes in them. Character is never used as a source of motivation; these people's inner life is never the principal cause of the action and seldom its principal result; the individual is seen from outside. Literature needs the film not only indirectly but also directly. (Willett, ed., *Brecht on Theatre,* 48)

As for the question of the hero, Brecht identified Chaplin as "in many ways . . . closer to the epic than the dramatic theatre's requirements" (Willett, 56). Brecht was well aware that its dependence on capital would tend to make film reproduce the worst aspects of the old theater of illusion; sound films, he said in 1935, were "one of the most blooming branches of the international narcotics traffic" (Willett, 90).

4. Marx was "the only spectator of my plays I'd ever come across. For a man

with interests like his must of necessity be interested in my plays, not because they are so intelligent but because he is—they are something for him to think about" (Willett, 23–24).

5. Willett, ed., *Brecht on Theatre,* 21, 24.

6. "Schwierigkeiten des epischen Theaters," November 1927, Willett, ed., *Brecht on Theatre,* 23.

7. In 1952, Brecht reiterated the point: "It is not true, though it is sometimes suggested, that epic theatre . . . proclaims the slogan: 'Reason this side, Emotion (feeling) that.' It by no means renounces emotion, least of all the sense of justice, the urge to freedom, and righteous anger." Willett, ed., *Brecht on Theatre,* 227.

8. Brecht uses the phrases specifically about his drama *Die Mutter,* but they are applicable to his ideas of epic theater in general. Willett, ed., *Brecht on Theatre,* 57.

9. Ibid., 79.

10. Brecht says *The Threepenny Opera* "is concerned with bourgeois conceptions not only in content, by representing them, but also through the manner in which it does so. It is a kind of report on life as any member of the audience would like to see it . . . at the same time, however, he sees a good deal that he has no wish to see." Willett, ed., *Brecht on Theatre,* 43.

11. Ibid., 44.

12. Wright, *Postmodern Brecht,* 31.

13. Ibid.

14. Ibid., 1.

15. Ibid., 50.

16. Ibid.

17. Walcott, "What the Twilight Says," 22–23.

18. Wright, *Postmodern Brecht,* 3.

19. "He and his brother were already creating their own little theatre, 'little men' made from twigs enacting melodramas of hunting and escape, but of cowboys and gangsters, not of overseers and maroons." "What the Twilight Says," 20.

20. Banham, Hill, and Woodyard, *Cambridge Guide to African and Caribbean Theatre,* 181, 183.

21. Walcott, "What the Twilight Says," 6.

22. "Meanings," *Savacou* 2, 1970. When an interviewer described his mother as "walking round the house quoting *The Merchant of Venice,*" Walcott interrupted: "Well, yeah, not quoting, standing up and doing it. Not walking around. She was performing, you know." Walcott, *Desert Island Discs,* BBC Radio 4, June 14, 1991.

23. Walcott, "Leaving School," 26.

24. Banham, Hill, and Woodyard, *Cambridge Guide to African and Caribbean Theatre,* 177.

25. Walcott, "What the Twilight Says," 4.

26. Ibid., 20.

27. Willett, ed., *Brecht on Theatre,* 126.
28. Walcott, "What the Twilight Says," 4, 7.
29. Ibid., 4.
30. Ibid., 21–22. The original edition has ""if to weep," not "whether to weep."
31. Ibid., 11, 12.
32. Omotoso, *The Theatrical into Theatre,* 155.
33. Ibid., 159. For the history of Walcott's theatre, see Bruce King, *Derek Walcott and West Indian Drama,* and Judy Stone, *Theatre.*
34. Walcott, "What the Twilight Says," 32.
35. Ibid., 4.
36. Walcott, *Antilles,* 65.
37. Ibid., 68.
38. Ibid.
39. Ibid., 66.
40. Banham, Hill, and Woodyard, *Cambridge Guide to African and Caribbean Theatre,* 183.
41. Walcott, "What the Twilight Says," 30.
42. Ibid.
43. Ibid., 22.
44. Omotoso, *The Theatrical into Theatre,* 12.
45. Ibid., 51.
46. Walcott, "What the Twilight Says," 16–17.
47. Omotoso, *The Theatrical into Theatre,* 52.
48. Walcott, "What the Twilight Says," 23–24.
49. Ibid., 33.
50. Ibid., 30–31.
51. Ibid., 3–4.
52. Ibid., 7.
53. Berger, *Ways of Seeing,* 33.
54. Walcott, "Meanings," 45.
55. Walcott, "What the Twilight Says," 10–11.
56. Ibid., 11–12.
57. Ibid., 11.
58. Ibid., 12.
59. Ibid., 13.
60. Omotoso, *The Theatrical into Theatre,* 145.
61. Lewis, *The Growth of the Modern West Indies,* 393, cited in Omotoso *The Theatrical into Theatre,* 120.
62. Berger, *Ways of Seeing,* 11.
63. Wright, *Postmodern Brecht,* 24, 25.
64. Walcott, "What the Twilight Says," 17–18.
65. Ibid., 5.

66. Ibid., 6, 7.

67. Ibid., 28.

68. Walcott, "The Ghost Dance." Since the dramatic texts given detailed analysis in the remainder of this study are mainly unpublished, or drafts, revisions, or performance scripts of published texts, it seems less confusing if quotations are consistently *not* annotated. The main text indicates when a published version is under discussion.

69. Walcott's *The Last Carnival* was performed in Swedish in Stockholm in the autumn of 1992. *Ti-Jean and His Brothers* (as *Ti-Jean e i suoi Fratelli*) was staged for the Sixty-Seventh Theatre Festival of San Miniato, Pisa, in July 1993.

70. Willett, ed., *Brecht on Theatre,* 44.

71. Ibid., 84–85.

72. Ibid., 27.

9. "All You Stick Together": The Epic Federation Dream

1. The Department of Extra-Mural Studies was instrumental in encouraging Caribbean playwrights by its publication in the Caribbean Plays Series of more than sixty plays. Among them were Walcott's *Malcauchon* (published later in New York as *Malcochon), The Sea at Dauphin, Ione, The Charlatan, Henri Christophe,* and *Ti-Jean and His Brothers,* three of which have not been published elsewhere. Omotoso, *The Theatrical into Theatre,* 166–68.

2. Quotations are from the original Foreword to *Drums and Colours* by Noel Vaz, published in *Caribbean Quarterly* 7. 1–2, 1962, and reprinted in *Caribbean Quarterly* 38.4, 1992. Quotations from the play are from the latter text.

3. Omotoso, *The Theatrical into Theatre,* 145.

4. Wright, *Postmodern Brecht,* 9, from her summary of recent theorizations of Brecht's position.

5. The tone of the dialogue reflects the gender attitudes of its time but in some ways is not as dated as it might seem. With a jokey ambivalence typical of him, Walcott makes Yette a strong woman and a leader of men in every sense.

6. The richness of this final chapter of Raleigh's story is demonstrated by Naipaul's *A Way in the World,* which engages with the same sequence of events as does Walcott's play. Naipaul cannot have seen *Drums and Colours,* because, although it was performed in his hometown, he spent the 1950s in England. Walcott's construction of Paco, the *mestizo,* in the Columbus scenes and the boyhood of Raleigh, prefigures Naipaul's centering of the real-life *mestizo* who accompanied Raleigh back to England and was with him on the scaffold. It seems unlikely that Walcott knew of the history of this man, as he would probably have used him in his drama if he had.

7. Both of these deaths may have been mimed on the stage's upper level.

8. Quoted in Omotoso *The Theatrical into Theatre,* 145.

9. King, *Derek Walcott and West Indian Drama,* 21.

10. V. S. Naipaul, *A Way in the World,* 157–205.

11. Burnett, ed., *Caribbean Verse,* 32–33.

12. Walcott, "I Have Moved Away from the Big Speech," interview with Questel, 5.1, 1981.

13. Thieme, *Derek Walcott,* 66.

14. Stone, *Theatre,* 103–6.

10. "The Moment of Stillness": The Arrivants' Last Carnival

1. Lowel Fiet, "Mapping a New Nile: Derek Walcott's Later Plays," in Brown, ed., *The Art of Derek Walcott,* 146.

2. Walcott, *Three Plays,* 1986.

3. Stone, *Theatre,* 115–18.

4. The premiere was at the Birmingham Playhouse on July 10, 1992. This production was directly the result of the fact that, unlike many of Walcott's plays, it was published. The director, John Adams, who had not known of the play, happened on a copy in a New York bookshop and decided to stage it as the final production of his tenure as director in Birmingham.

5. Stone, *Theatre,* 115.

6. King, *Derek Walcott and West Indian Drama,* 143–44.

7. Ibid.

8. In the version of the play published in 1986, the first act is presented in chronological sequence from Agatha's arrival in Trinidad to independence, and the journalist is not introduced until the 1970 opening of the second act, which then follows a straightforward pattern of chronological narration. The play was substantially rewritten for the 1992 Birmingham production. The rehearsal script is in a number of different typefaces and is dated at the end, "Stratford-on-Avon, 8th June 1992."

9. Lovelace, "The Last Carnival," in Hamner, ed., *Critical Perspectives,* 374.

10. Walcott, "What the Twilight Says," 18.

11. Walcott, *Midsummer,* XX, C.P., 481.

12. Dancing the cocoa is a feature of Trinidadian culture to which Naipaul gives significance in *A Way in the World.*

13. Stone, *Theatre,* 118.

14. Wright, *Postmodern Brecht,* 34.

15. Ibid., 26.

16. In the 1992 version, the speech is broken up with off-stage interruptions, presumably in acknowledgment that its length in the printed version was excessive.

17. The song has also been used by Abdul Malik, who was involved in the Black Power revolution in Trinidad in 1970, in a recording of his poetry (*More Power,* Port of Spain, DAMD Productions, 1982), where his young daughter sings it as backing to his words.

18. Walcott, "What the Twilight Says," 24.

19. Walcott, "I Have Moved Away from the Big Speech," interview with Questel, 1981.

20. "In your island, O Venus! I found standing only a symbolic gallows where my image hung."

21. Walcott, *Midsummer,* XX, C.P., 481.

22. Walcott, "The Spoiler's Return," C.P., 433.

11. "The Joy of the Ghost Dance": The American Epic

1. Ibid., 437–38. This summary is based on Brown's account of events.

2. Foucault, *The Archaeology of Knowledge,* 25.

3. Walcott, *Omeros,* XXXIV.i, 175.

4. Brown, *Bury My Heart at Wounded Knee,* 416.

5. Ibid., 439.

6. Letter from Duncan Smith to Burnett, April 21, 1993. I am indebted to Duncan Smith for sharing his personal knowledge of the production.

7. Bensen, "'The Ghost Dance' by Derek Walcott," unpublished review article, kindly supplied by Duncan Smith and quoted with the author's permission.

8. Brown, *Bury My Heart at Wounded Knee,* 426.

9. Walcott, speaking at the Olivier Theatre, National Theatre, London, May 23, 1991, said it took him three years to write *Omeros.*

10. Bensen, "'The Ghost Dance' by Derek Walcott."

11. Brown recounts some of their terrible experiences: Cheyennes fled from a nighttime military attack, for example, with "only a few horses, and scarcely any blankets, robes, or even moccasins. . . . During the first night of flight, twelve infants and several old people froze to death. The next night the men killed some of the ponies, disembowelled them, and thrust small children inside to keep them from freezing. The old people put their hands and feet in beside the children. For three days they tramped across the frozen snow . . . ," 306.

12. Bensen, "'The Ghost Dance' by Derek Walcott."

13. Brown, *Bury My Heart at Wounded Knee,* 146.

14. Duncan Smith, letter to Burnett, April 21, 1993.

15. Ibid.

16. Walcott, "I Have Moved Away from the Big Speech," interview with Questel, 1981, 11.

17. The poem uses the idea of Catherine's son's wound at XXXIV.iii, 176.

18. Walcott, *Omeros,* XXXV.ii, 178–79.

19. Ibid., XXXV.iii, 182.

20. Ibid., 181.

21. *Citizen Kane,* 1941, dir. Welles.

22. Walcott, *Omeros,* XLIII.i, 215.

23. Ibid.

24. Barrault on *Late Theatre,* BBC TV, London, January 26, 1994.

25. Walcott, "Walcott on Walcott," an interview with Scott, 1968, 1–2.

12. "The Echo of the Shape": Metamorphosis of the Homeric

1. Homer, *Iliad,* p. xiii.
2. Gilroy, *The Black Atlantic;* Bernal, *Black Athena.*
3. Steiner, speaking at the Hay-on-Wye Literary Festival, May 30, 1993.
4. Walcott in "The Old Bard Teaches a New Spell," BBC Radio 3, June 26, 1992.
5. Walcott, "The Poet in the Theatre."
6. Walcott, interview with Burnett, Stratford-on-Avon, July 1, 1992.
7. Walcott, on *The Arts Programme,* introduced by Florance, BBC Radio 2, June 26, 1992.
8. Ibid.
9. Ibid.
10. Walcott, interview with Burnett, Stratford-on-Avon, July 1, 1992.
11. Walcott, on *The Arts Programme,* introduced by Florance, BBC Radio 3, June 26, 1992.
12. Walcott, interview with Burnett, Stratford-on-Avon, July 1, 1992.
13. Walcott, on *The Arts Programme,* introduced by Florance, BBC Radio 3, June 26, 1992.
14. Walcott, interview with Burnett, Stratford-on-Avon, July 1, 1992.
15. Ibid.
16. Lawrence, "Translator's Note" to Homer, *The Odyssey,* 1935.
17. Rieu, introduction to his translation of Homer, *The Odyssey,* 1946, 10.
18. Walcott, interview with Burnett, Stratford-on-Avon, July 1, 1992.
19. Walcott, on *The Arts Programme,* introduced by Florance, BBC Radio 3, June 26, 1992.
20. Ibid.
21. Walcott, interview with Burnett, Stratford-on-Avon, July 1, 1992.
22. Ibid.
23. Ibid.
24. Homer, *Iliad,* 293.
25. Walcott, interview with Burnett, Stratford-on-Avon, July 1, 1992.
26. Homer, *Iliad,* 74. In Walcott's first draft, the Old Man of the Sea "resembles Eumaeus."
27. Ibid., 67.
28. Ibid., 288.
29. Walcott, interview with Burnett, Stratford-on-Avon, July 1, 1992.
30. Ibid.
31. Graves, *The Greek Myths,* Book II, 368.
32. Homer, *Iliad,* 70.
33. Ibid.
34. Bernal, *Black Athena.*
35. Stanford, *The Ulysses Theme.*
36. Walcott, interview with Burnett, Stratford-on-Avon, July 1, 1992.

37. Walcott, on *The Arts Programme,* introduced by Florance, BBC Radio 3, June 26, 1992.

38. Homer, *Iliad,* 285.

39. The recent history of Greece included a military dictatorship.

40. Homer, *Iliad,* 353.

41. Lawrence in Homer, *The Odyssey,* 3.

42. Homer, *Iliad,* 347, 349.

43. In an intriguing study of father-daughter relations, the pattern of the ruined father and the rescuing daughter is one of six types explored. Goulter, Minninger, *The Father-Daughter Dance.*

44. Homer, *Iliad,* 72.

45. Ibid., 182.

46. Ibid., 285.

47. Thieme, *Derek Walcott,* 189.

"To Praise Lovelong": Conclusion

1. Walcott, "As John to Patmos," C.P. 5; Bob Marley, "Redemption Song."

2. Walcott, *Desert Island Discs,* BBC Radio 4, London, June 14, 1991.

3. Walcott, "North and South," C.P., 405.

4. Walcott, *Arena,* February 20, 1993.

5. Revelation 22.2–3.

6. Walcott, "North and South," C.P., 407.

7. Mazrui, "The 'Other' as the 'Self' under Cultural Dependency," 361.

8. Walcott, interview with Burnett, London, June 21, 1988.

9. Benitez-Rojo, *The Repeating Island,* 28.

10. Walcott, on *Night Waves,* BBC Radio 3, April 14, 1998.

11. Walcott, "The Old Bard Teaches a New Spell," BBC Radio 3, June 26, 1992.

12. Walcott, *Another Life,* 16.ii, C.P., 250.

13. Walcott, on *Night Waves,* BBC Radio 3, April 14, 1998.

14. Bernabé, Chamoiseau, and Confiant, *Eloge de la Créolité,* 87, 83. Dash finds the *Eloge* "reductionist" and lacking in "ironic self-scrutiny" and "insistence on process (creolisation and not *créolité*)" (Dash, *Edouard Glissant,* 23). Walcott's work, however, would seem to meet his criteria.

15. Walcott, *Midsummer,* XXIII, C.P. 483; Coetzee, *Dusklands,* 26.

16. Walcott, *Another Life,* 8.iii, C.P., 196.

17. Walcott, "Roots," *In a Green Night,* 60.

18. Walcott, interview in Jaggi, "No Trouble in Paradise," *Guardian,* July 12, 1997.

19. Walcott, "Leaving School," 28.

20. Walcott, "Muse of History," 63.

21. Walcott, interview in Jaggi, "No Trouble in Paradise," *Guardian,* July 12, 1997.

22. Walcott, interview with Leone Ross, *Voice,* London, July 21, 1992.

23. Walcott, "Roots," *In a Green Night,* 60.

24. "If there is a poet Walcott seems to have a lot in common with, it's nobody English but rather the author of the *Iliad* and the *Odyssey.*" Brodsky, "The Sound of the Tide," 167.

25. Ibid., 173–75.

26. Walcott, speaking at the University of Milan, May 22, 1996.

27. "Leaving School," 30.

28. Walcott, interview in Jaggi, "No Trouble in Paradise," *Guardian,* July 12, 1997.

29. This has become increasingly true. In *Another Life,* for instance, from 1973, he uses the phrase "epicanthic Arawak," but in the later poem, "Hurucan," he follows the unfamiliar word with a "translation": "the epicanthic, almond-shaped eye," C.P., 217; 424.

30. Bernabé, Chamoiseau, and Confiant, *Eloge de la Créolité,* 112.

31. See for a related discussion, Burnett, "Hegemony or Pluralism?"

32. Walcott, "Elegy (for Warwick Walcott)," *In a Green Night,* 13.

33. Walcott, "As John to Patmos," C.P., 5.

34. Walcott, "Roots," *In a Green Night,* 61.

35. Walcott, "Return to D'Ennery; Rain," C.P. 29; "Muse of History," 54.

36. Burnett, "Whispers of Immortality," *Independent,* London, November 14, 1998.

37. Walcott, speaking at the Hay-on-Wye Literary Festival, May 30, 1993.

Bibliography

Works by Derek Walcott

Poetry (in chronological order)

25 Poems. Trinidad, privately printed, 1948; Barbados: Advocate, 1949.
Epitaph for the Young: A Poem in XII Cantoes. Barbados: Advocate, 1949.
Poems. Jamaica: Kingston City Printery, [1951].
In a Green Night. London: Cape, 1962.
Selected Poems. New York: Farrar, Straus, 1964.
The Castaway, and Other Poems. London: Cape, 1965.
The Gulf. New York: Farrar, Straus and Giroux, 1970.
Another Life. London: Cape, 1973; New York: Farrar, Straus and Giroux, 1974.
Sea Grapes. London: Cape; and New York: Farrar, Straus and Giroux, 1976.
The Star-Apple Kingdom. New York: Farrar, Straus and Giroux, 1979; London: Cape, 1980.
Selected Poetry. Ed. Wayne Brown. London: Heinemann, 1981.
The Fortunate Traveller. New York: Farrar, Straus and Giroux, 1981; London: Faber, 1982.
The Caribbean Poetry of Derek Walcott and the Art of Romare Beardon. New York: Limited Editions Club, 1983.
Midsummer. London: Faber; and New York: Farrar, Straus and Giroux, 1984.
Collected Poems 1948–1984. New York: Farrar, Straus and Giroux; and London: Faber, 1986.
The Arkansas Testament. New York: Farrar, Straus and Giroux, 1987; London: Faber, 1988.
Omeros. New York: Farrar, Straus and Giroux; and London: Faber, 1990.
Mappa del Nuovo Mondo. Trans. Barbara Bianchi, Gilberto Forti, and Roberto Mussapi. Milan: Adelphi, 1992.
Poems 1965–1980. London: Cape, 1992.
The Bounty. New York: Farrar, Straus and Giroux; and London: Faber, 1997.
Songs from the Capeman. Lyrics by Paul Simon and Derek Walcott. New York: Paul Simon Music, 1997. [Enclosure with compact disk.]
Tiepolo's Hound. New York: Farrar, Straus and Giroux; London: Faber, 2000.

Published Plays (in chronological order)

Henri Christophe, a Chronicle. Barbados: Advocate, [1950].
Harry Dernier, a Play for Radio Production. Barbados: Advocate, [1951].
The Charlatan. [Caribbean Plays Series]. Trinidad: Department of Extra-Mural Studies [premiered 1954].

The Sea at Dauphin. [Caribbean Plays Series]. Trinidad: Department of Extra-Mural Studies, 1954.

Wine of Me Country. Jamaica: University of the West Indies, [1956].

Ione, a Play with Music. Jamaica: University of the West Indies, [1957].

Jourmard, or a Comedy until the Last Minute. [Caribbean Plays Series], Trinidad: Department of Extra-Mural Studies [premiered 1959].

Drums and Colours. *Caribbean Quarterly* 7, 1–2, 1962; reprinted in *Caribbean Quarterly* 38.4, 1992.

Malcauchon (published later as *Malcochon*). [Caribbean Plays Series]. Trinidad: Department of Extra-Mural Studies, 1965.

Dream on Monkey Mountain, and Other Plays [The Sea at Dauphin; Ti-Jean and His Brothers; Malcochon, or the Six in the Rain; Dream on Monkey Mountain]. New York: Farrar, Straus and Giroux, 1970.

The Joker of Seville, and O Babylon! New York: Farrar, Straus and Giroux, 1978.

Remembrance, and Pantomime. New York: Farrar, Straus and Giroux, 1980.

Pantomime [shortened version]. In David Self and Andrew Bethell, eds., *Power*. London: Hutchinson, with Thames Television, 1981.

Ti-Jean and His Brothers [adapted as a children's picture-book, hand-lettered and illustrated by Stuart Hahn]. Trinidad: Paria Publishing, 1984.

Ti-Jean and His Brothers. In Errol Hill, ed., *Plays for Today*. Harlow: Longman, 1985.

Three Plays [The Last Carnival; Beef, No Chicken; A Branch of the Blue Nile]. New York: Farrar, Straus and Giroux, 1986.

The Odyssey. London: Faber; and New York: Farrar, Straus and Giroux, 1993.

Ti-Jean e i suoi fratelli; Sogno sul Monte della Scimmia. Trans. Annuska Palme Sanavio and Fernanda Steele. Milan: Adelphi, 1993.

Unpublished Plays, Drafts, and Rehearsal Scripts Used for This Study

The Ghost Dance. Unpublished script, premiered by the Cardboard Alley Players, directed by Duncan Smith at Hartwick College, Oneonta, New York on November 9, 1989.

The Last Carnival. Revised script for Birmingham Playhouse production, directed by John Adams, premiered July 10, 1992.

The Odyssey. Drafts [first, third, and fourth] prepared for the Royal Shakespeare Company production, written September 1991–March 1992, premiered July 2, 1992 [previews from June 24], directed by Gregory Doran.

Selected Essays and Other Prose (in alphabetical order; references are to the most recent edition)

"The Action is Panicky." *Sunday Guardian*. Trinidad, May 5, 1963; reprinted untitled in Susheila Nasta, ed., *Critical Perspectives on Sam Selvon*.

"Animals, Elemental Tales, and the Theater." In A. James Arnold, ed., *Monsters, Tricksters and Sacred Cows: Animal Tales and American Identities*. Charlottesville: University Press of Virginia, 1996.

The Antilles: Fragments of Epic Memory. London: Faber, 1993. Reprinted in *What the Twilight Says: Essays.*

"Café Martinique." [Short story.] *House and Garden* 157, 1985; reprinted in *What the Twilight Says: Essays.*

"Caligula's Horse." In Stephen Slemon and Helen Tiffin, eds., *After Europe*. Australia, Denmark and U.K.: Dangaroo, 1989.

"The Caribbean: Culture or Mimicry?" *Journal of InterAmerican Studies and World Affairs* 16.1, 1974; reprinted in Robert D. Hamner, ed., *Critical Perspectives on Derek Walcott.*

"A Colonial's-Eye View of the Empire." *TriQuarterly* 65, 1986.

"The Figure of Crusoe." Lecture, 1965. In Robert D. Hamner, ed., *Critical Perspectives on Derek Walcott.*

"Jackie Hinkson." *Massachusetts Review* 35.3/4, 1994.

"Leaving School." *London Magazine* 5.6, 1965; reprinted in Robert D. Hamner, ed., *Critical Perspectives on Derek Walcott.*

"Meanings." *Savacou* 2, 1970; reprinted in Robert D. Hamner, ed., *Critical Perspectives on Derek Walcott.*

"The Muse of History." In Orde Coombs, ed., *Is Massa Day Dead?* New York: Anchor Doubleday, 1974. Reprinted in John Hearne, ed., *Carifesta Forum,* [Jamaica], 1976, and in *What the Twilight Says: Essays.*

"Necessity of Negritude." [*Trinidad Guardian*, September 28, 1964]; reprinted in Robert D. Hamner, ed., *Critical Perspectives on Derek Walcott.*

"On Choosing Port of Spain." In David Frost, ed., *Trinidad and Tobago*. London: Deutsch, 1975.

"The Poet in the Theatre." *Poetry Review* 80.4, 1990–91.

"Poetry—Enormously Complicated Art." *Trinidad Guardian,* June 18, 1962.

"A Tribute to C.L.R. James." In Selwyn R. Cudjoe and William E. Cain, eds., *C.L.R. James: His Intellectual Legacies*. Amherst: University of Massachusetts Press, 1995.

"What the Twilight Says." In *Dream on Monkey Mountain, and Other Plays*. New York: Farrar, Straus and Giroux, 1970. Reprinted in *What the Twilight Says: Essays.*

What the Twilight Says: Essays. New York: Farrar, Straus and Giroux; and London: Faber, 1998.

"The White Devil." [Short story.] *Sunday Guardian*, Trinidad, December 25, 1966.

Selected Interviews, Interview-based Journalism, Broadcasts, and Public Appearances (in chronological order)

"Walcott on Walcott." An interview with Dennis Scott. *Caribbean Quarterly* 14.1–2, 1968.

Robert D. Hamner. "Conversation with Derek Walcott." *World Literature Written in English* 16.2, 1977.

Derek Walcott. "I Have Moved away from the Big Speech." Interview with Vic Questel. *Trinidad and Tobago Review* 5.1, 1981.
"An Interview with Nancy Schoenberger." *Threepenny Review* 15, 1983.
Derek Walcott. Poetry Workshop, Royal Festival Hall, London, June 18, 1988.
Derek Walcott, interview with Paula Burnett, London, June 21, 1988.
South Bank Show, with Melvyn Bragg. London Weekend Television, January 15, 1989.
"An Object Beyond One's Own Life." Interview with Luigi Sampietro. *Caribana* 2, 1991.
Derek Walcott, introducing a reading, the Brighton Festival, at the Royal Albion Hotel, Brighton, Sussex, May 16, 1991.
Derek Walcott, reading and questions, Olivier Theatre, National Theatre, London, May 23, 1991.
Derek Walcott, speaking at the International Writers Conference, on the theme of "The Legacy of Europe," Dublin, June 20, 1991.
Desert Island Discs, with Sue Lawley. BBC Radio 4, London, June 14, 1991.
"And the Dish Ran Away with the Spoon." *Developing Stories* (Banyan, Port of Spain). BBC2, London, May 21, 1992.
The Arts Programme, with John Florance. BBC Radio 2, London, June 26, 1992.
"The Old Bard Teaches a New Spell," with Oliver Taplin. BBC Radio 3, London, June 26, 1992.
Start the Week, with Melvyn Bragg. BBC Radio 4, London, June 29, 1992.
Interview with Paula Burnett, Stratford-on-Avon, July 1, 1992. Published as "Walcott, Man of the Theatre." *Caribbean Writer* 14, 2000.
Interview with Leone Ross. *The Voice,* London, July 21, 1992.
Interview with Julian May. BBC, summer 1992.
"Walcott Blasts Baron for Tourist Resort 'Greed.'" *The Voice,* London, October 27, 1992.
"Derek Walcott on *Omeros.*" Interview with Luigi Sampietro. *Caribana* 3, 1992–93.
Arena. BBC TV, with Stuart Hall, February 20, 1993.
Derek Walcott, speaking at the Hay-on-Wye Literary Festival, May 30, 1993.
Interview with Frances Stoner-Saunders at the Hay-on-Wye Literary Festival, BBC TV, London, June 1993.
"Derek Walcott: An Interview," with Lawrence Scott. *English and Media Magazine,* Autumn 1993.
Derek Walcott, speaking at the "Beautiful Translations," event at the Tate Gallery, London, May 1, 1995.
Derek Walcott. "A Tribute to C.L.R. James." [1991]. In Selwyn R. Cudjoe and William E. Cain, eds., *C.L.R. James: His Intellectual Legacies.* Amherst: University of Massachusetts Press, 1995.
Derek Walcott. Address to "Caribana Milano" conference, University of Milan, May 22, 1996.

William Baer, ed. *Conversations with Derek Walcott.* Jackson: University Press of Mississippi, 1996.
Maya Jaggi. "No Trouble in Paradise." *Guardian,* "The Week," July 12, 1997.
Maya Jaggi. "Paradise Fights Back." *Guardian,* "Guardian Weekend," December 13, 1997.
Interview with Antonio Benitez-Rojo. *Night Waves.* BBC Radio 3, London, April 14, 1998.
Paula Burnett. "Whispers of Immortality." *Independent,* November 14, 1998.

Other References

Achebe, Chinua. "An Image of Africa." *Massachusetts Review* 18.4, 1977; reprinted in *Research in African Literatures* 9.1, 1978; also in Robert D. Hamner, ed., *Joseph Conrad: Third World Perspectives.* Washington D.C: Three Continents Press, 1990; also in the Norton edition of Joseph Conrad, *Heart of Darkness.*
———. "The Novelist as Teacher." *New Statesman,* January 1965.
Alleyne, Mervyn C. *Roots of Jamaican Culture.* London: Pluto, 1988.
Allsopp, Richard. *Dictionary of Caribbean Usage.* Oxford: Oxford University Press, 1996.
Anderson, Benedict. *Imagined Communities.* London: Verso, [1983]; rev. ed., 1991.
Arnold, A. James. *Modernism and Negritude: The Poetry and Poetics of Aimé Césaire.* Cambridge, Mass.: Harvard University Press, 1981.
———, ed. *Monsters, Tricksters and Sacred Cows: Animal Tales and American Identities.* Charlottesville: University Press of Virginia, 1996.
Ashcroft, Bill, Gareth Griffiths, and Helen Tiffin. *The Empire Writes Back: Theory and Practice in Post-colonial Literatures.* London and New York: Routledge, 1989.
Auden, W. H. *The Dyer's Hand and Other Essays.* London: Faber, 1963.
Bakhtin, Mikhail. *The Dialogic Imagination.* Trans. Caryl Emerson and Michael Holquist. Austin: University of Texas, 1981.
Banham, Martin, Errol Hill, and George Woodyard. *Cambridge Guide to African and Caribbean Theatre.* Cambridge: Cambridge University Press, 1994.
Barthes, Roland. *Mythologies.* [1957]. Trans. Annette Lavers. London: Collins, 1973.
Baugh, Edward. *Derek Walcott: Memory as Vision: "Another Life."* Harlow: Longman, 1978.
Bedient, Calvin. "Derek Walcott: Contemporary." In Robert D. Hamner, ed., *Critical Perspectives on Derek Walcott.*
———. Review of *The Fortunate Traveller, Parnassus* 9.2, 1981.
Benitez-Rojo, Antonio. *The Repeating Island.* Trans. James Maraniss. Durham, N.C.: Duke University Press, 1992.

Benjamin, Walter. *Illuminations*. [1955]. Trans. Harry Zohn. London: Fontana, 1992.
Bensen, Robert. "'The Ghost Dance' by Derek Walcott" [unpublished review].
Berger, John. "The Infinity of Desire." *Guardian*, London, July 13, 2000.
———. *Ways of Seeing*. London: BBC and Penguin Books, 1972.
Bernabé, Jean, Patrick Chamoiseau, and Raphaël Confiant. *Eloge de la Créolité*. [1989]. Trans. M. B. Taleb-Khyar. Baltimore: Johns Hopkins University Press, 1990.
Bernal, Martin. *Black Athena: The Afroasiatic Roots of Classical Civilization*. [1987]; London: Vintage, 1991.
Berry, James. "Fantasy of an African Boy." *Poetry Review* 71.4.
Berry, Philippa, and Andrew Wernick, eds. *Shadow of Spirit: Postmodernism and Religion*. London: Routledge, 1992.
Bhabha, Homi. "DissemiNation: Time, Narrative, and the Margins of the Modern Nation." In Bhabha, ed., *Nation and Narration*. London and New York: Routledge, 1990.
———. *The Location of Culture*. London and New York: Routledge, 1994.
Bobb, June D. L. *Beating a Restless Drum: The Poetics of Kamau Brathwaite and Derek Walcott*. Trenton, N.J., and Asmara, Eritrea: Africa World Press, 1998.
Brathwaite, [Edward] Kamau. "Caliban's Guarden" [from the T. S. Eliot lectures, "Conversations with Caliban"]. *Wasafiri* 16, 1992.
———. *History of the Voice*. London: New Beacon, 1984.
Brodsky, Joseph. "Laureate of the Supermarkets." *Poetry Review* 81.4, 1991/2.
———. "The Sound of the Tide." In *Less Than One*. [1986]; London: Penguin, 1987.
———. *Watermark*. New York and London: Hamish Hamilton, 1992.
Brown, Dee. *Bury My Heart at Wounded Knee*. [1970]; London: Vintage, 1991.
Brown, Lloyd. *West Indian Poetry*. [1978]; London: Heinemann, 1984.
Brown, Paul. "'This Thing of Darkness I Acknowledge Mine': *The Tempest* and the Discourse of Colonialism." In Jonathan Dollimore and Alan Sinfield, eds., *Political Shakespeare*. Manchester: Manchester University Press, 1985.
Brown, Stewart, ed. *The Art of Derek Walcott*. Bridgend, Wales: Seren Books, 1991.
Brown, Stewart, Mervyn Morris, and Gordon Rohlehr, eds. *Voiceprint*. Harlow: Longman, 1989.
Brown, Wayne. "The Century of Exile." *Jamaica Journal* 14.3, 1973.
Brydon, Diana, and Helen Tiffin. *Decolonising Fictions*. Australia, Denmark, and U.K.: Dangaroo, 1993.
Burnett, Paula. "Derek Walcott's *Omeros*." *Wasafiri* 14, 1991.
———. "Elegies at Ebb Tide from St. Lucia" [review of Derek Walcott, *The Bounty*]. *Independent*, London, July 12, 1997.

———. "The Empire Writes Back" [report on award of Nobel Prize for Literature to Derek Walcott]. *New Statesman,* London, October 16, 1992.

———. "Epic, a Woman's Place: A Study of Derek Walcott's *Omeros* and Jean Binta Breeze's 'A River Called Wise.'" In Vicki Bertram, ed., *Kicking Daffodils: A Celebration of Women's Poetry.* Edinburgh: Edinburgh University Press, 1997.

———. "Hegemony or Pluralism? The Literary Prize and the Postcolonial Project in the Caribbean." *Commonwealth* 16.1, 1993.

———. "The Island Self as World Text in the Work of Derek Walcott and Romesh Gunesekera." In Isabella Maria Zoppi, ed., *Routes of the Roots: Geography and Literature in the English-Speaking Countries.* Rome: Bulzoni, 1998.

———. "The Sea and the Mirror" [review of Derek Walcott, *The Odyssey*]. *New Statesman,* London, July 10, 1992.

———. "The Ulyssean Crusoe and the Quest for Redemption in J. M. Coetzee's *Foe* and Derek Walcott's *Omeros.*" In Lieve Spaas and Brian Stimpson, eds., *Robinson Crusoe: Myths and Metamorphoses.*

———. "Walcott's Spellbinding Drama." *Caribbean Times,* London, July 7, 1992.

———. "'Where Else to Row, but Backward?' Addressing Caribbean Futures through Re-visions of the Past." *Ariel* 30.1, 1999.

———. "Whispers of Immortality." *Independent,* London, November 14, 1998.

———. "Writing Home: Constructing the Caribbean Subject in the Poetry of Derek Walcott." In Máire ní Fhlathúin, ed., *The Legacy of Colonialism: Gender and Cultural Identity in Postcolonial Societies.* Galway: Galway University Press, 1998.

———, ed. *Caribbean Verse in English.* London: Penguin, 1986.

Carpentier, Alejo. *The Lost Steps* [1953]. Trans. Harriet de Onis. London: Penguin, 1980.

Chamberlin, J. Edward. *Come Back to Me My Language: Poetry and the West Indies.* Toronto: McClelland and Stewart, 1993.

Chinweizu. *Decolonising the African Mind.* Lagos: Pero Press, 1987.

———. *The West and the Rest of Us.* Lagos: Pero Press, 1987.

Coetzee, J. M. *Dusklands.* [1974]. London, 1982.

Conrad, Joseph. *Heart of Darkness.* London: Penguin, 1995.

Coupe, Laurence. *Myth.* London: Routledge, 1997.

Cribb, T. J. "Defining a Voice: Derek Walcott." *Kunapipi* 20.3, 1998.

Dabydeen, David. "On Not Being Milton: Nigger Talk in England Today." In Geoffrey Davis and Hena Maes-Jelinek, eds., *Crisis and Creativity in the New Literatures in English.* Amsterdam: Rodopi, 1990.

Dash, J. Michael. *Edouard Glissant.* Cambridge: Cambridge University Press, 1995.

———. *The Other America: Caribbean Literature in a New World Context.* Charlottesville: University Press of Virginia, 1998.

Davis, Geoffrey, and Hena Maes-Jelinek, eds. *Crisis and Creativity in the New Literatures in English*. Amsterdam: Rodopi, 1990.

Deleuze, Gilles, and Felix Guattari. *Anti-Oedipus: Capitalism and Schizophrenia*. [1972]. Trans. Robert Hurley, Mark Seem, and Helen R. Lane. London: Athlone Press, 1984.

Dieke, Ikenna. *The Primordial Image: African, Afro-American and Caribbean Mythopoetic Text*. New York: Peter Lang, 1993.

Dollimore, Jonathan, and Alan Sinfield, eds. *Political Shakespeare*. Manchester: Manchester University Press, 1985.

Drayton, Richard, and Andaiye, eds. *Conversations with George Lamming*. London: Karia Press, 1992.

Eagleton, Terry. *Walter Benjamin, or Towards a Revolutionary Criticism*. London: Verso, 1981.

Eliade, Mircea. *The Myth of the Eternal Return: Cosmos and History*. London: Penguin, 1954.

Eliot, T. S. *Collected Poems*. London: Faber, 1969.

———. "*Ulysses*, Order and Myth." *The Dial*. November 1923.

Fanon, Frantz. *Black Skin, White Masks*. [1952]. Trans. Charles Lam Markmann. London: Pluto Press, 1986.

———. *The Wretched of the Earth*. [1961]. Trans. Constance Farrington. London: Penguin, 1967.

Figueroa, John. "The Poetry of Derek Walcott." Seminar, Commonwealth Institute, London, December 1, 1990.

Foucault, Michel. *The Archaeology of Knowledge*. [1969]. Trans. A. M. Sheridan Smith. London: Routledge, 1989.

Fox, Robert E. "Big Night Music: Derek Walcott's *Dream on Monkey Mountain* and the 'Splendours of Imagination.'" In Robert D. Hamner, ed., *Critical Perspectives on Derek Walcott*.

Froude, J. A. *The English in the West Indies*. London, 1888.

Frye, Northrop. "Myth." *Antaeus* 43, 1981.

Fukuyama, Francis. *The End of History and the Last Man*. London: Penguin, 1992.

Gardner, Helen, ed. *Metaphysical Poets*. London: Penguin, 1957.

Gilbert, Helen, and Joanne Tompkins. *Post-Colonial Drama: Theory, Practice, Politics*. London: Routledge, 1996.

Gilroy, Paul. *The Black Atlantic: Modernity and Double Consciousness*. London: Verso, 1993.

Goldstraw, Irma. *Derek Walcott: An Annotated Bibliography of His Works*. New York: Garland, 1984.

Goulter, Barbara, and Joan Minninger. *The Father-Daughter Dance*. [1993]; New York: Piatkus, 1994.

Graves, Robert. *Greek Myths*. [1955]; rev. ed., London: Penguin, 1960.

———. *The White Goddess*. London: Faber, 1961.

Greene, Graham. *"The Third Man" and "The Fallen Idol."* London: Penguin, 1976.
Gugelberger, Georg. *Marxism and African Literature.* London: James Currey, 1985.
Guillén, Nicolás. *West Indies, Ltd.* 1934.
Hackett, C. A. *Rimbaud.* Cambridge: Cambridge University Press, 1981.
Hamner, Robert D. *Derek Walcott.* [1981]. 2nd ed. New York: Twayne, 1993.
———. *Epic of the Dispossessed: Derek Walcott's "Omeros."* Columbia: University of Missouri Press, 1997.
———, ed. *Critical Perspectives on Derek Walcott.* Washington, D.C.: Three Continents Press, 1993.
Harris, Wilson. "Comedy and Modern Allegory." In Hena Maes-Jelinek, ed., *Wilson Harris: The Uncompromising Imagination.* Denmark, Australia, and U.K.: Dangaroo, 1991.
———. "Unfinished Genesis of the Imagination." Lecture given at the Essex Church, Palace Gardens Terrace, London, March 18, 1992.
Hawthorn, Jeremy. *Multiple Personality and the Disintegration of Literary Character.* London: Edward Arnold, 1983.
Heaney, Seamus. "The Murmur of Malvern." In *The Government of the Tongue.* London: Faber, 1988.
Hearne, John, ed. *Carifesta Forum.* [Jamaica], 1976.
Heath, Roy A. K. "Criticism in Art: A View from the Diaspora." *Ariel* 24.1, 1993.
Herbert, George. *The Temple.* [1633]; reprinted in Helen Gardner, ed., *Metaphysical Poets.* London: Penguin, 1957.
Herbert, Zbigniew. "The Price of Art." *Still Life with a Bridle.* Trans. John and Bogdana Carpenter. London: Cape, 1993.
Hoegburg, David. "The Anarchist's Mirror: Walcott's *Omeros* and the Epic Tradition." *Commonwealth Essays and Studies* 17.2, 1995.
Homer. *Iliad.* Trans. E. V. Rieu. London: Penguin, 1950.
———. *Odyssey.* Trans. T. E. Lawrence. New York: 1932.
———. *Odyssey.* Trans. E. V. Rieu. London: Penguin, 1946.
Hulme, Peter. *Colonial Encounters: Europe and the Native Caribbean 1492–1797.* [1986]; London: Routledge, 1992.
Hutcheon, Linda. "'Circling the Downspout of Empire': Post-Colonialism and Postmodernism." *Ariel* 20.4, 1989.
Ismond, Patricia. "Walcott versus Brathwaite." *Caribbean Quarterly* 17.3–4, 1971.
James, C.L.R. *Spheres of Existence.* London: Allison & Busby, 1980.
James, Louis. *Caribbean Literature in English.* London: Longman, 1999.
———, ed. *The Islands in Between.* Oxford: Oxford University Press, 1968.
Jameson, Fredric. *Postmodernism, or, The Cultural Logic of Late Capitalism.* London and New York: Verso, 1991.
———. *Signatures of the Visible.* London: Routledge, 1992.

Jones, Bridget. "With Crusoe the Slave and Friday the Boss: Derek Walcott's *Pantomime*." In Lieve Spaas and Brian Stimpson, eds., *Robinson Crusoe: Myths and Metamorphoses.*

Joseph, Margaret Paul. *Caliban in Exile: The Outsider in Caribbean Fiction.* New York: Greenwood, 1992.

Joyce, James. *A Portrait of the Artist as a Young Man.* [1916]; London: Penguin, 1960.

———. *Ulysses.* [1922]; London: Penguin, 1969.

Juneja, Renu. *Caribbean Transactions: West Indian Culture in Literature.* Basingstoke: Macmillan, 1996.

King, Bruce. "The *Collected Poems* and *Three Plays* of Derek Walcott." In Robert D. Hamner, ed., *Critical Perspectives on Derek Walcott.*

———. *Derek Walcott: A Caribbean Life.* New York and London: Oxford University Press, 2000.

———. *Derek Walcott and West Indian Drama: "Not Only a Playwright But a Company":The Trinidad Theatre Workshop, 1959–1993.* Oxford: Clarendon Press, 1995.

———, ed. *New National and Post-Colonial Literatures.* Oxford: Oxford University Press, 1996.

Krishnaswamy, Revathi. "Mythologies of Migrancy: Postcolonialism, Postmodernism and the Politics of (Dis)locations." *Ariel* 26.1, 1995.

Kristeva, Julia. *Desire in Language: A Semiotic Approach to Literature and Art.* Trans. Thomas Gora, Alice Jardine, and Leon S. Roudiez. Oxford: Blackwell, 1980.

———. "Foreign Body." *Transition* 59, 1993.

———. *Strangers to Ourselves.* Trans. Leon S. Roudiez. New York: Columbia University Press, 1991.

Lacan, Jacques. *See* Miller, Jacques-Alain

Lamming, George. *The Pleasures of Exile.* [1960]; part reprinted in John Hearne, ed., *Carifesta Forum.*

Lee, John Robert. "Introduction." In Jenny Palmer, *Saint Lucia.*

Lovelace, Earl. "Review of *The Last Carnival.*" In Robert D. Hamner, ed., *Critical Perspectives on Derek Walcott.*

Lewis, R. W. B. *The American Adam.* Chicago: University of Chicago Press, 1955.

Lowell, Robert. *Poems 1938–1949.* London: Faber, 1950.

Macdonald, Ian. *Jaffo the Calypsonian.* Leeds: Peepal Tree, 1994.

Maes-Jelinek, Hena, ed. *Wilson Harris: The Uncompromising Imagination.* Denmark, Australia, and U.K.: Dangaroo, 1991.

Mannoni, Octave. *Prospero and Caliban: The Psychology of Colonization.* [1950]. Trans. Pamela Powesland. Ann Arbor: University of Michigan Press, 1990.

Markham, E. A., ed. *Hinterland: Caribbean Poetry from the West Indies and Britain.* Newcastle: Bloodaxe, 1989.

Mazrui, Ali. "The 'Other' as the 'Self' under Cultural Dependency: The Impact of the Postcolonial University." In Gisela Brinker-Gabler, ed., *Encountering the Other(s)*. Albany: State University of New York Press, 1995.

Melville, Pauline. *The Ventriloquist's Tale*. London: Bloomsbury, 1997.

Memmi, Albert. *The Colonizer and the Colonized*. [1965]. Trans. Howard Greenfeld. London: Earthscan, 1990.

Miller, Jacques-Alain, ed. *The Seminar of Jacques Lacan: Book II; The Ego in Freud's Theory and in the Technique of Psychoanalysis 1954–1955*. Trans. Sylvana Tomaselli. Cambridge: Cambridge University Press, 1988.

Milne, Anthony. "Derek Walcott." *Express*, March 14, 1982.

Moi, Toril. *Sexual Textual Politics: Feminist Literary Theory*. London: Routledge, 1985.

Moore, Gerald. "Passion, Fire, and Music in Recent West Indian Poetry." Lecture, "Caribana Milano" Conference, University of Milan, May 22, 1996.

Moretti, Franco. *Modern Epic: The World System from Goethe to Garcia Marquez*. [1994]. Trans. Quintin Hoare. London: Verso, 1996.

Naipaul, V. S. "East Indian." *The Reporter*, June 17, 1965; reprinted in *The Overcrowded Barracoon*. [1972]; London: Penguin, 1976.

———. *In a Free State*. [1971]; London: Penguin, 1973.

———. *The Middle Passage*. [1962]; London: Penguin, 1969.

———. *A Way in the World*. London: Heinemann, 1994.

Nashe, Thomas. *The Unfortunate Traveller*. [1594]. Ed. H. F. B. Brett-Smith. Oxford: Basil Blackwell, 1927.

Nasta, Susheila, ed. *Critical Perspectives on Sam Selvon*. Washington, D.C.: Three Continents Press, 1988.

———. *Motherlands*. London: Women's Press, 1991.

Nettleford, Rex. *Inward Stretch, Outward Reach: A Voice from the Caribbean*. Basingstoke: Macmillan, 1993.

Niane, D. T., ed. *Sundiata*. [Paris: Présence Africaine, 1960]. Trans. G. D. Pickett. London: Longman, 1965.

Nixon, Rob. "Caribbean and African Appropriations of *The Tempest*." *Critical Inquiry*, Spring 1987.

Nyerere, Julius. "Who Shall Inherit the Earth?" *Guardian*, London, November 16, 1992.

Omotoso, Kole. *The Theatrical into Theatre*. London: New Beacon, 1982.

Palmer, Jenny. *Saint Lucia*. London and Basingstoke: Macmillan, 1998.

Pantin, Raoul. "Any Revolution Based on Race Is Suicidal." *Caribbean Quarterly* 1.8, 1973.

Parker, Michael, and Roger Starkey, eds. *Postcolonial Literatures: Achebe, Ngugi, Desai, Walcott*. Basingstoke: Macmillan, 1995.

Prown, Jules David. *American Painting*. Geneva: Skira, 1969.

Retamar, Roberto. "Caliban." In John Hearne, ed., *Carifesta Forum*.

Rhys, Jean. *Wide Sargasso Sea.* [1966]; London: Penguin: 1993.

Rimbaud, Arthur. *Lettre du Voyant.* 1871.

Rodman, Selden. *Tongues of Fallen Angels.* New York: New Direction Books, 1974.

Rodney, Walter. *The Groundings with My Brothers.* London: Bogle L'Ouverture, 1969.

———. *How Europe Underdeveloped Africa.* [London: Bogle L'Ouverture, 1972]; rev. ed., Washington, D.C.: Howard University Press, 1982.

Rohlehr. Gordon. "A Carrion Time." In *My Strangled City and Other Essays.* Trinidad: Longman, 1992.

———. "My Strangled City." In John Hearne, ed., *Carifesta Forum.* Reprinted in *My Strangled City and Other Essays.* Trinidad: Longman, 1992.

———. "Rohlehr on Brathwaite." In E. A. Markham, ed., *Hinterland.*

———. "The Shape of That Hurt." In Stewart Brown, Mervyn Morris, and Gordon Rohlehr, eds., *Voiceprint.* Harlow: Longman, 1989. Reprinted in *The Shape of That Hurt and Other Essays.* Trinidad: Longman, 1992.

Rushdie, Salman. *The Jaguar Smile.* London: Picador, 1987.

Said, Edward. *Culture and Imperialism.* London: Chatto and Windus, 1993.

———. *The World, the Text and the Critic.* London: Vintage, 1983.

Savory [Fido], Elaine. "Mother/lands: Self and Separation in the Work of Buchi Emecheta, Bessie Head and Jean Rhys." In Susheila Nasta, ed., *Motherlands.* London: Women's Press, 1991.

———. "Value Judgements on Art and the Question of Macho Attitudes: The Case of Derek Walcott." In Michael Parker and Roger Starkey, eds., *Postcolonial Literatures: Achebe, Ngugi, Desai, Walcott.*

Shakespeare, William. *Complete Works.* Ed. W. J. Craig. Oxford: Oxford University Press, 1905.

Sherlock, Philip. *West Indies.* London: Thames and Hudson, 1966.

Smith, Duncan. Letter to Paula Burnett, April 21, 1993 [unpublished].

Sontag, Susan. *Against Interpretation and Other Essays.* London: Deutsch, 1987.

Soyinka, Wole. *Art, Dialogue and Outrage.* [1988]; London: Methuen, 1993.

———. *Myth, Literature and the African World.* Cambridge: Cambridge University Press, 1976.

Spaas, Lieve, and Brian Stimpson, eds. *Robinson Crusoe: Myths and Metamorphoses.* Basingstoke: Macmillan, 1996.

Stanford, W. B. *The Ulysses Theme.* [1963]; Dallas: Spring Publications, 1992.

Stone, Judy. *Theatre.* [Studies in West Indian Literature]. Basingstoke: Macmillan, 1994.

Stratton, Florence. *Contemporary African Literature and the Politics of Gender.* London: Routledge, 1994.

Taylor, Patrick. "Myth and Reality in Caribbean Narrative: Derek Walcott's *Pantomime.*" *World Literature Written in English* 26.i, 1986; reprinted in Robert D. Hamner, ed., *Critical Perspectives on Derek Walcott.*

———. *The Narrative of Liberation: Perspectives on Afro-Caribbean Literature, Popular Culture and Politics*. Ithaca: Cornell University Press, 1989.

Terada, Rei. *Derek Walcott's Poetry: American Mimicry*. Boston: Northeastern University Press, 1992.

Thieme, John. *Derek Walcott*. Manchester: Manchester University Press, 1999.

Thomas, J. J. *Froudacity*. [1889]; London: New Beacon, 1969.

Toohey, Peter. *Reading Epic*. London: Routledge, 1992.

Treves, Frederick. *The Cradle of the Deep*. 1910.

Vendler, Helen. Review of Geoffrey Hartman, *Criticism in the Wilderness* [Yale, 1982]. *New Yorker*, May 3, 1982.

———. "Poet of Two Worlds." Review of Derek Walcott, *The Fortunate Traveller*. *New York Review of Books*, March 4, 1982.

West, T. G., ed. and trans. *Symbolism: An Anthology*. London: Methuen, 1980.

White, Allon. *Carnival, Hysteria and Writing*. Oxford: Clarendon, 1993.

Willett, John, ed. *Brecht on Theatre: The Development of an Aesthetic*. [1964]; London: Methuen, 1990.

Wright, Elizabeth. *Postmodern Brecht: A Re-Presentation*. London: Routledge, 1989.

Young, Robert. *Colonial Desire: Hybridity in Theory, Culture and Race*. London: Routledge, 1995.

———. *White Mythologies: Writing History and the West*. London: Routledge, 1990.

Zabus, Chantal. "A Calibanic Tempest in Anglophone and Francophone New World Writing." *Canadian Literature* 104, 1985.

Zamora, Lois Parkinson. *Writing the Apocalypse*. Cambridge: Cambridge University Press, 1989.

Films

Apocalypse Now. Dir. Francis Ford Coppola, 1979.

The Birth of a Nation. Dir. D. W. Griffith, 1915.

Citizen Kane. Dir. Orson Welles, 1941.

Do the Right Thing. Dir. Spike Lee, 1989.

Pather Panchali. Dir. Satyajit Ray, 1955.

The Third Man. Dir. Carol Reed, 1948.

Broadcasts and Recordings

Barrault, Jean-Louis. On *Late Theatre*. BBC TV, London, January 26, 1994.

Malik, Abdul. *More Power*. Port of Spain: DAMD Productions, 1982.

Night Waves. BBC Radio 3, London, April 14, 1998.

Okri, Ben. Interview with Melvyn Bragg. *Arts Review 1991*. ITV London, December 29, 1991.

Index

Paula Burnett, who lectures at Brunel University, London, is the editor of the Penguin anthology *Caribbean Verse in English* and the author of numerous studies in postcolonial literature, particularly that of the Caribbean.